President Gordon B. Hinckley

IN MEMORIUM

Gordon Bitner Hinckley, born June 23, 1910, in Salt Lake City, Utah, to Bryant S. and Ada Bitner Hinckley, died Jan. 27, 2008, at age 97, after a long life of dedicated service to God and his fellowman. A man of wit and wisdom, President Hinckley left behind a rich legacy. He had the distinction of being the longest-lived president of the Church.

Deseret News

Publisher
Jim M. Wall
Editor
Joe Cannon
Managing editor
Richard Hall
Assistant managing editor
Dave Schneider
Church News editor
Gerry Avant
Almanac editor
Shaun D. Stahle
Almanac assistant
Dell Van Orden
Church News staff
Greg Hill
R. Scott Lloyd
Jason Swensen
Scott Taylor
Sarah Jane Weaver
Church News Artist
John Clark
Deseret News Photo editor
Ravell Call
LDS Church graphics/maps
Gary Christensen

Church History Department

**Church Historian and Recorder
and Executive Director**
Elder Marlin K. Jensen
Assistant Executive Director
Elder Paul K. Sybrowsky
Assistant Church Historian / Recorder
Richard E. Turley Jr.
Managing Director
Steven L. Olsen
Almanac Chairman
Grant A. Anderson
Staff Contributions
Jeff Anderson
Mary Teresa Anderson
Mel Bashore
Jay Burrup
Clint Christensen
Scott Christensen
Marie Erickson
Matt Heiss
Gordon Irving
Mike Landon
Christine Marin
Blake Miller
Brian Reeves
William W. Slaughter
Sarah Sorenson
Jennifer A. St. Clair

TABLE OF CONTENTS

President Dieter F. Uchtdorf leads President Thomas S. Monson and President Henry B. Eyring in sustaining vote during solemn assembly.

NEWS IN REVIEW

GENERAL AUTHORITIES

CHURCH STATISTICS MAPS

TEMPLES FACTS

FEATURE PRESIDENT HINCKLEY

INDEX

How to contact us
The *Deseret News Church Almanac* is prepared and edited by the staff of the *Church News*, a section of the *Deseret News*, with the Family and Church History Department of The Church of Jesus Christ of Latter-day Saints. Copyright@ *Deseret News* 2008

Deseret News
30 East 100 South
Salt Lake City, Utah 84111

Mailing address
P.O. Box 1257
Salt Lake City, Utah
84110

E-mail address
churchnews@desnews.com

Visit
Church News
online
www.ldschurch.com

Statistical Profile

GROWTH IN MEMBERSHIP

12,868,606	13,193,999	13,428,061
2006	2007	3rd quarter 2008

Membership by area of the Church, or state in the U.S., or by country, see 149.

LDS Church News

MEMBERSHIP
(31 December 2007)

6,051,510

Members living
in the United States
and Canada

7,142,489

Members outside
North America

CHURCH UNITS
(31 December 2007)

2,790

Stakes

618

Districts

27,827

Wards and branches

348

Missions

CHURCH GROWTH
(31 December 2007)

93,698

Increase in children
of record

279,218

Converts

YOUTH
(31 December 2007)

491,993

Young Women (ages 12-17)

597,082

Young Men (ages 12-18)

MISSIONARIES
(31 December 2007)

52,686

Serving worldwide

Missionaries from the
Salt Lake City Mission
sit in front of the Salt
Lake Temple during the
Sunday morning session
of General Conference
April 1, 2007.

LDS Church News

Temple News

128

Temples in operation worldwide.

Four temples were dedicated in 2008:
- **Rexburg Idaho**
- **Curitiba Brazil**
- **Panama City Panama**
- **Twin Falls Idaho**

Nine temples announced in 2007-08:
- San Salvador, El Salvador
- Gilbert, Arizona
- Gila Valley, Arizona
- Phoenix, Arizona
- Calgary Alberta, Canada
- Kansas City, Missouri
- Philadelphia, Pennsylvania
- Cordoba, Argentina
- Rome, Italy

In total, **17 temples** have been announced or are under construction, bringing the total number of temples in operation, announced or planned to **145.**

The **Nuku'alofa Tonga Temple** was rededicated Nov. 4, 2007. Ground was broken in 2007-08 for **Cebu Phillipines, Manaus Brazil and San Salvador El Salvador temples.** See **Temples** starting on page 193.

President Thomas S. Monson was sustained 16th president of the Church during the 178th Annual General Conference.

Church's 16th president sustained in solemn assembly

Pres. Monson holds all priesthood keys

Since being called as a General Authority in October 1963, President Thomas S. Monson has addressed many general conferences. In April, during the 178th Annual General conference, he delivered his 90th.

See *Church News*, April 5, 2008, for complete comments, or: ldschurchnews.com.

During proceedings of the two-day conference, which convened Saturday, April 5, he was sustained in a solemn assembly as the 16th President of the Church, succeeding President Gordon B. Hinckley, who died Jan. 27.

> "I've always followed the philosophy, 'Serve where you're called, not where you've been or where you might be. Serve where you're called.'"
>
> —Pres. Monson

Prior to April general conference, reflecting on the momentous events that were about to take place, President Monson said in a *Church News* interview, "When you realize that hands will be raised in the traditional fashion, it's an overwhelming feeling of humility and gratitude for the faith of the membership of the Church. I've had those feelings when I've read the names for sustaining on previous occasions and when I was sustained on previous occasions,"

President Monson spoke of a "great loneliness" that he has felt since President Hinckley's passing. "I knew him so well. I worked with him in three First Presidencies. We knew how each other thought. And when I got word that he had passed away, I began to realize that the person with whom I had conversed on any subject was no longer here. There was really no one else. We were two men who were so close. We sat next to each other so many years.

"I was called to his bedside. President (Henry B.) Eyring (who was second counselor in the First Presidency) was with me. On Saturday, the day before he died, I said to his family, "I think we ought to come at three o'clock on the Sabbath day, and give Brother Hinckley a blessing." I called Brother (Boyd K.) Packer (then-Acting President of the Quorum of the Twelve) so he could be there with Brother Eyring and me because he's also been close to Brother Hinckley. That day, as the male members of Brother Hinckley's family, his doctor, and the little group that I had arranged for, put our hands on Brother Hinckley's head and gave him a blessing, I realized that it would not be long before he would be called home. I held his wrist and tapped it, one friend to another. Within three hours after the blessing, we got word that he had gone home to Heavenly Father."

Asked about his thoughts and feelings pertaining to the moment he realized that he was going to be the next president of the Church, the one who holds all the priesthood keys, President Monson said, "I've always followed the philosophy, 'Serve where you're called, not where you've been or where you might be. Serve where you're called.'

"I did that as a bishop, as a stake presidency member, as mission president and as an apostle. I've never speculated on what might lie ahead for me. I just never did. I didn't know but what President Hinckley would outlive me."

Speaking about following the spirit, President Monson said, "I don't know what prompts others, but I know what prompts me. When I get a feeling that I need to be somewhere and be doing something, whether it sounds plausible to me or not, I go. And I find that the thought came because the Lord knew that He didn't need to give Brother Monson a lot of advance notice. It makes me feel so good inside to think that I would get the call, or the inspiration, that the Lord knows who I am and that He knows that I will go."

Dave Newman

President Monson married Frances Johnson on Oct. 7, 1948, in the Salt Lake Temple.

Monsons celebrate 60th anniversary

An anniversary moment to be cherished forever

Certain moments ought to be frozen in time, to be cherished and remembered forever. One of those moments occurred Monday evening, Oct. 6, 2008, as President Thomas S. Monson and his wife, Sister Frances Monson, gathered with family, friends and associates to celebrate their 60th anniversary.

A meal had been served in an upstairs room of the Lion House in Salt Lake City. Several favorite songs were performed, a poem recited, and a tribute given by two sons, their daughter and a grandson.

Sister Monson expressed her appreciation for the evening and bore her testimony.

When President Monson stood to speak he made reference to meeting Frances Johnson at a streetcar stop as a university student, marking the beginning of their lives together.

President Monson then looked down at Sister Monson, and said to her. "I'd simply like to say that 60 years have certainly gone by fast, dear. Where did they go?"

He leaned down and kissed her, to the applause of all in the room.

MAJOR EVENTS
OCTOBER 2007 - SEPTEMBER 2008

Elder Quentin L. Cook of the Quorum of the Twelve meets volunteers in Poway California Stake, some of whom are sifting through ashes for items of value to homeowners.

OCTOBER 2007

Uplifting voice, visit brings comfort to fire-stricken areas

> "The scriptures are clear that the rain falls on the just and the unjust. ... Unfortunately, fires in San Diego County do the same thing."

SAN DIEGO, Calif.

Members of the Poway California Stake who lost their homes to wildfires that ravaged San Diego County at the end of October were buoyed up by a visit from Elder Quentin L. Cook of the Quorum of the Twelve.

Elder Cook spoke to about 30 family members during an intimate meeting in the stake center during a tour of the area Saturday, Oct. 27.

Members in the Poway stake were the hardest-hit by the fires, losing at least 18 homes.

Elder Cook blessed the people that they "might have peace, that there might dwell up in your hearts a feeling of well-being and of love and appreciation for the Savior and for those who are around you who are serving you and that you'll have a sense that you are loved.

Elder Cook visits with Errin Arnold and her daughter, McCall.

Also in the news in October 2007

AMBASSADOR PICNIC

Photo by Page Johnson
Zoran Jolevski, ambassador from Macedonia, and family greeted by BYU Living Legends.

Oct. 13: More than 20 ambassadors and diplomats and their families from 34 countries participated in the annual Western Family Picnic, sponsored by the Church's Office of Public and International Affairs, at the Marriott Ranch in Hume, Va.

CONSUL FAMILY DAY

Photo by Alan Gibby
Diplomatic families enjoy rides and games.

Oct. 20: Representing more than 40 countries, consuls general and their families participated in the seventh Consular Corps Family Day, hosted by the Church's Southern California Public Affairs Council at the Calamigos Ranch in Malibu, Calif.

FOSTER RESPECT, LOVE

Oct. 21: President Gordon B. Hinckley, in speaking at a multi-stake conference that originated from the Conference Center in Salt Lake City and broadcast by satellite to 107 Utah stakes, counseled members to foster love and mutual respect in families.

DIGITIZE RECORDS

Oct. 23: The U.S. National Archives and Records Administration and the Church's FamilySearch announced an agreement which, over time, will lead to the digitization of millions of historical documents.

DESERET INDUSTRIES DEDICATED

Oct. 24: Bishop Richard C. Edgley, first counselor in the Presiding Bishopric, dedicated a new 50,000-square-foot Deseret Industries Store in West Valley City, Utah, that will serve 36 stakes in the Salt Lake Valley. The facility also includes an LDS Employment Center and offices for LDS Family Services.

PERU CONSULATE VISITS

Oct. 26: Peruvian Consulate General Guido Loayza visited Church headquarters in Salt Lake City, Utah, to offer thanks to the Church for its ongoing assistance to victims of an 8.0-magnitude earthquake in southwest Peru in August 2007.

Courtesy David Utria
Peruvian Conculate Guido Loayza meets with Elder Claudio R.M. Costa.

HELPING HANDS IN AFRICA

Oct. 27: Tens of thousands of members of the Church in the Africa Southeast and Africa West areas spent the day participating in the Mormon Helping Hands day of service, volunteering hundreds of thousands of hours of community service in South Africa, Botswana, Zimbabwe, Namibia, Nigeria, Ghana, Liberia, Ivory Coast, Sierra Leone and Tanzania.

Courtesy Herve K. Koffi
Volunteer cares for infant.

MEMBER HOMES FLOODED IN MEXICO

Oct. 28: Intense torrential rains hit the Mexican state of Tabasco, leaving over 70 percent of the state inundated. More than 300 homes of LDS members were flooded and all 28 missionaries serving in Villahermosa lost their dwellings.

Courtesy Duane Hiatt
Villahermosa Mexico Gaviotas Stake meetinghouse partially submerged from flooding.

LDS Church News

Members gather on the grounds of the rededicated Nuku'alofa Tonga Temple on Nov. 4, 2007. The temple was originally dedicated in 1983.

NOVEMBER 2007

Reaping a devoted harvest in Pacific paradise of Tonga

NUKU'ALOFA, Tonga

The only Pacific nation to remain independent of western colonization, Tonga's national motto reflects the nation's spirituality: "God and Tonga Are My Inheritance."

There is no greater symbol of that national spirituality today than the Nuku'alofa Tonga Temple, rededicated Nov. 4 by Elder Russell M. Nelson of the Quorum of the Twelve.

Dubbed the "Friendly Islands" by visitors, nearly one in every two Tongans is a member of the Church.

"We reaped the harvest today of seeds that had been sown by the king of Tonga, who gave the land to the Lord in the first place," Elder Nelson told the *Church News* after the dedication.

Indeed, the people of Tonga have never forgotten their rich spiritual heritage, said Temple President Eric B. Shumway. "The dedication — the giving of a temple and its people back to God through covenant — is at the heart of the tradition that extends to 1839."

> "We reaped the harvest today of seeds that had been sown by the king of Tonga, who gave the land to the Lord in the first place."

LDS Church News

Elder Russell M. Nelson and his wife, Wendy, walk to cornerstone ceremony.

Also in the news in November 2007

GUATEMALAN FIRST LADY VISITS

Nov. 1: Guatemalan First Lady Wendy Widmann de Berger visited Church headquarters in Salt Lake City and toured Welfare Square and the Church's Humanitarian Center.

Deseret News

Guatemalan First Lady Wendy Widmann de Berger

COLORFUL TONGA CULTURAL PROGRAM

Nov. 3: Some 2,400 Tongan youth and young single adults, clad in

LDS Church News

Youth participants.

LDS Church News

Samoan dancer.

bright costumes, participated in a cultural program the night before the Nuku'alofa Tonga Temple was rededicated. The program, which drew thousands of Church members to Teufaiva Stadium, was attended by Tonga's king, his Majesty George Tupou V. Titled "A Treasure That Lasts," the program, through song and dance, portrayed the journey of a grieving couple who lost their only child to death, but returned to Tonga to find the gospel of Jesus Christ.

NEW BYU-HAWAII PRESIDENT

Nov. 6: Steven C. Wheelwright was inaugurated as the school's ninth president. President Henry B. Eyring, second counselor in the First Presidency, issued a charge to President Wheelwright to "lead the university to new heights of service, achievement and recognition."

FOUR GUIDEPOSTS

Nov. 13: President Thomas S. Monson, addressing students at BYU during the weekly campus devotional, suggested four guideposts that would assist them in their journeys through school and life itself. The guideposts are "glance forward," "look heavenward," "reach outward" and "press onward."

LDS Church News

President Thomas S. Monson and his wife, Frances.

BREAKS GROUND

Nov. 14: Elder Dallin H. Oaks of the Quorum of the Twelve broke ground for the Cebu Philippines Temple, the second temple that will be built in the Philippines.

Photo by Edwin Redrino

Elder Dallin H. Oaks leads groundbreaking in Cebu.

EL SALVADOR TEMPLE

Nov. 18: Plans for construction of a temple in San Salvador, El Salvador, were announced by the First Presidency. It will be the first temple in that Central America nation.

CHURCH HONORED IN BRAZIL

Nov. 22: the Brazilian Federal Senate recognized the Church for its humanitarian work and paid tribute to missionaries of the past 80 years. Specifically mentioned were 60,000 volunteers who spruced up 284 public schools in September 2007.

LDS Church News

Elder Claudio R.M. Costa meets with Brazilian reporter.

The image of the Savior is the image of a Christmas with hope.

DECEMBER 2007

Let love and peace permeate hearts

The peace and love that the Savior brought into the world were emphasized Dec. 2 by President Gordon B. Hinckley and his counselors, President Thomas S. Monson and President Henry B.

LDS Church News
Tabernacle Choir performs during First Presidency Christmas Devotional.

Eyring, at the annual First Presidency Christmas Devotional, which originated from the Conference Center in Salt Lake City and was telecast by satellite to members around the world.

In his address, President Hinckley said the world is full of people with sorrow, and for many of them life seems hopeless. Yet, he said, the image of the Savior "is the image of a Christmas with hope. May the spirit of the Babe of Bethlehem permeate our hearts with added love and peace."

President Monson said the Christmas spirit "is the spirit of the gospel of Jesus Christ, obedience to which will bring peace on earth because it means good will toward all men. The spirit of Christmas can mend wounded hearts and heal entire nations."

President Eyring said although there is darkness and cruelty in the world, "there is the light and love which the Savior has brought and is bringing into millions of hearts. We can choose on this Christmas and all the days which will follow to feel that light and that love."

LDS Church News
Pres. Gordon B. Hinckley shares his love of the Savior.

Also in the news in December 2007

TSUNAMI AID COMPLETE

December: Three years after a devastating tsunami, triggered by a 9.0-magnitude earthquake that resulted in the deaths of more than 220,000 people in a dozen countries, the Church Humanitarian Services completed its humanitarian projects in the region. In partnership with other international organizations, the Church, among other projects, constructed 902 homes, 15 schools, three health clinics, 24 village water systems and three community centers.

LDS Church News

Missionaries assist with the unloading of new fishing nets as part of the Church's humanitarian projects.

LATINO CHRISTMAS PROGRAM

Dec. 6-8: Speaking at the Church's annual Latino Christmas program in the Tabernacle on Temple Square, Elder Claudio R.M. Costa of the Presidency of the Seventy related many yuletide traditions found throughout Latin America. "The great and true Christmas gift for all humankind is Christ Himself," he said. Performed almost entirely in Spanish, "El Regalo de Navidad" – The Gift of Christmas – featured several choir performances during the program's three-day run.

LDS Church News

Latino choir performs during Christmas celebration in the Tabernacle.

FLOODING CLEANUP

Dec. 8: Nearly 3,000 members of the Church from 21 stakes in western Washington, wearing Mormon Helping Hands T-shirts, turned out to help clean up in the aftermath of severe flooding caused by a powerful Pacific storm that deluged the area Dec. 3-4. The first week after the storm hit, truckloads of food, blankets and other relief supplies, including more than 10,000 clean-up kits, arrived from the Church.

LDS Church News

Leaders and youth assemble to assist with flooding cleanup.

LIFELONG LEARNING

Dec. 14: Susan W. Tanner, Young Women general president, addressed the 1,079 graduates at the fall commencement exercises at BYU-Idaho and spoke about the importance of lifelong learning.

LDS Church News

Young Women General President Susan Tanner joins President Kim Clark, right, of BYU-Idaho and her husband, John S. Tanner.

EMBRACE TECHNOLOGIES

Dec. 15: Elder M. Russell Ballard of the Quorum of the Twelve counseled the more than 200 graduates at BYU-Hawaii's commencement exercises to embrace new technologies in their efforts to share the gospel.

LDS Church News

Elder M. Russell Ballard, accompanied by Elder W. Rolfe Kerr, right, and President Steven C. Wheelwright, left, of BYU-Hawaii leads procession of graduates.

LDS Church News

President Gordon B. Hinckley's chair is conspicuously empty beside his counselors, President Thomas S. Monson and President Henry B. Eyring prior to funeral services.

President Hinckley:
A life of extraordinary service

A fter a long life of dedicated service to God and his fellowman, President Gordon B. Hinckley, the 15th president of the Church, died Jan. 27 of causes incident to age. He was 97.

He was set apart and ordained as President of the Church on March 12, 1995, after serving for 14 years as a counselor to three Church presidents, 20 years as a member of the Quorum of the Twelve, and three years as an Assistant to the Twelve.

On Nov. 2, 2006, he became the longest-lived president of the 13 million member Church.

Despite being the longest-lived president in the history of the Church, President Hinckley kept up with his daily work schedule until the last week of his life. His nearly 13 years as president of the Church were marked with vigor and foresight, evidenced by his numerous major accomplishments and his lengthy travel schedule that took him across the globe many times.

His nearly 13 years as president of the Church were marked with vigor and foresight, evidenced by his numerous major accomplishments.

LDS Church News

President Thomas S. Monson consoles Elder Richard G. Hinckley at graveside.

Quorum of the Twelve members line entrance into Conference Center, as Hinckley family follows casket.

Also in the news in January 2008

In his last official public appearance, President Gordon B. Hinckley dedicates Utah State Capitol following four-year renovation, above and right.

Jan. 4: In his last official public appearance, President Hinckley rededicated the Utah State Capitol after extensive remodeling and renovation that had closed the 91-year-old building to the public since 2004. The Mormon Tabernacle Choir, along with the Orchestra at Temple Square and the Bells on Temple Square, were among musical groups that participated in the dedicatory services.

Jan. 15: President Henry B. Eyring, second counselor in the First Presidency, addressed BYU students in the Marriott Center and bore witness of divine power and deliverance, saying deliverance requires humility before God, prayer, a willingness to obey, and service to others out of love for them and for the Savior.

President Thomas S. Monson and his counselors, President Henry B. Eyring, left, and President Dieter F. Uchtdorf, make their first public appearance as the First Presidency during a news conference on Feb. 4.

FEBRUARY 2008

Thomas S. Monson named 16th president

President Thomas S. Monson, a counselor to Presidents Ezra Taft Benson, Howard W. Hunter and Gordon B. Hinckley, was set apart and ordained the 16th President of the Church during a sacred meeting in the Salt Lake Temple on Feb. 3. Called as his first counselor was President Henry B. Eyring, who had served as President Hinckley's second counselor. Called as President Monson's second counselor was President Dieter F. Uchtdorf of the Quorum of the Twelve. President Boyd K. Packer was set apart as president of the Quorum of the Twelve.

The following day, on Feb. 4, President Monson and his counselors held a press conference in the lobby of

President Monson answers questions during press conference.

"I am humbled as I stand before you today. I testify that this work in which we are engaged is the Lord's work, and I have felt His sustaining influence. I know that He will direct our efforts as we serve Him with faith and diligence."
— President Monson

the Church Office Building that was carried live on local TV and transmitted via the Church satellite system to meetinghouses across the world. Members of the Quorum of the Twelve sat to the sides of the new First Presidency, showing a united pledge of support for the Church's highest-ranking governing body.

Each member of the First Presidency made brief remarks and then President

Also in the news in February 2008

LDS Church News

Well-wishers line funeral route while waving handkerchiefs and canes in tribute to President Gordon B. Hinckley, who often greeted others with similar gestures of kindness and love.

"If we follow the guidelines which have been set before us in this meeting (Worldwide Leadership Training), we will draw closer to the Lord and bring more of heaven into our homes."
— Pres. Monson

Sister Cheryl C. Lant, Sister Julie B. Beck, Elder Dallin H. Oaks, Elder Jeffrey R. Holland and Susan W. Tanner participate in roundtable discussion concerning matters of the family.

Feb. 2: Funeral services for President Hinckley, who died Jan. 27, were held in the building that's an integral part of his legacy – the Conference Center in Salt Lake City. Sixteen thousand mourners gathered in the massive building across the street from Temple Square for the services that were telecast by satellite in 69 languages to more than 6,000 Church buildings across the world.

Feb. 9: In his first address since becoming President of the Church, President Monson counseled Church members attending the annual Worldwide Leadership Training Broadcast that the home remains the basis of a righteous life. Also participating in the satellite broadcast were President Boyd K. Packer, president of the Quorum of the Twelve, who used the Church's "Proclamation on the Family" as the basis of his counsel; and Elders Dallin H. Oaks and Jeffrey R. Holland of the Quorum

of the Twelve who shared their insights on families in a "roundtable" discussion with Relief Society General President Julie B. Beck, Young Women General President Susan W. Tanner and Primary General President Cheryl C. Lant.

Feb. 9: In song, dance and music, 2,000 children, youth and young single adults participated in a cultural program the night before the Rexburg Idaho Temple was dedicated that portrayed the settling of the Upper Snake River Valley in 1883 by Mormon pioneers. Themed "Come to God's Own Temple, Come," the cultural program was viewed by 3,500 people who packed Hart Auditorium on the BYU-Idaho campus, with thousands more watching via live satellite in stake centers throughout the temple district.

Feb. 10: President Monson dedicated the Rexburg Idaho Temple in four sessions, the third temple to be constructed in Idaho and the 125th temple throughout the world.

Feb. 25: The Church announced the establishment of The Church History Press, a new imprint for publishing works related to the Church's origin and growth. The department is contracting with Deseret Book Co. for printing and publishing, and the first product of the new venture will be the Joseph Smith Papers.

LDS Church News
Dancer performs during harvest dance.

LDS Church News
Members line up to attend dedication of the Rexburg Idaho Temple, third in Idaho, and 125th in Church.

LDS Church News

Statue of Samuel Smith, replicating the one at Provo Missionary Training Center, is displayed in Salt Lake Tabernacle during commemoration of his 200th birthday, at which Orem Institute Choir performs.

MARCH 2008

One million missionaries called since Samuel Smith

The 200th anniversary of the birth of Samuel H. Smith, brother of the Prophet Joseph and the first formal missionary in this dispensation, was commemorated March 9 in a meeting of his descendants and relatives in the Salt Lake Tabernacle.

Page of Samuel Smith's journal superimposed on William Whitaker's painting of him.

Samuel Smith was born March 13, 1808, and, as a missionary, traveled more than 4,000 miles between 1830 and 1833. A life-size statute of Samuel with a knapsack full of copies of the Book of Mormon is located at the Missionary Training Center in Provo, Utah.

Elder M. Russell Ballard of the Quorum of the Twelve and a great-

Since Samuel's first missionary service, more than 1 million missionaries have been called to serve in 348 missions, teaching in 176 nations, and in 164 languages.

great-grandson of Hyrum Smith, brother of Joseph and Samuel, spoke at the meeting, as did Ardeth G. Kapp, former Young Women general president, who told of the impact that Samuel Smith had on one of her ancestors.

Elder Ballard said, "Since Samuel's first missionary service, the Church has called over 1 million missionaries to serve in 348 missions, now teaching the gospel in 176 nations and in 164 languages and dialects. What a wonderful beginning to spreading the message of the Restoration to the people of the world."

Also in the news in March 2008

LDS Church News

Scores of Church members join others from Wells, Nev., to aid the victims of a magnitude-6 earthquake.

"Real progress occurs only in the hearts, minds and conduct of the members. The Church is only as strong as the goodness, faith and spirituality of each member. True progress takes place in the Church when there is personal spiritual progress in the membership."
— Pres. Monson

March 1: More than 200 members of the Church from Wells, Elko and Wendover, Nev., wearing yellow "LDS Helps Hands" T-shirts, turned out to help in the recovery process after a 6.0 magnitude earthquake rocked the town of Wells on Feb. 21, which caused damage to 75 percent of the homes of members of the Wells Ward.

March 15: President Monson addressed the BYU-Idaho's President's Club Banquet in Salt Lake City, declaring "There aren't many small decisions in the life of a person. Every decision you make will have an influence upon what you become, what you really are and what your potential beyond yourself can be."

March 16: Gathered in stake centers throughout Bolivia for a satellite broadcast that originated from a studio in the Conference Center in Salt Lake City, Church members and investigators listened to counsel and instruction from President Monson and other Church leaders.

March 28: In an effort to further memorialize the victims killed at Mountain Meadows more than 150 years before in southern Utah, Elder Marlin K. Jensen of the Seventy and Church historian told leaders of three descendant organizations in Carrollton, Ark., that the Church will seek National Historic Landmark designation for the site.

March 29: Speaking at the worldwide broadcast of the annual General Young Women Meeting, President Henry B. Eyring, first counselor in the First Presidency, described to the young women of the Church the Lord's guidelines for joy as they journey through mortal life. Young Women General President Susan W. Tanner and her counselors, Elaine S. Dalton and Mary N. Cook, also spoke.

"The way through difficulties has always been prepared for you, and you will find it if you exercise faith.... You must have faith to pray. You must have faith to ponder the word of God. You must have faith to do those things and to go to those places which invite the Spirit of Christ and the Holy Ghost."
— Pres. Eyring

LDS Church News

Banners in the colors of the Young Women Values are draped in Conference Center for General Young Women annual meeting.

LDS Church News

President Thomas S. Monson with counselors President Henry B. Eyring and President Dieter F. Uchtdorf greet Young Women general presidency.

President Dieter F. Uchtdorf leads the First Presidency in the sustaining of President Thomas S. Monson as 16th president of the Church in a sacred solemn assembly during the opening session of general conference.

APRIL 2008

Members worldwide raise hands to sustain prophet

President Thomas S. Monson was sustained by Church members worldwide – according to their quorums and groups – as prophet, seer and revelator, and the 16th President of The Church of Jesus Christ of Latter-day Saints in a solemn assembly on April 5.

Also at the solemn assembly, held in the Conference Center in Salt Lake City during the opening session of the 178th Annual General Conference, President Henry B. Eyring and President Dieter F. Uchtdorf were sustained as first and second counselors in the First Presidency, respectively.

Capacity crowds filled the 21,000-seat Conference Center and overflow areas on Temple Square for the conference, which was translated into 91 languages and transmitted by satellite to 170 countries.

The First Presidency had been functioning since a Feb. 3, 2008, meeting in the Salt Lake Temple where President

"As your hands were raised toward heaven, my heart was touched. I felt your love and support, as well as your commitment to the Lord."

— President Monson

Monson was ordained and set apart to succeed President Gordon B. Hinckley, at age 97, who died Jan. 27, 2008.

In addition to sustaining the new First Presidency, Church members also sustained Elder D. Todd Christofferson to the Quorum of the Twelve, filling the vacancy created by President Uchtdorf's call to the First Presidency; and Elder L. Whitney Clayton, a member of the First Quorum of the Seventy, to the Presidency of the Seventy, filling the vacancy left by Elder Christofferson.

In addition, a new Young Women general presidency, consisting of Elaine S. Dalton, president; Mary N. Cook, first counselor; and Ann M. Dibb, second counselor was sustained at the conference.

Also in the news in April 2008

April 1-4: In conjunction with April general conference, the general auxiliary organizations held training workshops for stake auxiliary leaders, which focused on how the stake leaders can help new ward auxiliary leaders learn their duties. The workshops, to be held yearly, replace the general auxiliary open houses that previously coincided with each general conference.

April 10: Elder L. Tom Perry of the Quorum of the Twelve addressed graduates of LDS Business College in the Assembly Hall on Temple Square, telling them that the greatest assurance to finding success and satisfaction in the decisions they make is to develop their character.

LDS Church News

Elder L. Tom Perry, with LDS Business College President Stephen K. Woodhouse, leads processional on Temple Square.

April 11: Speaking at the winter commencement exercises at BYU-Idaho, Elder M. Russell Ballard of the Quorum of the Twelve encouraged the 1,411 graduates "to reach out to others in the world to help change the perception and even the hearts of millions of our Heavenly Father's children by correcting misunderstandings by sharing with them the message of the

LDS Church News

Elder M. Russell Ballard, right, assisted by BYU-Idaho President Kim B. Clark, recognize some 1,400 graduates.

restored gospel of Jesus Christ."

April 24: Elder David A. Bednar of the Quorum of the Twelve told the 6,276 BYU graduates during the university's spring commencement exercises that a love for learning is central to the gospel because "the Atonement of Jesus Christ and the agency afforded . . . are divinely designed to facilitate our learning."

April 26: Plans to build two new temples in Arizona – one in Gilbert and the other in Gila Valley – were announced by President Monson, the first two temples he announced since becoming president of the Church on Feb. 3, 2008.

LDS Church News

Elder David A. Bednar and BYU President Cecil D. Samuelson walk in the snow to Marriott Center to award 6,276 degrees.

New temples were announced for Gilbert and the Gila Valley, bringing the number of temples in Arizona to four, 134 worldwide.

A large congregation gathers in the Marriott Center to hear counsel from President Thomas S. Monson. "Don't procrastinate what matters most," he said.

MAY 2008

Enjoy the journey, women are advised

More than 17,000 women participated in the 2008 Women's Conference, held May 1-2 on the BYU campus and co-sponsored by BYU and the Relief Society. During the conference, 209 presenters addressed topics based on the theme, "Awake, Arise and Come unto Him" (from Moroni 10:30-32), and included 96 concurrent sessions and four general sessions.

President Thomas S. Monson converses with his wife, Sister Frances Monson.

President Monson spoke at the closing general session, and counseled the women to find "joy in the journey," to enjoy today rather than just looking forward to what might come tomorrow. "I plead with you not to let the important things in life pass you by, planning instead for that illusive and non-existent future day when you'll have time to do all that you want to do.

> "Each one of you is living a life filled with much to do. I plead with you not to let the important things in life pass you by, planning instead for that illusive and non-existent future day when you'll have time to do all that you want to do. Instead, find joy in the journey — now."
> — President Monson

Instead, find joy in the journey – now. There is no tomorrow to remember if we don't do something today. Let us not procrastinate those things which matters most," he said.

During the two-day event, the women also participated in a number of service projects, including making newborn baby kits, school kits, hospital activity kits and hygiene kits.

Also in the news in May 2008

May 2-3: Responding rapidly after Cylone Nargis struck Myanmar's Irrawaddy Delta region, resulting in an estimated 100,000 deaths, the Church made a large donation, in partnership with CARE International, for the purchase of clean drinking water, tarps, blankets, basic food items and medical supplies for distribution to victims. A week later, the Church sent to Myanmar 142,000 pounds of emergency relief supplies, and another 13,000 first aid kits.

Getty Images
Survivors of Cyclone Nargis wait for a relief of food distribution. The Church provided medical supplies to Myanmar.

May 8: The president of the Dominican Republic, Leonel Fernandez Reyna, spoke to some 1,500 Church members at a meeting on the grounds of the Santo Domingo Dominican Republic Temple.

May 16: President Henry B. Eyring, first counselor in the First Presidency, dedicated a new building in Provo, Utah, for LDS Philanthropies, which is a department of the Presiding Bishopric's Office.

May 23-24: More than 600 Hong Kong members of the Church, responding to a call for help

LDS Church News
Service project leaders include: Elder Sam Chi Hong Wong, Bruce Lai, Ms. Zhao Li Zhen, Elder Stanley Wan.

from Church leaders, traveled to nearby Shenzhen, China, to assemble 10,000 necessities kits for earthquake victims of Sichuan, China.

May 24: President Monson announced the Church plans to build a new temple in Phoenix, Ariz., bringing to three the number of temples announced for Arizona within a month. The Phoenix temple is the 140th temple in operation or in construction or planning stages.

May 29: U.S. President George W. Bush, in Salt Lake City to participate in fundraisers for presumptive Republican Party presidential nominee, Sen. John McCain, visited with members of the First Presidency in an hour-long meeting in the Church Administration Building.

May 31: The evening before the Curitiba Brazil Temple was dedicated, thousands of members re-enacted in a grand cultural event in Curitiba's Arena da Baixada the history of the Church – from the First Vision in 1820 to the dedication of the Curitiba temple, which took place the next day. President Monson, in Brazil for the temple dedication, described the program as "very much like what you'd see at the opening ceremony for the Olympics."

LDS Church News
President Dieter F. Uchtdorf, Relief Society General President Julie B. Beck and President Thomas S. Monson tour Air Force One on May 28, 2008, during the visit of U.S. President George W. Bush to Salt Lake City.

LDS Church News
Immigrants from many nations were represented by performers in the Curitiba Brazil Temple cultural event.

Answering a call for volunteers, missionaries from Missouri St. Louis, Illinois Peoria and Illinois Nauvoo missions work together in Quincy, Ill. Their help came nearly 170 years after citizens in Quincy sheltered oppressed Latter-day Saints.

JUNE 2008

Church members work to protect Nauvoo House

Church members turned out in massive numbers to help victims of record-breaking flooding in four Midwestern states. Flood waters from the Mississippi, Cedar, Iowa and White rivers, which crested June 17-18, inundated several cities in Indiana, Illinois, Iowa and Wisconsin.

Members and missionaries filled sandbags that were set to protect the historic Nauvoo House.

Dozens of Church-member families were displaced from their homes, and approximately 60 Latter-day Saints homes sustained significant damage.

In response to the disaster, the Church sent 16 truckloads of supplies to the impacted areas.

In Nauvoo, Ill., missionaries and BYU

The historic sites director for the Community of Christ said he woke up knowing that the historic Nauvoo House would be threatened by the rising Mississippi. Worse was the fact that he didn't have a plan of action to protect it.

students in Nauvoo worked with Community of Christ members to sandbag the historic Nauvoo House, near the edge of the Mississippi River. Church members also participated in sandbagging efforts in other parts of Illinois, as well as in Indiana, Iowa and Wisconsin.

Also in the news in June 2008

LDS Church News

President Thomas S. Monson with Elder Russell M. Nelson and his wife, Wendy, left; and Elder Charles Didier and his wife, Lucie, participate in Curitiba Brazil Temple dedication.

LDS Church News

President Thomas S. Monson, left, with Elder Russell M. Nelson, right, meet with Brazil's vice president, Jose Alencar, center, with translator Edison Lopes.

June 1: The fifth temple in Brazil was dedicated in four sessions by President Monson in Curitiba, a little over three years after the ground was broken for the temple.

June 2: In Brazil for the dedication of the Curitiba Brazil Temple, President Monson and Elder Russell M. Nelson of the Quorum of the Twelve traveled to Brasilia to address 7,000 members gathered in Marina Hall, some coming from as far away as 600 miles. President Monson counseled the members about the choices they make in their lives. "Our choices determine our eternal destiny," he said.

June 2: While in Brasilia, President Monson and Elder Nelson paid a courtesy call on Brazil's Vice President José Alencar. They were accompanied by Elder Charles Didier of the Seventy and president of the Brazil Area, and Elder Ulisses Soares, a counselor in the Area presidency.

June 8: The 30th anniversary of the 1978 priesthood revelation that granted the priesthood to all worthy males regardless of race, was commemorated at a gathering in the Salt Lake Tabernacle. Speakers included Elder Sheldon F. Child of the Seventy and

three Church members of African-American descent: Fred A. Parker III, Catherine M. Stokes and Ahmad S. Corrbitt. Elder Child said that June 8, 1978, was a day never to be forgotten.

June 20: Ground for the sixth temple in Brazil was broken in Manaus by Elder Charles Didier of the Seventy and president of the Brazil Area.

June 21: Elder Dallin H. Oaks of the Quorum of the Twelve admonished the 235 graduates of BYU-Hawaii in Laie, Hawaii, not to become imprisoned by "voluntary slavery." "When we allow ourselves to be brought under the power of anything or anyone, we become a slave to that person or that thing," he said.

June 22: President Monson addressed new mission presidents and their wives at a sacrament meeting, held at the Missionary Training Center in Provo, Utah, during the 2008 Seminar for New Mission Presidents. President Henry B. Eyring addressed the mission leaders on June 23, President Dieter F. Uchtdorf on June 24, and President Boyd K. Packer on June 25.

June 23: BYU's Ballroom Dance Company, on a three-week performance tour of China, helped open the Olympic Cultural Festival, an international celebration prior to the Beijing 2008 Summer Olympics.

"When we allow ourselves to be brought under the power of anything or anyone, we become a slave to that person or that thing.... Prize your power of choice. Protect it against every surrender, every dilution, every threat. Hold to the values you have been taught by your worthy parents, by righteous teachers ....When we know the truth and act upon that truth, we can avoid the slavery of which I have spoken."

BYU

Audience in Beijing, China, enjoys BYU ballroom dancers' performance in Olympic Cultural Festival.

Pres. Thomas S. Monson and his wife, Frances, participate in the Days of '47 parade in downtown Salt Lake City.

JULY 2008

Days of '47 parade celebrates pioneering

"People come together and talent comes out of the woodwork for this huge undertaking."
— Sherrie Cottam

Oun a pleasant summer morning, crowds lined the streets of downtown Salt Lake City for the annual Pioneer Day parade July 24. All ages cheered as floats traveled the parade route, each with its own colorful and artistic representation of this year's theme, "Still Pioneering Together." As a celebration for Utah's pioneer heritage,

Woods Cross Utah Stake

the floats creatively represented pioneers from an array of areas.

"Most of the people didn't know anybody else and then, all of the sudden, they started working as a team and now they have lasting friendships," said Sherrie Cottam, religious float coordinator on the Days of '47 Parade committee.

Also in the news in July 2008

Sandy Utah Crescent South Stake

Magna Utah East Stake

Salt Lake Granger North Stake

Farmington Utah Stake

> "Gaining knowledge through scripture study requires some attributes and actions that most formal education endeavors do not; sincere desire, unwavering faith, prayer and the will and obedience to follow the Spirit's promptings. Virtually all humans upon the earth, no matter what their mental capacity, can experience the joy and rewards of lifetime gospel study.
> — Elder Hales

Elder Robert D. Hales addresses an audience of 22,000 attending the annual BYU Campus Education Week devotional.

AUGUST 2008

Learning is essential to eternal progress

Finna Patterson and her mother, Tess Buyanan, from the Philippines study Education week catalog.

Learning throughout a person's lifetime is an essential part of his or her eternal education, Elder Robert D. Hales told some 22,000 people gathered in the BYU Marriott Center for the university's annual Campus Education Week

Elder Hales said a few basic attributes are needed to become a lifelong learner, including courage, faithful desire, humility, patience, curiosity and a willingness to communicate and share knowledge.

devotional assembly Aug. 19. Elder Hales of the Quorum of the Twelve spoke on the theme of the week: "The Journey of Lifelong Learning."

Also in the news in August 2008

Aug. 9: The Mormon Tabernacle Choir participated in the Sun Valley (Idaho) Summer Symphony's annual fund-raising concert, held in central Idaho's newest performance venue, The Sun Valley Pavilion. The Summer Symphony director, Alasdair Neale, said the experience was "unforgettable."

Young women participate in cultural celebratiion dressed in native costume.

Aug. 9: The night before the Panama City Panama Temple was dedicated, a cast of 900 youth, who gathered from throughout Panama, danced and sang in a colorful cultural celebration in the spacious Figali Convention Center in Panama City. "I love to see young people have these great memory-building experiences," President Monson said.

Members stroll across grounds after dedication of Panama temple

Aug. 10: With the famed Panama Canal a short distance away, the Panama City Panama Temple, partially surrounded by a lush tropical forest, was dedicated in four sessions by President Monson.

Aug. 11: President Monson paid a visit to Panama's president, Martin Torrijos and his wife, First Lady Vivian Fernandez de Torrijos. The occasion marked the first time a Church president had met with a Panamanian president.

President Thomas S. Monson presents a family-themed statue to Panama President Martin Torrijos and Mrs. Vivian Fernandez de Torrijos.

Presidency of the Republic of Panama

Aug. 14: Speaking at BYU's commencement ceremonies, Elder Richard G. Scott of the Quorum of the Twelve offered several "simple yet profound" suggestions to the 2,559 graduates that would help them commence their post-graduate life.

Aug. 14: In honor of the 80th birthday of King Bhumibol Adulyadej of Thailand, Latter-day Saint Charities donated 980 wheelchairs to the Sai Jai Thai Foundation in Bangkok.

Youth from 14 stakes in south-central Idaho perform in cultural event.

Aug. 22-23: Prior to the dedication of the Twin Falls Idaho Temple, 3,200 youth from 14 stakes participated in a cultural production, which celebrated through music and dance the rich heritage of the area and the blessings of the Church to members who live in south-central Idaho's Magic Valley. Titled "Living Water," the production was staged in the rodeo arena of the Filer, Idaho, fairgrounds for four audiences, one on Aug. 22 and three on Aug. 23.

Late-summer flowers complement Twin Falls Idaho Temple on day of dedication.

Aug. 24: Idaho's fourth temple, located in Twin Falls near Shoshone Falls on the Snake River was dedicated in four sessions by President Monson.

Missionaries and members wearing "Helping Hands" T-shirts volunteer during clean up after Hurricane Ike.

SEPTEMBER 2008

Church aid loaded in trucks before hurricanes hit

Once temporal needs are met, members can begin to do things of a more spiritual nature, like look after their neighbors and find out how they can be helpful. Sometimes it leads them to seek their Heavenly Father in ways they haven't done before.

Immediately after Hurricane Ike struck Texas on Sept. 13, Church supplies reached victims.

Hurricane Ike left 48 dead in 10 states as it moved from Texas northeastward across the U.S. midsection, causing millions of dollars in damage and leaving 2.6 million people without power. Some 600 members took shelter in more than 20 Church buildings during the storm.

Prior to hitting the United States, Hurricane Ike wreaked havoc on Haiti, where the Church sent two planeloads of supplies to Port-au-Prince in response to the disaster. In addition to the supplies, the Church purchased food and other relief supplies in Haiti to be distributed to the victims.

The Church sent 80,640 hygiene kits (six truckloads); 8,064 cleaning kits (four truckloads); 11,520 blankets (two truckloads); four truckloads of water; and 4,800 food boxes. Each food box was designed to feed a family of four for a week to 10 days.

Also in the news in September 2008

September: In response to severe drought in Ethiopia, the Church sent 1.4 million pounds of Atmit – an easily digestible porridge made of oat flour, sugar, powdered milk and a vitamin/mineral mix – to the African nation. The first of 34 container loads reached Ethiopia Sept. 19. An estimated four million Ethiopians were in need of emergency assistance.

LDS Church News

Family, friends and law enforcement officers gather on the grounds of the Utah State Capitol for the dedication of a monument memorializing those who died in the line of duty. President Boyd K. Packer dedicated the monument built to honor with a bronze plaque each of the 126 fallen officers.

Nothing can divide a family that is willing to serve the Lord and keep His commandments.... Members must ask themselves what they are doing to strengthen their personal faith — and the faith of their families.
— Pres. Uchtdorf

Sept. 6: President Boyd K. Packer, president of the Quorum of the Twelve, dedicated the Utah Law Enforcement Memorial on the grounds of the Utah State Capitol, in honor of the 126 law enforcement officers who died in the line of duty in Utah.

Sept. 7: Members of 135 stakes in Utah's Wasatch and Utah counties gathered in the Marriott Center on the BYU campus and in scores of meetinghouses in the two counties for a combined satellite broadcast stake conference. President Dieter F. Uchtdorf, second counselor in the First Presidency; President Boyd K. Packer, president of the Quorum of the

Twelve; Elder Marlin K. Jensen of the Seventy; and Sister Ann M. Dibb, second counselor in the Young Women general presidency, addressed the conference.

LDS Church News

President Thomas S. Monson departs with his wife, Frances, and daughter, Ann Dibb, following conference.

Sept. 14: Speaking at the Salt Lake City North Stake Conference Broadcast originating in the Conference Center, President Monson counseled members of the Church from 77 stakes to respond to the Savior's plea, "Come follow me." Other speakers were Elder M. Russell Ballard of the Quorum of the Twelve, Elder Richard G. Hinckley of the Seventy and Primary General President Cheryl C. Lant.

September: Brigham Young University-Idaho reached an all-time high in students with 13,759 enrollment for the fall semester. The record is the result of more freshmen students accepting admission than expected.

"Let there be no anger among us, brothers and sisters. Let there be love among the membership of this great Church."
— Pres. Monson

Almost 14,000 students are enrolled in at BYU-Idaho due to a larger than anticipated freshman class, and returned missionaries.

LDS Church News

Local children watch as Elder David Frandsen, a Church service missionary and water engineer, and Robert Hokanson of Church Humanitarian Services inspect a clean water source in area outside Luputa, DR Congo.

2007 REPORT

During the past year, Humanitarian Services responded to **170** natural disasters in **52** countries. Members of the Church contributed **647,319** days of volunteer labor in Welfare and Humanitarian Services initiatives, providing aid to over 5 million people in 88 countries. The Church distributed **1,157,000** hygiene, newborn and school and cleaning kits to people in distress, along with **247,000** blankets and quilts and **9,742,000** pounds of clothing and shoes.

Clean water: An answer to villagers' prayers

Word spread quickly as two missionary couples traveled from village to village in early 2008 in the remote area surrounding Luputa, DR Congo. They had come to finalize the development of a Church-funded humanitarian project that would provide clean water to an estimated 160,000 people.

The villagers let out a loud African cheer, clapping and celebrating. Their prayers had been answered.

Local residents walk in downtown Luputa, a remote city of 110,000 people in DR Congo. The Church has begun work on a clean-water project in the area, the largest clean-water project the Church has undertaken to date, delivering water via pipeline from hilltop springs an estimated 20 miles to Luputa. The gravity-fed system requires no pump or electricity.

$259.8 million
Cash donations

$750.9 million
Value of material assistance

Humanitarian assistance rendered (1985-2007)

GENERAL AUTHORITIES, OFFICERS

The Quorum of Twelve Apostles, October 2008.

President Boyd K. Packer, Elder L. Tom Perry, Elder Russell M. Nelson,
Elder Dallin H. Oaks, Elder M. Russell Ballard, Elder Joseph B. Wirthlin,
back row, Elder Richard G. Scott, Elder Robert D. Hales, Elder Jeffrey R. Holland,
Elder David A. Bednar, Elder Quentin L. Cook, Elder D. Todd Christofferson.

THE FIRST PRESIDENCY
Thomas S. Monson

PRESIDENT

President Thomas S. Monson has been on the Lord's errand all his life, from serving as president of his ward's teachers quorum in his teens, to serving as bishop in his early 20s, to presiding over a mission in his early 30s, to becoming a member of the Quorum of the Twelve at age 36.

Thomas S. Monson

For the 22 years prior to being set apart as 16th President of the Church on Feb. 3, 2008, President Monson served as counselor to three presidents: second counselor to President Ezra Taft Benson and President Howard W. Hunter and, for nearly 13 years, first counselor to President Gordon B. Hinckley.

Five years after his call to the Twelve, he was given a special assignment for the work of the Church in Europe, requiring many visits with members behind the Iron Curtain in the German Democratic Republic, Czechoslovakia, Poland and Hungary. He had a key role in gaining permission from the East German government to build the Freiberg Germany Temple, which was dedicated in 1985, and in advancing the work of the Lord in other eastern European countries that were part of the communist bloc.

His life is associated with benevolence and compassion, serving others with a desire to nourish the weak and strengthen the weary. His role in the Church's welfare program has been characterized by one-on-one service.

He remembers how his father never spoke ill of another, and would leave the room when others spoke disrespectfully or negatively. He often speaks of his mother who taught him compassion by her acts of service to others, particularly those who were hungry or in need.

On one occasion, on a cold winter's night, a knock came at Bishop Monson's door. A German man living in Ogden began to weep as he told how his brother, a faithful member in Germany during World War II, and his family were moving from Germany to an apartment in Bishop Monson's ward. Then-Bishop Monson visited the apartment and found it woefully inadequate. The next morning during a ward welfare committee meeting, he described the challenge. Members offered their skills and services. When the family arrived three weeks later, they found new carpet and paint, adequate lighting and full cupboards. "The father . . . buried his head in my shoulder and repeated the words, 'Mein Bruder, mein Bruder, mein Bruder.' "

Family: Born Aug. 21, 1927, in Salt Lake City to G. Spencer and Gladys Condie Monson; two brothers and three sisters; married **Frances Beverly Johnson** in the Salt Lake Temple on Oct. 7, 1948; three children: two sons, Tom and Clark; one daughter, Ann Dibb; eight grandchildren and four great-grandchildren.

Church service: Called at age 22 as bishop of the Sixth-Seventh Ward in Salt Lake City, with some 1,080 members, including about 84 widows; called as counselor in a stake presidency at age 27; called as president of the Canadian Mission at age 31; served on several Church committees, including the Adult Correlation Committee and helped pioneer the home teaching program of the Church; sustained on Oct. 4, 1963, at age 36 to Quorum of the Twelve. As a member of the Quorum of the Twelve, he supervised the missions in western America, the South Pacific, Mexico, Central America and Europe. After a number of years and following the policy of rotation, the European missions were transferred to another member of the Twelve; however, Elder Monson retained responsibility for all countries behind the Iron Curtain. He was instrumental in the construction of the Freiberg Germany Temple, served as chairman of the Scriptures Publication Committee and supervised the process which resulted in new editions of the Standard Works of the Church. Called on Nov. 10, 1985, as second counselor to President Ezra Taft Benson; called in 1994 as second counselor to President Howard W. Hunter and in 1995 as first counselor to President Gordon B. Hinckley; ordained and set apart on Feb. 3, 2008, as President of The Church of Jesus Christ of Latter-day Saints.

Education: Graduated with honors from the University of Utah in 1948 with a degree in business; received an MBA from Brigham Young University, and received honorary Doctor of Laws degree from BYU, honorary Doctor of Humane Letters from Salt Lake Community College, and honorary Doctor of Business from the University of Utah.

Employment: Began working for *Deseret News* in 1948 as assistant classified advertising manager; shortly thereafter he became classified advertising manager; he became an officer of Newspaper Agency Corporation in 1952, became sales manager of Deseret News Press in 1953, and later became assistant general manager; served as president of the Printing Industry of Utah and later served as a director of the Printing Industries of America; named general manager of Deseret Press upon returning home from serving as a mission president in Canada; chairman of the Deseret News Board of directors for 19 years.

Civic: Has served nearly four decades on the National Executive Board of Boy Scouts of America; received Scouting's Silver Beaver and Silver Buffalo awards and International Scouting's highest award, the Bronze Wolf. In December 1981 President Monson was appointed by U.S. President Ronald Reagan to serve on the President's Task Force for Private Sector Initiatives. He served in this capacity until December 1982, when the work of the task force was completed.

Military Service: In 1945-1946, served active duty in U.S. Naval Reserve.

Henry B. Eyring

FIRST COUNSELOR IN FIRST PRESIDENCY

President Henry B. Eyring was set apart Feb. 3, 2008, as first counselor in the First Presidency to President Thomas S. Monson, and sustained April 5, 2008, in the solemn assembly of general conference.

He was sustained Oct. 6, 2007, and set apart Oct. 11, 2007, as second counselor in the First Presidency to President Gordon B. Hinckley.

He was sustained to the Quorum of the Twelve April 1, 1995, and ordained an apostle April 6, 1995, at age 61.

He was sustained to the First Quorum of the Seventy Oct. 3, 1992, and as first counselor in the Presiding Bishopric April 6, 1985.

Before being called as a General Authority he served as a regional representative, member of the Sunday School general board, and bishop.

Born May 31, 1933, in Princeton, N.J., to Henry and Mildred Bennion Eyring.

He received a bachelor's degree in physics from the University of Utah, and

Henry B. Eyring

master's and doctoral degrees from Harvard University in business administration. His passion was to teach; he became an assistant professor and associate professor at the Stanford Graduate School of Business in Palo Alto, Calif.

He served as the president of Ricks College, 1971-77, before being called as Deputy Commissioner, and then Commissioner, of Church Education.

He and his wife, **Kathleen Johnson Eyring,** are parents of six children and have 25 grandchildren.

President Eyring was reared by parents who valued education. His father was a chemistry professor at Princeton University and his mother had been a professor at the University of Utah and a doctoral candidate at the University of Wisconsin when she met and married her husband.

The Eyring home was a learning laboratory — filled with discussion about "deep, serious things" — where President Eyring learned to cherish religion and appreciate science and to respect others. Once President Eyring asked his father why he asked the gas station attendants questions. "Dad said, 'I never met a man I couldn't learn something from.' "

Dieter F. Uchtdorf

SECOND COUNSELOR IN FIRST PRESIDENCY

President Dieter F. Uchtdorf was set apart Feb. 3, 2008, as second counselor in the First Presidency to President Thomas S. Monson, and sustained April 5, 2008, in the solemn assembly in general conference.

He was sustained to the Quorum of the Twelve Oct. 2, 2004, and ordained an apostle Oct. 7, 2004, at age 63.

He was called to the Presidency of the Seventy Aug. 15, 2002, and sustained Oct. 5, 2002.

He was sustained to the First Quorum of the Seventy April 6, 1996.

He was sustained to the Second Quorum of the Seventy April 2, 1994.

Prior to being called as a General Authority, he was stake president and stake mission president.

He received his education in engineering, and later studied business administration and international management.

Dieter F. Uchtdorf

He is a former senior vice president for flight operations and chief pilot for Lufthansa German Airlines.

He was born Nov. 6, 1940, in Ostrava, the former Czechoslovakia, to Karl Albert and Hilde Else Opelt Uchtdorf, and grew up in Germany.

He married **Harriet Reich Uchtdorf;** they are parents of two children, and have six grandchildren.

His family joined the Church as a result of a missionary-minded, elderly woman who invited his grandmother to Church in East Germany. He was baptized two years after his family, when he turned 8 years old.

Reflecting on his life, he gives full credit to the teachings and the programs of the Church for what has happend to him.

In October 2006 general conference, he said: "Our motives and thoughts ultimately influence our actions. The testimony of the truthfulness of the restored gospel of Jesus Christ is the most powerful motivating force in our lives. Jesus repeatedly emphasized the power of good thoughts and proper motives: 'Look unto me in every thought; doubt not, fear not.' "

Boyd K. Packer

Set apart as President of the Quorum of the Twelve on Feb. 3, 2008. Previously set apart as Acting President of the Quorum of the Twelve on June 5, 1994, and again March 12, 1995. Sustained as an Assistant to the Twelve Sept. 30, 1961; sustained to the Quorum of the Twelve April 6, 1970, and ordained an apostle April 9, 1970, at age 45. Former supervisor of Seminaries and Institutes of Religion; former president of the New England States Mission. Received bachelor's and master's degrees from Utah State University, and Ed.D. in educational administration from BYU. Pilot in the Pacific Theater during World War II. Born Sept. 10, 1924, in Brigham City, Utah, a son of Ira Wight and Emma Jensen Packer. Wife, Donna Smith Packer; parents of 10 children.

L. Tom Perry

Sustained as an Assistant to the Twelve Oct. 6, 1972; sustained to the Quorum of the Twelve on April 6, 1974, and ordained an apostle April 11, 1974, at age 51. Served in the Marines in the Pacific during World War II. Graduated from Utah State University with a B.S. degree in finance; was controller, vice president and treasurer of department store organizations in Idaho, California and Boston, Mass. Former president of the Boston Stake and served as counselor in other stake presidencies and bishoprics. Born Aug. 5, 1922, in Logan, Utah, to L. Tom and Nora Sonne Perry. Wife, Virginia Lee; parents of three children. She died in 1974. Married Barbara Dayton in 1976.

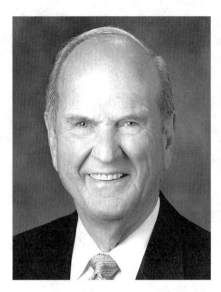

Russell M. Nelson

Sustained to the Quorum of the Twelve April 7, 1984, and ordained an apostle April 12, 1984, at age 59. Former Sunday School general president, regional representative, and stake president. Renowned surgeon and medical researcher. Received B.A. and M.D. degrees from University of Utah, and Ph.D. from University of Minnesota. Former president of the Society for Vascular Surgery and former chairman of the Council on Cardiovascular Surgery for the American Heart Association. Born Sept. 9, 1924, in Salt Lake City, Utah, to Marion C. and Edna Anderson Nelson. Wife, Dantzel White Nelson; parents of 10 children. She died Feb. 12, 2005. Married Wendy Watson on April 6, 2006.

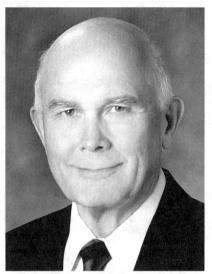

Dallin H. Oaks

Sustained to the Quorum of the Twelve April 7, 1984, and ordained an apostle May 3, 1984, at age 51. Graduate of BYU in accounting; J.D. cum laude The University of Chicago Law School; law clerk to U.S. Supreme Court Chief Justice Earl Warren, practiced law in Chicago; professor of law at The University of Chicago; nine years as BYU president; three-and-one-half years as a justice of the Utah Supreme Court; and five years as chairman of the board of the Public Broadcasting Service. Former regional representative and counselor in stake presidency. Born Aug. 12, 1932, in Provo, Utah, a son of Dr. Lloyd E. and Stella Harris Oaks. Wife, June Dixon Oaks died July 21, 1998; parents of six children. Married Kristen Meredith McMain on Aug. 25, 2000.

M. Russell Ballard

Sustained to the First Quorum of the Seventy April 3, 1976, and to the presidency of the quorum Feb. 21, 1980. Sustained to the Quorum of the Twelve Oct. 6, 1985, and ordained an apostle Oct. 10, 1985, at age 57. Attended the University of Utah; previously engaged in various business enterprises, including automotive, real estate, and investments. Was president of the Canada Toronto Mission, counselor in a mission presidency, and bishop. The grandson of Apostles Melvin J. Ballard and Hyrum Mack Smith, he was born Oct. 8, 1928, in Salt Lake City, Utah, to Melvin Russell Sr. and Geraldine Smith Ballard. Wife, Barbara Bowen Ballard; parents of seven children.

Joseph B. Wirthlin

Sustained as an Assistant to the Twelve April 4, 1975, to the First Quorum of the Seventy Oct. 1, 1976, and to the presidency of the quorum Aug. 28, 1986; sustained to the Quorum of the Twelve Oct. 4, 1986, and ordained an apostle Oct. 9, 1986, at age 69. Served in the Sunday School general presidency, as stake president's counselor, and bishop. Graduate of University of Utah in business management; former president of trade association. Born June 11, 1917, in Salt Lake City, Utah, to Joseph L. and Madeline Bitner Wirthlin. Wife, Elisa Young Rogers Wirthlin; parents of eight children. She died Aug. 16, 2006.

Richard G. Scott

Sustained to the First Quorum of the Seventy April 2, 1977, and to the quorum presidency Oct. 1, 1983; sustained to the Quorum of the Twelve Oct. 1, 1988, and ordained apostle Oct. 6, 1988, at age 59. Received B.S. degree in mechanical engineering from George Washington University, completed post-graduate work in nuclear engineering at Oak Ridge, Tenn. Worked on the staff of Adm. Hyman Rickover, developing military and private nuclear power reactors; was consultant to nuclear power industry. Former president of Argentina North Mission, regional representative, and counselor in stake presidency. Born Nov. 7, 1928, in Pocatello, Idaho, to Kenneth Leroy and Mary Eliza Whittle Scott. Wife, Jeanene Watkins; parents of seven children. She died May 15, 1995.

Robert D. Hales

Sustained as an Assistant to the Twelve April 4, 1975, and to the First Quorum of the Seventy Oct. 1, 1976; sustained as Presiding Bishop April 6, 1985; sustained to the Quorum of the Twelve April 2, 1994, and ordained an apostle April 7, 1994, at age 61. Former first counselor in the Sunday School general presidency, president of the England London Mission, regional representative, stake president's counselor, served as a branch president and bishop. Earned bachelor's degree from the University of Utah and master's degree in business administration from Harvard; served in the U.S. Air Force as jet fighter pilot; was an executive with four major national companies. Born Aug. 24, 1932, in New York City, N.Y., to John Rulon and Vera Marie Holbrook Hales. Wife, Mary Elene Crandall Hales; parents of two children.

Jeffrey R. Holland

Ordained an apostle June 23, 1994, at age 53, and sustained to the Quorum of the Twelve Oct. 1, 1994. Sustained to the First Quorum of the Seventy on April 1, 1989, while serving as president of Brigham Young University. Former Church Commissioner of Education, 1976-80; BYU president from 1980-89, former dean of College of Religion at BYU. Received bachelor's degree in English, and master's degree in religious education from BYU, and master's degree and doctorate in American studies from Yale University. Former regional representative, counselor in stake presidency, and bishop. Born Dec. 3, 1940, in St. George, Utah, to Frank D. and Alice Bentley Holland. Wife, Patricia Terry Holland; parents of three children.

David A. Bednar

Sustained to the Quorum of the Twelve Oct. 2, 2004; ordained an apostle Oct. 7, 2004, at age 52. Former Area Seventy, Area Authority, regional representative, stake president and bishop. Received bachelor's degree and master's degree from BYU, and doctorate from Purdue University. Professor of business management at Texas Tech University, and at University of Arkansas. President of Brigham Young University-Idaho from 1997-2004. Born June 15, 1952, in San Leandro, Calif., to Anthony G. and Lavina Whitney Bednar. Wife, Susan Kae Robinson; parents of three sons.

Quentin L. Cook

Sustained to the Second Quorum of the Seventy April 6, 1996; sustained to the First Quorum of the Seventy April 5, 1998; called to the Presidency of the Seventy Aug. 1, 2007; sustained to the Quorum of the Twelve Oct. 6, 2007, ordained an apostle Oct. 11, 2007, at age 67. Former area authority in the North America West Area, regional representative, stake president and counselor, and bishop. Former managing partner of a San Francisco Bay area law firm and president and CEO of a California healthcare system. Received bachelor's degree from Utah State University and juris doctorate from Stanford University. Born Sept. 8, 1940, in Logan, Utah, to J. Vernon and Bernice Kimball Cook. Wife, Mary Gaddie Cook; parents of three children.

D. Todd Christofferson

Sustained to the First Quorum of the Seventy April 3, 1993; called to the Presidency of the Seventy Aug. 15, 1998, and sustained Oct. 3, 1998; sustained to the Quorum of the Twelve April 5, 2008, ordained an apostle April 10, 2008, at age 63. Former regional representative, stake president, stake president's counselor, and bishop. Received bachelor's degree in English/international relations from BYU; juris doctorate from Duke University. Former associate general counsel of NationsBank Corp., (now Bank of America) in Charlotte, N.C.; practiced law in Washington, D.C., Tennessee and North Carolina, and was law clerk to the Hon. John J. Sirica, U.S. District Court for the District of Columbia, 1972-74. Born Jan. 24, 1945, in American Fork, Utah, to Paul V. and Jeanne Swenson Christofferson. Wife, Katherine Jacob Christofferson; parents of five children.

PRESIDENCY OF THE SEVENTY

Neil L. Andersen

Sustained to the First Quorum of the Seventy April 3, 1993, at age 41; called to the Presidency of the Seventy Aug. 15, 2005, and sustained Oct. 1, 2005. Former president of the France Bordeaux Mission and president of the Tampa Florida Stake. Received a bachelor's degree from BYU, received master's degree in business from Harvard University. His business interests included advertising, real estate development and health care, all based in Florida. Speaks French, Portuguese and Spanish. Born Aug. 9, 1951, in Logan, Utah, to Lyle P. and Kathryn Andersen. Wife, Kathy Sue Williams Andersen; parents of four children.

Ronald A. Rasband

Sustained to the First Quorum of the Seventy April 1, 2000, at age 49; called to the Presidency of the Seventy Aug. 15, 2005, and sustained Oct. 1, 2005. Former president of New York New York North Mission, high councilor and bishop. Was self-employed businessman and previously was president and chief operations officer of Huntsman Chemical Corporation. Attended University of Utah and received an honorary doctorate of business and commerce from Utah Valley State College in Orem, Utah. Born Feb. 6, 1951, in Salt Lake City, Utah, to Rulon Hawkins and Verda Anderson Rasband. Wife, Melanie Twitchell Rasband; parents of five children.

Claudio R.M. Costa

Sustained to the Second Quorum of the Seventy April 2, 1994, at age 45; sustained to the First Quorum of the Seventy March 31, 2001; called to the Presidency of the Seventy Aug. 1, 2007, and sustained Oct. 6, 2007. Former president of the Brazil Manaus Mission, regional representative, stake president's counselor and bishop. Graduated from Colegio Pio XII, attended Paulista School of Marketing, Paulista Institute of Gems and Precious Metals. Former CES associate area director, diamond cutter and finance director of Diversified Almeida Prado Co. Born March 25, 1949, in Santos, Brazil, to Nelson Mendes and Luzia Tassar Simoes Costa. Wife, Margareth Fernandes Morgado Mendes Costa; parents of four children.

Steven E. Snow

Sustained to the First Quorum of the Seventy March 31, 2001, at age 51; called to the Presidency of the Seventy Aug. 1, 2007, and sustained Oct. 6, 2007. Former Area Authority Seventy in the Utah South Area, president of the California San Fernando Mission, stake president and bishop. Received bachelor's degree in accounting from Utah State University and juris doctorate from Brigham Young University. Was senior partner in law firm of Snow Nuffer and formerly deputy county attorney for Washington County, Utah. Born Nov. 23, 1949, in St. George, Utah, to Gregg E. and Viola Jean Goates Snow. Wife, Phyllis Squire Snow; parents of four sons.

Walter F. Gonzalez

Sustained to the First Quorum of the Seventy March 31, 2001, at age 48; sustained to the Presidency of the Seventy Oct. 6, 2007. Former Area Authority Seventy, serving as second counselor in the South America North Area presidency, and was previously regional representative, mission president, stake president and area public affairs director. Received bachelor's degree at Indiana University and a technician's certificate at CEMLAD Institute. Formerly Church Educational System director for South America North Area and a CES employee. Born Nov. 18, 1952, in Montevideo, Uruguay, to Fermin Gabino and Victoria Dolores Nunez Gonzalez. Wife, Zulma Anahir Nunez Gonzalez; parents of four children.

L. Whitney Clayton

Sustained to the First Quorum of the Seventy March 31, 2001, at age 51; sustained to the Presidency of the Seventy April 5, 2008. Former Area Authority Seventy in the North America West Area, regional representative, mission president's counselor, high councilor, and bishop. Received bachelor's degree in finance from the University of Utah and law degree from the University of Pacific. Was an attorney and shareholder with Call, Clayton, and Jensen, a California law firm. Born Feb. 24, 1950, in Salt Lake City, Utah, to L. Whitney and Elizabeth Graham Touchstone Clayton. Wife, Kathy Ann Kipp Clayton; parents of seven children.

PRESIDENCY OF THE SEVENTY

Jay E. Jensen

Called to the Second Quorum of the Seventy June 6, 1992, at age 50, and sustained Oct. 3, 1992. Sustained to the First Quorum of the Seventy April 1, 1995. Called to the Presidency of the Seventy Aug. 1, 2008, and sustained Oct. 4, 2008. Former president of the Colombia Cali Mission, stake president's counselor and bishop. Former director of CES curriculum, and later director of scripture coordination for the Church Curriculum Department. Received bachelor's, master's, and doctoral degrees in Spanish and history, Church history and doctrine, and education, respectively, from BYU. Born Feb. 5, 1942, in Payson, Utah, to Ruel W. and Ethel Otte Jensen. Wife, Lona Lee Child Jensen; parents of six children.

FIRST QUORUM OF THE SEVENTY

Marcos A. Aidukaitis

Sustained to the First Quorum of the Seventy April 5, 2008, at age 48. Former Area Seventy in Brazil Area, president of Brazil Brasilia Mission and stake president. Was partner at MAV Distribution. Received bachelor's degree in mechanical engineering from BYU, master's degree of business administration from BYU's Marriott School of Management. Born Aug. 30, 1959, in Porto Alegre, Brazil, to Antony and Maria Dittrich Aidukaitis. Wife, Luisa Englert Aidukaitis; parents of five children.

Carlos H. Amado

Sustained to the Second Quorum of the Seventy April 1, 1989, at age 44; called to the First Quorum of the Seventy June 6, 1992, and sustained Oct. 3, 1992. Former president of the Guatemala Guatemala City Mission, where he was assigned to reopen the El Salvador San Salvador Mission, chairman of the Guatemala City Temple Committee, regional representative, stake president and counselor, bishop, and branch president. Received degree from the Technical Vocational Institute of Guatemala City; former technical draftsman, and later, area director for the Church Educational System. Born Sept. 25, 1944, in Guatemala City, Guatemala, to Carlos and Rosario Funes de Amado. Wife, Mayavel Pineda Amado; parents of five children.

David S. Baxter

Sustained to the First Quorum of the Seventy April 1, 2006, at age 51. Former Area Seventy and second counselor in the Europe West Area presidency, mission president's counselor, stake president and bishop. Received bachelor of science degree in business management from the University of Wales; was senior executive for British Telecom. Born Feb. 7, 1955, in Stirling, Scotland, to Allan D. and Ellen S. Steel Baxter. Wife, Dianne Lewars Baxter; parents of four children.

Shayne M. Bowen

Sustained to the First Quorum of the Seventy April 1, 2006, at age 51. Former Area Seventy in the Idaho Area, president of Spain Barcelona Mission, stake president, high councilor, bishop, high priests group instructor, and elders quorum president. Received bachelor's degree in English from BYU, chartered underwriter and chartered financial consultant from American College; was owner of an insurance agency. Born Aug. 29, 1954, in Rigby, Idaho, to Lyle and Jacqueline Neeley Bowen. Wife, Lynette Mortensen Bowen; parents of seven children.

Gérald Caussé

Sustained to the First Quorum of the Seventy April 5, 2008, at age 44. Former Area Seventy in Europe West Area, stake president and counselor, and high priests group leader. Was general manager for Pomona, France's largest food distributor. Received equivalent of a master's degree in business administration from ESSEC Business School in Paris with emphasis in finance and marketing. Served in military in a NATO Agency. Born May 20, 1963, in Bordeaux, France, to Jean and Marie Blanche Bonnet Caussé. Wife, Valérie Badin Caussé; parents of five children.

Craig C. Christensen

Sustained to the Second Quorum of the Seventy Oct. 5, 2002, at age 46; sustained to the First Quorum of the Seventy April 5, 2008. Former Area Authority Seventy, president of the Mexico Mexico City East Mission from 1995-98, high councilor, bishop and missionary in Chile. Received a bachelor's degree in accounting from Brigham Young University and an MBA from the University of Washington; real estate developer and franchised automobile dealer. Born March 18, 1956, in Salt Lake City, Utah, to Sheron Glen and Colleen Cloward Christensen. Wife, Debora Bliss Jones Christensen, parents of four children.

Gary J. Coleman

Called to the Second Quorum of the Seventy June 6, 1992, at age 50, and sustained Oct. 3, 1992; sustained to First Quorum of the Seventy April 5, 1997. Former president of the California Arcadia Mission, counselor to two mission presidents, stake president's counselor, and bishop. Was associate director and instructor at Weber State University Institute of Religion. Received bachelor's degree in physical education from Washington State University, master's degree and doctorate from BYU in counseling and guidance. Born Sept. 18, 1941, in Wenatchee, Wash., to Benton Joseph and Evalin Barrett Coleman. Wife, Judith Renee England Coleman; parents of six children.

Spencer J. Condie

Sustained to the Second Quorum of the Seventy April 1, 1989, at age 48; sustained to the First Quorum of the Seventy Oct. 3, 1992. Former president of the Austria Vienna Mission, regional representative, stake president and bishop. Former professor at Brigham Young University. Born Aug. 27, 1940, in Preston, Idaho, to Spencer C. and Josie Peterson Condie. Wife, Dorothea Speth Condie; parents of five children.

Lawrence E. Corbridge

Sustained to the First Quorum of the Seventy April 5, 2008, at age 58. Former president of the Chile Santiago North Mission, stake president, high councilor and bishop. Was partner and senior attorney in Salt Lake City law firm. Received bachelor's degree in business management and finance from BYU, and juris doctorate from BYU's J. Reuben Clark Law School . Born April 6, 1949, in Moscow, Idaho, to Ivan and Agnes Howe Corbridge. Wife, Jacquelyn Gayle Shamo Corbridge; parents of five children.

Benjamin De Hoyos

Sustained to the First Quorum of the Seventy April 2, 2005, at age 51. Former Area Seventy in the Mexico South Area, president of Mexico Tuxtla Gutierrez Mission, stake president and counselor, high councilor, and branch president. Received bachelor's degree in education from Normal Superior Benavente, master's degree in business management from Chapultepec University. Was Church Educational System director of Mexico South Area. Born Feb. 20, 1953 in Monterrey, N.L., Mexico, to Alfredo and Sara Estrada de De Hoyos. Wife, Evelia Genesta De Hoyos; parents of six children.

John B. Dickson

Called to the Second Quorum of the Seventy June 6, 1992, at age 48, and sustained Oct. 3, 1992. Sustained to the First Quorum of the Seventy April 1, 1995. Former president of the Mexico Mexico City North Mission, stake president, and stake president's counselor. Was vice president of sawmill and timber company. Received bachelor's degree from Brigham Young University in business administration. Born July 12, 1943, in Tacoma, Wash., to John H. and Helen Baird Dickson. Wife, Delores Jones Dickson; parents of eight children.

Charles Didier

Sustained to the First Quorum of the Seventy Oct. 3, 1975, at age 39; served in the Presidency of the Seventy from Aug. 15, 1992, to Aug. 15, 1995; called to the presidency for the second time Aug. 15, 2001, and sustained Oct. 6, 2001; served until Aug. 1, 2007. Sunday School general president from 1994-95. Former president of France Switzerland Mission and regional representative; converted to Church in 1957; fluent in five languages, French, Flemish, English, Spanish and German. Received bachelor's degree in economics from University of Liege in Belgium; served as officer in the Belgian Air Force Reserve. Born Oct. 5, 1935, in Ixelles, Belgium, to Andre and Gabrielle Colpaert Didier. Wife, Lucie Lodomez Didier; parents of two children.

David F. Evans

Sustained to the First Quorum of the Seventy April 2, 2005, at age 53. Former president of Japan Nagoya Mission, stake president and counselor, bishop and bishop's counselor, stake Young Men president and elders quorum president. Received bachelor's degree in community health education from the University of Utah and juris doctorate from BYU. Was partner and practicing attorney with Durham, Jones and Pinegar law firm, and an executive in investment banking business. Born Aug. 11, 1951, in Salt Lake City, Utah, to David C. and Joy Frewin Evans. Wife, Mary Dee Shepherd Evans; parents of eight children.

Enrique R. Falabella

Sustained to the First Quorum of the Seventy March 31, 2007, at age 56. Former Area Seventy in the Central America Area, regional representative, stake president, bishop and stake mission president. Received degree in agronomy from the University of San Carlos in Guatemala and studied marketing at the University of Costa Rica. Formerly agronomical engineer for Bayer. Born May 9, 1950, in Guatemala City, Guatemala, to Udine and Leonor Arellano Falabella. Wife, Blanca Lidia Sanchez Falabella; parents of five children.

Eduardo Gavarret

Sustained to the First Quorum of the Seventy April 5, 2008, at age 51. Former president of Paraguay Asuncion Mission, Area Authority Seventy, regional representative, stake president and bishop. Former employment included pharmaceutical sales and management in several South American countries. Graduated from the Escuela Superior de Administracion Empresas in business administration, and received master of business administration degree in marketing from Instituto Nacional de Posgraduacão in Brazil. Born May 11, 1956, in Minas, Uruguay, to Juan and Elsa Inzaurralde Gaverret. Wife, Norma Gorgorso Gavarrei; parents of three children.

Carlos A. Godoy

Sustained to the First Quorum of the Seventy April 5, 2008, at age 47. Former Area Seventy in the Brazil Area, president of Brazil Belem Mission, high councilor, bishop and regional welfare agent. Employed in various business positions before starting his own company as a business consultant in organizational change management. Received bachelor's degree in economics and political science from Pontificia Universidade Católica and master's degree in organizational behavior from BYU. Served in Brazilian army. Born Feb. 4, 1961, in Porto Alegre, Brazil, to Moacir and Ivone Poersch Godoy. Wife, Mônica Soares Brandao Godoy; parents of four children.

Christoffel Golden Jr.

Sustained to the First Quorum of the Seventy March 31, 2001, at age 48. Former Area Authority Seventy in the Africa Southeast Area, stake president and counselor, and bishop. Received bachelor's degree in political science and post graduate honors degree in international politics from the University of South Africa. After a long and varied business career, served as Church Educational System director for Africa Southeast Area. Born June 1, 1952, in Johannesburg, South Africa, to Christoffel and Maria S. Oosthuisen Golden. Wife, Diane Norma Hulbert Golden; parents of four children.

C. Scott Grow

Sustained to the First Quorum of the Seventy April 2, 2005, at age 56. Former Area Seventy in the North America Northwest and Idaho Areas, president of Uruguay Montevideo Mission, stake president and counselor, high councilor Young Men president, and bishop's counselor. Received bachelor's degree in accounting from BYU. Worked at major accounting and business consulting firms before establishing his own accounting partnership. Born May 5, 1949, in Moscow, Idaho, to Cecil W. and Elsie Mae Lee Grow. Wife, Rhonda Lee Patten Grow; parents of eight children.

Bruce C. Hafen

Sustained to the First Quorum of the Seventy April 6, 1996, at age 55. Former regional representative, counselor in stake presidency and counselor in bishopric. Former president of Ricks College and provost at Brigham Young University. Received bachelor's degree in political science and humanities from Brigham Young University and juris doctorate from University of Utah. Born Oct. 30, 1940, in St. George, Utah, to Orval and Ruth Clark Hafen. Wife, Marie Kartchner Hafen; parents of seven children.

Donald L. Hallstrom

Sustained to the First Quorum of the Seventy April 1, 2000, at age 50. Former Area Authority Seventy, regional representative, stake president, and bishop. Former president and owner of real estate economics company. Received bachelor's degree in economics from BYU. Born July 27, 1949, in Honolulu, Hawaii, to James E. and Betty Jo Lambert Hallstrom. Wife, Diane Clifton Hallstrom; parents of four children.

James J. Hamula

Sustained to the First Quorum of the Seventy April 5, 2008, at age 50. Former Area Seventy in the North America Southwest Area, president of the Washington D.C. South Mission, stake president and bishop. Was attorney and shareholder in an Arizona law firm. Received bachelor's and master's degrees in political science/philosophy from BYU, and juris doctorate from BYU. Born Nov. 20, 1957, in Long Beach, Calif., to Joseph Frank and Joyce Evelyn Jacobs Hamula. Wife, Joyce Anderson Hamula; parents of six children.

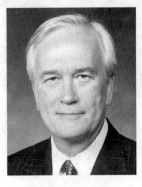

Keith K. Hilbig

Sustained to the Second Quorum of the Seventy March 31, 2001, at age 59; sustained to the First Quorum of the Seventy April 1, 2006. Former Area Authority Seventy, regional representative, president of Switzerland Zurich Mission, stake president, bishop, temple ordinance worker and Europe East and North America Northwest Area presidencies. Received bachelor's degree in European history from Princeton University and law degree from Duke University. Formerly international legal counsel for the Church in Europe. Born March 13, 1942, in Milwaukee, Wis., to Karl Herbert and Mildred Bower Hilbig. Wife, Susan Rae Logie Hilbig; parents of six children.

Richard G. Hinckley

Sustained to the First Quorum of the Seventy April 2, 2005, at age 63. Former temple sealer, president of Utah Salt Lake City Mission, stake president and counselor, high councilor, bishop, and elder's quorum president. Received bachelor's degree in economics from University of Utah and MBA from Stanford University. Formerly executive and owner in private business ventures. Served in U.S. Army Reserve. Born May 2, 1941, in Salt Lake City, Utah, to Gordon B. and Marjorie Pay Hinckley. Wife, Jane Freed Hinckley; parents of four children.

Marlin K. Jensen

Church Historian and Recorder, was sustained to the First Quorum of the Seventy April 1, 1989, at age 46; served in the Presidency of the Seventy from Aug. 15, 1998, to Aug. 15, 2001. Was general president of the Sunday School from Oct. 7, 2000, to Oct. 6, 2001. Former president of the New York Rochester Mission, regional representative, stake president, and bishop. Received bachelor's degree in German from Brigham Young University and juris doctorate from University of Utah; was attorney specializing in business and estate planning. Born May 18, 1942, in Ogden, Utah, to Keith G. and Lula Hill Jensen. Wife, Kathleen Bushnell Jensen; parents of eight children.

Daniel L. Johnson

Sustained to the First Quorum of the Seventy April 1, 2006, at age 59. Former Area Seventy in the Mexico North Area, president of Ecuador Guayaquil North Mission, counselor to mission president and stake president, and bishop. Received bachelor's degree in accounting and economics from BYU; former executive in international companies, as well as holding Church and family farming positions throughout the United States and Latin America. Born Dec. 15, 1946, in Colonia Juarez, Mexico, to Leroy and Rita Skousen Johnson. Wife, LeAnn Holman Johnson; parents of six children.

Kenneth Johnson

Sustained to the Second Quorum of the Seventy March 31, 1990, at age 49; sustained to the First Quorum of the Seventy April 3, 1993. Former regional representative and stake president; converted to the Church in 1959. Graduated from Norwich City College in England and did graduate work at the City and Guilds of London Institute of Printing; former college instructor and partner in a British insurance brokerage firm. Born July 5, 1940, in Norwich, England, to Bertie A.M. and Ada Hutson Johnson. Wife, Pamela Wilson Johnson; parents of one son.

Paul V. Johnson

Sustained to the First Quorum of the Seventy April 2, 2005, at age 50. Former Area Seventy in the Utah Salt Lake City Area, counselor in stake presidency, high councilor, bishop, and ward Young Men president. Received bachelor's degree in zoology and master's degree in counseling and guidance from BYU, and doctorate in instructional technology from Utah State University. Formerly Church Educational System administrator of Religious Education and Elementary and Secondary Education. Born June 24, 1954, in Gainesville, Fla., to Vere Hodges and Winifred Amacher Johnson. Wife, Leslie Jill Washburn Johnson; parents of nine children.

Yoshihiko Kikuchi

Sustained to the First Quorum of the Seventy Oct. 1, 1977, at age 36; first native-born Japanese called as General Authority. Former president of Hawaii Honolulu Mission, Tokyo temple president, stake president and counselor to mission president; converted to the Church in 1955. Graduated from Asia University of Tokyo in business psychology and management; former regional sales manager over Japan for a cookware company, president of a Japanese food import company. Born July 25, 1941, to Hatsuo and Koyo Ideda Kikuchi in Hokkaido, Japan. Wife, Toshiko Koshiya Kikuchi; parents of four children.

Paul E. Koelliker

Sustained to the First Quorum of the Seventy April 2, 2005, at age 62. Former temple sealer, stake president, high councilor, bishop, high priests group leader, elders quorum president, and counselor in ward Young Men presidency. Received bachelor's degree in business administration from University of Utah. Formerly managing director of Church Temple Department, as well as working in senior managerial positions for the Church. Born March 12, 1943, in Pittsburg, Calif., to Edward Conrad and Lois Bernice Olson Koelliker. Wife, Freda Ann Neilson Koelliker; parents of seven children.

Erich W. Kopischke

Sustained to the First Quorum of the Seventy March 31, 2007, at age 50. Former Area Seventy in the Europe Central Area, president of the Germany Berlin Mission, stake president, district president, high councilor, bishop's counselor and branch president. Served in German military, 1977-1978. Attended vocational school. Was Church Educational System coordinator in Germany. Born Oct. 20, 1956, in Elmshom, Germany, to Kurt and Helga Haupt Kopischke. Wife, Christiane Glück Kopischke; parents of seven children.

John M. Madsen

Called to the Second Quorum of the Seventy June 6, 1992, at age 53, and sustained Oct. 3, 1992; sustained to the First Quorum of the Seventy April 5, 1997. Former president of the England Southwest Mission, member of the Melchizedek Priesthood MIA general board and Young Men general board, and regional representative. Was BYU religion professor. Received bachelor's degree in zoology from Washington State University and master's degree and doctorate in education from BYU. Born April 24, 1939, in Washington, D.C. to Louis L. and Edith Louise Gundersen Madsen. Wife, Diane Dursteler Madsen; parents of six children.

Richard J. Maynes

Sustained to the Second Quorum of the Seventy April 5, 1997, at age 46; sustained to the First Quorum of the Seventy March 31, 2001. Former president of the Mexico Monterrey Mission. Received bachelor's degree from Brigham Young University, and MBA degree from the American Graduate School of International Management. Was owner and president of Raymond Production Systems Inc. Born Oct. 29, 1950, in Berkeley, Calif., to Stan and Betty Maynes. Wife, Nancy J. Purrington Maynes; parents of four children.

Lynn A. Mickelsen

Sustained to the Second Quorum of the Seventy March 31, 1990, at age 54, and to the First Quorum of the Seventy April 3, 1993. Former president of the Colombia Cali Mission, regional representative, stake president, and bishop. Attended Ricks College and graduated from BYU. Served on a hospital board and in farm associations; formerly self-employed as a farmer and potato shipper. Born July 21, 1935, in Idaho Falls, Idaho, to Lloyd P. and Reva Faye Willmore Mickelsen. Wife, Jeanine Andersen Mickelsen; parents of nine children.

Marcus B. Nash

Sustained to the First Quorum of the Seventy April 1, 2006, at age 49. Former Area Seventy in the North America Northwest Area, stake president, bishop, Young Men president and elders quorum president. Received bachelor's degree in international relations and law degree, both from BYU. Was partner in a major law firm in Seattle, Wash. Born March 26, 1957, in Seattle, Wash., to Brent and Beverly Bell Nash. Wife, Shelley Hatch Nash; parents of five children.

Dennis B. Neuenschwander

Sustained to the Second Quorum of the Seventy April 6, 1991, at age 51; sustained to First Quorum of the Seventy Oct. 1, 1994; called to Presidency of the Seventy Aug. 15, 2000, and sustained Oct. 7, 2000; served until April 3, 2004. Former president of the Austria Vienna East Mission and counselor in mission presidency. Was manager of International Area of Acquisitions Division of the Church Genealogical Department. Received bachelor's degree from BYU, master's degree and doctorate in Russian literature from Syracuse University in New York. Born Oct. 6, 1939, in Salt Lake City, Utah, to George Henry and Genevieve Bramwell Neuenschwander. Wife, LeAnn Clement Neuenschwander; parents of four children. She died July 13, 2007.

Glenn L. Pace

Sustained as second counselor in the Presiding Bishopric April 6, 1985, at age 45; sustained to the First Quorum of the Seventy Oct. 3, 1992. Former president of the Australia Sydney North Mission, bishop's counselor, stake clerk, and elders quorum president. Received bachelor's and master's degrees in accounting from BYU; certified public accountant; former managing director of Church Welfare Services. Born March 21, 1940, in Provo, Utah, to Kenneth LeRoy and Elizabeth A. Wilde Pace. Wife, Jolene Clayson Pace; parents of six children.

Allan F. Packer

Sustained to the First Quorum of the Seventy April 5, 2008, at age 59. Former president of Spain Malága Mission, member of Young Men general board, stake president's counselor, bishop and counselor, and Young Men president. Was in-field representative for the Church's Missionary Department and vice president of various companies. Received bachelor's degree in electronic engineering technology from BYU. Born July 7, 1948, in Brigham City, Utah, to Boyd K. and Donna Smith Packer. Wife, Terri Anne Bennett Packer; parents of eight children.

Kevin W. Pearson

Sustained to the First Quorum of the Seventy April 5, 2008, at age 51. Former president of Washington Tacoma Mission, bishop, bishop's counselor, elder's quorum president and Young Men president. Was CEO of a health care information company. Received bachelor's degree in finance from University of Utah, master's degree in business administration and corporate finance from Harvard Business School. Born April 10, 1957, to Wayne F. and Velda Labrum Pearson. Wife, June Langeland Pearson; parents of six children.

Anthony D. Perkins

Sustained to the First Quorum of the Seventy April 1, 2006, at age 45. Former president of the Taiwan Taipei Mission, counselor in district presidency, branch president and elders quorum president. Received bachelor's degree in finance from BYU, MBA from the University of Pennsylvania's Wharton School, and master's degree in international studies from University of Pennsylvania. Was senior partner in a management consulting firm. Born July 22, 1960, in Cortez, Colo., to Larry Lazelle and Sunny Kimballa Luther Perkins. Wife, Christine Abbott Perkins; parents of six children.

Paul B. Pieper

Sustained to the First Quorum of the Seventy April 2, 2005, at age 47. Former president of Russia St. Petersburg Mission, counselor in stake presidency, high councilor and branch president. Studied international relations at BYU, then received bachelor's degree in political science and juris doctorate, both from University of Utah. Was attorney and international development consultant. Born Oct. 7, 1957, in Pocatello, Idaho, to Dee M. and Norma Bowen Pieper. Wife, Melissa Tuttle Pieper; parents of six children.

Rafael E. Pino

Sustained to the First Quorum of the Seventy April 5, 2008, at age 52. Former Area Seventy in the South America North Area, president of the Argentina Rosario Mission, stake president, high councilor and bishop. Worked for the Church in a variety of capacities, including Member and Statistical Records Division and Temporal Affairs. Received a certificate in administration in Caracas, Venezuela. Born Oct. 27, 1955, in Valencia, Venezuela, to Arturo and Josefina Gimenez Pino. Wife, Patricia Monica Dassler Pino; parents of three children.

Bruce D. Porter

Sustained to the Second Quorum of the Seventy April 1, 1995, at age 42; sustained to the First Quorum of the Seventy April 5, 2003. Former stake president's counselor, stake mission president, bishop and branch president. Was a professor of political science at BYU and former executive director of the U.S. Board for International Broadcasting; was research fellow at Harvard University, and served as a corporate analyst for the Northrop Corporation and a staff member of the U.S. Senate Armed Services Committee. Graduated from BYU and earned M.A. and Ph.D. degrees from Harvard University. Born in Albuquerque, N.M., Sept. 18, 1952, to Lyle Kay and Wilma Holmes Porter. Wife, Susan Elizabeth Holland Porter; parents of four children.

Carl B. Pratt

Sustained to the First Quorum of the Seventy April 5, 1997, at age 55. Former area authority, mission president in Spain, regional representative, temple sealer, stake president's counselor, and bishop's counselor. Was law clerk in U.S. 10th Circuit Court of Appeals, attorney in private practice, and served 19 years as legal counsel for the Church in South America. Received bachelor's degree from University of Arizona, and juris doctorate from Arizona State University. Born Oct. 30, 1941, in Monterrey, Mexico, to Carl Barton and LaVern Whetten Pratt. Wife, Karen Ann Yeoman Pratt; parents of eight children.

Lynn G. Robbins

Sustained to the Second Quorum of the Seventy April 5, 1997, at age 44; sustained to the First Quorum of the Seventy April 1, 2000. Former president of the Uruguay Montevideo Mission, high councilor, bishop and bishop's counselor. Was co-founder and former senior vice president of Franklin Quest. Received bachelor's degree from Utah State University and master's degree from American Graduate School of International Management. Born Oct. 27, 1952, to Joshua Grant and Evelyn Reed Robbins; raised in Springville, Utah. Wife, Jan Neilson Robbins; parents of seven children.

Cecil O. Samuelson

President of BYU, was sustained to the First Quorum of the Seventy Oct. 1, 1994, at age 53; served in the Presidency of the Seventy from Aug. 15, 2001, to April 5, 2003. Former regional representative and stake president. Received bachelor's, master's and medical degrees from the University of Utah; served residency and fellowship at Duke University Medical Center. Was a physician and senior vice president of Intermountain Health Care, and former vice president of health services, professor of medicine and dean of the School of Medicine at the University of Utah. Born Aug. 1, 1941, in Salt Lake City, Utah, to Cecil Osborn Sr. and Janet Brazier Mitchell Samuelson. Wife, Sharon Giauque Samuelson; parents of five children.

Ulisses Soares

Sustained to the First Quorum of the Seventy April 2, 2005, at age 46. Former president of the Portugal Porto Mission, regional welfare agent, stake president, high councilor, stake executive secretary, bishop's counselor, and elders quorum president. Received bachelor's degree in accounting and economics from Pontificia Catholic University, master's degree in business administration from National Institute of Post Graduate Study. Was director of temporal affairs for the Church in Brazil. Born Oct. 2, 1958, in Sao Paulo, Brazil, to Apparecido and Mercedes Carecho Soares. Wife, Rosana Fernandes Morgado Soares; parents of three children.

Gary E. Stevenson

Sustained to the First Quorum of the Seventy April 5, 2008, at age 52. Former president of the Japan Nagoya Mission, counselor in stake presidency, and bishop and counselor. Was chief operating officer of Icon Health and Fitness Inc. Received bachelor's degree in business administration from Utah State University. Served on BYU Marriott School of Business National Advisory Council and Utah State University Foundation Board. Born Aug. 6, 1955, in Ogden, Utah, to Evan Noel and Vera Jean Hall Stevenson. Wife, Lesa Jean Higley Stevenson; parents of four children.

Michael J. Teh

Sustained to the First Quorum of the Seventy March 31, 2007, at age 41. Former Area Seventy in the Philippines Area, mission president's counselor, stake president's counselor, high councilor, stake clerk, bishop and bishop's counselor. Received bachelor's degree in business administration from De La Salle University in Manila. Was recorder at Manila Philippines Temple. Born June 25, 1965, in Davao City, Philippines, to Martin and Norma Uy Teh. Wife, Grace May Weedon Teh; parents of three children.

José A. Teixeira

Sustained to the First Quorum of the Seventy April 5, 2008, at age 47. Former Area Seventy in Portugal, president of Brazil Sao Paulo South Mission, stake president and counselor, bishop's counselor, district president, and high priest group leader. Former area finance manager and later international controller for the Church in Europe and Africa. Attended IAT Technical Improvement Institute in Lisbon, Portugal. Served in the Portuguese Air Force. Born Feb. 24, 1961, in Vila Real, Portugal, to Fernando and Benilde Teixeira. Wife, Maria Filomena Lopes Teles Grilo Teixeira; parents of three children.

Octaviano Tenorio

Sustained to the First Quorum of the Seventy March 31, 2007, at age 64. Former Area Seventy in the Mexico South Area, president of the Mexico Tuxtla Gutierrez Mission, regional representative, stake president, stake president's counselor and branch president. Received certificate in finance from the Academia Practica de Comercio. Former Mexico City Mexico Temple recorder. Born Oct. 31, 1942, in Tilapan, Veracruz, Mexico, to Octaviano and Flora Dominguez Tenorio. Wife, Rosa Elva Valenzuela Tenorio; parents of five children.

Francisco J. Viñas

Sustained to the Second Quorum of the Seventy April 6, 1996, at age 49; sustained to the First Quorum of the Seventy April 5, 1998. Former Area Authority Seventy in the Europe West Area, president of Argentina Salta Mission, regional representative, stake president, counselor, bishop, and branch president. Was Church Educational System director and coordinator for Uruguay and Spain. Born Dec. 28, 1946, in Montevideo, Uruguay, to Rafael and Sacramento Serrano de Viñas. Wife, Cristina Helenas Gaminara de Vinas; parents of three children.

William R. Walker

Sustained to the Second Quorum of the Seventy April 6, 2002, at age 57; sustained to the First Quorum of the Seventy April 5, 2008. Former president of the Japan Tokyo South Mission, stake president and bishop. Received bachelor's degree in international relations from Brigham Young University. Formerly held a number of executive positions in investment banking and other business fields. Born May 25, 1944, to J. Harris and Beth Russell Walker; raised in Raymond, Alberta, Canada. Wife, Vicki Van Wagenen Walker; parents of five children.

F. Michael Watson

Sustained to the First Quorum of the Seventy April 5, 2008, at age 65. Former sealer in Bountiful Utah Temple, stake president, stake mission president, bishop, branch president, and elders quorum president. Served as assistant secretary and secretary to the First Presidency, assistant secretary and secretary to the Quorum of the Twelve. Received bachelor's degree in business and office administration from Utah State University. Served three years in U.S. Army. Born March 9, 1943, in Spring City, Utah, to Frank C. and Genniel Baxter Watson. Wife, Jolene Mann Watson; parents of 12 children.

Lance B. Wickman

Church General Counsel, was sustained to the Second Quorum of the Seventy April 2, 1994, at age 53; sustained to the First Quorum of the Seventy April 1, 2000. Served as regional representative, stake president, and bishop. Received bachelor's degree from University of California at Berkeley and juris doctorate from Stanford University. Former partner in the international law firm of Latham and Watkins in San Diego, Calif. Born Nov. 11, 1940, in Seattle, Wash., to Alton C. and Irene Marilyn Carlson Wickman. Wife, Patricia Farr Wickman; parents of five children.

Jorge F. Zeballos

Sustained to the First Quorum of the Seventy April 5, 2008, at age 52. Former Area Seventy, president of Chile Concepcion Mission, regional representative, stake president and bishop. Former mining engineer and manager of corporate affairs of large Chilean mining company. Receive bachelor's degree in civil engineering from Santa Maria University, master's degree in business administration from BYU. Born July 19, 1955, in Ovalle, Chile, to Alberto and Ines Zeballos. Wife, Carmen Gloria Valenzuela Zeballos; parents of five children.

Claudio D. Zivic

Sustained to the First Quorum of the Seventy March 31, 2007, at age 58. Former Area Seventy in the South America South Area, president of the Spain Bilbao Mission, regional representative, temple ordinance worker, stake president's counselor, high councilor, bishop and bishop's counselor. Received a degree in accounting from the University of Buenos Aires. Was CPA, working in manufacturing and marketing fields. Born Dec. 19, 1948, in Buenos Aires, Argentina, to Sergio Zivic and Eleonora Zalewski de Zivic. Wife, Dina Noemi Alvarez Zivic; parents of five children.

W. Craig Zwick

Sustained to the First Quorum of the Seventy April 1, 1995, at age 47. Former president of the Chile Santiago South Mission, stake Young Men president, stake mission president's counselor, high councilor, and bishop's counselor. Was executive director of the Utah Department of Transportation, former building contractor. Received bachelor of science degree in business management from the University of Utah. Born June 30, 1947, in Salt Lake City, Utah, to William E. and Audrey McDonough Zwick. Wife, Janet Johnson Zwick; parents of four children.

THE SECOND QUORUM OF THE SEVENTY

Mervyn B. Arnold

Sustained to the Second Quorum of the Seventy April 5, 2003, at age 54. Former president of the Costa Rica San Jose Mission, counselor in stake presidency, high councilor and bishop. Received bachelor's degree in business and master's degree in public administration, both from BYU. Founder and co-owner of a building and development company. Following retirement from business, became director of Training and Field Services in the Church Missionary Department. Born July 19, 1948, in Salt Lake City, Utah, to John E.S. and Jasmine Bennion Arnold. Wife, Devonna Kress Arnold; parents of six children.

Douglas L. Callister

Sustained to the Second Quorum of the Seventy April 1, 2000, at age 61. Former Area Authority Seventy, regional representative, president of Minnesota Minneapolis Mission, temple sealer, stake president and bishop. Received bachelor's degree from BYU, juris doctorate from University of Southern California, and L.L.M. degree (master's of law) from Harvard University. Former tax attorney. Born Feb. 17, 1939, in Glendale, Calif., to Reed Eddington and Norinne Richards Callister. Wife, Jeannette McKibben Callister; parents of six children.

Tad R. Callister

Sustained to the Second Quorum of the Seventy April 5, 2008, at age 62. Former Area Seventy, regional representative, president of Canada Toronto East Mission and mission president's counselor, temple ordinance worker, stake president and counselor, bishop, and stake mission president. Was president of a Boy Scout Council. Former attorney. Received bachelor's degree in accounting from BYU, juris doctorate from UCLA, master's degree in tax law from New York University Law School. Born Dec. 17, 1945, in Glendale, Calif., to Reed and Norinne Richards Callister. Wife, Kathryn Saporiti Callister; parents of six children.

Craig A. Cardon

Sustained to the Second Quorum of the Seventy April 1, 2006, at age 57. Former president of Italy Rome Mission, stake president and counselor, high councilor and bishop. Received bachelor's degree in accounting from Arizona State University, master's degree in public administration from Harvard University; was co-owner of family business, primarily in real estate development. Born Dec. 30, 1948, in Mesa, Ariz., to Wilford Pratt and Vilate Allen Cardon. Wife, Deborah Dana Cardon; parents of eight children.

Shirley D. Christensen

Sustained to the Second Quorum of the Seventy April 5, 2003, at age 64. Former president of the Argentina Resistencia Mission, counselor in stake presidency, regional welfare agent, high councilor, bishop, and branch president. Studied political science at BYU. Was fruit grower. Born Jan. 8, 1939, in Preston, Idaho, to LaGrand and Blanche Naef Christensen. Wife, Geniel Johnson Christensen; parents of seven children (one deceased). She died Oct. 2, 2005.

Don R. Clarke

Sustained to the Second Quorum of the Seventy April 1, 2006, at age 60. Former president of Bolivia Santa Cruz Mission, stake president, assistant director of Church hosting, high councilor, stake Young Men president and bishop, Received associate degree from Ricks College, bachelor's degree in business from BYU, and MBA from Washington State University. Held senior executive positions and CEO in several companies. Born Dec. 11, 1945, in Rexburg, Idaho, to Raymond Ernest and Gladys Lydia Larsen Clarke. Wife, Mary Anne Jackson Clarke; parents of six children.

James M. Dunn	Keith R. Edwards	Stanley G. Ellis

Sustained to the Second Quorum of the Seventy Oct. 5, 2002, at age 62. Former Area Authority Seventy, president of the Colombia Bogota Mission 1980-83, stake president, high councilor and bishop. Received juris law degree from University of Utah and degree in Latin American studies from Brigham Young University. Founding partner in Jardine, Linebaugh & Dunn. Born April 16, 1940, in Pocatello, Idaho, to Bill E. and Melba Meyers Dunn. Wife, Penny Barker Dunn; parents of six children.

Sustained to the Second Quorum of the Seventy April 1, 2006, at age 64. Former Area Seventy in the North America Southwest Area, president of Zimbabwe Harare Mission, stake president and counselor, high councilor, bishop and counselor, regional welfare director, assistant temple recorder and temple ordinance worker. Received bachelor's degree in political science from BYU and juris doctorate from University of Utah. Was senior partner in law firm. Born March 16, 1942, in Boulder City, Nev., to Elbert Bird and Mary Reid Edwards. Wife, Judith Higgins Edwards; parents of seven children.

Sustained to the Second Quorum of the Seventy April 1, 2006, at age 59. Former Area Seventy in the North America Southwest Area, president of Brazil Sao Paulo North Mission, stake president and counselor, high councilor, bishop's counselor and elders quorum president. Received bachelor's degree in government studies from Harvard University and juris doctorate from BYU. Was financial consultant. Born Jan. 22, 1947, in Burley, Idaho, to Stephen B. and Hazel Taylor Ellis. Wife, Kathryn Kloepfer Ellis; parents of nine children.

Daryl H. Garn

Sustained to the Second Quorum of the Seventy Oct. 5, 2002, at age 63. Former Area Authority Seventy, regional representative, mission president's counselor, stake president, high councilor and bishop. Received bachelor's degree from Utah State University and doctor of dental surgery degree from Western Reserve, and master of science degree from Temple University; orthodontist. Born Dec. 28, 1938, in Tremonton, Utah, to Uel A. and Lolita Hodges Garn. Wife, Irene Hall Garn; parents of six children.

Larry W. Gibbons

Sustained to the Second Quorum of the Seventy April 1, 2006, at age 63. Former Area Seventy, regional representative, and stake president and counselor. Was a major in U.S. Army. Attended Stanford University, received medical degree from University of Utah., and master's degree in public health from Harvard University. Former president and medical director of medical clinic in Dallas, Texas. Born July 30, 1942, in Logan, Utah, to Andrew H. and Lola Heaton Gibbons. Wife, LaDawn Anderson Gibbons; parents of two children.

Spencer V. Jones

Sustained to the Second Quorum of the Seventy Oct. 5, 2002, at age 57. Former full-time Area Authority Seventy serving in the Dominican Republic at the time of his call, former president of the Chile Antofagasta Mission, area executive secretary, high councilor and bishop. Received bachelor's degree from BYU; businessman and business owner. Born Sept. 17, 1945, in Safford, Ariz., to Virgil Worth and Nellie Mae Baker Jones; Wife, Joyce Elizabeth Mathews Jones; parents of three children.

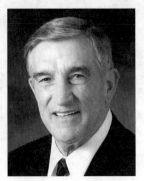

Won Yong Ko

Sustained to the Second Quorum of the Seventy April 2, 2005, at age 59. Former Area Seventy in the Asia North Area, regional representative, national director of public affairs for Korea, stake president, high councilor, stake executive secretary and bishop's counselor. Received bachelor's degree electrical engineering from Seoul National University. Served in South Korean army for three years. Formerly president and CEO of a major information systems and telecommunications company and an international computer company. Born Oct. 15, 1945, in Pusan, South Korea, to Chang Soo and Sang Soon Lee Kim. Wife, Eun Hee Kim Ko; parents of two children

Clate W. Mask Jr.

Sustained to the Second Quorum of the Seventy April 5, 2003, at age 60. Former president of Spain Barcelona Mission, high councilor, bishop and branch president. Received bachelor's degree in English from BYU and master's degree in education from Cal State-Northridge. Was Church Educational System coordinator. Born Aug. 20, 1942, in El Paso, Texas, to Clate W. and Marva Gonzalez Mask. Wife, Carol Garns Mask; parents of six children.

Robert C. Oaks

Sustained to the Second Quorum of the Seventy April 1, 2000, at age 64; served in the Presidency of the Seventy from Oct. 2, 2004, to Aug. 1, 2007. Former stake president, mission president's counselor, district president's counselor, high councilor and bishop's counselor. Received bachelor's degree in military science from Air Force Academy, master's in business administration from Ohio State University, and attended Naval War College. Former senior vice president of operations at U.S. Airway, retired four-star Air Force general. Born Feb. 14, 1936, in Los Angeles, Calif., to Charles E. and Ann Bonnett Oaks. Wife, Gloria Unger Oaks; parents of six children.

William W. Parmley

Sustained to the Second Quorum of the Seventy April 5, 2003, at age 67. Former Area Authority Seventy, regional representative, stake president and counselor, and bishop. Received bachelor's degree in physics from Harvard and medical degree from Johns Hopkins Medical School. Was chief of cardiology at University of California/San Francisco. Born Jan. 22, 1936, in Salt Lake City, Utah, to Thomas Jennison and Martha LaVern Watts Parmley. Wife, Shanna Lee Parmley; parents of four children.

Wolfgang H. Paul

Sustained to the Second Quorum of the Seventy April 2, 2005, at age 65. Former Area Seventy in Europe Central and East areas, president of Germany Dresden Mission and Germany Hamburg Mission, regional representative, counselor in stake presidency, stake Young Men president, bishop, branch president, high priests group leader, and elders quorum president. Graduated from the German Federal Government Administration Academy and formerly a government officer in Germany; was director of temporal affairs for the Church in Europe. Born Feb. 28, 1940, in Munster, Germany, to Johann and Berta Starbati Paul. Wife, Helga Klappert Paul; parents of three children.

W. Douglas Shumway

Sustained to the Second Quorum of the Seventy April 5, 2003, at age 62. Former president of the Bolivia Santa Cruz Mission, counselor in stake presidency and bishop. Received bachelor's degree in business management from BYU. Was self-employed as owner of Whiting Brothers Investment Company. Born May 8, 1940, in St. Johns, Ariz., to Wilford and Mabel Shumway. Wife, Dixie Ann Jarvis Shumway; parents of eight children.

Lowell M. Snow

Sustained to the Second Quorum of the Seventy April 2, 2005, at age 61. Former Area Seventy in the Utah North Area, area executive secretary, Church hosting director, president of Mississippi Jackson Mission, counselor in stake presidency, bishop, branch president, and stake and ward Young Men president. Received bachelor's degree in life sciences from BYU; master's degree in education, guidance and counseling from Wayne State University; and juris doctorate from University of Utah. Was corporate and self-employed attorney, and commissioned officer in U.S. Army. Born Jan. 2, 1944, in St. George, Utah, to Rulon and Marian Miller Snow. Wife, Tamara Means Snow; parents of five children.

Paul K. Sybrowsky

Sustained to the Second Quorum of the Seventy April 2, 2005, at age 60. Former president of Canada Toronto West Mission, stake president, high councilor, stake executive secretary, bishop and bishop's counselor. Received bachelor's degree in social science from BYU. Served in U.S. Army Reserve and Utah Air National Guard. Was executive for multinational information services and software development companies and later self-employed. Born Aug. 22, 1944, in Salt Lake City, Utah, to Paul H. and Betty Ann Sybrowsky. Wife, Lynne Prior Sybrowsky; parents of nine children.

Kent D. Watson

Sustained to the Second Quorum of the Seventy April 5, 2008, at age 64. Former president of Taiwan Taichung Mission, interim president of Taiwan Kaaohsiung Mission, stake president's counselor, bishop, branch president, ward clerk and Scoutmaster. Was chief executive officer of an international accounting firm. Received bachelor's and master's degrees in accounting from BYU. Born May 8, 1943, in Cedar City, Utah, to L. Dee and Joyce Judd Watson. Wife, Connie Lingmann Watson; parents of five children.

Robert S. Wood

Sustained to the Second Quorum of the Seventy April 3, 1999, at age 62. Former Area Authority Seventy, regional representative, stake president, high councilor, and bishop. Received bachelor's degree in history from Stanford University, master's and doctoral degrees in political science from Harvard University. Former Chester W. Nimitz Chair of National Security and Foreign Affairs, U.S. Naval War College. Born Dec. 25, 1936, in Idaho Falls, Idaho, to John Albert (Jack) and Blanche Wood. Wife, Dixie Leigh Jones Wood; parents of four children.

THE THIRD QUORUM OF THE SEVENTY

Area Seventies residing in Africa Southeast, Africa West, Europe and Europe East Areas make up the Third Quorum of the Seventy

AFRICA SOUTHEAST AREA

Colin H. Bricknell, Garith C. Hill, Kapumba T. Kola, Allen P. Young

AFRICA WEST AREA

Richard K. Ahadjie, David W. Eka, Declan O. Madu, Alexander A. Odume, Adesina J. Olukanni, Norbert K. Ounleu

EUROPE AREA

Milton Camargo, Andrew M. Ford, Alfredo L.

Gessati, Frerich J. Görts, Patrick Kearon, Stephen C. Kerr, Christiaan H. Kleijweg, Faustino López, Per G. Malm, J. Michel Paya, Fernando A.R. Da Rocha, Eivind Sterri, Louis Weidmann, Johann A. Wondra

EUROPE EAST AREA

Aleksandr N. Manzhos, Sergiy N. Mikulin, Anatoly K. Reshetnikov, Gvido Senkans

THE FOURTH QUORUM OF THE SEVENTY

Area Seventies residing in the Caribbean, Central America, Mexico, South America North and South America West Areas make up the Fourth Quorum of the Seventy

CARIBBEAN

Jorge M. Alvarado, Miguel A. Lee, Ysrael A. Tolentino

CENTRAL AMERICA AREA

Pedro E. Abularach, Nelson L. Altamirano, Carlos L. Astorga, Jose E. Boza, Rafael E. Castro, I. Poloski Cordon, Luis G. Duarte, Carlos F. Rivas

MEXICO AREA

Jose L. Alonso, Sergio M. Anaya, Manuel Araiz, Jorge D. Arrevillaga, Hector Avila, David R. Brown, David Cabrera, Mario L. Carlos, Mosiah S. Delgado, Julio C. González, Manuel Gonzalez, S. Horacio Guzmán, Luis S.

Hernandez, Miguel Hidalgo, Glendon Lyons, Juan A. Machuca, Abelardo Morales, Raymundo Morales, Juan M. Rodriguez, Jorge A. Rojas, José L. Torres

SOUTH AMERICA NORTH AREA

Fernando E. Calderon, César A. Dávila, Javier Ibañez, B. Renato Maldonado, Gamaliel Osorno, Ruben D. Torres

SOUTH AMERICA WEST AREA

Vladimiro J. Campero, César H. Hooker, F. Rene Loli, Enrique J. Montoya, Alexander A. Nuñez, A. Rolando Oyola, Richard C. Zambrano

THE FIFTH QUORUM OF THE SEVENTY

Area Seventies residing in the Idaho, North America Northwest, North America West, Utah North, Utah Salt Lake City, and Utah South Areas make up the Fifth Quorum of the Seventy

IDAHO AREA

Robert E. Chambers, Kim B. Clark, Ronald J. Hammond, K. Brett Nattress, Brent H. Nielson, Gary W. Walker

NORTH AMERICA NORTHWEST AREA

Marvin T. Brinkerhoff, R. Bruce Merrell, Melvin R. Perkins, James C. Perry, G. Perrin Walker

NORTH AMERICA WEST AREA

Nelson D. Córdova, John C. Dalton, Larry R. Lawrence, William F. Reynolds, Donald P. Tenney, Frank V. Trythall, Scott D. Whiting

UTAH NORTH AREA

G. Lynn Brenchley, Wynn R. Dewsnup, J. Roger Fluhman, Robert H. Garff, Donald J. Keyes, Errol S. Phippen

UTAH SALT LAKE CITY AREA

LeGrand R. Curtis Jr., Michael H. Holmes, Jon M. Huntsman, Kent H. Murdock, John C. Pingree, Patrick H. Price, Dale G. Renlund

UTAH SOUTH AREA

D. Fraser Bullock, Donald J. Butler, I. Lee Ence, Daniel M. Jones, Lamont W. Moon, Russell T. Osguthorpe, Gary L. Pocock, Jay L. Sitterud, Ronald A. Stone, Richard W. Wheeler

THE SIXTH QUORUM OF THE SEVENTY

Area Seventies residing in the North America Central, North America Northeast, North America Southeast and North America Southwest Areas comprise the Sixth Quorum of the Seventy

NORTH AMERICA CENTRAL AREA

Randy D. Funk, Stephen W. Hansen, Joseph T. Hicken, Richard K. Melchin, Maury W. Schooff, Terrence C. Smith

NORTH AMERICA NORTHEAST AREA

Nolan D. Archibald, John J. Chipman, Clayton M. Christensen, David L. Cook, Gary L. Crittenden, Matthew J. Eyring,Ralph W. Hardy Jr., J. Willard Marriott Jr., W.T. David Murray, Neil E. Pitts, Robert B. Smith

NORTH AMERICA SOUTHEAST AREA

John S. Anderson, M. Anthony Burns, J. Devn Cornish, Robert C. Gay, David H. Ingram, Stephen D. Posey, John C. Taggart

NORTH AMERICA SOUTHWEST AREA

Wilford W. Andersen, Stephen L. Fluckiger, James B. Gibson, Robert W. Lees, James B. Martino, Michael D. Pickerd, D. Chad Richardson, J. Romeo Villarreal, Perry M. Webb

THE SEVENTH QUORUM OF THE SEVENTY

Area Seventies residing in Brazil, Chile and South America South Areas comprise the Seventh Quorum of the Seventy

BRAZIL AREA

Climato C.A.Almeida, Homero S. Amato, Gutenberg G. Amorím, Fernando J.D. Araújo, Marcelo Bolfarini, Flávio A. Cooper, Ronaldo da Costa, Luiz C. França, Paulo H. Itinose, Joni L. Koch, Alfredo Heliton de Lemos, Domingos S. Linhares, Carlos S. Obata, Adilson de Paula Parrella, Pedro J. Penha, Paulo R. Puerta, A. Ricardo Sant'Ana, Natã C. Tobias, Carlos A.C. Villanova,

CHILE AREA

Juan C. Barros, Gabriel A. Campos, Daniel M. Cañoles, G. Guillermo Garcia, Mario E. Guerra, Hernan I. Herrera, Fernando Maluenda, Dinar M. Reyes, Gerardo L. Rubio

SOUTH AMERICA SOUTH AREA

Rubén V. Alliaud, Sergio E. Avila, Ernesto A. Da Silva, Heber O. Diaz, Juan A. Etchegaray, Daniel A. Moreno, Rubén L. Spitale

THE EIGHTH QUORUM OF THE SEVENTY

Area Seventies residing in Asia, Asia North, Pacific and the Philippines Areas comprise the Eighth Quorum of the Seventy

ASIA AREA

Victor Kah Keng Chen, Chu-Jen Chia, Kuo Chiang Chung, Yu Chen (Philip) Ho, Joshua Subandriyo, Stanley Wan, Chi Hong (Sam) Wong

ASIA NORTH AREA

Koichi Aoyagi, Yoon Hwan Choi, Pita F. Hopoate, Tohru Hotta, Tetsuji Ishii, Bin Kikuchi, Yong Hwan Lee, Satoshi Nishihara, Kazuhiko Yamashita

PACIFIC AREA

James Dunlop, Sione M. Fineanganofo, David J. Hoare, William K. Jackson, Douglas W. Jessop, Peter F. Meurs, Michael A. Roberts, Dirk Smibert, Hans T. Sorensen, Jean A. Tefan, Terence M. Vinson, Taniela B. Wakolo

PHILIPPINES AREA

Federico F. Costales, Edgardo E. Fernando, Julio G. Gaviola, Jovencio A. Guanzon, Benson E. Misalucha, Fabian L. Sinamban, Miguel R. Valdez

THE PRESIDING BISHOPRIC

Richard C. Edgley

Called as first counselor in the Presiding Bishopric Dec. 27, 1995; sustained April 6, 1996. Sustained as second counselor to Presiding Bishop Robert D. Hales on Oct. 3, 1992, at age 56, and as second counselor to Presiding Bishop Merrill J. Bateman on April 2, 1994. Former stake president and bishop. Was managing director of the Church's Finance and Records Department, board member of various Church-related corporations. Received bachelor's degree in political science from BYU and master's degree in business administration from Indiana University. Born Feb. 6, 1936, in Preston, Idaho, to Phenoi Harrison and Ona Crockett Edgley. Wife, Pauline Nielson Edgley; parents of six children.

H. David Burton

Called as Presiding Bishop Dec. 27, 1995; sustained April 6, 1996. Sustained as first counselor to Presiding Bishop Robert D. Hales on Oct. 3, 1992, at age 54, and first counselor to Presiding Bishop Merrill J. Bateman on April 2, 1994. Former stake president and temple sealer. Former secretary to the Presiding Bishopric for 14 years. Received bachelor's degree in economics from the University of Utah and master's degree from University of Michigan in business administration. Born April 26, 1938, in Salt Lake City, Utah, to Harold Nelson and Blanche Mabel Swanson Burton. Wife, Barbara Matheson Burton; parents of five children.

Keith B. McMullin

Called as second counselor in the Presiding Bishopric Dec. 27, 1995, at age 54; sustained April 6, 1996. Former president of Germany Frankfurt Mission, stake president, bishop and counselor, and high councilor. Was managing director of Church Welfare Services. Received bachelor's degree in banking and finance from University of Utah. Born Aug. 18, 1941, in St. George, Utah, to Lawrence and Margaret Savage McMullin. Wife, Carolyn Jean Gibbs McMullin; parents of eight children.

HISTORICAL LISTING OF GENERAL AUTHORITIES
PRESIDENTS OF THE CHURCH

1. Joseph Smith Jr. — Born December 23, 1805, in Sharon, Windsor, Co., Vermont, Joseph Smith Jr. was the fifth of eleven children of Joseph Smith and Lucy Mack. He worked on the family farm in Vermont and later in western New York.

Married Emma Hale Jan. 18, 1827; they had seven children. Received the Melchizedek Priesthood (ordained apostle) in May-June 1829 by Peter, James, and John (D&C 20:2, 27:12); sustained as First Elder of the Church April 6, 1830, at age 24; ordained high priest June 3, 1831, by Lyman Wight, sustained as president of the High Priesthood Jan. 25, 1832, at age 26 at a conference at Amherst, Lorain Co., Ohio.

A series of remarkable spiritual experiences prepared him for his prophetic calling. Beginning in 1820 at Palmyra, New York, Joseph Smith saw God the Father and Jesus Christ in vision. Through revelation, he translated and published the Book of Mormon, organized The Church of Jesus Christ of Latter-day Saints on April 6, 1830, and received revelations to guide the Church. By inspiration, he called apostles and other Church leaders, defined doctrines, and taught the principles and ordinances that lead to exaltation. Under his leadership, Latter-day Saints founded communities in Ohio, Missouri, and Illinois.

On June 27, 1844, at Carthage, Illinois, Joseph Smith died a martyr, at age 38.

2. Brigham Young — Born June 1, 1801, at Whitingham, Windham Co., Vermont, to John Young and Abigail Howe.

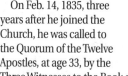

On Feb. 14, 1835, three years after he joined the Church, he was called to the Quorum of the Twelve Apostles, at age 33, by the Three Witnesses to the Book of Mormon: Oliver Cowdery, David Whitmer, and Martin Harris. He was sustained as president of the Quorum of the Twelve Apostles April 14, 1840.

As successor to Joseph Smith, he led the migration west in 1846–47 to the Rocky Mountains and founded Salt Lake City. He was sustained as president of the Church on December 27, 1847. As Church president and territorial governor of Utah, he established Latter-day Saint settlements in Utah and throughout the American West. Under his direction, construction commenced on the Salt Lake, St. George, Logan and Manti temples.

He brought the telegraph and the railroad to Utah and encouraged cooperative industry among Latter-day Saints, and he encouraged excellence and refinement in every aspect of life.

He died Aug. 29, 1877, in Salt Lake City at age 76 after nearly 30 years as Church president.

3. John Taylor — Born November 1, 1808, in Milnthorpe, Westmorland, England. An 1832 immigrant to Toronto, Canada, he was a cooper and part-time Methodist minister. He and his wife, Leonora, joined the Church in 1836. Two years later, on Dec. 19, 1838, he became an apostle under the hands of Brigham Young and Heber C. Kimball, at age 30. He was sustained as president of the Quorum of the Twelve Apostles Oct. 6, 1877.

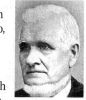

He enjoyed close association with Joseph Smith and Brigham Young. He accompanied Joseph Smith to Carthage, Illinois, in June 1844, and was seriously wounded when Joseph Smith was killed. He was sustained as president of the Church on October 10, 1880, during one of the most challenging periods in Church history.

The Church was persecuted for the

practice of plural marriage and many Latter-day Saints were being fined, imprisoned and denied the vote due to their beliefs and practices. He organized members to meet this trial of their faith and for the last 2 1/2 years of his life administered the affairs of the Church from seclusion resulting from anti-polygamy legislation. After seven eventful years as president, he died July 25, 1887, in Kaysville, Utah, at age 78.

4. Wilford Woodruff — Born March 1, 1807, at Avon (Farmington), Hartford Co., Connecticut, to Aphek Woodruff and Beulah Thompson.

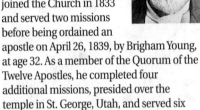

A miller by trade, he joined the Church in 1833 and served two missions before being ordained an apostle on April 26, 1839, by Brigham Young, at age 32. As a member of the Quorum of the Twelve Apostles, he completed four additional missions, presided over the temple in St. George, Utah, and served six years as Church historian. He was sustained as Church president on April 7, 1889, at age 82.

As president of the Church, he dedicated temples in Salt Lake City and Manti, Utah, oversaw the organization of the Genealogical Society, and re-emphasized the value of historical record-keeping. After much pondering and prayer, he received a revelation that the Latter-day Saints should cease the practice of plural marriage.

In 1890, he wrote the Manifesto, testifying that the Church had ceased teaching the practice of plural marriage. In addition to being the Lord's mouthpiece for that revelation, President Woodruff also left a legacy that emphasized missionary and temple work. He died in San Francisco, Calif., on Sept. 2, 1898, at age 91.

5. Lorenzo Snow — Born April 3, 1814, at Mantua, Portage Co., Ohio, to Oliver Snow and Rosetta Leonora Pettibone. As a youth, he preferred academic study

to an apprenticeship. Study of Hebrew and theology led to his conversion to the Church in 1836. He spent the rest of his life in service as a missionary, apostle and Church president.

He was ordained apostle Feb. 12, 1849, by Heber C. Kimball, at age 34; sustained as counselor to President Brigham Young April 8, 1873; sustained as assistant counselor to President Brigham Young May 9, 1874; sustained as president of the Quorum of the Twelve Apostles April 7, 1889; began serving as president of the Church Sept. 13, 1898, at age 84.

He helped the Church recover from the challenges of the previous decades. He stabilized Church finances as he encouraged members to pay their tithes and offerings, promising them that the "windows of heaven would be opened." He expanded Church missionary efforts. He opened a new era in Latter-day Saint history in the 20th Century.

He died in Salt Lake City on Oct. 10, 1901, at age 87.

6. Joseph Fielding Smith — Born Nov. 13, 1838, in Far West, Caldwell, Co., Missouri, to Hyrum Smith and Mary Fielding.

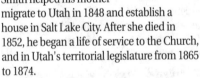

In 1844, his father was martyred along with his uncle, the Prophet Joseph Smith. Young Joseph F. Smith helped his mother migrate to Utah in 1848 and establish a house in Salt Lake City. After she died in 1852, he began a life of service to the Church, and in Utah's territorial legislature from 1865 to 1874.

He was ordained apostle by Brigham Young and named counselor to the First Presidency July 1, 1866, at age 27; set apart as a member of the Quorum of the Twelve Apostles Oct. 8, 1867; released as counselor to the First Presidency at the death of President Young Aug. 29, 1877; sustained as second counselor to President John Taylor Oct. 10, 1880; released at the death of President Taylor July 25, 1887; sustained as second counselor to President Wilford

Woodruff April 7, 1889; sustained as second counselor to President Lorenzo Snow Sept. 13, 1898; sustained as first counselor to Lorenzo Snow Oct. 6, 1901, not set apart to this position; released at the death of President Snow Oct. 10, 1901. He became president of the Church on Oct. 17, 1901.

While ushering the Church into the 20th Century, Joseph F. Smith brought Latter-day Saints to a better appreciation of early Church history. He worked to improve the public image of the Church by developing important Church historical sites in New York, Missouri, and Illinois, building a visitors' bureau, and expanding Church missionary and educational systems. He clarified important doctrines, served numerous missions, and directed the construction of a new headquarters complex for an expanding Church.

After 17 years as Church president, Joseph F. Smith died on Nov. 19, 1918, in Salt Lake City, at age 80.

7. Heber Jeddy Grant — Born Nov. 22, 1856, in Salt Lake City, Utah, to Jedediah Morgan Grant and Rachel Ridgeway Ivins. He was raised by his widowed mother. By the time he was 15, he had begun a successful business career and had been ordained to the office of seventy. Ten years later, he was ordained to the Quorum of the Twelve Apostles on Oct. 16, 1882, at age 25, where he served for 37 years. He became president of the Quorum of the Twelve Nov. 23, 1916.

After becoming Church president on Nov. 23, 1918, at age 62, he dedicated three new temples, developed the Welfare Program, and helped Latter-day Saints cope with the tragedy of World War II. His business experience enabled him to modernize Church organizations and procedures. His missionary efforts, including extensive speaking engagements and friendships with national business leaders, brought the Church to the attention of the nation.

After 27 years as president, he died in Salt Lake City, Utah, on May 14, 1945, at age 88.

8. George Albert Smith — Born on April 4, 1870, in Salt Lake City, Utah, to John Henry Smith and Sarah Farr. Married Lucy Emily Woodruff May 25, 1892 (she died Nov. 5, 1937); they had three children.

His father and grandfather, George A. Smith, were counselors to Church presidents. While employed in the Federal Land Office for Utah, he was called to the Quorum of the Twelve Apostles on Oct. 8, 1903, at age 33, by Joseph F. Smith. He was sustained as president of the Quorum of the Twelve July 1, 1943.

Despite fragile health and impaired eyesight, he had a distinguished career as a Church leader. He became president of the Church on May 21, 1945, at age 75. He organized the Church's massive welfare assistance to Europe following World War II. He also championed Scouting among Latter-day Saints. Through numerous other civic and Church responsibilities, President Smith lived that portion of his personal creed that declared, "I would be a friend to the friendless and find joy in ministering to the needs of the poor" (*Improvement Era* Mar. 1932, 295).

After six years as president, he died in Salt Lake City on his 81st birthday, April 4, 1951.

9. David Oman McKay — Born in Huntsville, Weber Co., Utah on Sept. 8, 1873, to David McKay and Jennette Eveline Evans, he studied at the Weber Stake Academy and the University of Utah to prepare for a career in education. After completing formal schooling and a mission, he married his college sweetheart, Emma Ray Riggs, Jan. 2, 1901. She died Nov. 14, 1970.

Five years after their marriage, on April 9,

1906, he was called as an apostle, at age 32, beginning a life of service in the Church's highest councils. He was sustained as second counselor to President Heber J. Grant Oct. 6, 1934; sustained as second counselor to President George Albert Smith May 21, 1945; and sustained as president of the Quorum of the Twelve Apostles Sept. 30, 1950.

He was sustained president of the Church on April 9, 1951, at age 77. He expanded the vision of the Church's worldwide mission, and under his administration, the first non-English speaking stakes outside of the United States were created. He also strengthened Church membership with a renewed emphasis on the value of family life and education.

After 44 years in the Quorum of the Twelve, and 19 years as president of the Church, he died on Jan. 18, 1970, in Salt Lake City, Utah, at age 96.

10. Joseph Fielding Smith — Born July 19, 1876, in Salt Lake City, Utah, to Joseph F. Smith and Julina Lambson. He spent his entire life in Church service. During nearly three-quarters of a century, he was a missionary, Church 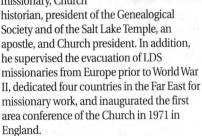 historian, president of the Genealogical Society and of the Salt Lake Temple, an apostle, and Church president. In addition, he supervised the evacuation of LDS missionaries from Europe prior to World War II, dedicated four countries in the Far East for missionary work, and inaugurated the first area conference of the Church in 1971 in England.

He married Louie E. Shurtliff April 26, 1898 (she died March 30, 1908); they had two children. Married Ethel G. Reynolds Nov. 2, 1908 (she died Aug. 26, 1937); they had nine children. Married Jessie Ella Evans April 12, 1938 (she died Aug. 3, 1971).

He was ordained apostle April 7, 1910, by Joseph F. Smith, at age 33; sustained as acting president of the Quorum of the Twelve Apostles Sept. 30, 1950; sustained as president of the Quorum of the Twelve Apostles April 9, 1951; sustained as counselor in the First Presidency Oct. 29, 1965.

He became president of the Church on Jan. 23, 1970, at age 93. As one of the Church's most prolific writers, Joseph Fielding Smith's numerous books and articles helped educate generations of Latter-day Saints about the history and doctrine of the Church. Under President Smith's administration, missionary work continued to grow, the Ogden and Provo temples were dedicated, several Church departments were restructured, and the Church magazines were consolidated.

On July 2, 1972, President Smith died quietly at his home in Salt Lake City, at age 95.

11. Harold Bingham Lee — Born on March 28, 1899, in Clifton, Oneida Co., Idaho, to Samuel M. Lee and Louisa Bingham. In Idaho, and later in Utah, he developed careers in education, business, and government. As president of the Salt Lake Pioneer Stake during the Great Depression, he initiated a program of self-help and relief that grew into the welfare system of the Church.

He married Fern Lucinda Tanner Nov. 14, 1923 (she died Sept. 24, 1962); they had two children. Married Freda Joan Jensen June 17, 1963.

After his call to the Quorum of the Twelve Apostles on April 10, 1941, by Heber J. Grant, at age 42, he continued to work with the welfare program, which served needy individuals and communities in many countries. He initiated organizational changes to improve the coordination of efforts at Church headquarters and among all Latter-day Saint congregations. These helped the Church prepare for its rapid expansion of members, activities, and influence of the decades that followed.

He was sustained as president of the Quorum of the Twelve Jan. 23, 1970; sustained as first counselor to President Joseph Fielding Smith Jan. 23, 1970.

He became president of the Church on July 7, 1972, at age 73. As Church president, he traveled often and frequently addressed the youth of the Church.

After only 18 months as Church president, he died on Dec. 26, 1973, in Salt Lake City, at age 74.

12. Spencer Woolley Kimball — Born on March 28, 1895, in Salt Lake City, Utah, to Andrew Kimball and Olive Woolley, Spencer W. Kimball grew up in Thatcher, Ariz. After completing a mission and marrying Camilla Eyring on Nov. 16, 1917, they settled  in Safford, Ariz., to raise their family and run an insurance business. They had four children. Years of Church and community leadership preceded his calling as an apostle when he was ordained by Heber J. Grant on Oct. 7, 1943, at age 48. He was set apart as acting president of the Quorum of the Twelve Apostles Jan. 23, 1970; set apart as president of the Quorum of the Twelve July 7, 1972. Overcoming severe health problems, he became Church president on Dec. 30, 1973, at the age of 78. He led the Church with spiritual power and energetic determination during a period of dramatic vitality and growth. His administration produced significant advances in doctrinal understanding, member unity, and gospel expansion worldwide. In the 12 years of his presidency, the number of operating temples doubled, the number of missionaries increased by 50 percent, and the priesthood was extended to all worthy male members.

He died in Salt Lake City on Nov. 5, 1985, at age 90.

13. Ezra Taft Benson — Born on Aug. 4, 1899, in Whitney, Franklin Co., Idaho, to George T. Benson and Sarah Dunkley, he learned early the principle of hard work on the family farm. He served a mission to Great Britain and after his return was  married to his sweetheart, Flora Amussen, on Sept. 10, 1926; they had six children. He received his education in agriculture and went on to hold many important positions within the industry.

He was ordained an apostle on Oct. 7, 1943, by President Heber J. Grant, at age 44, after having been president of two stakes. From 1953 to 1961, he served as Secretary of Agriculture in the cabinet of U. S. President Dwight D. Eisenhower. He was set apart as president of the Quorum of the Twelve Apostles Dec. 30, 1973.

On Nov. 10, 1985, he became president of the Church, at age 86. Having a resolute testimony of the power of the Book of Mormon, he emphasized the importance of it in daily scripture study, missionary efforts, and gospel teaching. His love of freedom, home, and family were also evident in his addresses and counsel to Church members. Despite his failing health, the Church continued to grow under his administration, temples were dedicated, and missionary work expanded around the world, particularly in eastern Europe.

He died in Salt Lake City, Utah, on May 30, 1994, at age 94.

14. Howard William Hunter — Born Nov. 14, 1907, in Boise, Ada Co., Idaho, to John William Hunter and Nellie Marie Rasmussen.

He had a love for music in his youth. After high school, his band, 'Hunter's Croonaders,' toured for five months on the SS President Jackson, which gave him the opportunity to see many exotic sites in Asia.

He married Clara May (Claire) Jeffs June 10, 1931, she died Oct. 9, 1983; they had three children (one died in infancy). He married Inis Bernice Egan on April 12, 1990.

Upon his marriage to Clara May Jeffs in 1931, he gave up his music career in favor of a stable family life. He studied law and became a successful lawyer in California. Various positions of priesthood leadership prepared him for his call to the apostleship in 1959. He was ordained an apostle Oct. 15, 1959, by David O. McKay, and set apart as Acting President of the Quorum of the Twelve Nov. 10, 1985.

After 35 years as an apostle, he became president of the Church on June 5, 1994, at age 86. During his short presidency, he challenged all members of the Church to become temple worthy, prior to a decade of increased temple building, and invited members who had become offended to come back to the Church. He traveled as often as his health permitted, dedicating two temples and commemorating the 150th anniversary of the martyrdom of Joseph and Hyrum Smith in Nauvoo and Carthage, Ill.

He died March 3, 1995, in Salt Lake City, Utah, at age 87.

15. Gordon Bitner Hinckley – Born June 23, 1910, in Salt Lake City, Utah, to Bryant S. and Ada Bitner Hinckley. As a young man, he earned a reputation as an outstanding writer and speaker because of his ability with words. After graduating from the University of Utah in 1932 with a major in English, he served a mission in the British Isles from 1933-1935.

Upon his return home, he reported to the First Presidency in an interview that led to employment with the Church as secretary of the then-recently formed Radio, Publicity, and Mission Literature Committee. Except for a short period during World War II, he worked for the Church for nearly 25 years, where he pioneered the adaptation of Church materials, particularly historical, for radio and later television programming and prepared various materials for missionaries. In 1951, he was called as executive secretary of the General Missionary Committee.

On April 29, 1937, he married Marjorie Pay in the Salt Lake Temple. They had five children. She died April 6, 2004. Prior to being called as a General Authority, he was a third-generation stake president and served on the Sunday School General Board.

He was sustained as an Assistant to the Twelve April 6, 1958. Three-and-a-half years later, on Sept. 30, 1961, he was sustained a member of the Quorum of the Twelve and was ordained an apostle on Oct. 5, 1961, at age 51. He served in the Twelve for 20 years and then served 14 years as a counselor to three Church presidents: Presidents Spencer W. Kimball, from 1981-1985; Ezra Taft Benson, from 1985-1994; and Howard W. Hunter, from 1994-1995. He was ordained and set apart as the 15th president of the Church on March 12, 1995, at age 84.

As president of the Church, President Hinckley had a strong desire to be out among the people and during his presidency he traveled more than a million miles and spoke to hundreds of thousands of members in more than 60 nations in Africa, Asia, the Pacific, Europe, and North, Central and South America. He was the first Church president to visit mainland China, West Africa, Russia and Ukraine.

A man of wit and wisdom, President Hinckley left behind a rich legacy. He envisioned the concept of small temples – perhaps the hallmark of his presidency – which helped fulfill his desire to provide temples close to members wherever they were. During the 12 years of his presidency, 79 new temples were announced worldwide. He dedicated 63 of the 77 temples that were dedicated during the same period. During the time he served in the First Presidency, he dedicated or rededicated 95 of the 124 temples then in operation. His leadership advanced the Church on every front, and construction of the massive Conference Center in Salt Lake City will forever be linked with his legacy.

He was awarded 10 honorary degrees, and in 2004, was given the United States' highest civil award, the Presidential Medal of Freedom, by President George Bush.

He died Jan. 27, 2008, at age 97, after a long life of dedicated service to God and his fellowman. He had the distinction of being the longest-lived president of the Church.

16. Thomas Spencer Monson — See current FIRST PRESIDENCY.

ASSISTANT PRESIDENTS OF THE CHURCH

1. Oliver Cowdery — Born Oct. 3, 1806, at Wells, Rutland Co., Vermont, to William Cowdery and Rebecca Fuller. Received Melchizedek Priesthood (ordained apostle) in May-June 1829, by Peter, James and John (D&C 20:2, 27:12); 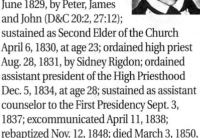 sustained as Second Elder of the Church April 6, 1830, at age 23; ordained high priest Aug. 28, 1831, by Sidney Rigdon; ordained assistant president of the High Priesthood Dec. 5, 1834, at age 28; sustained as assistant counselor to the First Presidency Sept. 3, 1837; excommunicated April 11, 1838; rebaptized Nov. 12, 1848; died March 3, 1850, at Richmond, Ray Co., Missouri, at age 43.

2. Hyrum Smith — Born Feb. 9, 1800, at Tunbridge, Orange Co., Vermont, to Joseph Smith Sr. and Lucy Mack. Ordained high priest in June 1831 by Joseph Smith; sustained as assistant counselor to the First Presidency Sept. 3, 1837, at  age 37; sustained as second counselor to President Joseph Smith Nov. 7, 1837; given all the priesthood formerly held by Oliver Cowdery (including apostle); ordained Patriarch to the Church and assistant president Jan. 24, 1841, by Joseph Smith, at age 40; martyred June 27, 1844, at Carthage Jail, Carthage, Hancock Co., Illinois, at age 44.

FIRST COUNSELORS IN THE FIRST PRESIDENCY

1. Sidney Rigdon — Born Feb. 19, 1793, at Saint Clair Township, Allegheny Co., Pennsylvania, to William Rigdon and Nancy Bryant. Ordained high priest in June 1831 by Lyman Wight; set apart as first counselor to President Joseph Smith March 18, 1833, at age 40; excommunicated Sept. 8, 1844; died July 14, 1876, at Friendship, Allegany Co., New York, at age 83.

2. Heber Chase Kimball — Born June 14, 1801, at Sheldon, Franklin Co., Vermont, to Solomon Farnham Kimball and Anna Spaulding. Ordained apostle Feb. 14, 1835, under the hands of Oliver Cowdery, David Whitmer, and Martin Harris, at age 33; sustained as first counselor to President Brigham Young Dec. 27, 1847, at age 46; died June 22, 1868, at Salt Lake City, Salt Lake Co., Utah, at age 67.

3. George Albert Smith — Born June 26, 1817, at Potsdam, Saint Lawrence Co., New York, to John Smith and Clarissa Lyman. Ordained apostle April 26, 1839, by Heber C. Kimball at age 21;  sustained as first counselor to President Brigham Young Oct. 7, 1868, at age 51; died Sept. 1, 1875, at Salt Lake City, Salt Lake Co., Utah, at age 58.

4. John Willard Young — Born Oct. 1, 1844, at Nauvoo, Hancock Co., Illinois, to Brigham Young and Mary Ann Angell. Ordained apostle Feb. 4, 1864, by Brigham Young. Sustained as counselor to President Brigham Young April 8, 1873, at age 28; sustained as assistant counselor to President Young May 9, 1874; sustained as first counselor to President Young Oct. 7, 1876, at age 32; released at death of President Young Aug. 29, 1877; sustained as a counselor to the Twelve Apostles Oct. 6, 1877; released Oct. 6, 1891; died Feb. 11, 1924, at New York City, New York, at age 79.

5. George Quayle Cannon — Born Jan. 11, 1827, at Liverpool, Lancashire Co., England, to George Cannon and Ann Quayle. Ordained an apostle Aug. 26, 1860, by Brigham Young, at age 33; sustained as counselor to President Young April 8,

1873, at age 46; sustained as assistant counselor to President Young May 9, 1874; released at death of President Young Aug. 29, 1877; sustained as first counselor to President John Taylor Oct. 10, 1880; released at death of President Taylor July 25, 1887; sustained as first counselor to President Wilford Woodruff April 7, 1889; sustained as first counselor to President Lorenzo Snow Sept. 13, 1898; died April 12, 1901, at Monterey, Monterey Co., California, at age 74.

6. Joseph Fielding Smith — See PRESIDENTS OF THE CHURCH, No. 6.

7. John Rex Winder — Born Dec. 11, 1821, at Biddenham, Kent Co., England, to Richard Winder and Sophia Collins. Ordained high priest March 4, 1872, by Edward Hunter; sustained as second counselor to Presiding Bishop William B. Preston

April 8, 1887, at age 65; sustained as first counselor to President Joseph F. Smith Oct. 17, 1901, at age 79; died March 27, 1910, at Salt Lake City, Salt Lake Co., Utah, at 88.

8. Anthon Henrik Lund — Born May 15, 1844, at Aalborg, Jutland, Denmark, to Henrik Lund and Anne C. Andersen. Ordained apostle Oct. 7, 1889, by George Q. Cannon, at age 45; sustained as second counselor to President

Joseph F. Smith Oct. 17, 1901, at age 57; sustained as first counselor to President Smith April 7, 1910; sustained as first counselor to President Heber J. Grant Nov. 23, 1918; died March 2, 1921, at Salt Lake

City, Salt Lake Co., Utah, at age 76.

9. Charles William Penrose — Born Feb. 4, 1832, at London, Surrey Co., England, to Richard Penrose and Matilda Sims. Ordained apostle July 7, 1904, by Joseph F. Smith, at age 72; sustained as second counselor to President

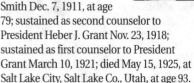

Smith Dec. 7, 1911, at age 79; sustained as second counselor to President Heber J. Grant Nov. 23, 1918; sustained as first counselor to President Grant March 10, 1921; died May 15, 1925, at Salt Lake City, Salt Lake Co., Utah, at age 93.

10. Anthony Woodward Ivins — Born Sept. 16, 1852, at Toms River, Ocean Co., New Jersey, to Israel Ivins and Anna Lowrie. Ordained apostle Oct. 6, 1907, by Joseph F. Smith, at age 55; sustained as second counselor to President Heber J. Grant

March 10, 1921, at age 68; sustained as first counselor to President Grant May 28, 1925; died Sept. 23, 1934, at Salt Lake City, Salt Lake Co., Utah, at age 82.

11. Joshua Reuben Clark Jr. — Born Sept. 1, 1871, at Grantsville, Tooele Co., Utah, to Joshua Reuben Clark and Mary Louise Woolley. Sustained as second counselor to President Heber J. Grant, April 6, 1933, at age 61; sustained as first counselor

to President Grant, Oct. 6, 1934; ordained apostle Oct. 11, 1934, at age 63, by President Grant; sustained as first counselor to President George Albert Smith May 21, 1945; sustained as second counselor to President David O. McKay April 9, 1951; sustained as first counselor to President McKay June 12, 1959; died Oct. 6, 1961, at Salt Lake City, Salt Lake Co., Utah, at age 90.

12. Stephen L Richards — Born June 18, 1879, at Mendon, Cache Co., Utah, to Stephen Longstroth Richards and Emma

Louise Stayner. Ordained apostle Jan. 18, 1917, by Joseph F. Smith, at age 37; sustained as first counselor to President David O. McKay April 9, 1951, at age 71; died May 19, 1959, at Salt Lake City, Salt Lake Co., Utah, at age 79.

13. Joshua Reuben Clark Jr. — See No. 11 above.

14. Henry Dinwoodey Moyle — Born April 22, 1889, at Salt Lake City, Salt Lake Co., Utah, to James H. Moyle and Alice E. Dinwoodey. Ordained apostle April 10, 1947, by George Albert Smith, at age 57; sustained as second counselor to President David O. McKay June 12, 1959, at age 70; sustained as first counselor to President McKay Oct. 12, 1961; died Sept. 18, 1963, at Deer Park, Osceola Co., Florida, at age 74.

15. Hugh Brown Brown — Born Oct. 24, 1883, at Granger, Salt Lake Co., Utah, to Homer Manly Brown and Lydia Jane Brown. Sustained as Assistant to the Twelve Oct. 4, 1953, at age 69; ordained an apostle April 10, 1958, by David O. McKay, at age 74; sustained as counselor in the First Presidency June 22, 1961; sustained as second counselor to President McKay Oct. 12, 1961; sustained as first counselor to President McKay Oct. 4, 1963; released at death of President McKay Jan. 18, 1970, and resumed position in the Quorum of the Twelve Apostles; died Dec. 2, 1975, at Salt Lake City, Salt Lake Co., Utah, at age 92.

16. Harold Bingham Lee — See PRESIDENTS OF THE CHURCH, No. 11.

17. Nathan Eldon Tanner — Born May 9, 1898, at Salt Lake City, Salt Lake Co., Utah, to Nathan William Tanner and Sarah Edna Brown. Sustained as Assistant to the Twelve Oct. 8, 1960, at age 62; ordained apostle Oct.

11, 1962, at age 64; sustained as second counselor to President David O. McKay Oct. 4, 1963; sustained as second counselor to President Joseph Fielding Smith Jan. 23, 1970; sustained as first counselor to President Harold B. Lee July 7, 1972; sustained as first counselor to President Spencer W. Kimball Dec. 30, 1973; died Nov. 27, 1982, at Salt Lake City, Salt Lake Co., Utah, at age 84.

18. Marion George Romney — Born Sept. 19, 1897, in Colonia Juarez, Mexico, to George Samuel Romney and Teressa Artemesia Redd. Sustained as Church's first Assistant to the Twelve April 6, 1941, at age 43; ordained apostle Oct. 11, 1951, at age 54; sustained as second counselor to President Harold B. Lee July 7, 1972; sustained as second counselor to President Spencer W. Kimball Dec. 30, 1973; sustained as first counselor to President Kimball Dec. 2, 1982; released at the death of President Kimball Nov. 5, 1985, and resumed position in the Quorum of Twelve Apostle; became president of the Quorum of the Twelve Nov. 10, 1985; died May 20, 1988, at Salt Lake City, Salt Lake Co., Utah, at age 90.

19. Gordon Bitner Hinckley – See PRESIDENTS OF THE CHURCH, No. 15.

20. Thomas Spencer Monson — See current FIRST PRESIDENCY.

21. Henry Bennion Eyring – See current FIRST PRESIDENCY.

SECOND COUNSELORS IN THE FIRST PRESIDENCY

1. Frederick Granger Williams — Born Oct. 28, 1787, at Suffield, Hartford, Co., Connecticut, to William Wheeler Williams and Ruth Granger. Called by revelation March 1832 to be a high priest and counselor to President Joseph Smith (D&C 81:1);  ordained high priest by Miles H. Jones; set apart as second counselor to President Smith March 18, 1833, at age 45; rejected Nov. 7, 1837; excommunicated March 17, 1839; restored to fellowship April 8, 1840; died Oct. 10, 1842, at Quincy, Adams Co., Illinois, at age 54.

2. Hyrum Smith — See ASSISTANT PRESIDENTS OF THE CHURCH, No. 2.

3. William Law — Born Sept. 8, 1809, at Tyrone Co., North Ireland. Set apart as second counselor to President Joseph Smith Jan. 24, 1841, at age 31; excommunicated April 18, 1844; died Jan. 19, 1892, at Shullsburg, Lafayette Co., Wisconsin, at age 82.

4. Willard Richards — Born June 24, 1804, at Hopkinton, Middlesex Co., Massachusetts, to Joseph Richards and Rhoda Howe. Ordained apostle April 14, 1840, by Brigham Young, at age 35; sustained as second counselor to President Young Dec. 27,  1847, at age 43; died March 11, 1854, at Salt Lake City, Salt Lake Co., Utah, at age 49.

5. Jedediah Morgan Grant — Born Feb. 21, 1816, at Windsor, Broome Co., New York, to Joshua Grant and Athalia Howard. Set apart as one of the First Seven Presidents of the Seventy Dec. 2, 1845, at age 29; ordained apostle April 7, 1854, by Brigham Young, at  age 38; sustained as second counselor to President Young April 7, 1854; died Dec. 1, 1856, at Salt Lake City, Salt Lake Co., Utah, at age 40.

6. Daniel Hanmer Wells — Born Oct. 27, 1814, at Trenton, (now Barnveld) Oneida Co., New Jersey, to Daniel Wells and Catherine Chapin. Set apart as second counselor to President Young Jan. 4, 1857, at age 42; released at death of President Young  Aug. 29, 1877; sustained as a counselor to the Twelve Apostles Oct. 6, 1877; died March 24, 1891, at Salt Lake City, Salt Lake Co., Utah, at age 76.

7. Joseph Fielding Smith — See PRESIDENTS OF THE CHURCH, No. 6.

8. Rudger Clawson — Born March 12, 1857, at Salt Lake City, Salt Lake Co., Utah, to Hiram Bradley Clawson and Margaret Gay Judd. Ordained apostle Oct. 10, 1898, by Lorenzo Snow, at age 41; sustained as second counselor to President Snow  Oct. 6, 1901, at age 44, not set apart to this position; released at death of President Snow Oct. 10, 1901, and resumed position in the Quorum of the Twelve Apostles; sustained as president of the Quorum of the Twelve Apostles March 17, 1921; died June 21, 1943, in Salt Lake City, Salt Lake Co., Utah at age 86.

9. Anthon Henrik Lund — See FIRST COUNSELORS IN THE FIRST PRESIDENCY, No. 8.

10. John Henry Smith — Born Sept. 18, 1848, at Carbunca (now part of Council Bluffs), Pottawattamie Co., Iowa, to George Albert Smith and Sarah Ann Libby. Ordained apostle Oct. 27, 1880, by Wilford Woodruff, at age 32; sustained as second  counselor to President Joseph F. Smith April 7, 1910, at age 61; died Oct. 13, 1911, at Salt Lake City, Salt Lake Co., Utah, at 63.

11. Charles William Penrose — See FIRST COUNSELORS IN THE FIRST PRESIDENCY, No. 9.

12. Anthony Woodward Ivins — See FIRST COUNSELORS IN THE FIRST PRESIDENCY, No. 10.

13. Charles Wilson Nibley — Born Feb. 5, 1849, at Hunterfield, Midlothian Region, Scotland, to James Nibley and Jane Wilson. Ordained high priest June 9, 1901, by Joseph F. Smith; sustained as Presiding Bishop of the Church Dec. 4, 1907, at age 58; sustained as second counselor to President Heber J. Grant, May 28, 1925, at age 76; died Dec. 11, 1931, at Salt Lake City, Salt Lake Co., Utah, at age 82.

14. Joshua Reuben Clark Jr. — See FIRST COUNSELORS IN THE FIRST PRESIDENCY, No. 11.

15. David Oman McKay — See PRESIDENTS OF CHURCH, No. 9.

16. Joshua Reuben Clark Jr. — See FIRST COUNSELORS IN THE FIRST PRESIDENCY, No. 11.

17. Henry Dinwoodey Moyle — See FIRST COUNSELORS IN THE FIRST PRESIDENCY, No. 14.

18. Hugh Brown Brown — See FIRST COUNSELORS IN THE FIRST PRESIDENCY, No. 15.

19. Nathan Eldon Tanner — See FIRST COUNSELORS IN THE FIRST PRESIDENCY, No. 17.

20. Marion George Romney — See FIRST COUNSELORS IN THE FIRST PRESIDENCY, No. 18.

21. Gordon Bitner Hinckley – See PRESIDENTS OF THE CHURCH, No. 15.

22. Thomas Spencer Monson — See current FIRST PRESIDENCY.

23. James Esdras Faust – Born July 31, 1920, in Delta, Millard Co., Utah, to George A. Faust and Amy Finlinson. Sustained an Assistant to the Twelve Oct. 6, 1972, at age 52, and to the Presidency of the Seventy Oct. 1, 1976; sustained to the Quorum of the Twelve Sept. 30, 1978, ordained apostle Oct. 1, 1978, at age 58; sustained as second counselor to President Gordon B. Hinckley March 12, 1995; died Aug. 10, 2007, at Salt Lake City, Salt Lake Co., Utah, at age 87.

24. Henry Bennion Eyring – See current FIRST PRESIDENCY.

25. Dieter Friedrich Uchtdorf – See current FIRST PRESIDENCY.

OTHER COUNSELORS IN THE FIRST PRESIDENCY

1. Jesse Gause — Born about 1784 at East Marlborough, Chester Co., Virginia, to William and Mary Beverly Gause. Converted from the Shaker sect, he was baptized about the end of 1831. Set apart as counselor to Joseph Smith March 8, 1832; sent on a mission Aug. 1, 1832. Excommunicated Dec. 3, 1832. Died about 1836.

2. John Cook Bennett — Born Aug. 3, 1804, at Fair Haven, Bristol Co., Massachusetts, to J. and N. Bennett. Presented as assistant president with the First Presidency April 8, 1841, at age 36 (See *History of the Church* 4:341); disfellowshipped May 25, 1842; excommunicated latter part of 1842; died Aug. 5, 1867, in Polk City, Polk Co., Iowa at age 63.

3. Amasa Mason Lyman — Born March 30, 1813, at Lyman, Crafton Co., New Hampshire, to Roswell Lyman and Martha Mason. Ordained apostle Aug. 20, 1842, by Brigham Young, at age 29; replaced in the Quorum of the

Twelve Apostles Jan. 20, 1843, due to reinstatement of Orson Pratt; appointed counselor to the First Presidency about Feb. 4, 1843; retired from the First Presidency with death of Joseph Smith June 27, 1844; returned to the Quorum of the Twelve Apostles Aug. 12, 1844; deprived of apostleship Oct. 6, 1867; excommunicated May 12, 1870; died Feb. 4, 1877, at Fillmore, Millard Co., Utah, at age 63. Blessings restored after death on Jan. 12, 1909.

4. Joseph Fielding Smith — See PRESIDENTS OF CHURCH, No. 6.

5. Lorenzo Snow — See PRESIDENTS OF CHURCH, No. 5.

6. Brigham Young Jr. — Born Dec. 18, 1836, at Kirtland, Geauga Co., Ohio, to Brigham Young and Mary Ann Angell. Ordained apostle Feb. 4, 1864, by Brigham Young, at age 27; sustained to the Quorum of the Twelve Apostles Oct. 9, 1868;  sustained as counselor to President Young April 8, 1873, at age 36; sustained as assistant counselor to President Young May 9, 1874; released at President Young's death Aug. 29, 1877, and resumed position in the Quorum of the Twelve Apostles; sustained as president of the Quorum of the Twelve Apostles Oct. 17, 1901; died April 11, 1903, in Salt Lake City, Salt Lake Co., Utah, at age 66.

7. Albert Carrington — Born Jan. 8, 1813, at Royalton, Windsor Co., Vermont, to Daniel Van Carrington and Isabella Bowman. Ordained apostle July 3, 1870, by Brigham Young, at age 57; sustained as counselor to President Young April 8, 1873, at age 60; sustained as assistant counselor to President Young May 9, 1874; released at death of President Young Aug. 29, 1877; excommunicated Nov. 7, 1885; rebaptized Nov. 1, 1887; died Sept. 19, 1889, at Salt Lake City, Salt Lake Co., Utah, at age 76.

8. John Willard Young — See FIRST COUNSELORS IN THE FIRST PRESIDENCY, No. 4.

9. George Quayle Cannon — See FIRST COUNSELORS IN THE FIRST PRESIDENCY, No. 5.

10. Hugh Brown Brown — See FIRST COUNSELORS IN THE FIRST PRESIDENCY, No. 15.

11. Joseph Fielding Smith — See PRESIDENTS OF THE CHURCH, No. 10.

12. Henry Thorpe Beal Isaacson — Born Sept. 6, 1898, at Ephraim, Sanpete Co., Utah, to Martin Isaacson and Mary Jemima Beal. Ordained high priest Oct. 1, 1941, by Charles A. Callis; sustained as second counselor to Presiding Bishop LeGrand  Richards Dec. 12, 1946, at age 48; sustained as first counselor to Presiding Bishop Joseph L. Wirthlin April 6, 1952; sustained as Assistant to the Twelve Sept. 30, 1961; sustained as counselor in the First Presidency Oct. 28, 1965, at age 67; released at death of President David O. McKay Jan. 18, 1970; resumed position as Assistant to the Twelve Apostles Jan. 23, 1970; died Nov. 9, 1970, at Salt Lake City, Salt Lake Co., Utah, at age 72.

13. Alvin Rulon Dyer — Born Jan. 1, 1903, at Salt Lake City, Salt Lake Co., Utah, to Alfred R. Dyer and Harriet Walsh. Ordained high priest Oct. 2, 1927, by Joseph Fielding Smith; sustained an Assistant to the Twelve Oct. 11, 1958, at age 55;  ordained apostle Oct. 5, 1967, by David O. McKay, at age 64; sustained as counselor in the First Presidency April 6, 1968; released at death of President McKay Jan. 18, 1970; resumed position as Assistant to the Twelve Apostles Jan. 23, 1970; sustained a member of First Quorum of the Seventy Oct. 1, 1976; died March 6, 1977, at Salt Lake City, Salt Lake Co., Utah, at age 74.

14. Gordon Bitner Hinckley – See PRESIDENTS OF THE CHURCH, No. 15.

ASSISTANT COUNSELORS IN THE FIRST PRESIDENCY

1. Oliver Cowdery — See ASSISTANT PRESIDENTS OF THE CHURCH, No. 1.

2. Joseph Smith Sr. — Born July 12, 1771, at Topsfield, Essex Co., Massachusetts, to Asael Smith and Mary Duty. Ordained high priest June 3, 1831, by Lyman Wight; ordained Patriarch to the Church Dec. 18, 1833, at age 62; sustained as assistant counselor to the First Presidency Sept. 3, 1837, at age 66; died Sept. 14, 1840, at Nauvoo, Hancock Co., Illinois, at age 69.

3. Hyrum Smith — See ASSISTANT PRESIDENTS OF THE CHURCH, No. 2.

4. John Smith — Born July 16, 1781, at Derryfield, Hillsboro Co., New Hampshire, to Asael Smith and Mary Duty. Ordained high priest June 3, 1833, by Lyman Wight; sustained as assistant counselor to the First Presidency Sept. 3, 1837, at age 56; released at the death of Joseph Smith June 27, 1844; ordained Patriarch to the Church Jan. 1, 1849, at age 67; died May 23, 1854, at Salt Lake City, Salt Lake Co., Utah, at age 72.

5. Lorenzo Snow — See PRESIDENTS OF THE CHURCH, No. 5.

6. Brigham Young Jr. — See OTHER COUNSELORS IN THE FIRST PRESIDENCY, No. 6.

7. Albert Carrington — See OTHER COUNSELORS IN THE FIRST PRESIDENCY, No. 7.

8. John Willard Young — See FIRST COUNSELORS IN THE FIRST PRESIDENCY, No. 4.

9. George Quayle Cannon — See FIRST COUNSELORS IN THE FIRST PRESIDENCY, No. 5.

QUORUM OF THE TWELVE APOSTLES

1. Thomas Baldwin Marsh — Born Nov. 1, 1800, at Acton, Middlesex Co., Massachusetts, to James Marsh and Molly Law. Ordained apostle April 25, 1835, under the hands of Oliver Cowdery, David Whitmer, and Martin Harris, at Kirtland, Ohio, at age 35; sustained as president of the Quorum of the Twelve Apostles May 2, 1835; excommunicated March 17, 1839; rebaptized July 16, 1857; died January 1866, at Ogden, Weber Co., Utah, at age 66.

2. David Wyman Patten — Born Nov. 14, 1799, at Theresa, Jefferson Co., New York, to Benenio Patten and Abigail Cole. Ordained apostle Feb. 15, 1835, under the hands of Oliver Cowdery, David Whitmer, and Martin Harris, at Kirtland, Ohio, at age 35; killed Oct. 25, 1838, at the Battle of Crooked River, Missouri, at age 38.

Note: David Patten was actually older than Thomas B. Marsh when called to the Twelve, but he did not know his age at that time. Subsequent records showed he was actually older by almost a year.

3. Brigham Young — See PRESIDENTS OF THE CHURCH, No. 2.

4. Heber Chase Kimball — See FIRST COUNSELORS IN THE FIRST PRESIDENCY, No. 2.

5. Orson Hyde — Born Jan. 8, 1805, at Oxford, New Haven Co., Connecticut, to Nathan Hyde and Sally Thorp. Ordained apostle Feb. 15, 1835, under the hands of Oliver Cowdery, David Whitmer, and Martin Harris, at Kirtland, Ohio, at age 30; dropped from Quorum May 4, 1839; restored to Quorum June 27, 1839; sustained as president of the Quorum of the Twelve Apostles Dec. 27, 1847; Brigham Young, on April 10, 1875, took Hyde from his original position in the quorum and placed him in the order he would have been in when he was restored to fellowship had he come into the quorum at that time (See *"Succession in the Priesthood"* by John Taylor, p. 16.); died

Nov. 28, 1878, at Spring City, Sanpete Co., Utah, at age 73.

6. William E. McLellin — Born Jan. 18, 1806, in Smith Co., Tenn. Ordained apostle Feb. 15, 1835, under the hands of Oliver Cowdery, David Whitmer, and Martin Harris, at Kirtland, Ohio, at age 29; excommunicated May 11, 1838; died April 24, 1883, at Independence, Jackson Co., Missouri, at age 77.

7. Parley Parker Pratt — Born April 12, 1807, at Burlington, Otsego Co., New York, to Jared Pratt and Charity Dickinson. Ordained apostle Feb. 21, 1835, under the hands of Joseph Smith, Oliver Cowdery, and David Whitmer, at Kirtland, Ohio, at age 27; assassinated May 13, 1857, near Van Buren, Crawford Co., Arkansas, at age 50.

8. Luke Johnson — Born Nov. 3, 1807, at Pomfret, Windsor Co., Vermont, to John Johnson and Elsa Jacobs. Ordained apostle Feb. 15, 1835, by Oliver Cowdery, David Whitmer, and Martin Harris, at Kirtland, Ohio, at age 27; excommunicated April 13, 1838; rebaptized in 1846 at Nauvoo, Illinois; died Dec. 9, 1861, at Salt Lake City, Salt Lake Co., Utah, at age 54.

9. William B. Smith — Born March 13, 1811, at Royalton, Windsor Co., Vermont, to Joseph Smith Sr. and Lucy Mack. Ordained apostle Feb. 15, 1835, under the hands of Oliver Cowdery, David Whitmer, and Martin Harris, at Kirtland, Ohio, at age 23; dropped from the quorum May 4, 1839; restored to quorum May 25, 1839; dropped from the quorum Oct. 6, 1845; excommunicated Oct. 19, 1845; died Nov. 13, 1893, at Osterdock, Clayton Co., Iowa, at age

82.

10. Orson Pratt — Born Sept. 19, 1811, at Hartford, Washington, Co., New York, to Jared Pratt and Charity Dickinson. Ordained apostle April 26, 1835, under the hands of Oliver Cowdery, David Whitmer, and Martin Harris, at Kirtland, Ohio, at age 23; excommunicated Aug. 20, 1842; rebaptized Jan. 20, 1843, and ordained to former office in the Quorum of the Twelve Apostles. Brigham Young took him from his original position in the quorum in 1875 and placed him in the order he would have been in when he was restored to fellowship had he come into the quorum at that time; died Oct. 3, 1881, at Salt Lake City, Salt Lake Co., Utah, at age 70.

11. John Farnham Boynton — Born Sept. 20, 1811, at Bradford, Essex Co., Massachusetts, to Eliphalet Boynton and Susannah Nichols. Ordained apostle Feb. 15, 1835, under the hands of Oliver Cowdery, David Whitmer and Martin Harris, at Kirtland, Ohio, at age 23; disfellowshipped Sept. 3, 1837; excommunicated 1837; died Oct. 20, 1890, at Syracuse, Onondaga Co., New York, at age 79.

12. Lyman Eugene Johnson — Born Oct. 24, 1811, at Pomfret, Windsor Co., Vermont, to John Johnson and Elsa Jacobs. Ordained apostle Feb. 14, 1835, under the hands of Oliver Cowdery, David Whitmer and Martin Harris, at Kirtland, Ohio, at age 23; excommunicated April 13, 1838; died Dec. 20, 1859, at Prairie du Chien, Crawford Co., Wisconsin, at age 45.

13. John Edward Page — Born Feb. 25, 1799, at Trenton Township, Oneida Co., New York, to Ebenezer and Rachel Page. Ordained apostle Dec. 19, 1838, under the hands of Brigham Young and Heber C. Kimball at Far West,

Missouri, at age 39; disfellowshipped Feb. 9, 1846; excommunicated June 27, 1846; died Oct. 14, 1867, at De Kalb Co., Illinois, at age 68.

14. John Taylor — See PRESIDENTS OF THE CHURCH, No. 3.

15. Wilford Woodruff — See PRESIDENTS OF THE CHURCH, No. 4.

16. George Albert Smith — See FIRST COUNSELORS IN THE FIRST PRESIDENCY, No. 3.

17. Willard Richards — See SECOND COUNSELORS IN THE FIRST PRESIDENCY, No. 4.

18. Lyman Wight — Born May 9, 1796, at Fairfield, Herkimer Co., New York, to Levi Wight and Sarah Corbin. Ordained apostle April 8, 1841, by Joseph Smith, at Nauvoo, Illinois, at age 44; excommunicated Dec. 3, 1848; died March 31, 1858, in Dexter, Texas, at age 63.

19. Amasa Mason Lyman — See OTHER COUNSELORS IN THE FIRST PRESIDENCY, No. 3.

20. Ezra Taft Benson — Born Feb. 22, 1811, at Mendon, Worcester Co., Massachusetts, to John Benson and Chloe Taft. Ordained apostle July 16, 1846, by Brigham Young at Council Bluffs, Iowa, at age 35; died Sept. 3, 1869, at Ogden, Weber Co., Utah, at age 58.

21. Charles Coulsen Rich — Born Aug. 21, 1809, near Big Bone, Boone Co., Kentucky, to Joseph Rich and Nancy O. Neal. Ordained apostle Feb. 12, 1849, by Brigham Young, at Salt Lake City, Utah, at age 39; died Nov. 17, 1883, at Paris, Bear Lake Co., Idaho, at age 74.

22. Lorenzo Snow — See PRESIDENTS OF THE CHURCH, No. 5.

23. Erastus Snow — Born Nov. 9, 1818, at Saint Johnsbury, Caledonia Co., Vermont, to Levi Snow and Lucina Streeter. Ordained apostle Feb. 12, 1849, by Brigham Young, at age 30; died May 27, 1888, at Salt Lake City, Salt Lake Co., Utah, at age 69.

24. Franklin Dewey Richards — Born April 2, 1821, at Richmond, Berkshire Co., Massachusetts, to Phinehas Richards and Wealthy Dewey. Ordained apostle Feb. 12, 1849, by Heber C. Kimball, at age 27; sustained as president of the Quorum of the Twelve Apostles Sept. 13, 1898; died Dec. 9, 1899, at Ogden, Weber Co., Utah, at age 78.

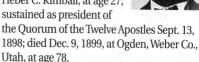

25. George Quayle Cannon — See FIRST COUNSELORS IN THE FIRST PRESIDENCY, No. 5.

26. Joseph Fielding Smith — See PRESIDENTS OF THE CHURCH, No. 6.

27. Brigham Young Jr. — See OTHER COUNSELORS IN THE FIRST PRESIDENCY, No. 6.

28. Albert Carrington — See OTHER COUNSELORS IN THE FIRST PRESIDENCY, No. 7.

29. Moses Thatcher — Born Feb. 2, 1842, at Springfield Sangamon Co., Ill., to Hezekiah Thatcher and Alley Kitchen. Ordained apostle April 7, 1879, by John Taylor, at age 37; dropped from the Quorum of the Twelve Apostles April 6, 1896; died Aug. 21, 1909, at Logan, Cache Co., Utah, at age 67.

30. Francis Marion Lyman — Born Jan. 12, 1840, at Good Hope, McDonough Co., Illinois, to Amasa Mason Lyman and Maria Louisa Tanner.

Ordained apostle Oct. 27, 1880, by John Taylor, at age 40; sustained as president of the Quorum of the Twelve Apostles Oct. 6, 1903; died Nov. 18, 1916, at Salt Lake City, Salt Lake Co., Utah, at age 76.

31. John Henry Smith — See SECOND COUNSELORS IN THE FIRST PRESIDENCY, No. 10.

32. George Teasdale — Born Dec. 8, 1831, at London, Middlesex Co., England, to William Russell Teasdale and Harriett H. Tidey. Ordained apostle Oct. 16, 1882, by John Taylor, at age 50; died June 9, 1907, at Salt Lake City, Salt Lake Co., Utah, at age 75.

33. Heber Jeddy Grant — See PRESIDENTS OF THE CHURCH, No. 7.

34. John Whittaker Taylor — Born May 15, 1858, at Provo, Utah Co., Utah, to John Taylor and Sophia Whittaker. Ordained apostle April 9, 1884, by John Taylor, at age 25; resigned Oct. 28, 1905; excommunicated March 28, 1911; died Oct. 10, 1916, at Salt Lake City, Salt Lake Co., Utah, at age 58. Blessings restored May 21, 1965.

35. Marriner Wood Merrill — Born Sept. 25, 1832, at Sackville, Westmoreland Co., New Brunswick, Canada, to Nathan Alexander Merrill and Sarah Ann Reynolds. Ordained apostle Oct. 7, 1889, by Wilford Woodruff, at age 57; died Feb. 6, 1906, at Richmond, Cache Co., Utah, at age 73.

36. Anthon Henrik Lund — See FIRST COUNSELORS IN THE FIRST PRESIDENCY, No. 8.

37. Abraham Hoagland Cannon — Born March 12, 1859, at Salt Lake City, Salt Lake Co., Utah, to George Quayle Cannon and Elizabeth Hoagland. Sustained as one of the First Seven Presidents of the Seventy Oct. 8, 1882, at age 23; ordained apostle Oct. 7, 1889, by Joseph F. Smith, at age 30; died July 19, 1896, at Salt Lake City, Salt Lake Co., Utah, at age 37.

38. Matthias Foss Cowley — Born Aug. 25, 1858, at Salt Lake City, Salt Lake Co., Utah, to Matthias Cowley and Sarah Elizabeth Foss. Ordained apostle Oct. 7, 1897, by George Q. Cannon, at age 39; resigned Oct. 28, 1905; priesthood suspended May 11, 1911; restored to full membership April 3, 1936; died June 16, 1940, at Salt Lake City, Salt Lake Co., Utah, at age 81.

39. Abraham Owen Woodruff — Born Nov. 23, 1872, at Salt Lake City, Salt Lake Co., Utah, to Wilford Woodruff and Emma Smith. Ordained apostle Oct. 7, 1897, by Wilford Woodruff, at age 24; died June 20, 1904, at El Paso, El Paso Co., Texas, at age 31.

40. Rudger Clawson — See SECOND COUNSELORS IN THE FIRST PRESIDENCY, No. 8.

41. Reed Smoot — Born Jan. 10, 1862, at Salt Lake City, Salt Lake Co., Utah, to Abraham Owen Smoot and Anne Kestine Morrison. Ordained apostle April 8, 1900, by Lorenzo Snow, at age 38; served in the U.S. Senate, 1903-32; died Feb. 9, 1941, at St. Petersburg, Pinellas Co., Florida, at age 79.

42. Hyrum Mack Smith — Born March 21, 1872, at Salt Lake City, Salt Lake Co., Utah, to Joseph Fielding Smith and Edna Lambson. Ordained apostle Oct. 24, 1901, by Joseph F. Smith, at age 29;

died Jan. 23, 1918, at Salt Lake City, Salt Lake Co., Utah, at age 45.

43. George Albert Smith — See PRESIDENTS OF THE CHURCH, No. 8.

44. Charles William Penrose — See FIRST COUNSELORS IN THE FIRST PRESIDENCY, No. 9.

45. George Franklin Richards — Born Feb.  23, 1861, at Farmington, Davis Co., Utah, to Franklin Dewey Richards and Nanny Longstroth. Ordained apostle April 9, 1906, by Joseph F. Smith, at age 45; sustained as acting Patriarch to the Church Oct. 8, 1937; released from this position Oct. 3, 1942; sustained as president of the Quorum of the Twelve Apostles May 21, 1945; died Aug. 8, 1950, at Salt Lake City, Salt Lake Co., Utah, at age 89.

46. Orson Ferguson Whitney — Born July  1, 1855, at Salt Lake City, Salt Lake Co., Utah, to Horace Kimball Whitney and Helen Mar Kimball. Ordained apostle April 9, 1906, by Joseph F. Smith, at age 50; died May 16, 1931, at Salt Lake City, Salt Lake Co., Utah, at age 75.

47. David Oman McKay — See PRESIDENTS OF THE CHURCH, No. 9.

48. Anthony Woodward Ivins — See FIRST COUNSELORS IN THE FIRST PRESIDENCY, No. 10.

49. Joseph Fielding Smith — See PRESIDENTS OF THE CHURCH, No. 10.

50. James Edward Talmage — Born Sept.  21, 1862, at Hungerford, Berkshire Co., England, to James J. Talmage and Susannah Preater. Ordained apostle Dec. 8, 1911, by Joseph F. Smith, at age 49; died July 27, 1933, at Salt Lake City, Salt Lake Co., Utah, at age 70.

51. Stephen L Richards — See FIRST

COUNSELORS IN THE FIRST PRESIDENCY, No. 12.

52. Richard Roswell Lyman — Born Nov.  23, 1870, at Fillmore, Millard Co., Utah, to Francis Marion Lyman and Clara Caroline Callister. Ordained apostle April 7, 1918, by Joseph F. Smith, at age 47; excommunicated Nov. 12, 1943; rebaptized Oct. 27, 1954; died Dec. 31, 1963, at Salt Lake City, Salt Lake Co., Utah, at age 93.

53. Melvin Joseph Ballard — Born Feb. 9,  1873, at Logan, Cache Co., Utah, to Henry Ballard and Margaret Reid McNeil. Ordained apostle Jan. 7, 1919, by Heber J. Grant, at age 45; died July 30, 1939, at Salt Lake City, Salt Lake Co., Utah, at age 66.

54. John Andreas Widtsoe — Born Jan. 31,  1872, at Daloe, Island of Froyen, Trondhjem, Norway, to John A. Widtsoe and Anna Karine Gaarden. Ordained apostle March 17, 1921, by Heber J. Grant, at age 49; died Nov. 29, 1952, at Salt Lake City, Salt Lake Co., Utah, at age 80.

55. Joseph Francis Merrill — Born Aug. 24,  1868, at Richmond, Cache Co., Utah, to Marriner Wood Merrill and Mariah Loenza Kingsbury. Ordained apostle Oct. 8, 1931, by Heber J. Grant, at age 63; died Feb. 3, 1952, at Salt Lake City, Salt Lake Co., Utah, at age 83.

56. Charles Albert Callis — Born May 4, 1865, at Dublin, Dublin Co., Ireland, to John Callis and Susanna Charlotte Quillam. Ordained apostle Oct. 12, 1933, by Heber J. Grant, at age 68; died Jan. 21, 1947, in

Jacksonville, Duval Co., Florida, at age 81.

57. Joshua Reuben Clark Jr. — See FIRST COUNSELORS IN THE FIRST PRESIDENCY, No. 11.

58. Alonzo Arza Hinckley — Born April 23, 1870, at Cove Fort, Millard Co., Utah, to Ira Nathaniel Hinckley and Angeline Wilcox Noble. Ordained apostle Oct. 11, 1934, by Heber J. Grant, at age 64; died Dec. 22, 1936, at Salt Lake City, Salt Lake Co., Utah, at age 66.

59. Albert Ernest Bowen — Born Oct. 31, 1875, at Henderson Creek, Oneida Co., Idaho, to David Bowen and Annie Schackelton. Ordained apostle April 8, 1937, by Heber J. Grant, at age 61; died July 15, 1953, at Salt Lake City, Salt Lake Co., Utah, at age 77.

60. Sylvester Quayle Cannon — Born June 10, 1877, at Salt Lake City, Salt Lake Co., Utah, to George Quayle Cannon and Elizabeth Hoagland. Sustained as Presiding Bishop of the Church June 4, 1925, at age 47; sustained as Associate to the Quorum of the Twelve Apostles April 6, 1938; ordained apostle April 14, 1938, by Heber J. Grant; sustained as a member of the Quorum of the Twelve Apostles Oct. 6, 1939, at age 62; died May 29, 1943, at Salt Lake City, Salt Lake Co., Utah, at age 65.

61. Harold Bingham Lee — See PRESIDENTS OF THE CHURCH, No. 11.

62. Spencer Woolley Kimball — See PRESIDENTS OF THE CHURCH, No. 12.

63. Ezra Taft Benson — See PRESIDENTS OF THE CHURCH, No. 13.

64. Mark Edward Petersen — Born Nov. 7,

1900, at Salt Lake City, Salt Lake Co., Utah, to Christian Petersen and Christine M. Andersen. Ordained apostle April 20, 1944, by Heber J. Grant, at age 43; died Jan. 11, 1984, at Salt Lake City, Salt Lake Co., Utah, at age 83.

65. Matthew Cowley — Born Aug. 2, 1897, at Preston, Franklin Co., Idaho, to Matthias Foss Cowley and Abbie Hyde. Ordained apostle Oct. 11, 1945, by George Albert Smith, at age 48; died Dec. 13, 1953, at Los Angeles, Los Angeles Co., California, at age 56.

66. Henry Dinwoodey Moyle — See FIRST COUNSELORS IN THE FIRST PRESIDENCY, No. 14.

67. Delbert Leon Stapley — Born Dec. 11, 1896, at Mesa, Maricopa Co., Arizona, to Orley S. Stapley and Polly M. Hunsaker. Ordained apostle Oct. 5, 1950, by George Albert Smith, at age 53; died Aug. 19, 1978, at Salt Lake City, Salt Lake Co., Utah, at age 81.

68. Marion George Romney — See FIRST COUNSELORS IN THE FIRST PRESIDENCY, No. 18.

69. LeGrand Richards — Born Feb. 6, 1886, at Farmington, Davis Co., Utah, to George Franklin Richards and Alice Almira Robinson. Sustained Presiding Bishop of the Church April 6, 1938, at age 52; ordained apostle April 10, 1952, by David O. McKay, at age 66; died Jan. 11, 1983, at Salt Lake City, Salt Lake Co., Utah, at age 96.

70. Adam Samuel Bennion — Born Dec. 2, 1886, at Taylorsville, Salt Lake Co., Utah, to Joseph Bennion and Mary A.

Sharp. Ordained apostle April 9, 1953, by David O. McKay, at age 66; died Feb. 11, 1958, at Salt Lake City, Salt Lake Co., Utah, at 71.

71. Richard Louis Evans — Born March 23, 1906, at Salt Lake City, Salt Lake Co., Utah, to John A. Evans and Florence Neslen. Sustained as member of the First Council of the Seventy Oct. 7, 1938, at age 32; ordained apostle Oct. 8, 1953, by David O. McKay, at age 47; died Nov. 1, 1971, at Salt Lake City, Salt Lake Co., Utah, at age 65.

72. George Quayle Morris — Born Feb. 20, 1874, at Salt Lake City, Salt Lake Co., Utah, to Elias Morris and Mary L. Walker. Sustained as Assistant to the Quorum of the Twelve Apostles Oct. 6, 1951, at age 77; ordained apostle April 8, 1954, by David O. Mc-Kay, at age 80; died April 23, 1962, at Salt Lake City, Salt Lake Co., Utah, at age 88.

73. Hugh Brown Brown — See FIRST COUNSELORS IN THE FIRST PRESIDENCY, No. 15.

74. Howard William Hunter — See PRESIDENTS OF THE CHURCH, No. 14.

75. Gordon Bitner Hinckley – See PRESIDENTS OF THE CHURCH, No. 15.

76. Nathan Eldon Tanner — See FIRST COUNSELORS IN THE FIRST PRESIDENCY, No. 17.

77. Thomas Spencer Monson — See current FIRST PRESIDENCY.

78. Boyd Kenneth Packer — See current QUORUM OF THE TWELVE.

79. Marvin Jeremy Ashton — Born May 6, 1915, in Salt Lake City, Salt Lake Co., Utah, to Marvin O. Ashton and Rachel Jeremy. Sustained Assistant to the Twelve Apostles Oct. 3, 1969, at age 54; ordained apostle on Dec. 2, 1971, by Harold B. Lee at age 56; died Feb. 25, 1994, at Salt Lake City, Salt Lake

Co., Utah, at age 78.

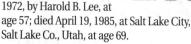

80. Bruce Redd McConkie — Born July 29, 1915, at Ann Arbor, Washtenaw Co., Michigan, to Oscar Walter McConkie and Vivian Redd. Sustained to First Council of the Seventy Oct. 6, 1946, at age 31; ordained apostle Oct. 12, 1972, by Harold B. Lee, at age 57; died April 19, 1985, at Salt Lake City, Salt Lake Co., Utah, at age 69.

81. Lowell Tom Perry — See current QUORUM OF THE TWELVE.

82. David Bruce Haight — Born Sept. 2, 1906, in Oakley, Idaho, to Hector C. Haight and Clara Tuttle. Sustained as Assistant to the Quorum of the Twelve Apostles April 6, 1970, at age 63; ordained apostle Jan 8, 1976, by Spencer W. Kimball, at age 69; sustained to the Quorum of the Twelve April 3, 1976; died July 31, 2004, at Salt Lake City, Salt Lake Co., Utah, at age 97.

83. James Esdras Faust – See SECOND COUNSELORS IN THE FIRST PRESIDENCY, NO. 23.

84. Neal Ash Maxwell — Born July 6, 1926, in Salt Lake City, Utah, to Clarence H. Maxwell and Emma Ash. Sustained as Assistant to the Quorum of the Twelve Apostles April 6, 1974, at age 47; to the Presidency of the Seventy, Oct. 1, 1976; and ordained apostle July 23, 1981, by Nathan Eldon Tanner, at age 55; sustained to the Quorum of the Twelve Oct. 3, 1981; died July 21, 2004, at Salt Lake City, Salt Lake Co., Utah, at age 78.

85. Russell Marion Nelson — See current QUORUM OF THE TWELVE.

86. Dallin Harris Oaks — See current QUORUM OF THE TWELVE.

87. Melvin Russell Ballard Jr. — See current QUORUM OF THE TWELVE.

88. **Joseph Bitner Wirthlin** — See current QUORUM OF THE TWELVE.

89. **Richard Gordon Scott** — See current QUORUM OF THE TWELVE.

90. **Robert Dean Hales** — See current QUORUM OF THE TWELVE.

91. **Jeffrey Roy Holland** — See current QUORUM OF THE TWELVE.

92. **Henry Bennion Eyring** – See current FIRST PRESIDENCY.

93. **Dieter Friedrich Uchtdorf** – See current FIRST PRESIDENCY.

94. **David Allan Bednar** — See current QUORUM OF THE TWELVE.

95. **Quentin LaMar Cook** – See current QUORUM OF THE TWELVE.

96. **David Todd Christofferson** – See current QUORUM OF THE TWELVE.

OTHER APOSTLES

1. **Joseph Smith Jr.** — See PRESIDENTS OF THE CHURCH, No. 1.

2. **Oliver Cowdery** — See ASSISTANT PRESIDENTS OF THE CHURCH, No. 1.

3. **Hyrum Smith** — See ASSISTANT PRESIDENTS OF THE CHURCH, No. 2.

4. **Amasa Mason Lyman** — See OTHER COUNSELORS IN THE FIRST PRESIDENCY, No. 3.

5. **Jedediah Morgan Grant** — See SECOND COUNSELORS IN THE FIRST PRESIDENCY, No. 5.

6. **John Willard Young** — See FIRST COUNSELORS IN THE FIRST PRESIDENCY, No. 4.

7. **Daniel Hanmer Wells** — See SECOND COUNSELORS IN THE FIRST PRESIDENCY, No. 6.

8. **Joseph Angell Young** — Born Oct. 14, 1834, in Kirtland, Geauga Co., Ohio, to Brigham Young and Mary Ann Angell. Ordained apostle Feb. 4, 1864, by Brigham Young, at age 29; died Aug. 5, 1875, at Manti, Sanpete Co., Utah, at age 40.

9. **Brigham Young Jr.** — See OTHER COUNSELORS IN THE FIRST PRESIDENCY, No. 6.

10. **Joseph Fielding Smith** — See PRESIDENTS OF THE CHURCH, No. 6.

11. **Sylvester Quayle Cannon** — See QUORUM OF THE TWELVE, No. 60.

12. **Alvin Rulon Dyer** — See OTHER COUNSELORS IN THE FIRST PRESIDENCY, No. 13.

PATRIARCHS TO THE CHURCH

1. Joseph Smith Sr. — See ASSISTANT COUNSELORS IN THE FIRST PRESIDENCY, No. 2.

2. Hyrum Smith — See ASSISTANT PRESIDENTS OF THE CHURCH, No. 2.

William Smith — See QUORUM OF THE TWELVE, No. 9. Ordained Patriarch to the Church May 24, 1845, by the Quorum of the Twelve and then gave patriarchal blessings, but was rejected by the Church membership at the General Conference held Oct. 6, 1845. There was no patriarch until the ordination of John Smith, uncle of Joseph Smith, on Jan. 1, 1849.

3. John Smith — See ASSISTANT COUNSELORS IN THE FIRST PRESIDENCY, No. 4.

4. John Smith — Born Sept. 22, 1832, at
Kirtland, Geauga Co., Ohio, the eldest son of Hyrum Smith and Jerusha Barden, nephew of Joseph Smith. Ordained Patriarch to the Church Feb. 18, 1855, by Brigham Young, at age 22; died Nov. 5, 1911, at Salt

Lake City, Salt Lake Co., Utah, at age 79.

5. Hyrum Gibbs Smith — Born July 8, 1879,
at South Jordan, Salt Lake Co., Utah, the eldest son of Hyrum Fisher Smith and Annie Maria Gibbs. Ordained high priest and Patriarch to the Church May 9, 1912, by Joseph F. Smith,

at age 32; died Feb. 4, 1932, at Salt Lake City, Salt Lake Co., Utah, at age 52.

(From 1932 to 1937, no Patriarch to the Church was sustained.)

George Franklin Richards — See QUORUM OF THE TWELVE, No. 45. (Served as acting Patriarch.)

6. Joseph Fielding Smith — Born Jan. 30,
1899, at Salt Lake City, Salt Lake Co., Utah, the eldest son of Hyrum Mack Smith and Ida E. Bowman. Ordained high priest and Patriarch to the Church Oct. 8, 1942, by Heber J. Grant, at age 43; released Oct. 6,

1946, due to ill health; died Aug. 29, 1964, in Salt Lake City, Salt Lake Co., Utah, at age 65.

7. Eldred Gee Smith — Born Jan. 9, 1907, at Lehi, Utah Co., Utah, the eldest son of Hyrum Gibbs Smith and Martha Electa Gee. Ordained high priest May 23, 1938, by J. Reuben Clark Jr.; ordained Patriarch to the Church April 10, 1947, by George Albert Smith, at age 40; named emeritus General Authority Oct. 6, 1979.

(No Patriarch to the Church has been sustained since Oct. 6, 1979.)

FIRST COUNCIL OF THE SEVENTY

(Functioned from February 1835 to October 1976)

1. Hazen Aldrich — Chosen and ordained one of the First Seven Presidents Feb. 28, 1835; released April 6, 1837, having previously been ordained high priest.

2. Joseph Young — Born April 7, 1797, at Hopkinton, Middlesex Co., Massachusetts, to John Young and Abigail Howe. Ordained seventy Feb. 28, 1835, under the hands of Joseph Smith, Sidney Rigdon, and Frederick G. Williams; chosen and ordained one of the First  Seven Presidents Feb. 28, 1835, at age 37; died July 16, 1881, at Salt Lake City, Salt Lake Co., Utah, at age 84.

3. Levi Ward Hancock — Born April 7, 1803, at Springfield, Hampden, Co., Massachusetts, to Thomas Hancock and Amy Ward. Ordained seventy Feb. 28, 1835, under the hands of Joseph Smith, Sidney Rigdon, and Frederick G. Williams; chosen and ordained one of  the First Seven Presidents Feb. 28, 1835, at age 31; released April 6, 1837, having supposedly previously been ordained high priest; restored to former place in the First Council Sept. 3, 1837, as he had not been ordained high priest; died June 10, 1882, at Washington, Washington Co., Utah, at age 79.

4. Leonard Rich — Chosen and ordained one of the First Seven Presidents Feb. 28, 1835; released April 6, 1837, having previously been ordained high priest.

5. Zebedee Coltrin — Born Sept. 7, 1804, at Ovid, Seneca Co., New York, to John Coltrin Jr. and Sarah Graham. Chosen and ordained one of the First Seven Presidents Feb. 28, 1835, at age 30; released April 6, 1837, having previously been ordained high priest; died July 21, 1887, at Spanish Fork, Utah Co., Utah, at age 82.

6. Lyman Royal Sherman — Born May 22, 1804, at Salem, Essex Co., Massachusetts, to Elkanah Sherman and Asenath Hulbert. Chosen and ordained one of the First Seven Presidents Feb. 28, 1835, at age 30; released April 6, 1837, having previously been ordained high priest; died Jan. 27, 1839, at age 34.

7. Sylvester Smith — Chosen and ordained one of the First Seven Presidents Feb. 28, 1835; released April 6, 1837, having previously been ordained high priest.

8. John Gould — Born May 11, 1808. Ordained seventy and set apart as one of the First Seven Presidents April 6, 1837, by Sidney Rigdon and Hyrum Smith, at age 28; released Sept. 3, 1837, to be ordained high priest. Died May 9, 1851, at age 42.

9. James Foster — Born April 1, 1775, at Morgan Co., New Hampshire. Ordained seventy April 6, 1837, under the hands of Sidney Rigdon and Hyrum Smith; set apart as one of the First Seven Presidents April 6, 1837, at age 62; died Dec. 21, 1841, at Morgan Co., Illinois, at age 66.

10. Daniel Sanborn Miles — Born July 23, 1772, at Sanbornton, Belknap Co., New Hampshire, to Josiah Miles and Marah Sanborn. Ordained seventy April 6, 1837, by Hazen Aldrich; set apart as one of the First Seven Presidents April 6, 1837, by Sidney Rigdon and Hyrum Smith, at age 64; died in autumn of 1845, at Hancock Co., Illinois, at age 73.

11. Josiah Butterfield — Born March 13 or 18, 1795, at Saco, York Co., Maine, to Abel and Mary or Mercy Butterfield. Ordained seventy April 6, 1837, under the hands of Sidney Rigdon and Hyrum Smith; set apart as one of the First Seven Presidents April 6, 1837, at age 42; excommunicated Oct. 7, 1844; died in April 1871 at Monterey Co., California, at age 76.

12. Salmon Gee — Born Oct. 16, 1792, at Lyme, New London Co., Connecticut, to Zopher Gee and Esther Beckwith. Ordained seventy April 6, 1837, under the hands of Sidney Rigdon and Hyrum Smith; set apart as one of the First Seven Presidents April 6, 1837, at age 44; fellowship withdrawn March 6, 1838; died Sept. 13, 1845, at Ambrosia, Lee Co., Iowa, at age 52; posthumously reinstated Sept. 14, 1967.

13. John Gaylord — Born July 12, 1797, in

Pennsylvania, to Chauncey Gaylord. Ordained seventy Dec. 20, 1836, by Hazen Aldrich; set apart as one of the First Seven Presidents April 6, 1837, at age 39, by Sidney Rigdon and others; excommunicated Jan. 13, 1838; rejoined the Church at Nauvoo, Illinois, Oct. 5, 1839; died July 17, 1878, at age 81.

14. Henry Harriman — Born June 9, 1804, at Rowley, Essex Co., Massachusetts, to Enoch Harriman and Sarah Brocklebank. Ordained seventy March 1835, under the hands of Joseph Smith and Sidney Rigdon; set apart as one of the First Seven Presidents Feb. 6, 1838, by Joseph Young and others, at age 33; died May 17, 1891, at Huntington, Emery Co., Utah, at 86.

15. Zera Pulsipher — Born June 24, 1789, at Rockingham, Windham Co., Vermont, to John Pulsipher and Elizabeth Dutton. Ordained seventy March 6, 1838, under the hands of Joseph Young and James Foster; set apart as one of the First Seven Presidents March 6, 1838, at age 48; released April 12, 1862; died Jan. 1, 1872, at Hebron, Washington Co., Utah, at age 82.

Roger Orton was excommunicated Nov. 30, 1837; returned to the Church; sustained as one of the First Seven Presidents April 7, 1845, but was never set apart and did not function; dropped from this position Oct. 6, 1845.

16. Albert Perry Rockwood — Born June 5, 1805, at Holliston, Middlesex Co., Massachusetts, to Luther Rockwood and Ruth Perry. Ordained seventy Jan. 5, 1839, under the hands of Joseph Young, Henry Harriman, and Zera Pulsipher; set apart as one of the First Seven Presidents Dec. 2, 1845, by Brigham Young and others, at age 40; died Nov. 26, 1879, at Sugar House, Salt Lake Co., Utah, at age 74.

17. Benjamin Lynn Clapp — Born Aug. 19, 1814, at West Huntsville, Madison Co., Alabama, to Ludwig Lewis Clapp and Margaret Ann Loy. Ordained seventy Oct. 20, 1844, under the

hands of Joseph Young and Levi W. Hancock; set apart as one of the First Seven Presidents Dec. 2, 1845, by Brigham Young and others, at age 31; excommunicated April 7, 1859; died Oct. 31, 1865 in Woodbridge, Calif., at age 51.

18. Jedediah Morgan Grant — See SECOND COUNSELORS IN THE FIRST PRESIDENCY, No. 5.

19. Horace Sunderlin Eldredge — Born Feb. 6, 1816, at Brutus, Cayuga Co., New York, to Alanson Eldredge and Esther Sunderlin. Ordained seventy Oct. 13, 1844, by Joseph Young; sustained as one of the First Seven Presidents Oct. 7, 1854, at age 38; died Sept. 6, 1888, at Salt Lake City, Salt Lake Co., Utah, at age 72.

20. Jacob Gates — Born March 9, 1811, at Saint Johnsbury, Caledonia Co., Vermont, to Thomas Gates and Patty Plumley. Ordained seventy Dec. 19, 1838, under the hands of Joseph Smith and Sidney Rigdon; sustained as one of the First Seven Presidents April 6, 1860, at age 49; set apart Oct. 8, 1862, by Orson Hyde; died April 14, 1892, at Provo, Utah Co., Utah, at age 81.

21. John Van Cott — Born Sept. 7, 1814, at Canaan, Columbia Co., New York, to Losee Van Cott and Lovinia Pratt. Ordained seventy Feb. 25, 1847, by Joseph Young; sustained as one of the First Seven Presidents Oct. 8, 1862, at age 48; set apart by John Taylor; died Feb. 18, 1883, at Salt Lake City, Salt Lake Co., Utah, at age 68.

22. William Whittaker Taylor — Born Sept. 11, 1853, at Salt Lake City, Salt Lake Co., Utah, to John Taylor and Harriet Whittaker. Ordained seventy Oct. 11, 1875, by

Orson Pratt; sustained as one of the First Seven Presidents April 7, 1880, at age 26; set apart by John Taylor; died Aug. 1, 1884, at Salt Lake City, Salt Lake Co., Utah, at age 30.

23. Abraham Hoagland Cannon — See QUORUM OF THE TWELVE, No. 37.

Theodore Belden Lewis — Born Nov. 18, 1843, at St. Louis, St. Louis Co., Missouri, to Thomas Anderson Lewis and Martha J. O. Belden. Ordained high priest at Nephi, Utah (date not known); sustained as one of the First Seven Presidents Oct. 8, 1882, at age 38; on Oct. 9, when he was to be set apart, he reported that he was already a high priest, so he was not set apart and did not function in this position.

24. Seymour Bicknell Young — Born Oct. 3, 1837, at Kirtland, Geauga Co., Ohio, to Joseph Young and Jane Adeline Bicknell. Ordained seventy Feb. 18, 1857, by Edmund Ellsworth; set apart by Franklin D. Richards as one of the First Seven Presidents Oct. 14,  1882, at age 45; sustained April 8, 1883; died Dec. 15, 1924, at Salt Lake City, Salt Lake Co., Utah, at age 87.

25. Christian Daniel Fjelsted — Born Feb. 20, 1829, at Amagar, Sundbyvester Co., Denmark, to Hendrick Ludvig Fjelsted and Ann Catrine Hendriksen. Ordained seventy Feb. 5, 1859, by William H. Walker; sustained as one of the First Seven Presidents April 6,  1884, at age 55; set apart by Wilford Woodruff; died Dec. 23, 1905, at Salt Lake City, Salt Lake Co., Utah, at age 76.

26. John Morgan — Born Aug. 8, 1842, at Greensburg, Decatur Co., Indiana, to Gerrard Morgan and Ann Eliza Hamilton. Ordained seventy Oct. 8, 1875, by Joseph Young; sustained as one of the First Seven Presidents Oct. 5, 1884, at age 42; set apart by Wilford Woodruff; died Aug. 14, 1894, at Preston,

Franklin Co., Idaho, at 52.

27. Brigham Henry Roberts — Born March 13, 1857, at Warrington, Lancashire Co., England, to Benjamin Roberts and Ann Everington. Ordained seventy March 8, 1877, by Nathan T. Porter. Sustained as one of the First Seven Presidents Oct. 7, 1888, at age 31; set apart by Lorenzo Snow; died Sept. 27, 1933, at Salt Lake City, Salt Lake Co., Utah, at age 76.

28. George Reynolds — Born Jan. 1, 1842, at Marylebone, London Co., London, England, to George Reynolds and Julia Ann Tautz. Ordained seventy March 18, 1866, by Israel Barlow; sustained as one of the First Seven Presidents April 5, 1890, at age 48; set apart by Lorenzo  Snow; died Aug. 9, 1909, at Salt Lake City, Salt Lake Co., Utah, at age 67.

29. Jonathan Golden Kimball — Born June 9, 1853, at Salt Lake City, Salt Lake Co., Utah, to Heber Chase Kimball and Christeen Golden. Ordained seventy July 21, 1886, by William M. Allred; sustained as one of the First Seven Presidents April 5, 1892, at age 38; set apart by Francis M. Lyman; died in an automobile accident Sept. 2, 1938, near Reno, Nevada, at age 85.

30. Rulon Seymour Wells — Born July 7, 1854, at Salt Lake City, Salt Lake Co., Utah, to Daniel Hanmer Wells and Louisa Free. Ordained seventy Oct. 22, 1875, by Brigham Young; sustained as one of the First Seven Presidents April 5, 1893, at age 38; set apart by George Q. Cannon; died May 7, 1941, at Salt Lake City, Salt Lake Co., Utah, at age 86.

31. Edward Stevenson — Born May 1, 1820, at Gibraltar, England, to Joseph Stevenson and Elizabeth Stevens. Ordained seventy

May 1, 1844, by Joseph Young; sustained as one of the First Seven Presidents Oct. 7, 1894, at age 74; set apart by Brigham Young Jr.; died Jan. 27, 1897, at Salt Lake City, Salt Lake Co., Utah, at age 76.

32. Joseph William McMurrin — Born Sept. 5,  1858, at Tooele, Tooele Co., Utah, to Joseph McMurrin and Margaret Leaning. Ordained seventy April 21, 1884, by Royal Barney; sustained as one of the First Seven Presidents Oct. 5, 1897, at age 39; set apart Jan. 21, 1898, by Anthon H. Lund; died Oct. 24, 1932, at Los Angeles, Los Angeles Co., California, at age 74.

33. Charles Henry Hart — Born July 5, 1866,  at Bloomington, Bear Lake Co., Idaho, to James Henry Hart and Sabina Scheib. Ordained seventy Aug. 10, 1890, by John Henry Smith; sustained as one of the First Seven Presidents April 9, 1906, at age 39; set apart by Joseph F. Smith; died Sept. 29, 1934, at Salt Lake City, Salt Lake Co., Utah, at age 68.

34. Levi Edgar Young — Born Feb. 2, 1874, at Salt Lake City, Salt Lake Co.,  Utah, to Seymour Bicknell Young and Ann Elizabeth Riter. Ordained seventy June 18, 1897, by Seymour B. Young; sustained as one of the First Seven Presidents Oct. 6, 1909, at age 35; set apart Jan. 23, 1910, by John Henry Smith; died Dec. 13, 1963, at Salt Lake City, Salt Lake Co., Utah, at age 89.

35. Rey Lucero Pratt — Born Oct. 11, 1878, at Salt Lake City, Salt Lake Co., Utah, to Helaman Pratt and Emeline Victoria Billingsley. Ordained seventy Sept. 23, 1911, by Rulon S. Wells; sustained as one of the First Seven Presidents Jan. 29, 1925, at age 46; set apart April 7, 1925, by Anthony W. Ivins; died April 14, 1931, at Salt Lake City, Salt Lake Co., Utah at age 52.

36. Antoine Ridgeway Ivins — Born May 11, 1881, at St. George, Washington Co., Utah, to Anthony Woodward Ivins and Elizabeth A. Snow. Ordained seventy Dec. 28,  1913, by Fred E. Barker; sustained as one of the First Seven Presidents Oct. 4, 1931, at age 50; ordained high priest June 11, 1961, by David O. McKay; died Oct. 18, 1967, at Salt Lake City, Salt Lake Co., Utah, at age 86.

37. Samuel Otis Bennion — Born June 9, 1874, at Taylorsville, Salt Lake Co., Utah, to John Rowland Bennion and Emma Jane  Terry. Ordained seventy March 14, 1904, by Samuel Gerrard; sustained as one of the First Seven Presidents April 6, 1933, at age 58; set apart by Heber J. Grant; died March 8, 1945, at Salt Lake City, Salt Lake Co., Utah, at age 70.

38. John Harris Taylor — Born June 28, 1875, at Salt Lake City, Salt Lake Co., Utah, to Thomas E. Taylor and Emma L. Harris. Ordained  seventy Jan. 24, 1896, by Heber J. Grant; sustained as one of the First Seven Presidents Oct. 6, 1933, at age 58; set apart by Heber J. Grant; died May 28, 1946, at Salt Lake City, Salt Lake Co., Utah, at age 70.

39. Rufus Kay Hardy — Born May 28, 1878, at Salt Lake City, Salt Lake Co., Utah, to Rufus H. Hardy and Annie Kay. Ordained seventy  July 2, 1897, by John Henry Smith; sustained to the First Council of the Seventy Oct. 6, 1934, at age 56; set apart Feb. 7, 1935, by Heber J. Grant; died March 7, 1945, at Salt Lake City, Salt Lake Co., Utah, at age 66.

40. Richard Louis Evans — See QUORUM OF THE TWELVE, No. 71.

41. Oscar Ammon Kirkham — Born Jan. 22, 1880, at Lehi, Utah Co., Utah, to James Kirkham and Martha Mercer. Ordained seventy Feb. 26, 1905, by

Joseph W. McMurrin; sustained to the First Council of the Seventy Oct. 5, 1941, at age 61; set apart by Heber J. Grant; died March 10, 1958, at Salt Lake City, Salt Lake Co., Utah, at 78.

42. Seymour Dilworth Young — See FIRST QUORUM OF THE SEVENTY, No. 24.

43. Milton Reed Hunter — Born Oct. 25, 1902, at Holden, Millard Co., Utah, to John E. Hunter and Margaret Teeples. Ordained seventy Aug. 31, 1928, by Rulon S. Wells; sustained to the First Council of the Seventy April 6, 1945, at age 42; ordained high priest June 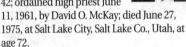 11, 1961, by David O. McKay; died June 27, 1975, at Salt Lake City, Salt Lake Co., Utah, at age 72.

44. Bruce Redd McConkie — See QUORUM OF THE TWELVE, No. 80.

45. Marion Duff Hanks — See PRESIDENCY OF THE SEVENTY, No. 6.

46. Albert Theodore Tuttle — See PRESIDENCY OF THE SEVENTY, No. 4.

47. Paul Harold Dunn — See PRESIDENCY OF THE SEVENTY, No. 7.

48. Hartman Rector Jr. — See FIRST QUORUM OF THE SEVENTY, No. 25.

49. Loren Charles Dunn — See FIRST QUORUM OF SEVENTY, No. 26.

50. Rex Dee Pinegar — See PRESIDENCY OF THE SEVENTY, No. 23.

51. Gene Raymond Cook – See FIRST QUORUM OF THE SEVENTY, NO. 28.

On Oct. 3, 1975, the First Quorum of the Seventy was reconstituted with the sustaining of three members, Elders Charles Didier, William R. Bradford, and George P. Lee. Four additional members, Elders Carlos E. Asay, M. Russell Ballard, John H. Groberg, and Jacob de Jager, were sustained April 3, 1976. On Oct. 1, 1976, the members of the First Council of the Seventy and the Assistants to the Quorum of the Twelve Apostles were released and sustained to the First Quorum of the Seventy. A Presidency of the First Quorum of the Seventy was sustained.

ASSISTANTS TO THE TWELVE

(Functioned from April 1941 to October 1976)

1. Marion George Romney — See FIRST COUNSELORS IN THE FIRST PRESIDENCY, No. 18.

2. Thomas Evans McKay — Born Oct. 29, 1875, at Huntsville, Weber Co., Utah, to David McKay and Jennette Eveline Evans. Sustained as Assistant to the Quorum of the Twelve Apostles April 6, 1941, and set apart May 23, 1941, by Heber J. Grant, at age 65; died Jan. 15, 1958, at Salt Lake Co., Utah, at age 82.

3. Clifford Earl Young — Born Dec. 7, 1883, at Salt Lake City, Salt Lake Co., Utah, to Seymour Bicknell Young and Ann Elizabeth Riter. Sustained as Assistant to the Quorum of the Twelve Apostles April 6, 1941, and set apart May 23, 1941, by President Grant, at age 57; died Aug. 21, 1958, at Salt Lake City, Salt Lake Co., Utah, at age 74.

4. Alma Sonne — See FIRST QUORUM OF THE SEVENTY, No. 8.

5. Nicholas Groesbeck Smith — Born June 20, 1881, at Salt Lake City, Salt Lake Co., Utah, to John Henry Smith and Josephine Groesbeck. Sustained an Assistant to the Quorum of the Twelve Apostles April 6, 1941; set apart Oct. 1, 1941, by Heber J. Grant, at age 60; died Oct. 27, 1945, at Salt Lake City, Salt Lake Co., Utah, at age 64.

6. George Quayle Morris — See QUORUM OF THE TWELVE, No. 72.

7. Stayner Richards — Born Dec. 20, 1885, at Salt Lake City, Salt Lake Co., Utah, to Stephen Longstroth Richards and Emma Louise Stayner. Sustained as Assistant to the Quorum of the Twelve Apostles Oct. 6, 1951, and set

apart Oct. 11, 1951, by David O. McKay, at age 65; died May 28, 1953, at Salt Lake City, Salt Lake Co., Utah, at age 67.

8. ElRay LaVar Christiansen — Born July 13, 1897, at Mayfield, Sanpete Co., Utah, to Parley Christiansen and Dorthea C. Jensen. Sustained as Assistant to the Quorum of the Twelve Apostles Oct. 6, 1951, and set apart Oct. 11, 1951, by Stephen L Richards, at age 54; died Dec. 2, 1975, at Salt Lake City, Salt Lake Co., Utah, at age 78.

9. John Longden — Born Nov. 4, 1898, at Oldham, Lancashire Co., England, to Thomas Johnson Longden and Lizetta Taylor. Sustained as Assistant to the Quorum of the Twelve Apostles Oct. 6, 1951, and set apart Oct. 11, 1951, by J. Reuben Clark Jr., at age 52; died Aug. 30, 1969, at Salt Lake City, Salt Lake Co., Utah, at age 70.

10. Hugh Brown Brown — See FIRST COUNSELORS IN THE FIRST PRESIDENCY, No. 15.

11. Sterling Welling Sill — See FIRST QUORUM OF THE SEVENTY, No. 9.

12. Gordon Bitner Hinckley – See PRESIDENTS OF THE CHURCH, No. 15.

13. Henry Dixon Taylor — See FIRST QUORUM OF THE SEVENTY, No. 10.

14. William James Critchlow Jr. — Born Aug. 21, 1892, at Brigham City, Box Elder Co., Utah, to William James Critchlow and Anna C. Gregerson. Sustained as Assistant to the Quorum of the Twelve Apostles Oct. 11, 1958, and set apart Oct. 16, 1958, by David O. McKay, at age 66; died Aug. 29, 1968, at Ogden, Weber Co., Utah, at age 76.

15. Alvin Rulon Dyer — See OTHER COUNSELORS IN THE FIRST PRESIDENCY, No. 13.

16. Nathan Eldon Tanner — See FIRST COUNSELORS IN THE FIRST PRESIDENCY, No. 17.

17. Franklin Dewey Richards — See PRESIDENCY OF THE SEVENTY, No. 1.

18. Theodore Moyle Burton — See FIRST QUORUM OF THE SEVENTY, No. 12.

19. Henry Thorpe Beal Isaacson — See OTHER COUNSELORS IN THE FIRST PRESIDENCY, No. 12.

20. Boyd Kenneth Packer — See current QUORUM OF THE TWELVE.

21. Bernard Park Brockbank — See FIRST QUORUM OF SEVENTY, No. 13.

22. James Alfred Cullimore — See FIRST QUORUM OF THE SEVENTY, No. 14.

23. Marion Duff Hanks — See PRESIDENCY OF THE SEVENTY, No. 6.

24. Marvin Jeremy Ashton — See QUORUM OF THE TWELVE, No. 79.

25. Joseph Anderson — See FIRST QUORUM OF THE SEVENTY, No. 15.

26. David Bruce Haight — See QUORUM OF THE TWELVE, No. 82.

27. William Hunter Bennett — See FIRST QUORUM OF SEVENTY, No. 16.

28. John Henry Vandenberg — See PRESIDING BISHOPS, No. 9.

29. Robert Leatham Simpson — See FIRST QUORUM OF THE SEVENTY, No. 18.

30. Oscar Leslie Stone — See FIRST QUORUM OF THE SEVENTY, No. 19.

31. James Esdras Faust – See SECOND COUNSELORS IN THE FIRST PRESIDENCY, NO. 23.

32. Lowell Tom Perry — See current QUORUM OF THE TWELVE.

33. John Thomas Fyans — See PRESIDENCY OF THE SEVENTY, No. 3.

34. Neal Ash Maxwell — See QUORUM OF THE TWELVE, No. 84.

35. William Grant Bangerter — See PRESIDENCY OF SEVENTY, No. 8.

36. Robert Dean Hales — See current QUORUM OF THE TWELVE.

37. Adney Yoshio Komatsu — See FIRST QUORUM OF SEVENTY, No. 22.

38. Joseph Bitner Wirthlin — See current QUORUM OF THE TWELVE.

On Oct. 1, 1976, the Assistants to the Quorum of the Twelve were released and sustained to the First Quorum of the Seventy.

PRESIDENCY OF THE SEVENTY

(From Oct. 3, 1975, to April 1, 1989, served as the Presidency of the First Quorum of the Seventy; from April 1, 1989, to April 1997, served as the Presidency of both the First and Second Quorums of the Seventy; since April 1997, served as the Presidency of all Quorums of the Seventy.)

1. Franklin Dewey Richards — Born Nov. 17, 1900, in Ogden, Weber Co., Utah, to Charles C. Richards and Louisa L. Peery. Sustained as Assistant to the Quorum of the Twelve Apostles Oct. 8, 1960, at age 59; sustained to First Quorum of the Seventy Oct. 1, 1976;  served in Presidency of the First Quorum of the Seventy, Oct. 1, 1976, to Oct. 1, 1983; died Nov. 13, 1987, at Salt Lake City, Salt Lake Co., Utah, at age 86.

2. James Esdras Faust – See SECOND COUNSELORS IN THE FIRST PRESIDENCY, NO. 23.

3. John Thomas Fyans — Born May 17, 1918, at Moreland, Bingham Co., Idaho, to Joseph Fyans and Mae Farnsworth. Sustained as Assistant to the Quorum of the Twelve Apostles April 6, 1974, at age 55; sustained to First Quorum of the Seventy Oct. 1, 1976; served in  Presidency of the First Quorum of the Seventy, Oct. 1, 1976, to Oct. 6, 1985; named emeritus General Authority Sept. 30, 1989; died May 18, 2008, at Sandy, Salt Lake Co., Utah, at age 90.

4. Albert Theodore Tuttle — Born March 2, 1919, in Manti, Sanpete Co., Utah, to Albert M. Tuttle and Clarice Beal. Sustained to First Council of the Seventy April 6, 1958, at age 39; sustained to First Quorum of the Seventy Oct. 1, 1976; served in Presidency of the  First Quorum of the Seventy, Oct. 1, 1976, to Feb. 22, 1980; died Nov. 28, 1986, at Salt Lake City, Salt Lake Co., Utah, at age 67.

5. Neal Ash Maxwell — See QUORUM OF THE TWELVE, No. 84.

6. Marion Duff Hanks — Born Oct. 13, 1921, in Salt Lake City, Salt Lake Co., Utah, to Stanley Alonzo Hanks and Maude Frame. Sustained to First Council of the Seventy Oct. 4, 1953, at age 31, and as Assistant to the Quorum of the Twelve  Apostles April 6, 1968; sustained to the First Quorum of the Seventy Oct. 1, 1976; served in the Presidency of the First Quorum of the Seventy from Oct. 1, 1976-April 5, 1980, and from Oct. 6, 1984-Aug. 15, 1992; named emeritus General Authority Oct. 3, 1992.

7. Paul Harold Dunn — Born April 24, 1924, at Provo, Utah Co., Utah, to Joshua Harold Dunn and Geneve Roberts. Sustained to First Council of the Seventy April 6, 1964, at age 39; sustained to First Quorum of the Seventy Oct. 1, 1976; served in Presidency of the First Quorum of the Seventy, Oct. 1, 1976, to Feb. 22, 1980; named emeritus General Authority Sept. 30, 1989; died Jan. 9, 1998, at Salt Lake City, Salt Lake Co., Utah, at age 73.

8. William Grant Bangerter — Born June 8, 1918, at Granger, Salt Lake Co., Utah, to William Henry Bangerter and Isabelle Bawden. Sustained as Assistant to the Quorum of the Twelve Apostles April 4, 1975, at age 56; sustained to  First Quorum of the Seventy Oct. 1, 1976; served in Presidency of the First Quorum of the Seventy from Sept. 30, 1978, to April 5, 1980, and from Feb. 17, 1985, to Sept. 30, 1989; named emeritus General Authority Sept. 30, 1989.

9. Carlos Egan Asay — Born June 12, 1926, in Sutherland, Millard Co., Utah, to A.E. Lyle Asay and Elsie Egan. Sustained to the First Quorum of the Seventy April 3, 1976, at age 49; served in Presidency of the Seventy  from Feb. 22, 1980, to Aug. 15,

1986, and from Oct. 1, 1989, to Aug. 15, 1996; named emeritus General Authority Oct. 5, 1996; died April 10, 1999, in Bountiful, Davis Co., Utah, at age 72.

10. Melvin Russell Ballard Jr. — See current QUORUM OF THE TWELVE.

11. Dean LeRoy Larsen — Born March 24, 1927, at Hyrum, Cache Co., Utah, to Edgar Niels Larsen and Gertrude Prouse. Sustained to First Quorum of the Seventy Oct. 1, 1976, at age 49; served in Presidency of the Seventy, Feb. 22, 1980, to Aug. 15, 1993; named emeritus General Authority Oct. 4, 1997.

12. Royden Glade Derrick — Born Sept. 7, 1915, at Salt Lake City, Salt Lake Co., Utah, to Hyrum H. Derrick and Margaret Glade. Sustained to First Quorum of the Seventy Oct. 1, 1976, at age 61; served in Presidency of the First Quorum of the Seventy, April 5, 1980, to Oct. 6, 1984; named emeritus General Authority Sept. 30, 1989.

13. George Homer Durham — Born Feb. 4, 1911, at Parowan, Iron Co., Utah, to George H. Durham and Mary Ellen Marsden. Sustained to First Quorum of the Seventy April 2, 1977, at age 66; served in Presidency of the First Quorum of the Seventy, Oct. 1, 1981, until his death Jan. 10, 1985, at Salt Lake City, Salt Lake Co., Utah, at age 73.

14. **Richard Gordon Scott** — See current QUORUM OF THE TWELVE.

15. Marion Duff Hanks — See PRESIDENCY OF THE SEVENTY, No. 6.

16. William Grant Bangerter — See PRESIDENCY OF THE SEVENTY, No. 8.

17. Jack H Goaslind Jr. — Born April 18, 1928, in Salt Lake City, Utah, to Jack H. Goaslind and Anita Jack. Sustained to the First Quorum of the Seventy Sept. 30, 1978, at age 50; served in

the Presidency of the Seventy, Oct. 6, 1985, to Aug. 15, 1987, and from Aug. 15, 1995, to Aug. 15, 1998; named emeritus General Authority Oct. 3, 1998.

18. Robert LeGrand Backman — Born March 22, 1922, in Salt Lake City, Salt Lake Co., Utah, to LeGrand P. Backman and Edith Price. Sustained to the First Quorum of the Seventy April 1, 1978, at age 56; served in the Presidency of the Seventy, Oct. 6, 1985, to Aug. 15, 1992; named emeritus General Authority Oct. 3, 1992.

19. Joseph Bitner Wirthlin — See current QUORUM OF THE TWELVE.

20. Hugh Wallace Pinnock – Born Jan. 15, 1934, in Salt Lake City, Salt Lake Co., Utah, to Lawrence Sylvester Pinnock and Florence Boden. Sustained to the First Quorum of the Seventy Oct. 1, 1977, at age 43; served in the Presidency of the Seventy, Oct. 4, 1986, to Oct. 1, 1989; died Dec. 15, 2000, in Salt Lake City, Salt Lake Co., Utah, at age 66.

21. James Martin Paramore — Born May 6, 1928, in Salt Lake City, Salt Lake Co., Utah, to James F. Paramore and Ruth C. Martin. Sustained to First Quorum of the Seventy April 2, 1977, at age 48, and served in the Presidency of the Seventy, Aug. 15, 1987, to Aug. 15, 1993; named emeritus General Authority Oct. 3, 1998.

22. John Richard Clarke — Born April 4, 1927, at Rexburg, Madison Co., Idaho, to John Roland Clarke and Nora L. Redford. Sustained as second counselor in Presiding Bishopric Oct. 1, 1976, at age 49, and to the First Quorum of the Seventy, April 6, 1985; served in the Presidency of the Seventy, Oct. 1, 1988, to Aug. 15, 1993; named emeritus General Authority Oct. 4, 1997.

23. Rex Dee Pinegar — Born Sept. 18, 1931, in

Orem, Utah Co., Utah, to John E. Pinegar and Grace Murl Ellis. Sustained to the First Council of the Seventy Oct. 6, 1972, at age 41; sustained to First Quorum of the Seventy Oct. 1, 1976; served in the Presidency of the Seventy, Sept. 30, 1989, to Aug. 15, 1995; named emeritus General Authority Oct. 6, 2001.

24. Carlos Egan Asay — See PRESIDENCY OF THE SEVENTY, No. 9.

25. Charles Amand Andre Didier – See current FIRST QUORUM OF THE SEVENTY.

26. Lloyd Aldin Porter — Born June 30, 1931, in Salt Lake City, Salt Lake Co., Utah, to J. Lloyd Porter and Revon Hayward. Sustained to the First Quorum of the Seventy April 4, 1987, at age 55; sustained to the Second Quorum of the Seventy April 1, 1989; sustained to the First Quorum of the Seventy April 6, 1991; served in the Presidency of the Seventy, Aug. 15, 1992, to Aug. 15, 2001; named emeritus General Authority Oct. 6, 2001

27. Joe Junior Christensen — Born July 21, 1929, in Banida, Franklin Co., Idaho, to Joseph A. Christensen and Goldie Miles. Sustained to First Quorum of the Seventy April 1, 1989, at age 59; served in the Presidency of the Seventy, Aug. 15, 1993, to Aug. 15, 1999; named emeritus General Authority Oct. 2, 1999.

28. Monte James Brough — Born June 11, 1939, in Randolph, Rich Co., Utah, to Richard Muir Brough and Gwendolyn Kearl. Sustained to the Second Quorum of the Seventy Oct. 1, 1989, at age 49; sustained to the First Quorum of the Seventy April 6, 1991; served in the Presidency of the Seventy from Aug. 15, 1993, to Aug. 15, 1998; named emeritus General Authority Oct. 6, 2007.

29. Warren Eugene Hansen — Born Aug. 23, 1928, in Tremonton, Box Elder Co., Utah, to Warren E. Hansen and Ruth Steed. Sustained to the First Quorum of the Seventy April 1, 1989, at age 60; served in the Presidency of the Seventy, Aug. 15, 1993, to Aug. 15, 1998; named emeritus General Authority Oct. 3, 1998.

30. Jack H Goaslind Jr. — See PRESIDENCY OF THE SEVENTY, No. 17.

31. Harold Gordon Hillam – Born Sept. 1, 1934, in Sugar City, Madison Co., Idaho, to Gordon R. Hillam and Florence Evelyn Skidmore. Sustained to the Second Quorum of the Seventy March 31, 1990, at age 54; sustained to the First Quorum of the Seventy April 6, 1991; served in the Presidency of the Seventy from Aug. 15, 1995, to Aug. 15, 2000; named emeritus General Authority Oct. 1, 2005.

32. Earl Carr Tingey – Born June 11, 1934, in Bountiful, Davis Co., Utah, to William W. Tingey and Sylvia Carr. Called to the First Quorum of the Seventy Dec. 5, 1990, at age 56, and sustained April 6, 1991; served in the Presidency of the Seventy from Aug. 15, 1996, to Aug. 1, 2008; named emeritus General Authority Oct. 4, 2008.

33. David Todd Christofferson – See current QUORUM OF THE TWELVE.

34. Marlin Keith Jensen — See current FIRST QUORUM OF THE SEVENTY.

35. David Eugene Sorensen – Born June 29, 1933, in Aurora, Millard Co., Utah, to Alma Sorensen and Metta Amelia Helquist. Called to the Second Quorum of the Seventy June 6, 1992, at age 58, and sustained Oct. 3, 1992; sustained to the First Quorum of the Seventy April 1, 1995; served in the Presidency of the Seventy from Aug. 15, 1998, to Aug. 15, 2005; named emeritus General Authority Oct. 1, 2005.

36. Benjamin Berry Banks — Born April 4,

1932, in Murray, Salt Lake Co., Utah, to Ben F. Banks and Samantha Berry. Sustained to the Second Quorum of the Seventy April 1, 1989, at age 56; called to the First Quorum of the Seventy June 6, 1992, and sustained Oct. 3, 1992; served in the Presidency of the Seventy, Aug. 15, 1999, to Aug. 15, 2002; named emeritus General Authority Oct. 5, 2002.

37. Dennis Bramwell Neuenschwander — See current FIRST QUORUM OF THE SEVENTY.

38. Charles Amand Andre Didier – See current FIRST QUORUM OF THE SEVENTY.

39. Cecil Osborn Samuelson Jr. – See current FIRST QUORUM OF THE SEVENTY.

40. Dieter Friedrich Uchtdorf – See current FIRST PRESIDENCY.

41. Merrill Joseph Bateman – Born June 19, 1936, in Lehi, Utah Co., Utah, to Joseph Frederic Bateman and Belva Smith. Called to the Second Quorum of the Seventy June 6, 1992, at age 55, and sustained Oct. 3, 1992; sustained as Presiding Bishop April 2, 1994, and  served until Nov. 2, 1995; when he was named president of BYU; called to the First Quorum of the Seventy Nov. 2, 1995, and sustained April 6, 1996; served in the Presidency of the Seventy from April 5, 2003, after being released as president of BYU, to Aug. 1, 2007; named emeritus Oct. 6, 2007.

42. John Holbrook Groberg – Born June 17, 1934, in Idaho Falls, Bonneville Co., Idaho, to Delbert V. Groberg and Jennie Holbrook. Sustained to the First Quorum of the Seventy April 3, 1976, at age 41; sustained to the Presidency of the Seventy, April 3, 2004,  and served until Aug. 15, 2005; named emeritus General Authority Oct. 1, 2005.

43. Robert Charles Oaks – See current SECOND QUORUM OF THE SEVENTY.

44. Neil Linden Andersen – See current PRESIDENCY OF THE SEVENTY.

45. Ronald A Rasband – See current PRESIDENCY OF THE SEVENTY.

46. Quentin LaMar Cook – See current QUORUM OF THE TWELVE.

47. Claudio Roberto Mendez Costa – See current PRESIDENCY OF THE SEVENTY.

48. Steven Erastus Snow — See current PRESIDENCY OF THE SEVENTY.

49. Walter Fermin Gonzalez — See current PRESIDENCY OF THE SEVENTY.

50. Lyndon Whitney Clayton — See current PRESIDENCY OF THE SEVENTY.

51. Jay Edwin Jensen — See current PRESIDENCY OF THE SEVENTY.

FIRST QUORUM OF THE SEVENTY

The organization of the First Quorum of the Seventy was announced Oct. 3, 1975, and the first members of the quorum were sustained in general conference.

The following year, on Oct. 1, 1976, members of the First Council of the Seventy and the Assistants to the Twelve were released in general conference and called to the First Quorum of the Seventy.

1. Franklin Dewey Richards — See PRESIDENCY OF THE SEVENTY, No. 1.

2. James Esdras Faust – See SECOND COUNSELORS IN THE FIRST PRESIDENCY, NO. 23.

3. John Thomas Fyans — See PRESIDENCY OF THE SEVENTY, No. 3.

4. Albert Theodore Tuttle — See PRESIDENCY OF THE SEVENTY, No. 4.

5. Neal Ash Maxwell — See QUORUM OF THE TWELVE, No. 84.

6. Marion Duff Hanks — See PRESIDENCY OF THE SEVENTY, No. 6.

7. Paul Harold Dunn — See PRESIDENCY OF THE SEVENTY, No. 7.

8. Alma Sonne — Born March 5, 1884, at Logan, Cache Co., Utah, to Niels C. Sonne and Elisa Peterson. Sustained as Assistant to the Quorum of the Twelve Apostles April 6, 1941, at age 57; sustained to First Quorum of the Seventy Oct. 1, 1976; died Nov. 27, 1977, at Logan, Cache Co., Utah, at age 93.

9. Sterling Welling Sill — Born March 31, 1903, at Layton, Davis Co., Utah, to Joseph Albert Sill and Marietta Welling. Sustained as Assistant to the Quorum of the Twelve Apostles April 6, 1954, at age 51; sustained to First Quorum of the Seventy Oct. 1, 1976; named emeritus General Authority Dec. 31, 1978; died May 25, 1994, in Salt Lake City, Salt Lake Co., Utah, at age 91.

10. Henry Dixon Taylor — Born Nov. 22, 1903, in Provo, Utah Co., Utah, to Arthur N. Taylor and Maria Dixon. Sustained as Assistant to the Quorum of the Twelve Apostles April 6, 1958, at age 54; sustained to First Quorum of the Seventy Oct. 1, 1976; named emeritus General Authority Sept. 30, 1978; died Feb. 24, 1987, at Salt Lake City, Salt Lake Co., Utah, at age 83.

11. Alvin Rulon Dyer — See OTHER COUNSELORS IN THE FIRST PRESIDENCY, No. 13.

12. Theodore Moyle Burton — Born March 27, 1907, at Salt Lake City, Salt Lake Co., Utah, to Theodore T. Burton and Florence Moyle. Sustained as Assistant to the Quorum of the Twelve Apostles Oct. 8, 1960, at age 53; sustained to First Quorum of the Seventy Oct. 1, 1976; named emeritus General Authority Sept. 30, 1989; died Dec. 22, 1989, at Salt Lake City, Salt Lake Co., Utah, at age 82.

13. Bernard Park Brockbank — Born May 24, 1909, at Salt Lake City, Salt Lake Co., Utah, to Taylor P. Brockbank and Sarah LeCheminant. Sustained as Assistant to the Quorum of the Twelve Apostles Oct. 6, 1962, at age 53; sustained to First Quorum of the Seventy Oct. 1, 1976; named emeritus General Authority Oct. 4, 1980; died Oct. 11, 2000, at Holladay, Salt Lake Co., Utah at age 91.

14. James Alfred Cullimore — Born Jan. 17, 1906, at Lindon, Utah Co., Utah, to Albert Lorenzo Cullimore and Luella Keetch. Sustained an Assistant to the Quorum of the Twelve Apostles April 6, 1966, at age 60; sustained to First Quorum of the Seventy Oct. 1, 1976; named emeritus General Authority Sept. 30, 1978; died June 14, 1986, at Salt Lake City, Salt Lake Co., Utah, at age 80.

15. Joseph Anderson — Born Nov. 20, 1889, at Salt Lake City, Salt Lake Co., Utah, to George

Anderson and Isabella Watson. Sustained as Assistant to the Quorum of the Twelve Apostles April 6, 1970, at age 80; sustained to First Quorum of the Seventy Oct. 1, 1976; named emeritus General Authority Dec. 31, 1978; died March 13, 1992, at Salt Lake City, Salt Lake Co., Utah, at age 102.

16. William Hunter Bennett — Born Nov. 5, 1910, at Taber, Alberta, Canada, to William Alvin Bennett and Mary Walker. Sustained as Assistant to the Quorum of the Twelve Apostles April 6, 1970, at age 59; sustained to First Quorum of the Seventy Oct. 1, 1976; named emeritus General Authority Dec. 31, 1978; died July 23, 1980, at Bountiful, Davis Co., Utah, at age 69.

17. John Henry Vandenberg — See PRESIDING BISHOPS, No. 9.

18. Robert Leatham Simpson — Born Aug. 8, 1915, at Salt Lake City, Salt Lake Co., Utah, to Heber C. Simpson and Lillian Leatham. Sus-tained as first counselor to Presiding Bishop John H. Vandenberg Sept. 30, 1961, at age 46; sustained as Assistant to the Quorum of the Twelve Apostles April 6, 1972; sustained to First Quorum of the Seventy Oct. 1, 1976; named emeritus General Authority Oct. 1, 1989; died April 15, 2003, at St. George, Washington Co., Utah, at age 87.

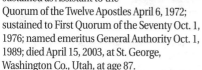

19. Oscar Leslie Stone — Born May 28, 1903, at Chapin, Idaho, to Frank J. Stone and Mable Crandall. Sustained as Assistant to the Quorum of the Twelve Apostles, Oct. 6, 1972, at age 69; sustained to First Quorum of the Seventy, Oct. 1, 1976; named emeritus General Authority Oct. 4, 1980; died April 26, 1986, at Salt Lake City, Salt Lake Co., Utah, at age 82.

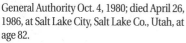

20. William Grant Bangerter — See PRESIDENCY OF THE SEVENTY, No. 8.

21. Robert Dean Hales — See current QUORUM OF THE TWELVE.

22. Adney Yoshio Komatsu — Born Aug. 2, 1923, at Honolulu, Honolulu Co., Oahu, Hawaii, to Jizaemon Komatsu and Misao Tabata. Sustained as Assistant to the Quorum of the Twelve Apostles, April 4, 1975, at age 51; sustained to the First Quorum of the Seventy Oct. 1, 1976; named emeritus General Authority Oct. 2, 1993.

23. Joseph Bitner Wirthlin — See current QUORUM OF THE TWELVE.

24. Seymour Dilworth Young — Born Sept. 7, 1897, at Salt Lake City, Salt Lake Co., Utah, to Seymour Bicknell Young Jr. and Carlie Louine Clawson. Sustained to the First Council of the Seventy April 6, 1945, at age 47; sustained to the First Quorum of the Seventy Oct. 1, 1976; named emeritus General Authority Sept. 30, 1978; died July 9, 1981, at Salt Lake City, Salt Lake Co., Utah, at age 83.

25. Hartman Rector Jr. — Born Aug. 20, 1924, at Moberly, Randolph Co., Missouri, to Hartman Rector and Vivian Fay Garvin. Sustained to the First Council of the Seventy April 6, 1968, at age 43; sustained to the First Quorum of the Seventy Oct. 1, 1976; named emeritus General Authority Oct. 1, 1994.

26. Loren Charles Dunn — Born June 12, 1930, in Tooele, Tooele Co., Utah, to Alex F. Dunn and Carol Horsfall. Sustained to the First Council of the Seventy April 6, 1968, at age 37, and to the First Quorum of the Seventy Oct. 1, 1976; named emeritus General Authority Oct. 7, 2000; died May 16, 2001, at Boston, Suffolk Co., Mass., at age 70.

27. Rex Dee Pinegar — See PRESIDENCY OF THE SEVENTY, No. 23.

28. Gene Raymond Cook – Born Sept. 1, 1940, in Lehi, Utah Co., Utah, to Clarence H. Cook and Cora Myrl Thornton. Sustained to the First Council of the Seventy Oct. 3, 1975, at age 34; sustained to the First Quorum of the Seventy Oct. 1, 1976; named emeritus General Authority Oct. 6, 2007.

29. Charles Amand Andre Didier – See current FIRST QUORUM OF THE SEVENTY.

30. William Rawsel Bradford – Born Oct. 25, 1933, in Springville, Utah Co., to Rawsel W. Bradford and Mary Waddoups. Sustained to First Quorum of the Seventy Oct. 3, 1975, at age 41; named emeritus General Authority Oct. 4, 2003.

31. George Patrick Lee — Born March 23, 1943, at Towaoc, Ute Mountain Indian Reservation, Colorado, to Pete Lee and Mae K. Asdzaatchii. Sustained to First Quorum of the Seventy Oct. 3, 1975, at age 32; excommunicated Sept. 1, 1989.

32. Carlos Egan Asay — See PRESIDENCY OF THE SEVENTY, No. 9.

33. Melvin Russell Ballard Jr. — See current QUORUM OF THE TWELVE.

34. John Holbrook Groberg – See PRESIDENCY OF THE SEVENTY, No. 42.

35. Jacob de Jager — Born Jan. 16, 1923, at The Hague, South Holland, Netherlands, to Alexander Philippis de Jager and Maria Jacoba Cornelia Scheele. Sustained to the First Quorum of the Seventy April 3, 1976, at age 53; named emeritus General Authority Oct. 2, 1993; died Feb. 25, 2004, in Salt Lake City, Salt Lake Co., Utah, at age 81.

36. Vaughn J Featherstone — Born March 26, 1931, in Stockton, Tooele Co., Utah, to Stephen E. Featherstone and Emma M. Johnson. Sustained as second

counselor in the Presiding Bishopric April 6, 1972, at age 41; sustained to the First Quorum of the Seventy Oct. 1, 1976; named emeritus General Authority Oct. 6, 2001.

37. Dean LeRoy Larsen — See PRESIDENCY OF THE SEVENTY, No. 11.

38. Royden Glade Derrick — See PRESIDENCY OF THE SEVENTY, No. 12.

39. Robert Earl Wells — Born Dec. 28, 1927, in Las Vegas, Clark Co., Nevada, to Robert Stephen Wells and Zella Verona Earl. Sustained to the First Quorum of the Seventy Oct. 1, 1976, at age 48; named emeritus General Authority Oct. 4, 1997.

40. George Homer Durham — See PRESIDENCY OF THE SEVENTY, No. 13.

41. James Martin Paramore — See PRESIDENCY OF THE SEVENTY, No. 21.

42. Richard Gordon Scott — See current QUORUM OF THE TWELVE.

43. Hugh Wallace Pinnock — See PRESIDENCY OF THE SEVENTY, No. 20.

44. Friedrich Enzio Busche — Born April 5, 1930, in Dortmund, Germany, to Friedrich Busche and Anna Weber. Sustained to the First Quorum of the Seventy Oct. 1, 1977, at age 47; named emeritus General Authority Oct, 7, 2000.

45. Yoshihiko Kikuchi — See current FIRST QUORUM OF THE SEVENTY.

46. Ronald Eugene Poelman — Born May 10, 1928, in Salt Lake City, Salt Lake Co., Utah, to Hendrick Poelman and Ella May Perkins. Sustained to the First Quorum of the Seventy April 1, 1978, at age 49; named emeritus General Authority Oct. 3, 1998.

47. Derek Alfred Cuthbert — Born Oct. 5, 1926, at Nottingham, Derbyshire Co., England, to Harry Cuthbert and Hilda May Freck.

Sustained to the First Quorum of the Seventy April 1, 1978, at age 51; died April 7, 1991, at Salt Lake City, Salt Lake Co., Utah, at age 64.

48. Robert LeGrand Backman — See PRESIDENCY OF THE SEVENTY, No. 18.

49. Rex Cropper Reeve Sr. — Born Nov. 23, 1914, at Hinckley, Millard Co.,  Utah, to Arthur H. Reeve and Mary A. Cropper. Sustained to First Quorum of the Seventy April 1, 1978, at age 63; named emeritus General Authority Sept. 30, 1989; died July 18, 2005, in Murray, Salt Lake Co., at age 90.

50. Fred Burton Howard – Born March 24, 1933, in  Logan, Cache Co., to Fred P. Howard and Beatrice Ward. Sustained to the First Quorum of the Seventy Sept. 30, 1978, at age 45; named emeritus General Authority Oct. 1, 2005.

51. Teddy Eugene Brewerton — Born March 30, 1925, at Raymond, Alberta, Canada, to Lee  Brewerton and Jane Fisher. Sustained to the First Quorum of the Seventy, Sept. 30, 1978, at age 53; named emeritus General Authority Sept. 30, 1995.

52. Jack H Goaslind Jr. — See PRESIDENCY OF THE SEVENTY, No. 17.

53. Angel Abrea – Born Sept. 13, 1933, in Buenos Aires, Argentina, to Edealo  Abrea and Zulema Estrada. Sustained to First Quorum of the Seventy April 4, 1981, at age 47; named emeritus General Authority Oct. 4, 2003.

54. John Kay Carmack — Born May 10, 1931, in Winslow, Navajo Co., Ariz., to  Cecil E. Carmack and Gladys Bushman. Sustained to the First Quorum of the Seventy April 7, 1984, at age 52; named emeritus General Authority Oct. 6, 2001.

55. Russell Carl Taylor — Born Nov. 25, 1925, at Red Mesa, Conejos Co., Colorado, to Leo Sanford  Taylor and Florence Stella Dean. Sustained to First Quorum of the Seventy April 7, 1984, at age 58; sustained to Second Quorum of the Seventy April 1, 1989; released Sept. 30, 1989.

56. Robert B Harbertson — Born April 19, 1932, at Ogden, Weber Co. Utah, to Brigham Y.  Harbertson and Gladys Venice Lewis. Sustained to First Quorum of the Seventy April 7, 1984, at age 51; sustained to Second Quorum of the Seventy April 1, 1989; released Sept. 30, 1989.

57. Devere Harris — Born May 30, 1916, at Portage, Box Elder Co. Utah, to Robert Crumbell Harris  and Sylvia Green. Sustained to First Quorum of the Seventy April 7, 1984, at age 67; sustained to Second Quorum of the Seventy April 1, 1989; released Sept. 30, 1989; died July 6, 2006, in Logan, Cache Co., Utah, at age 90.

58. Spencer Hamlin Osborn — Born July 8, 1921, at Salt Lake City, Salt Lake Co., Utah, to William W.  Osborn and Alice M. Hamlin. Sustained to First Quorum of the Seventy April 7, 1984, at age 62; sustained to Second Quorum of the Seventy April 1, 1989; released Sept. 30, 1989; died May 1, 2006, in Salt Lake City, Salt Lake Co., Utah, at age 84.

59. Phillip Tadje Sonntag — Born July 13, 1921, at Salt Lake City, Salt Lake Co., Utah, to Richard  Peter Sonntag and Lena Emma Tadje. Sustained to First Quorum of the Seventy April 7, 1984, at age 62; sustained to Second Quorum of the Seventy April

1, 1989; released Sept. 30, 1989.

60. John Sonnenberg — Born April 11, 1922, at Schneidemuhle, Germany, to Otto Paul Sonnenberg and Lucille Mielke. Sustained to First Quorum of the Seventy Oct. 6, 1984, at age 62; sustained to Second Quorum of the Seventy April 1, 1989; released Sept. 30, 1989.

61. Ferril Arthur Kay — Born July 15, 1916, at Annabella, Sevier Co., Utah, to Samuel Arthur Kay and Medora Hooper. Sustained to First Quorum of the Seventy Oct. 6, 1984, at age 68; sustained to Second Quorum of the Seventy April 1, 1989; released Sept. 30, 1989; died Dec. 13, 2005, in Kirkland, King Co., Wash., at age 89.

62. Keith Wilson Wilcox — Born May 15, 1921, at Hyrum, Cache Co., Utah, to Irving C. Wilcox and Nancy Mary Wilson. Sustained to First Quorum of the Seventy Oct. 6, 1984, at age 63; sustained to Second Quorum of the Seventy April 1, 1989; released Sept. 30, 1989.

63. Victor Lee Brown — See PRESIDING BISHOPS, No. 10.

64. Harold Burke Peterson — Born Sept. 19, 1923, in Salt Lake City, Salt Lake Co., Utah, to Harold A. Peterson and Juna Tye. Sustained as first counselor in Presiding Bishopric April 6, 1972, at age 48; sustained to the First Quorum of the Seventy April 6, 1985; named emeritus General Authority Oct. 2, 1993.

65. John Richard Clarke — See PRESIDENCY OF THE SEVENTY, No. 22.

66. Hans Benjamin Ringger — Born Nov. 2, 1925, in Zurich, Switzerland, to Carl Ringger and Maria Reif. Sustained to the First Quorum of the Seventy April

6, 1985, at age 59; named emeritus General Authority Sept. 30, 1995.

67. Waldo Pratt Call — Born Feb. 5, 1928, at Colonia Juarez, Chihuahua, Mexico, to Charles Helaman Call and Hannah Skousen. Sustained to First Quorum of the Seventy April 6, 1985, at age 57; sustained to Second Quorum of the Seventy April 1, 1989; released Oct. 6, 1990.

68. Helio da Rocha Camargo — Born Feb. 1, 1926, at Resende, Rio de Janeiro, Brazil, to Jose Medeiros de Camargo and Else Ferreira da Rocha. Sustained to First Quorum of the Seventy April 6, 1985, at age 59; sustained to Second Quorum of the Seventy April 1, 1989; released Oct. 6, 1990.

69. Hans Verlan Andersen — Born Nov. 6, 1914, in Logan, Cache Co., Utah, to Hans Andersen and Mynoa Richardson. Sustained to the First Quorum of the Seventy April 6, 1986, at age 71; sustained to the Second Quorum of the Seventy April 1, 1989; released Oct. 5, 1991; died July 16, 1992, at Orem, Utah Co., Utah, at age 77.

70. George Ivins Cannon — Born March 9, 1920, in Salt Lake City, Salt Lake Co., Utah, to George J. Cannon and Lucy Grant. Sustained to the First Quorum of the Seventy April 6, 1986, at age 66; sustained to the Second Quorum of the Seventy April 1, 1989; released Oct. 5, 1991.

71. Francis Marion Gibbons — Born April 10, 1921, in St. Johns, Apache Co., Arizona, to Andrew S. Gibbons and Adeline Christensen. Sustained to the First Quorum of the Seventy April 6, 1986, at age 64; sustained to the Second Quorum of the Seventy April

1, 1989; released Oct. 5, 1991.

72. Gardner Hale Russell — Born Aug. 12, 1920, in Salt Lake City, Salt Lake Co., Utah, to Harry J. Russell and Agnes Gardner. Sustained to the First Quorum of the Seventy April 6, 1986, at age 65; sustained to the Second Quorum of the Seventy April 1, 1989; released Oct. 5, 1991.

73. George Richard Hill III — Born Nov. 24, 1921, in Ogden, Weber Co., Utah, to George Richard Hill Jr. and Elizabeth O. McKay. Sustained to the First Quorum of the Seventy April 4, 1987, at age 65; sustained to the Second Quorum of the Seventy April 1, 1989; released Oct. 3, 1992; died April 22, 2001, at Salt Lake City, Salt Lake Co., Utah, at age 79.

74. John Roger Lasater — Born Dec. 8, 1931, in Farmington, Davis Co., Utah, to Robert B. Lasater and Rowena Saunders. Sustained to the First Quorum of the Seventy April 4, 1987, at age 55; sustained to the Second Quorum of the Seventy April 1, 1989; released Oct. 3, 1992.

75. Douglas James Martin — Born April 20, 1927, in Hastings, New Zealand, to George Martin and Jesse Jamieson. Sustained to the First Quorum of the Seventy April 4, 1987, at age 59; sustained to the Second Quorum of the Seventy April 1, 1989; released Oct. 3, 1992.

76. Alexander Baillie Morrison — Born Dec. 22, 1930, in Edmonton, Alberta, Canada, to Alexander S. Morrison and Christina Wilson. Sustained to the First Quorum of the Seventy April 4, 1987, at age 56; sustained to the Second Quorum of the Seventy April 1, 1989; sustained to the First Quorum of the Seventy April 6, 1991; named emeritus Oct. 7, 2000.

77. Lloyd Aldin Porter — See PRESIDENCY OF THE SEVENTY, No. 26.

78. Glen Larkin Rudd — Born May 18, 1918, in Salt Lake City, Salt Lake Co., Utah, to Charles P. Rudd and Gladys Harman. Sustained to First Quorum of the Seventy April 4, 1987, at age 68; sustained to the Second Quorum of the Seventy April 1, 1989; released Oct. 3, 1992.

79. Douglas Hill Smith — Born May 11, 1921, in Salt Lake City, Salt Lake Co., Utah, to Virgil H. Smith and Winifred Pearl Hill. Sustained to the First Quorum of the Seventy April 4, 1987, at age 65; sustained to the Second Quorum of the Seventy April 1, 1989; released Oct. 3, 1992.

80. Lynn Andrew Sorensen — Born Sept. 25, 1919, in Salt Lake City, Salt Lake Co., Utah, to Ulric Andrew Sorensen and Ferny Boam. Sustained to the First Quorum of the Seventy April 4, 1987, at age 67; sustained to the Second Quorum of the Seventy April 1, 1989; released Oct. 3, 1992.

81. Robert Edward Sackley — Born Dec. 17, 1922, in Lismore, New South Wales, Australia, to Cecil James Sackley and Mary Duncan. Sustained to the First Quorum of the Seventy April 2, 1988, at age 65; sustained to the Second Quorum of the Seventy April 1, 1989; died Feb. 22, 1993, near Brisbane, Australia, at age 70.

82. Larry Lionel Kendrick — Born Sept. 19, 1931, in Baton Rouge, East Baton Rouge Parish, La., to Bonnie Delen Kendrick and Edna Campbell Forbes. Sustained to the First Quorum of the Seventy April 2, 1988, at age 56; sustained to the Second Quorum of the

Seventy April 1, 1989; sustained to the First Quorum of the Seventy April 6, 1991; named emeritus General Authority Oct. 6, 2001.

83. Monte James Brough – See PRESIDENCY OF THE SEVENTY, No. 28.

84. Albert Choules Jr. — Born Feb. 15, 1926, in Driggs, Teton Co., Idaho, to Albert Choules and Rula Wilson. Sustained to the First Quorum of the Seventy Oct. 1, 1988, at age 62; sustained to the Second Quorum of the Seventy April 1, 1989; released Oct. 1, 1994.

85. Lloyd Preal George Jr. — Born Sept. 17, 1920, in Kanosh, Millard Co., Utah, to Preal George and Artemesia Palmer. Sustained to the First Quorum of the Seventy Oct. 1, 1988, at age 68; sustained to the Second Quorum of the Seventy April 1, 1989; released Oct. 1, 1994; died May 13, 1996, at Salt Lake City, Salt Lake Co., Utah, at age 75.

86. Gerald Eldon Melchin — Born May 24, 1921, in Kitchener, Ontario, Can-ada, to Arthur Melchin and Rosetta Willis. Sus-tained to the First Quorum of the Seventy on Oct. 1, 1988, at age 67; sustained to the Second Quorum of the Seventy April 1, 1989; released Oct. 1, 1994.

87. Joe Junior Christensen — See PRESIDENCY OF THE SEVENTY, No. 27.

88. Warren Eugene Hansen Jr. — See PRESIDENCY OF THE SEVENTY, No. 29.

89. Jeffrey Roy Holland — See current QUORUM OF THE TWELVE.

90. Marlin Keith Jensen — See current FIRST QUORUM OF THE SEVENTY.

91. Earl Carr Tingey – See PRESIDENCY OF THE SEVENTY, No. 32.

92. Harold Gordon Hillam – See PRESIDENCY OF THE SEVENTY, No. 31.

93. Carlos Humberto Amado — See current FIRST QUORUM OF THE SEVENTY.

94. Benjamin Berry Banks — See PRESIDENCY OF THE SEVENTY, NO. 36.

95. Spencer Joel Condie — See current FIRST QUORUM OF THE SEVENTY.

96. Robert Kent Dellenbach – Born May 10, 1937, in Salt Lake City, Salt Lake Co., Utah, to Frank Dellenbach and Leona Conshafter. Sustained to the Second Quorum of the Seventy March 31, 1990, at age 52; called to the First Quorum of the Seventy June 6, 1992, and sustained Oct. 3, 1992; named emeritus General Authority Oct. 6, 2007.

97. Henry Bennion Eyring – See current FIRST PRESIDENCY.

98. Glenn Leroy Pace — See current FIRST QUORUM OF THE SEVENTY.

99. Floyd Melvin Hammond — Born Dec. 19, 1933, in Blackfoot, Bingham Co., Idaho, to Floyd Milton Hammond and Ruby Hoge. Sustained to the Second Quorum of the Seventy April 1, 1989, at age 55; sustained to the First Quorum of the Seventy April 3, 1993; named emeritus General Authority Oct. 1, 2005.

100. Kenneth Johnson — See current FIRST QUORUM OF THE SEVENTY.

101. Lynn Alvin Mickelsen — See current FIRST QUORUM OF THE SEVENTY.

102. Neil Linden Andersen – See current PRESIDENCY OF THE SEVENTY.

103. David Todd Christofferson – See current QUORUM OF THE TWELVE.

104. Cree-L Kofford – Born July 11, 1933, in Santaquin, Utah Co., Utah, to Cree Clarence Kofford and Melba Nelson. Sustained to Second Quorum of the Seventy April 6, 1991, at age 57; sustained to First Quorum of the Seventy April 2, 1994; named emeritus General Authority Oct. 4, 2003.

105. Dennis Bramwell Neuenschwander – See current FIRST QUORUM OF THE SEVENTY.

106. Andrew Wayne Peterson — Born June 8, 1947, in San Francisco, San Francisco Co., Calif., to Wayne Leo Peterson and Virginia Parker.

Sustained to First Quorum of the Seventy Oct. 1, 1994, at age 47; named emeritus General Authority Oct. 2, 1999; died Dec. 31, 2003, in Salt Lake City, Salt Lake Co., Utah, at age 56.

107. Cecil Osborn Samuelson Jr. – See current FIRST QUORUM OF THE SEVENTY.

108. John Baird Dickson — See current FIRST QUORUM OF THE SEVENTY.

109. Jay Edwin Jensen – See current PRESIDENCY OF THE SEVENTY.

110. David Eugene Sorensen – See PRESIDENCY OF THE SEVENTY, No. 35.

111. William Craig Zwick — See current FIRST QUORUM OF THE SEVENTY.

112. Merrill Joseph Bateman – See PRESIDENCY OF THE SEVENTY, No. 41.

113. Dallas Nielsen Archibald — Born July 24, 1938, in Logan, Cache Co., Utah, to Ezra Wilson Archibald and Marguerite Nielsen. Called to the Second Quorum of the Seventy June 6, 1992, at age 53, and sustained Oct. 3, 1992; sustained to First Quorum of the Seventy April 6, 1996; drowned in a boating accident Dec. 14, 1998, near Concepcion, Chile, at age 60.

114. Dieter Friedrich Uchtdorf – See current FIRST PRESIDENCY.

115. Bruce Clark Hafen — See current FIRST QUORUM OF THE SEVENTY.

116. Gary Jerome Coleman —See current FIRST QUORUM OF THE SEVENTY.

117. John Max Madsen — See current FIRST QUORUM OF THE SEVENTY.

118. Wm. Rolfe Kerr – Born June 29, 1935, in Tremonton, Box Elder Co., Utah , to Clifton G.M. Kerr and Irene Pack. Sustained to the Second Quorum of the Seventy April 6, 1996, at age 60; sustained to the First Quorum of the Seventy April 5, 1997; named emeritus General Authority Oct. 6, 2007.

119. Carl Barton Pratt — See current FIRST QUORUM OF THE SEVENTY.

120. Sheldon Fay Child – Born May 8, 1938, in Ogden, Weber Co., Utah, to Mark Fay Child and Viola Criddle. Sustained to the Second Quorum of the Seventy April 6, 1996, at age 57; sustained to the First Quorum of the Seventy April 5, 1998; named emeritus General Authority Oct. 4, 2008.

121. Quentin LaMar Cook – See current QUORUM OF THE TWELVE.

122. Francisco Jose Vinas — See current FIRST QUORUM OF THE SEVENTY.

123. Lance Bradley Wickman — See current FIRST QUORUM OF THE SEVENTY.

124. Lynn Grant Robbins — See current FIRST QUORUM OF THE SEVENTY.

125. Donald Larry Hallstrom — See current FIRST QUORUM OF THE SEVENTY.

126. Ronald A Rasband – See current PRESIDENCY OF THE SEVENTY.

127. Claudio Roberto Mendez Costa – See current PRESIDENCY OF THE SEVENTY.

128. Richard John Maynes — See current FIRST QUORUM OF THE SEVENTY.

129. Lyndon Whitney Clayton – See current PRESIDENCY OF THE SEVENTY.

130. Christoffel Golden Jr. — See current FIRST QUORUM OF THE SEVENTY.

131. Walter Fermin Gonzalez – See current PRESIDENCY OF THE SEVENTY.

132. Steven Erastus Snow — See current PRESIDENCY OF THE SEVENTY.

133. Bruce Douglas Porter – See current FIRST QUORUM OF THE SEVENTY.

134. Benjamin De Hoyos – See current FIRST QUORUM OF THE SEVENTY.

135. David Frewin Evans – See current FIRST QUORUM OF THE SEVENTY.

136. Cecil Scott Grow – See current FIRST QUORUM OF THE SEVENTY.

137. Richard Gordon Hinckley – See current FIRST QUORUM OF THE SEVENTY.

138. Paul Vere Johnson – See current FIRST QUORUM OF THE SEVENTY.

139. Paul Edward Koelliker – See current

FIRST QUORUM OF THE SEVENTY.

140. **Paul Bowen Pieper** – See current FIRST QUORUM OF THE SEVENTY.

141. **Ulisses Soares** – See current FIRST QUORUM OF THE SEVENTY.

142. **Keith Karlton Hilbig** – See current FIRST QUORUM OF THE SEVENTY.

143. **David Steward Baxter** – See current FIRST QUORUM OF THE SEVENTY.

144. **Shayne Martell Bowen** – See current FIRST QUORUM OF THE SEVENTY.

145. **Daniel Leroy Johnson** – See current FIRST QUORUM OF THE SEVENTY.

146. **Marcus Bell Nash** – See current FIRST QUORUM OF THE SEVENTY.

147. **Anthony Duane Perkins** – See current FIRST QUORUM OF THE SEVENTY.

148. **Enrique Rienzi Salvatore Falabella** – See current FIRST QUORUM OF THE SEVENTY.

149. **Erich Willi Horst Kopischke** – See current FIRST QUORUM OF THE SEVENTY.

150. **Michael John Uy Teh** – See current FIRST QUORUM OF THE SEVENTY.

151. **Octaviano Tenorio** – See current FIRST QUORUM OF THE SEVENTY.

152. **Claudio Daniel Zivic** – See current FIRST QUORUM OF THE SEVENTY.

153. **Craig Cloward Christensen** – See current FIRST QUORUM OF THE SEVENTY

154. **William Russell Walker** — See current FIRST QUORUM OF THE SEVENTY

155. **Marcus Antony Aidukaitis** – See current FIRST QUORUM OF THE SEVENTY.

156. **Gérald Jean Caussé** – See current FIRST QUORUM OF THE SEVENTY.

157. **Lawrence Edward Corbridge** – See current FIRST QUORUM OF THE SEVENTY.

158. **Eduardo Gavarret** – See current FIRST QUORUM OF THE SEVENTY.

157. **Carlos Augusto Godoy** – See current FIRST QUORUM OF THE SEVENTY.

159. **James Joseph Hamula** – See current FIRST QUORUM OF THE SEVENTY.

160. **Allan Forrest Packer** – See current FIRST QUORUM OF THE SEVENTY.

161. **Kevin Wayne Pearson** – See current FIRST QUORUM OF THE SEVENTY.

162. **Rafael Eduardo Pino** – See current FIRST QUORUM OF THE SEVENTY.

163. **Gary Evan Stevenson** – See current FIRST QUORUM OF THE SEVENTY.

164. **José Augusto Teixeira** – See current FIRST QUORUM OF THE SEVENTY.

165. **Frank Michael Watson** – See current FIRST QUORUM OF THE SEVENTY.

166. **Jorge Fernando Zeballos** – See current FIRST QUORUM OF THE SEVENTY.

SECOND QUORUM OF THE SEVENTY

The Second Quorum of the Seventy was created April 1, 1989, in response to the "continued rapid growth of the Church." (*Church News*, April 8, 1989.)

The initial members of the Second Quorum were those General Authorities serving under a five-year call (called from April 1984 to October 1988) in the First Quorum of the Seventy. General Authorities in the Second Quorum are now generally called for six years.

1. Russell Carl Taylor — See FIRST QUORUM OF THE SEVENTY, No. 55.

2. Robert B Harbertson — See FIRST QUORUM OF THE SEVENTY, No. 56.

3. Devere Harris — See FIRST QUORUM OF THE SEVENTY, No. 57.

4. Spencer Hamlin Osborn — See FIRST QUORUM OF THE SEVENTY, No. 58.

5. Philip Tadje Sonntag — See FIRST QUORUM OF THE SEVENTY, No. 59.

6. John Sonnenberg — See FIRST QUORUM OF THE SEVENTY, No. 60.

7. Ferril Arthur Kay — See FIRST QUORUM OF THE SEVENTY, No. 61.

8. Keith Wilson Wilcox — See FIRST QUORUM OF THE SEVENTY, No. 62.

9. Waldo Pratt Call — See FIRST QUORUM OF THE SEVENTY, No. 67.

10. Helio Da Rocha Camargo — See FIRST QUORUM OF THE SEVENTY, No. 68.

11. Hans Verlan Andersen — See FIRST QUORUM OF THE SEVENTY, No. 69.

12. George Ivins Cannon — See FIRST QUORUM OF THE SEVENTY, No. 70.

13. Francis Marion Gibbons — See FIRST QUORUM OF THE SEVENTY, No. 71.

14. Gardner Hale Russell — See FIRST QUORUM OF THE SEVENTY, No. 72.

15. George Richard Hill III — See FIRST QUORUM OF THE SEVENTY, No. 73.

16. John Roger Lasater — See FIRST QUORUM OF THE SEVENTY, No. 74.

17. Douglas James Martin — See FIRST QUORUM OF THE SEVENTY, No. 75.

18. Alexander Baillie Morrison — See FIRST QUORUM OF THE SEVENTY, No. 76.

19. Lloyd Aldin Porter — See PRESIDENCY OF THE SEVENTY, NO. 26.

20. Glen Larkin Rudd — See FIRST QUORUM OF THE SEVENTY, No. 78.

21. Douglas Hill Smith — See FIRST QUORUM OF THE SEVENTY, No. 79.

22. Lynn Andrew Sorensen — See FIRST QUORUM OF THE SEVENTY, No. 80.

23. Robert Edward Sackley — See FIRST QUORUM OF THE SEVENTY, No. 81.

24. Larry Lionel Kendrick — See FIRST QUORUM OF THE SEVENTY, No. 82.

25. Monte James Brough — See PRESIDENCY OF THE SEVENTY, No. 28.

26. Albert Choules Jr. — See FIRST QUORUM OF THE SEVENTY, No. 84.

27. Lloyd Preal George Jr. — See FIRST QUORUM OF THE SEVENTY, No. 85.

28. Gerald Eldon Melchin — See FIRST QUORUM OF THE SEVENTY, No. 86.

29. Carlos Humberto Amado — See current FIRST QUORUM OF THE SEVENTY.

30. Benjamin Berry Banks — See PRESIDENCY OF THE SEVENTY, No. 36.

31. Spencer Joel Condie — See current FIRST QUORUM OF THE SEVENTY.

32. Floyd Melvin Hammond – See FIRST QUORUM OF THE SEVENTY, No. 99.

33. Malcolm Seth Jeppsen — Born Nov. 1, 1924, in Mantua, Box Elder Co., Utah, to Conrad Jeppsen and Laurine Nielsen. Sustained to the Second Quorum of the Seventy April 1, 1989, at age 64; released Oct. 1, 1994.

34. Richard Powell Lindsay — Born March 18, 1926, in Salt Lake City, Salt Lake Co., Utah, to Samuel Bennion Lindsay and Mary Alice Powell. Sustained to the Second Quorum of the Seventy April 1, 1989, at age 63; released Oct. 1, 1994.

35. Merlin Rex Lybbert — Born Jan. 31, 1926, in Cardston, Alberta, Canada, to Charles Lester

Lybbert and Delvia Reed. Sustained to the Second Quorum of the Seventy April 1, 1989, at age 63; released Oct. 1, 1994; died July 6, 2001, at Salt Lake City, Salt Lake Co., Utah, at age 75.

36. Horacio Antonio Tenorio — Born March 6, 1935, in Mexico City, Distrito Federal, Mexico, to Leopoldo Horacio Tenorio and Blanca Otilia Oriza Arenas. Sustained to the Second Quorum of the Seventy April 1, 1989, at age 54; released Oct. 1, 1994.

37. Eduardo Ayala — Born May 3, 1937, in Coronel, Chile, to Magdonio Ayala and Maria Aburto. Sustained to the Second Quorum of the Seventy March 31, 1990, at age 52; released Sept. 30, 1995.

38. LeGrand Raine Curtis — Born May 22, 1924, in Salt Lake City, Salt Lake Co., Utah, to Alexander R. Curtis and Genevieve Raine. Sustained to the Second Quorum of the Seventy March 31, 1990, at age 66; released Sept. 30, 1995.

39. Clinton Louis Cutler — Born Dec. 27, 1929, in Salt Lake City, Salt Lake Co., Utah, to Benjamin Lewis Cutler and Hellie Helena Sharp. Sustained to the Second Quorum of the Seventy March 31, 1990, at age 60; died April 9, 1994, at South Jordan, Salt Lake Co., Utah, at age 64.

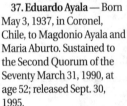

40. Robert Kent Dellenbach — See FIRST QUORUM OF THE SEVENTY, No. 96.

41. Harold Gordon Hillam – See PRESIDENCY OF THE SEVENTY, No. 31.

42. Kenneth Johnson — See current FIRST QUORUM OF THE SEVENTY.

43. Helvecio Martins — Born July 27, 1930, in Rio de Janeiro, Brazil, to Honorio Martins and Benedicta Francisca. Sustained to the Second Quorum of the Seventy March 31, 1990, at age 59; released Sept. 30, 1995, died May 14, 2005.

44. Lynn Alvin Mickelsen — See current FIRST QUORUM OF SEVENTY.

45. J Ballard Washburn — Born Jan. 18, 1929, in Blanding, San Juan Co., Utah, to Alvin Lavell Washburn and Wasel Black. Sustained to the Second Quorum of the Seventy March 31, 1990, at age 61; released Sept. 30, 1995.

46. Durrel Arden Woolsey — Born June 12, 1926, at Escalante, Garfield Co., Utah, to Willis A. Woolsey and Ruby Riddle. Sustained to the Second Quorum of the Seventy March 31, 1990, at age 63; released Sept. 30, 1995.

47. Rulon Gerald Craven — Born Nov. 11, 1924, in Murray, Salt Lake Co., Utah, to Gerald and Susie Craven. Called to the Second Quorum of the Seventy Dec. 5, 1990, at age 66, and sustained April 6, 1991; released Oct. 5, 1996.

48. William McKenzie Lawrence — Born Oct. 28, 1926, in Salt Lake City, Salt Lake Co., Utah, to Richard Sterling Lawrence and Thelma McKenzie. Called to the Second Quorum of the Seventy Jan. 1, 1991, at age 64, and sustained April 6, 1991; released Oct. 5, 1996.

49. Julio Enrique Davila — Born May 23, 1932, in Bucaramunga, Colombia, to Julio E. Davila Villamicar and Rita Penalosa de Davila.

Sustained to the Second Quorum of the Seventy April 6, 1991, at age 58; released Oct. 5, 1996.

50. Graham Watson Doxey — Born March 30, 1927, in Salt Lake City, Salt Lake Co., Utah, to Graham H. Doxey and Leone Watson. Sustained to the Second Quorum of the Seventy April 6, 1991, at age 64; released Oct. 5, 1996.

51. Cree-L Kofford – See FIRST QUORUM OF THE SEVENTY, No. 104.

52. Joseph Carl Muren — Born Feb. 5, 1936, in Richmond, Contra Costa Co., California, to Joseph S. Muren and Alba Maria Cairo. Sustained to the Second Quorum of the Seventy April 6, 1991, at age 55; released Oct. 5, 1996.

53. Dennis Bramwell Neuenschwander – See current FIRST QUORUM OF THE SEVENTY.

54. Jorge Alfonso Rojas — Born Sept. 27, 1940, in Delicias, Chihuahua, Mexico, to Rodolfo Rojas and Hilaria Ornelas. Sustained to the Second Quorum of the Seventy April 6, 1991, at age 50; released Oct. 5, 1996.

55. Han In Sang — Born Dec. 10, 1938, in Seoul, Korea, to Han Chang Soo and Lee Do Ho. Called to the Second Quorum of the Seventy June 1, 1991, at age 52, and sustained Oct. 5, 1991; released Oct. 5, 1996.

56. Stephen Douglas Nadauld — Born May 31, 1942, in Idaho Falls, Bonneville Co., Idaho, to Sterling Dwaine Nadauld and Lois Madsen. Called to the Second Quorum of the Seventy June 1, 1991, at age 49, and sustained Oct. 5, 1991; released Oct. 5, 1996.

57. Sam Koyei Shimabukuro — Born June 7, 1925, in Waipahu, Honolulu Co., Oahu, Hawaii, to Kame Shimabukuro and Ushi Nakasone. Called to the Second Quorum of the Seventy July 13, 1991, at age 66, and sustained Oct. 5, 1991; released Oct. 5, 1996.

58. Lino Alvarez — Born July 18, 1944, in Arteaga, Coahuila, Mexico, to Lino Alvarez and Margarita Vasquez. Called to the Second Quorum of the Seventy June 6, 1992, at age 47, and sustained Oct. 3, 1992; released Oct. 4, 1997.

59. Dallas Nielsen Archibald — See FIRST QUORUM OF THE SEVENTY, No. 113.

60. Merrill Joseph Bateman – See PRESIDENCY OF THE SEVENTY, No. 41.

61. Chellus Max Caldwell — Born Dec. 4, 1933, in Salt Lake City, Salt Lake Co., to Chellus M. and Electa J. Caldwell. Called to the Second Quorum of the Seventy June 6, 1992, at age 58, and sustained Oct. 3, 1992; released Oct. 4, 1997.

62. Gary Jerome Coleman — See current FIRST QUORUM OF THE SEVENTY.

63. John Baird Dickson — See current FIRST QUORUM OF THE SEVENTY.

64. John Emerson Fowler — Born Nov. 10, 1944, in Redding, Shasta Co., California, to R. Walter Fowler and Lois Manita Clayton. Called to the Second Quorum of the Seventy June 6, 1992, at age 47, and sustained Oct. 3, 1992; released Oct. 4, 1997.

65. Jay Edwin Jensen — See current FIRST QUORUM OF THE SEVENTY.

66. Augusto Alandy Lim — Born May 4, 1934, in Santa Cruz, Philippines, to Leon B. Lim and Beatriz R. Alandy. Called to the Second Quorum of the Seventy June 6, 1992, at age 58, and sustained Oct. 3, 1992; released Oct. 4, 1997.

67. John Max Madsen — See current FIRST QUORUM OF THE SEVENTY.

68. Victor Dallas Merrell — Born Jan. 25, 1936, in Basalt, Bingham Co., Idaho, to Victor Lybbert Merrell and Beatrice Jensen. Called to the Second Quorum of the Seventy June 6, 1992, at age 56, and sustained Oct. 3, 1992; released Oct. 4, 1997.

69. David Eugene Sorensen — See PRESIDENCY OF THE SEVENTY, No. 35.

70. Frank David Stanley — Born Sept. 11, 1935, in Salt Lake City, Salt Lake Co., Utah, to O. Frank Stanley and Winifred Parker. Called to the Second Quorum of the Seventy June 6, 1992, at age 56, and sustained Oct. 3, 1992; released Oct. 4, 1997.

71. Kwok Yuen Tai — Born June 30, 1941, in Hong Kong, to Lung Hing Tai and Yau Yin Chu. Sustained to the Second Quorum of the Seventy June 6, 1992, at age 50, and sustained Oct. 3, 1992; released Oct. 4, 1997.

72. Lowell Dale Wood — Born Jan. 23, 1933, in Cardston, Alberta, Canada, to Wm. Dale Wood and Donna Wolf. Called to the Second Quorum of the Seventy June 6, 1992, at age 59, and sustained Oct. 3, 1992; died March 7, 1997, in Apia, Samoa, at age 64.

73. Claudio Roberto Mendes Costa — See current PRESIDENCY OF THE SEVENTY.

74. William Don Ladd — Born July 14, 1933, in San Mateo, Putnam Co., Fla., to Joseph Donald Ladd and Phyllis Rose Anderson. Sustained to the Second Quorum of the Seventy April 2, 1994, at age 60; released Oct. 7, 2000.

75. James Ostermann Mason — Born June 19, 1930, in Salt Lake City, Salt Lake Co., Utah, to A. Stanton Mason and Neoma Thorup. Sustained to the Second Quorum of the Seventy April 2, 1994, at age 63; released Oct. 7, 2000.

76. Dieter Friedrich Uchtdorf – See current FIRST PRESIDENCY.

77. Lance Bradley Wickman — See current FIRST QUORUM OF THE SEVENTY.

78. Bruce Douglas Porter – See current FIRST QUORUM OF THE SEVENTY.

79. Lowell Edward Brown — Born June 18, 1937, In Preston, Franklin Co., Idaho, to Lowell Brown and Helen Peterson. Sustained to the Second Quorum of the Seventy April 6, 1996, at age 58; released Oct. 5, 2002.

80. Sheldon Fay Child – See FIRST QUORUM OF THE SEVENTY, No. 120.

81. Quentin LaMar Cook — See current QUORUM OF THE TWELVE.

82. Wm. Rolfe Kerr – See FIRST QUORUM OF THE SEVENTY, No. 118.

83. Dennis Ericksen Simmons — Born June 27, 1934, in Beaver Dam, Box Elder Co., Utah, to Thomas Yates Simmons and Sylvia Ericksen. Sustained to the Second Quorum of the Seventy April 6, 1996, at age 61; released Oct. 1, 2005.

84. Jerald Lynn Taylor — Born March 22, 1937, in Colonia Dublan, Mexico, to Loren LeRoy Taylor and Lillian Hatch. Sustained to the Second Quorum of the Seventy April 6, 1996, at age 59; released Oct. 5, 2002.

85. Francisco Jose Vinas — See current FIRST QUORUM OF THE SEVENTY.

86. Richard Bitner Wirthlin — Born March 15, 1931, in Salt Lake City, Salt Lake Co., Utah, to Joseph L. Wirthlin and Madeline Bitner. Sustained to the Second Quorum of the Seventy April 6, 1996, at age 65; released Oct. 6, 2001.

87. Richard David Allred — Born Aug. 3, 1932, in Salt Lake City, Salt Lake Co., Utah, to Elwood B. Allred and Glendora Malcom. Sustained to the Second Quorum of the Seventy April 5, 1997, at age 64; released Oct. 5, 2002.

88. Eran Abegg Call — Born Dec. 2, 1929, in Colonia Dublan, Mexico, to Anson Bowen Call and Julie Sarah Abegg. Sustained to the Second Quorum of the Seventy April 5, 1997, at age 67; released Oct. 7, 2000.

89. Richard Ernest Cook — Born Sept. 7, 1930, in Pleasant Grove, Utah Co., Utah, to Ernest William Cook and Clara Blackhurst. Sustained to the Second Quorum of the Seventy April 5, 1997, at age 66; released Oct. 6, 2001.

90. Duane Bird Gerrard – Born April 22, 1938, in Murray, Salt Lake Co., Utah, to Leonard Gerrard and Mildred Bird. Sustained to Second Quorum of the Seventy April 5, 1997, at age 58; released Oct. 4, 2003.

91. Wayne Mitchell Hancock — Born July 16, 1931, in Safford, Graham Co., Ariz., to Wayne M.P. Hancock and Phyllis Lines. Sustained to the Second Quorum of the Seventy April 5, 1997, at age 65; released Oct. 6, 2001.

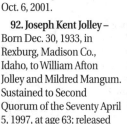

92. Joseph Kent Jolley – Born Dec. 30, 1933, in Rexburg, Madison Co., Idaho, to William Afton Jolley and Mildred Mangum. Sustained to Second Quorum of the Seventy April 5, 1997, at age 63; released Oct. 4, 2003.

93. Richard John Maynes — See current FIRST QUORUM OF THE SEVENTY.

94. Dale Emerson Miller — Born April 2, 1936, in Los Angeles, Los Angeles Co., Calif., to Wade Elliott Miller and Romania Davis. Sustained to the Second Quorum of the Seventy April 5, 1997, at age 61; released Sept. 30, 2006.

95. Lynn Grant Robbins — See current FIRST QUORUM OF THE SEVENTY.

96. Donald Lafayette Staheli — Born Oct.19, 1931, in St. George, Washington Co., Utah, to Lafayette Staheli and Grace Sullivan. Sustained to the Second Quorum of the Seventy April 5, 1997, at age 65; released Sept. 30, 2006.

97. Richard Eyring Turley Sr. — Born Dec. 29, 1930, in El Paso, El Paso Co., Texas, to Edward Vernon Turley and Winifred Louise Roche. Sustained to the Second Quorum of the Seventy April 5, 1997, at age 66; released Oct. 7, 2000.

98. Athos Marques Amorim — Born June 14, 1932, in Rio de Janeiro, Brazil, to Antonio Marques Amorim and Maria Carlota Martins Ferreira. Sustained to the Second Quorum of the Seventy April 4, 1998, at age 65; released Oct. 5, 2002.

99. E Ray Bateman – Born Oct. 20, 1937, in Sandy, Salt Lake Co., Utah, to Marlon Samuel Bateman and Mary Armstrong. Sustained to the Second Quorum of the Seventy April 4, 1998, at age 60; released Oct. 2, 2004.

100. Val Rigby Christensen – Born Sept. 27, 1935, in Hooper, Weber Co., Utah, to Leonard Christensen and Jennie Lowe Rigby. Sustained to the Second Quorum of the Seventy April 4, 1998, at age 62; released Oct. 2, 2004.

101. Ronald Tomlinson Halverson — Born Dec. 18, 1936, in Ogden, Weber Co., Utah, to Marlow Halverson and Hilda Tomlinson. Sustained to the Second Quorum of the Seventy April 4, 1998, at age 61; released Sept. 30, 2006.

102. Earl Merrill Monson — Born July 26, 1932, in Salt Lake City, Salt Lake Co., Utah, to Charles Horald Monson and Ortencia Hendricks Merrill. Sustained to the Second Quorum of the Seventy April 4, 1998, at age 65; released Oct. 5, 2002.

103. Merrill Clayton Oaks – Born Jan. 12, 1936, in Twin Falls, Twin Falls Co., Idaho, to Lloyd E. Oaks and Stella Harris. Sustained to the Second Quorum of the Seventy April 4, 1998, at age 62; released Oct. 2, 2004.

104. Horace Bryan Richards — Born March 18, 1934, in Salt Lake City, Salt Lake Co., Utah, to Horace B. Richards and LynnAnne Taylor. Sustained to the Second Quorum of the Seventy April 4, 1998, at age 64; released Sept. 30, 2006.

105. Ned Bardeane Roueche — Born Aug. 5, 1934, in Salt Lake City, Salt Lake Co., to Leonard C. Roueche and Ruth Lee. Sustained to the Second Quorum of the Seventy April 4, 1998, at age 63; released Oct. 1, 2005.

106. Don Lee Tobler – Born July 25, 1933, in Provo, Utah Co., Utah, to Donald Tobler and Louise Shoell. Sustained to Second Quorum of the Seventy April 4, 1998, at age 64; released Oct. 4, 2003.

107. Gordon Taylor Watts – Born Feb. 23, 1935, in South Weber, Davis Co., Utah, to Elwood Taylor Watts and Edna Davis. Sustained to the Second Quorum of the Seventy April 4, 1998, at age 63; released Oct. 2, 2004.

108. Stephen Allan West – Born March 23, 1935, in Salt Lake City, Salt Lake Co., Utah, to Allan Morrell West and Ferne Page. Sustained to the Second Quorum of the Seventy April 4, 1998, at age 63; released Oct. 2, 2004.

109. Robert Jay Whetten — Born April 12, 1943, in Chuichupa, Chihuahua, Mexico, to Glen A. Whetten and Ada May Judd. Sustained to the Second Quorum of the Seventy April 4, 1998, at age 54; released Sept. 30, 2006.

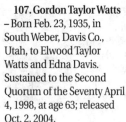

110. Raphael Hunter Wood — Born July 11, 1931, in Salt Lake City, Salt Lake Co., Utah, to Ray G. Wood and Mary Hunter. Sustained to the Second Quorum of the Seventy April 4, 1998, at age 66; released Oct. 6, 2001.

111. Adhemar Damiani — Born Dec. 18, 1939, in Sao Paulo, Sao Paulo State, Brazil, to Antonio and Maria Damiani. Sustained to the Second Quorum of the Seventy April 3, 1999, at age 59; released Oct. 1, 2005.

112. Stephen Berg Oveson — Born July 9, 1936, in Grass Valley, Sherman Co., Ore., to Merrill M. Oveson and Mal Berg. Sustained to the Second Quorum of the Seventy April 3, 1999, at age 62; released Oct. 1, 2005.

113. David Rodger Stone — Born June 16, 1936, in Buenos Aires, Argentina, to Hubert J. Stone and Ethel R. Grant. Sustained to the Second Quorum of the Seventy April 3, 1999, at age 62; released Sept. 30, 2006.

114. Harvey Bruce Stucki — Born Dec. 1, 1937, in St. George, Washington Co., Utah, to Harvey Stucki and Anna Hilda Wittwer. Sustained to the Second Quorum of the Seventy April 3, 1999, at age 61; released Sept. 30, 2006.

115. Richard Henry Winkel — Born May 17, 1942, in Oakland, Almeda Co., Calif., to Francis Benjamin Winkel and Karen Hart. Sustained to the Second Quorum of the Seventy April 3, 1999, at age 56; released Sept. 30, 2006.

116. Robert Stephen Wood — See current SECOND QUORUM OF THE SEVENTY.

117. Douglas Lane Callister — See current SECOND QUORUM OF THE SEVENTY.

118. Darwin B. Christenson — Born Aug. 11, 1935, in Firth, Bingham Co., Idaho, to Lars H. Christenson and Olive Brough. Sustained to the Second Quorum of the Seventy April 1, 2000, at age 64; released Oct. 1, 2005.

119. Keith Crockett – Born Jan. 15, 1934, in Pima, Graham Co., Ariz., to Wilford Woodruff Crockett III and Jacy Boggs. Sustained to the Second Quorum of the Seventy April 1, 2000, at age 66; released Oct. 2, 2004.

120. Himan Aldridge Gillespie — Born May 22, 1935, in Riverside, Riverside Co., Calif., to Lionel Aldridge Gillespie and Amelia Eileen Baird. Sustained to the Second Quorum of the Seventy April 1, 2000, at age 64; released Oct. 1, 2005.

121. Robert Charles Oaks — See current SECOND QUORUM OF THE SEVENTY.

122. Keith Karlton Hilbig — See current FIRST QUORUM OF THE SEVENTY.

123. Robert Frank Orton — Born Aug. 24, 1936, in Reno, Washoe Co., Nev., to H. Frank Orton and Gwen Riggs. Sustained to the Second Quorum of the Seventy March 31, 2001, at age 64; released Oct. 6, 2007.

124. Wayne Skeen Peterson — Born Oct. 6, 1939, in Ogden, Weber Co., Utah, to Rulon P. Peterson and Naomi Skeen. Sustained to the Second Quorum of the Seventy March 31, 2001, at age 61; released Oct. 6, 2007.

125. Ralph Conrad Schultz — Born March 11, 1938, in North Bend, Coos Co., Ore., to Ralph C. Schultz and Dorothy Bushong. Sustained to the Second Quorum of the Seventy March 31, 2001, at age 63; released Oct. 6, 2007.

126. Robert Ricky Steuer – Born Dec. 6, 1943, in Milwaukee, Milwaukee Co., Wisc., to Fritz Steuer and Hulda Hanel. Sustained to the Second Quorum of the Seventy March 31, 2001, at age 57; released Oct. 4, 2008.

127. Harley Ross Workman — Born Dec. 31, 1940, in Salt Lake City, Salt Lake Co., Utah, to Harley Workman and Lucille Ramsey. Sustained to the Second Quorum of the Seventy March 31, 2001, at age 60; released Oct. 6, 2007.

128. Gerald Niels Lund – Born Sept. 12, 1939, in Fountain Green, Sanpete Co., Utah, to Jewell G. Lund and Evelyn Mortensen. Sustained to the Second Quorum of the Seventy April 6, 2002, at age 62; released Oct. 4, 2008.

129. William Russell Walker — See current FIRST QUORUM OF THE SEVENTY.

130. Craig Cloward Christensen — See current FIRST QUORUM OF THE SEVENTY.

131. James Meyers Dunn — See current SECOND QUORUM OF THE SEVENTY.

132. Donald Rex Gerratt — Born April 9, 1936, in Heyburn, Minidoka Co., Idaho., to Donald Wayne Gerratt and Ann Bailey. Sustained to the Second Quorum of the Seventy Oct. 5, 2002, at age 66; released Oct. 6, 2007.

133. Daryl Hodges Garn — See current SECOND QUORUM OF THE SEVENTY.

134. Spencer Virgil Jones — See current SECOND QUORUM OF THE SEVENTY.

135. Mervyn Bennion Arnold — See current SECOND QUORUM OF THE SEVENTY.

136. Shirley Dean Christensen — See current SECOND QUORUM OF THE SEVENTY.

137. Clate Wheeler Mask Jr. — See current SECOND QUORUM OF THE SEVENTY.

138. William Watts Parmley — See current SECOND QUORUM OF THE SEVENTY.

139. Wilford Douglas Shumway — See current SECOND QUORUM OF THE SEVENTY.

140. Won Yong Ko – See current SECOND QUORUM OF THE SEVENTY.

141. Wolfgang Heinz Jürgen Paul – See current SECOND QUORUM OF THE SEVENTY.

142. Lowell Miller Snow – See current SECOND QUORUM OF THE SEVENTY

143. Paul Kay Sybrowsky – See current SECOND QUORUM OF THE SEVENTY

144. Craig Allen Cardon – See current SECOND QUORUM OF THE SEVENTY.

145. Don Ray Clarke – See current SECOND QUORUM OF THE SEVENTY.

146. Keith Reid Edwards – See current SECOND QUORUM OF THE SEVENTY.

147. Stanley Gareld Ellis – See current SECOND QUORUM OF THE SEVENTY.

148. Larry Wayne Gibbons – See current SECOND QUORUM OF THE SEVENTY.

149. Tad Richards Callister – See current SECOND QUORUM OF THE SEVENTY.

150. Kent Dee Watson – See current SECOND QUORUM OF THE SEVENTY.

PRESIDING BISHOPS

1. Edward Partridge —
Born Aug. 27, 1793, at
Pittsfield, Berkshire Co.,
Massachusetts, to William
Partridge and Jemima
Bidwell. Called by revelation
to be the First Bishop of the
Church Feb. 4, 1831, at age 37
(D&C 41:9); died May 27, 1840, at Nauvoo,
Hancock Co., Illinois, at age 46.

2. Newel Kimball Whitney
— Born Feb. 5, 1795, at
Marlborough, Windham Co.,
Vermont, to Samuel Whitney
and Susanna Kimball. Called
by revelation to be the First
Bishop of Kirtland (D&C
72:8); sustained as First
Bishop of the Church Oct. 7, 1844, at age 49;
sustained as Presiding Bishop of the Church
April 6, 1847; died Sept. 23, 1850, at Salt Lake
City, Salt Lake Co., Utah, at age 55.

George Miller — Born Nov. 25, 1794, at
Orange Co., Virginia, to John Miller and
Margaret Pfeiffer. Sustained as Second Bishop
of the Church Oct. 7, 1844, at age 49; dropped
prior to 1847; disfellowshipped Oct. 20, 1848.

3. Edward Hunter — Born
June 22, 1793, at Newton,
Delaware Co., Pennsylvania,
to Edward Hunter and
Hannah Maris. Sustained as
Presiding Bishop of the
Church April 7, 1851, at age
57; died Oct. 16, 1883, at Salt
Lake City, Salt Lake Co.,
Utah, at age 90.

4. William Bowker Preston
— Born Nov. 24, 1830, at
Halifax, Franklin Co.,
Virginia, to Christopher
Preston and Martha Mitchell
Clayton. Sustained as
Presiding Bishop of the
Church April 6, 1884, at age
53; released due to ill health Dec. 4, 1907; died
Aug. 2, 1908, at Salt Lake City, Salt Lake Co.,
Utah, at age 77.

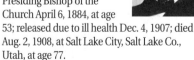

5. Charles Wilson Nibley — See SECOND
COUNSELORS IN THE FIRST PRESIDENCY,
No. 13.

6. Sylvester Quayle Cannon — See
QUORUM OF THE TWELVE, No. 60.

7. LeGrand Richards — See QUORUM OF
THE TWELVE, No. 69.

8. Joseph Leopold Wirthlin — Born Aug. 14,
1893, at Salt Lake City, Salt
Lake Co., Utah, to Joseph
Wirthlin and Emma
Hillstead. Sustained as
second counselor to
Presiding Bishop LeGrand
Richards April 6, 1938, at age
44; sustained as first
counselor to Bishop Richards Dec. 12, 1946;
sustained as Presiding Bishop of the Church
April 6, 1952, at age 58; released Sept. 30, 1961;
died Jan. 25, 1963, at Salt Lake City, Salt Lake
Co., Utah, at age 69.

9. John Henry Vandenberg — Born Dec. 18,
1904, at Ogden, Weber Co.,
Utah, to Dirk Vandenberg
and Maria Alkema. Sustained
as Presiding Bishop of the
Church Sept. 30, 1961, at age
56; sustained as Assistant to
the Quorum of the Twelve
Apostles April 6, 1972;
sustained to First Quorum of the Seventy Oct.
1, 1976; named emeritus General Authority
Dec. 31, 1978; died June 3, 1992, at Sandy, Salt
Lake Co., Utah, at age 87.

10. Victor Lee Brown — Born July 31, 1914, at
Cardston, Alberta, Canada,
to Gerald Stephen Brown
and Maggie Calder Lee.
Sustained as second
counselor to Presiding
Bishop John H. Vandenberg
Sept. 30, 1961, at age 47;
sustained as Presiding
Bishop of the Church April 6, 1972; sustained to
First Quorum of the Seventy April 6, 1985;
named emeritus General Authority Sept. 30,
1989; died March 26, 1996, at Salt Lake City, Salt
Lake Co., Utah at age 81.

11. Robert Dean Hales — See current
QUORUM OF THE TWELVE.

12. Merrill Joseph Bateman — See
PRESIDENCY OF THE SEVENTY, No. 41.

13. Harold David Burton — See current
PRESIDING BISHOPRIC.

FIRST COUNSELORS TO PRESIDING BISHOPS

1. Isaac Morley — Born March 11, 1786, at Montague, Hampshire Co., Massachusetts, to Thomas Morley and Editha Marsh. Set apart as first counselor to Presiding Bishop Edward Partridge June 6, 1831, at age 45; released at the death of Bishop Partridge May 27, 1840; died June 24, 1865, at Fairview, Sanpete Co., Utah, at age 79.

2. Leonard Wilford Hardy — Born Dec. 31, 1805, at Bradford, Essex Co., Massachusetts, to Simon Hardy and Rhoda Hardy. Sustained as first counselor to Presiding Bishop Edward Hunter Oct. 6, 1856, at age 50; died July 31, 1884, at Salt Lake City, Salt Lake Co., Utah, at age 78.

3. Robert Taylor Burton — Born Oct. 25, 1821, at Amhertsburg, Ontario, Canada, to Samuel Burton and Hannah Shipley. Sustained as second counselor to Presiding Bishop Edward Hunter Oct. 9, 1874, at age 52; sustained as first counselor to Presiding Bishop William B. Preston Oct. 5, 1884; died Nov. 11, 1907, at Salt Lake City, Salt Lake Co., Utah, at age 86.

4. Orrin Porter Miller — Born Sept. 11, 1858, at Mill Creek, Salt Lake Co., Utah, to Reuben G. Miller and Ann Craynor. Sustained as second counselor to Presiding Bishop William B. Preston Oct. 24, 1901, at age 43; sustained as first counselor to Presiding Bishop Charles W. Nibley Dec. 4, 1907, at age 49; died July 7, 1918, at Salt Lake City, Salt Lake Co., Utah at age 59.

5. David Asael Smith — Born May 24, 1879, at Salt Lake City, Salt Lake Co., Utah, to Joseph Fielding Smith and Julina Lambson. Sustained as second counselor to Presiding Bishop Charles W. Nibley Dec. 4, 1907, at age 28; sustained as first counselor to Bishop Nibley July 18, 1918; sustained as first counselor to Presiding Bishop Sylvester Q. Cannon June 4, 1925; released April 6, 1938; died April 6, 1952, at Salt Lake City, Salt Lake Co., Utah, at age 72.

6. Marvin Owen Ashton — Born April 8, 1883, at Salt Lake City, Salt Lake Co., Utah, to Edward T. Ashton and Effie W. Morris. Sustained as first counselor to Presiding Bishop LeGrand Richards April 6, 1938, at age 54; died Oct. 7, 1946, at Salt Lake City, Salt Lake Co., Utah, at age 63.

7. Joseph Leopold Wirthlin — See PRESIDING BISHOPS, No., 8.

8. Henry Thorpe Beal Isaacson — See OTHER COUNSELORS IN THE FIRST PRESIDENCY, No. 12.

9. Robert Leatham Simpson — See FIRST QUORUM OF THE SEVENTY, No. 18.

10. Harold Burke Peterson — See FIRST QUORUM OF THE SEVENTY, No. 64.

11. Henry Bennion Eyring — See current FIRST PRESIDENCY.

12. Harold David Burton — See current PRESIDING BISHOPRIC.

13. Richard Crockett Edgley — See current PRESIDING BISHOPRIC.

SECOND COUNSELORS TO PRESIDING BISHOPS

1. John Corrill — Born Sept. 17, 1794, at Worcester Co., Massachusetts. Set apart as second counselor to Presiding Bishop Edward Partridge June 6, 1831, at age 36; released Aug. 1, 1837; excommunicated March 17, 1839.

2. Titus Billings — Born March 25, 1793, at Greenfield, Franklin Co., Massachusetts, to Ebenezer Billings and Esther Joyce. Set apart as second counselor to Presiding Bishop Edward Partridge Aug. 1, 1837, at age 44; released at the death of Bishop Partridge May 27, 1840; died Feb. 6, 1866, at Provo, Utah Co., Utah, at age 72.

3. Jesse Carter Little — Born Sept. 26, 1815, at Belmont, Waldo Co., Maine, to Thomas Little and Relief White. Sustained as second counselor to Presiding Bishop Edward Hunter Oct. 6, 1856, at age 41; resigned summer of 1874; died Dec. 26, 1893, at Salt Lake City, Salt Lake Co., Utah, at age 78.

4. Robert Taylor Burton — See FIRST COUNSELORS IN THE PRESIDING BISHOPRIC, No. 3.

5. John Quayle Cannon — Born April 19, 1857, at San Francisco, San Francisco Co., California, to George Quayle Cannon and Elizabeth Hoagland. Sustained as second counselor to Presiding Bishop William B. Preston Oct. 5, 1884, at age 27; excommunicated Sept. 5, 1886; rebaptized May 6, 1888; died Jan. 14, 1931, at Salt Lake City, Salt Lake Co., Utah, at 73.

6. John Rex Winder — See FIRST COUNSELORS IN THE FIRST PRESIDENCY, No. 7.

7. Orrin Porter Miller — See FIRST COUNSELORS IN THE PRESIDING BISHOPRIC, No. 4.

8. David Asael Smith — See FIRST COUNSELORS IN THE PRESIDING BISHOPRIC, No. 5.

9. John Wells — Born Sept. 16, 1864, at Carlton, Nottinghamshire, England, to Thomas Potter Wells and Sarah Cook. Sustained as second counselor to Presiding Bishop Charles W. Nibley July 18, 1918, at age 53; sustained as second counselor to Presiding Bishop Sylvester Q. Cannon June 4, 1925; released April 6, 1938, when Bishop Cannon was released; died April 18, 1941, at Salt Lake City, Salt Lake Co., Utah, at age 76.

10. Joseph Leopold Wirthlin — See PRESIDING BISHOPS, No. 8.

11. Henry Thorpe Beal Isaacson — See OTHER COUNSELORS IN THE FIRST PRESIDENCY, No. 12.

12. Carl William Buehner — Born Dec. 27, 1898, at Stuttgart, Wuerttemberg, Germany, to Carl F. Buehner and Anna B. Geigle. Sustained as second counselor to Presiding Bishop Joseph L. Wirthlin April 6, 1952, at age 53; released Sept. 30, 1961; died Nov. 18, 1974, at Salt Lake City, Salt Lake Co., Utah, at age 75.

13. Victor Lee Brown — See PRESIDING BISHOPS, No. 10.

14. Vaughn J Featherstone — See FIRST QUORUM OF THE SEVENTY, No. 36.

15. John Richard Clarke — See PRESIDENCY OF THE SEVENTY, No. 22.

16. Glenn Leroy Pace — See current FIRST QUORUM OF THE SEVENTY.

17. Richard Crockett Edgley — See current PRESIDING BISHOPRIC.

18. Keith B. McMullin — See current PRESIDING BISHOPRIC.

LENGTH OF SERVICE
IN FIRST PRESIDENCY AND QUORUM OF THE TWELVE

(As of October 2008)

Name	Date of service, (Age at time)	Length of service	†Total Years as General Authority
David O. McKay	Apr 1906 (32) - Jan 1970 (96)	63 yrs 9 mos	
Heber J. Grant	Oct 1882 (25) - May 1945 (88)	62 yrs 7 mos	
Joseph Fielding Smith	Apr 1910 (33) - Jul 1972 (95)	62 yrs 3 mos	
Wilford Woodruff	Apr 1839 (32) - Sep 1898 (91)	59 yrs 5 mos	
***Lorenzo Snow**	Feb 1849 (34) - Oct 1901 (87)	52 yrs 8 mos	
Joseph F. Smith	Jul 1866 (27) - Nov 1918 (80)	52 yrs 4 mos	
Franklin D. Richards	Feb 1849 (27) - Dec 1899 (78)	50 yrs 10 mos	
Ezra Taft Benson	Oct 1943 (44) - May 1994 (94)	50 yrs 7 mos	
John Taylor	Dec 1838 (30) - Jul 1887 (78)	48 yrs 7 mos	
George Albert Smith	Oct 1903 (33) - Apr 1951 (81)	47 yrs 6 mos	
Gordon B. Hinckley	Oct 1961 (51) - Jan 2008 (97)	46 yrs 3 mos	49 yrs 9 mos
Orson Pratt	Apr 1835 (23) - Aug 1842 / Jan 1843 - Oct 1881 (70)	46 yrs 1 mo	
• **Thomas S. Monson**	Oct 1963 (36) - present	45 yrs	
Rudger Clawson	Oct 1898 (41) - Jun 1943 (86)	44 yrs 8 mos	
George F. Richards	Apr 1906 (45) - Aug 1950 (89)	44 yrs 4 mos	
Orson Hyde	Feb 1835 (30) - May 1839 / Jun 1839 - Nov 1878 (73)	43 yrs 8 mos	
Brigham Young	Fcb 1835 (33) - Aug 1877 (76)	42 yrs 6 mos	
Stephen L Richards	Jan 1917 (37) - May 1959 (79)	42 yrs 4 mos	
Spencer W. Kimball	Oct 1943 (48) - Nov 1985 (90)	42 yrs 1 mo	
Reed Smoot	Apr 1900 (38) - Feb 1941 (79)	40 yrs 10 mos	
*George Q. Cannon	Aug 1860 (33) - Apr 1901 (74)	40 yrs 8 mos	
Mark E. Petersen	Apr 1944 (43) - Jan 1984 (83)	39 yrs 9 mos	
Erastus Snow	Feb 1849 (30) - May 1888 (69)	39 yrs 3 mos	
• Boyd K. Packer	Apr 1970 (45) - present	38 yrs 6 mos	47 yrs
Marion G. Romney	Oct 1951 (54) - May 1988 (90)	36 yrs 7 mos	47 yrs 1 mo
George A. Smith	Apr 1839 (21) - Sep 1875 (58)	36 yrs 5 mos	
Francis M. Lyman	Oct 1880 (40) - Nov 1916 (76)	36 yrs 1 mo	
Howard W. Hunter	Oct 1959 (51) - Mar 1995 (87)	35 yrs 5 mo	
Charles C. Rich	Feb 1849 (39) - Nov 1883 (74)	34 yrs 9 mos	
*Brigham Young Jr.	Oct 1868 (31) - Apr 1903 (66)	34 yrs 6 mos	
• L. Tom Perry	Apr 1974 (51) - present	34 yrs 6 mos	36 yrs
Heber C. Kimball	Feb 1835 (33) - Jun 1868 (67)	33 yrs 4 mos	
Harold B. Lee	Apr 1941 (42) - Dec 1973 (74)	32 yrs 8 mos	

John A. Widtsoe	Mar 1921 (49) - Nov 1952 (80)	31 yrs 8 mos	
Anthon H. Lund	Oct 1889 (45) - Mar 1921 (76)	31 yrs 5 mos	
John Henry Smith	Oct 1880 (32) - Oct 1911 (63)	31 yrs	
LeGrand Richards	Apr 1952 (66) - Jan 1983 (96)	30 yrs 9 mos	44 yrs 9 mos
James E. Faust	Oct 1978 (58) - Aug 2007 (87)	28 yrs 10 mos	34 yrs 10 mos
David B. Haight	Jan 1976 (69) - Jul 2004 (97)	28 yrs 6 mos	34 yrs 3 mos
J. Reuben Clark Jr.	Apr 1933 (61) - Oct 1961 (90)	28 yrs 6 mos	
Delbert L. Stapley	Oct 1950 (53) - Aug 1978 (81)	27 yrs 10 mos	
Anthony W. Ivins	Oct 1907 (55) - Sep 1934 (82)	26 yrs 11 mos	
Richard R. Lyman	Apr 1918 (47) - Nov 1943 (72)	25 yrs 7 mos	
Amasa M. Lyman	Aug 1842 (29) - Oct 1867 (54)	25 yrs 2 mos	
Orson F. Whitney	Apr 1906 (50) - May 1931 (75)	25 yrs 1 mo	
George Teasdale	Oct 1882 (50) - Jun 1907 (75)	24 yrs 8 mo	
• Russell M. Nelson	Apr 1984 (59) - present	24 yrs 6 mos	
• Dallin H. Oaks	Apr 1984 (51) - present	24 yrs 6 mos	
Ezra T. Benson	Jul 1846 (35) - Sep 1869 (58)	23 yrs 2 mos	
• M. Russell Ballard	Oct 1985 (57) - present	23 yrs	32 yrs 6 mos
Neal A. Maxwell	Jul 1981 (55) - Jul 2004 (78)	23 yrs	30 yrs 3 mos
Parley P. Pratt	Feb 1835 (27) - May 1857 (50)	22 yrs 3 mos	
Marvin J. Ashton	Dec 1971 (56) - Feb 1994 (78)	22 yrs 2 mos	24 yrs 4 mos
• Joseph B. Wirthlin	Oct 1986 (69) - present	22 yrs	33 yrs 6 mos
James E. Talmage	Dec 1911 (49) - Jul 1933 (70)	21 yrs 7 mos	
John W. Taylor	Apr 1884 (25) - Oct 1905 (47)	21 yrs 6 mos	
Charles W. Penrose	Jul 1904 (72) - May 1925 (93)	20 yrs 10 mos	
#Daniel H. Wells	Jan 1857 (42) - Aug 1877 (62)	20 yrs 7 mos	34 yrs 2 mos
Melvin J. Ballard	Jan 1919 (45) - Jul 1939 (66)	20 yrs 6 mos	
Joseph F. Merrill	Oct 1931 (63) - Feb 1952 (83)	20 yrs 4 mos	
N. Eldon Tanner	Oct 1962 (64) - Nov 1982 (84)	20 yrs 1 mo	22 yrs 1 mo
• Richard G. Scott	Oct 1988 (59) - present	20 yrs	31 yrs 6 mos
Richard L. Evans	Oct 1953 (47) - Nov 1971 (65)	18 yrs 1 mo	33 yrs 1 mo
Hugh B. Brown	Apr 1958 (74) - Dec 1975 (92)	17 yrs 8 mos	22 yrs 2 mos
Moses Thatcher	Apr 1879 (37) - Apr 1896 (54)	17 yrs	
Henry D. Moyle	Apr 1947 (57) - Sep 1963 (74)	16 yrs 5 mos	
Marriner W. Merrill	Oct 1889 (57) - Feb 1906 (73)	16 yrs 4 mos	
Hyrum Mack Smith	Oct 1901 (29) - Jan 1918 (45)	16 yrs 3 mos	
Albert E. Bowen	Apr 1937 (61) - Jul 1953 (77)	16 yrs 3 mos	
*Albert Carrington	Jul 1870 (57) - Nov 1885 (72)	15 yrs 4 mos	
• Robert D. Hales	Apr 1994 (61) - present	14 yrs 6 mos	33 yrs 6 mos
• Jeffrey R. Holland	Jun 1994 (53) - present	14 yrs 4 mos	19 yrs 4 mos
Joseph Smith	Apr 1830 (24) - Jun 1844 (38)	14 yrs 2 mos	
Willard Richards	Apr 1840 (35) - Mar 1854 (49)	13 yrs 11 mos	

Name	Service		
• Henry B. Eyring	Apr 1995 (61) - present	13 yrs 6 mos	23 yrs 6 mos
Charles A. Callis	Oct 1933 (68) - Jan 1947 (81)	13 yrs 3 mos	
Bruce R. McConkie	Oct 1972 (57) - Apr 1985 (69)	12 yrs 6 mos	38 yrs 6 mos
Sidney Rigdon	Mar 1833 (40) - Jun 1844 (51)	11 yrs 3 mos	
William Smith	Feb 1835 (23) - Oct 1845 (34)	10 yrs 8 mos	
John R. Winder	Oct 1901 (79) - Mar 1910 (88)	8 yrs 5 mos	22 yrs 11 mos
Matthew Cowley	Oct 1945 (48) - Dec 1953 (56)	8 yrs 2 mos	
George Q. Morris	Apr 1954 (80) - Apr 1962 (88)	8 yrs	10 yrs 6 mos
Matthias F. Cowley	Oct 1897 (39) - Oct 1905 (47)	8 yrs	
*+Oliver Cowdery	Apr 1830 (23) - Apr 1838 (31)	8 yrs	
Lyman Wight	Apr 1841 (44) - Dec 1848 (52)	7 yrs 8 mos	
John E. Page	Dec 1838 (39) - Feb 1846 (47)	7 yrs 2 mos	
Abraham H. Cannon	Oct 1889 (30) - Jul 1896 (37)	6 yrs 9 mos	13 yrs 9 mos
*+Hyrum Smith	Sep 1837 (37) - Jun 1844 (44)	6 yrs 9 mos	
*John Smith	Sep 1837 (56) - Jun 1844 (62)	6 yrs 9 mos	
Abraham O. Woodruff	Oct 1897 (24) - Jun 1904 (31)	6 yrs 8 mos	
Charles W. Nibley	May 1925 (76) - Dec 1931 (82)	6 yrs 7 mos	24 yrs
Sylvester Q. Cannon	Apr 1938 (60) - May 1943 (65)	5 yrs 1 mo	18 yrs
Adam S. Bennion	Apr 1953 (66) - Feb 1958 (71)	4 yrs 10 mos	
Frederick G. Williams	Mar 1833 (45) - Nov 1837 (50)	4 yrs 8 mos	
*#John Willard Young	Apr 1873 (28) - Aug 1877 (32)	4 yrs 4 mos	18 yrs 6 mos
Thorpe B. Isaacson	Oct 1965 (67) - Jan 1970 (71)	4 yrs 3 mos	23 yrs 1 mo
• Dieter F. Uchtdorf	Oct 2004 (63) - present	4 yrs	14 yrs 6 mos
• David A. Bednar	Oct 2004 (52) - present	4 yrs	
Thomas B. Marsh	Apr 1835 (35) - Mar 1839 (39)	3 yrs 11 mos	
David W. Patten	Feb 1835 (35) - Oct 1838 (38)	3 yrs 8 mos	
William E. M'Lellin	Feb 1835 (29) - May 1838 (32)	3 yrs 3 mos	
William Law	Jan 1841 (31) - Apr 1844 (34)	3 yrs 3 mos	
Luke Johnson	Feb 1835 (27) - Apr 1838 (30)	3 yrs 2 mos	
Lyman E. Johnson	Feb 1835 (23) - Apr 1838 (26)	3 yrs 2 mos	
*Joseph Smith Sr.	Sep 1837 (66) - Sep 1840 (69)	3 yrs	6 yrs 9 mos
Jedediah M. Grant	Apr 1854 (38) - Dec 1856 (40)	2 yrs 8 mos	11 yrs
John F. Boynton	Feb 1835 (23) - Sep 1837 (25)	2 yrs 7 mos	
Alonzo A. Hinckley	Oct 1934 (64) - Dec 1936 (66)	2 yrs 2 mos	
Alvin R. Dyer	Apr 1968 (65) - Jan 1970 (67)	1 yr 9 mos	18 yrs 5 mos
• Quentin L. Cook	Oct 2007 (67) - present	1 yr	12 yrs 6 mos
• D. Todd Christofferson	Apr 2008 (63) - present	6 mos	15 yrs 6 mos

Bold Face denotes Church president.

• Currently serving.

†Includes service in the First Council of the Seventy, Assistants to the Twelve, First and Second Quorums of the Seventy, Presiding Bishopric, or as Church Patriarch.

* Served as assistant counselor in the First Presidency.

Served in the First Presidency under Brigham Young; after President Young's death sustained as counselor to Twelve Apostles.

+ Served as Assistant President of the Church

See **GROWTH OF CHURCH** chart on page 325.

GENERAL OFFICERS OF THE CHURCH
SUNDAY SCHOOL

T hough a few small Sunday School groups met regularly in Latter-day Saint communities before the Saints' westward exodus, Sunday School did not begin as a Church institution until after their arrival in the Salt Lake Valley in 1847.

Richard Ballantyne was a convert to the Church who, as a Presbyterian in his native Scotland, had organized a Sunday School. In Salt Lake City, disturbed by observing the children at play on the Sabbath day, he saw the need for a Sunday School.

In May 1849, he began plans to start a Sunday School. He built a structure on the northeast corner of 100 West and 300 South streets in Salt Lake City to serve both as his home and a place to hold a Sunday School. A monument on that corner today (now 200 West) commemorates the location of the first Sunday School, which was held Dec. 9, 1849, and involved 50 children. The following year, a meetinghouse was built for the Salt Lake 14th Ward, in which Brother Ballantyne was second counselor in the bishopric. An expanded Sunday School was moved into the new building and divided into a number of smaller classes, with additional teachers and two assistant superintendents.

Other wards in the valley and elsewhere followed the example of Brother Ballantyne and started Sunday Schools. They were somewhat autonomous, devising their own curricula and having their own administration, but functioning under the direction of the ward bishop.

With the coming of Johnston's Army to Utah, the Sunday School movement was suspended as many of the Saints moved south, but with the lessening of tensions in 1860, the Sunday School was resumed. By 1870, more than 200 Sunday Schools had been formed.

On Nov. 11, 1867, the Deseret Sunday School Union was organized by interested Church leaders, including President Brigham Young. Elder George Q. Cannon of the Quorum of the Twelve became the first general superintendent of the Sunday School. Its functions were to determine lesson topics and source materials and to address topics of punctuality, grading, prizes and rewards, recording and increasing attendance, music, elementary catechism, and libraries. The general Sunday School fostered uniformity in the theretofore disparate and independent Sunday Schools in the Church.

In 1866, prior to formation of the general Sunday School, a publication called the *Juvenile Instructor* was founded privately by Elder Cannon who also served as editor. It featured material on the scriptures, musical compositions and aids to gospel instruction. The publication became the official voice of the Deseret Sunday School Union, which purchased it from the Cannon family in January 1901. In 1929, the name was changed to the *Instructor*. It was discontinued in 1970 when the Church magazine structure was changed.

In early 1877, the sacrament was instituted as part of Sunday School. The practice continued until 1980, when Sunday meetings were consolidated into a three-hour block, with sacrament administered only during sacrament meeting.

The Deseret Sunday School Union continued to grow through the 1900s. Stake Sunday School superintendencies were designated to supervise ward Sunday Schools. General meetings of the Sunday School were held twice a year in connection with general conference. Five new classes for older children and youth were added in the early 1900s, followed shortly by the introduction of adult classes.

A Sunday School general board was introduced in the 1870s. In the 1900s, it was expanded and members traveled extensively to provide advice and support for local programs.

An effort in 1971 to correlate all Church functions under priesthood leadership affected the Sunday School. Dynamic changes followed, including centralized curriculum planning and writing, and an eight-year cycle of scripture instruction (later shortened to four years) for adult classes, focusing in turn on the Old Testament and Pearl of Great Price, the New Testament, the Book of Mormon, and the Doctrine and Covenants and Church History. Later, the size of the general board was reduced, and stake boards were discontinued.

On June 25, 1972, with Russell M. Nelson as presiding officer of the Sunday School, the title was changed from superintendent to president, and the title of assistants to counselors.

With the introduction of the consolidated meeting schedule in 1980, children's Sunday

School classes were discontinued, that function being filled by the Primary. In recent years, Sunday School curriculum for adults has included a Gospel Doctrine class and additional classes on Gospel Essentials, family history, and family relations.

A modified Church curriculum implemented Jan. 1, 1995, provided that classes for youth ages 14-18 study the scriptures using the Gospel Principles or Gospel Doctrine courses of study. Under the modified plan, youth ages 12-13 on alternate years study presidents of the Church and preparing for exaltation.

Throughout 1999, the Church observed the sesquicentennial of the Sunday School program by opening the 1949 centennial box and putting together a bicentennial box, the latter representative of a global Sunday School program. The new bicentennial box will be opened in 2049. The Museum of Church History and Art held a yearlong exhibit, "Sunday School: 150 Years of Teaching the Gospel," which opened July 6, 1998. Attending the reception were former members of the1949 Deseret Sunday School Union General Board who had watched the centennial box closed 50 years earlier.

An administrative change in the general presidency of the Sunday School was announced at general conference April 3, 2004. Members of the Seventy were relieved from the responsibility of serving in auxiliary presidencies, and a new Sunday School general presidency, composed of non-General Authorities, was called. Members of the Seventy had served in the Sunday School general presidency since Oct. 6, 1979.

Sources: *Encyclopedia of Mormonism*; *Jubilee History of Latter-day Saints Sunday Schools*, published by the Deseret Sunday School Union; *Church News*, July 1, 1972; First Presidency letter to General Authorities and priesthood leaders, April 21, 1994; "Exhibit serves as beginning of Sunday School celebration," by Sarah Jane Weaver, *Church News*, July 11, 1998.

SUNDAY SCHOOL OFFICERS
(As of October 2008)

 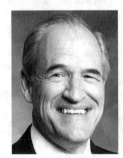 

| Daniel K. Judd | A. Roger Merrill | William D. Oswald |
| First Counselor | President | Second Counselor |

President – A. Roger Merrill, 3 Apr 2004 – present. Born in Salt Lake City, Utah, to Ariel Cardon and Edith Horsley Merrill, he grew up in Carmel, Calif.; served as an Area Authority Seventy, stake president and counselor, member of Melchizedek Priesthood General Committee, high councilor, bishop and branch president; senior consultant for a leadership training company and partner in own consulting firm; received bachelor's degree from BYU; wife, Rebecca Rippy Merrill; parents of seven children.

First Counselor – Daniel K. Judd, 3 Apr 2004 - present. Born in Kanab, Utah, to LeRoy P. and Phyllis Farnsworth Judd; served as stake president, bishop, ward mission leader and Young Men president; chairman of the Department of Ancient Scripture at BYU; received B.S. degree in zoology from Southern Utah University, M.S. degree in family science and Ph.D. in counseling psychology from BYU; wife, Kaye Seegmiller Judd; parents of four children.

Second Counselor – William D. Oswald, 3 Apr 2004 - present. Born in Salt Lake City, Utah, to William McKinley and Belle Davenport MacVichie Oswald; previously served as first counselor in the Sunday School general presidency and on the Sunday School general board, was president of the Russia Vladivostok Mission, regional representative, bishop and branch president; attorney; received bachelor's degree in history and juris doctorate from University of Utah; wife, Mavis Morris Oswald; parents of six children.

1. Superintendent, George Q. Cannon (as apostle, counselor in First Presidency) - Nov 1867-Apr 1901. See photo, FIRST COUNSELORS IN THE FIRST PRESIDENCY, No. 5.

First Assistants, George Goddard - Jun 1872-Jan 1899; Karl G. Maeser - Jan 1899-Feb 1901.

Second Assistants, John Morgan - Jun 1883-Jul 1894; Karl G. Maeser - Jul 1894-Jan 1899; George Reynolds - Jan 1899-May 1901.

2. Superintendent, Lorenzo Snow (as president of the Church) - May 1901-Oct 1901. See photo, PRESIDENTS OF THE CHURCH, No. 5.

First Assistant, George Reynolds - May 1901-Oct 1901.

Second Assistant, Jay M. Tanner - May 1901-Oct 1901.

3. Superintendent, Joseph F. Smith (as president of the Church) - Nov 1901-Nov 1918. See photo, PRESIDENTS OF THE CHURCH, No. 6.

First Assistants, George Reynolds - Nov 1901-May 1909, David O. McKay (as apostle) - May 1909-Nov 1918.

Second Assistants, Jay M. Tanner - Nov 1901-April 1906; David O. McKay (as apostle) - Jan 1907-May 1909; Stephen L Richards - May 1909-Nov 1918.

4. Superintendent, David O. McKay (as apostle) - Dec 1918-Oct 1934. See photo, PRESIDENTS OF THE CHURCH, No. 9.

First Assistant, Stephen L Richards (as apostle) - Dec 1918-Oct 1934.

Second Assistant, George D. Pyper - Dec 1918-Oct 1934.

5. Superintendent, George D. Pyper - Oct 1934-Jan 1943.

First Assistant, Milton Bennion - Oct 1934-May 1943.

Second Assistant, George R. Hill - Oct 1934-May 1943.

6. Superintendent, Milton Bennion - May 1943-Sep 1949.

First Assistant, George R. Hill - May 1943-Sep 1949.

Second Assistant, Albert Hamer Reiser - May 1943-Sep 1949.

7. Superintendent, George R. Hill - Sep 1949-Nov 1966.

First Assistants, Albert Hamer Reiser - Sep 1949-Oct 1952; David Lawrence McKay - Oct 1952-Nov 1966.

Second Assistants, David Lawrence McKay - Sep 1949-Oct 1952; Lynn S. Richards - Oct 1952-Nov 1966.

8. Superintendent, David Lawrence McKay - Nov 1966-Jun 1971.

First Assistant, Lynn S. Richards - Nov 1966-Jun 1971.

Second Assistant, Royden G. Derrick - Nov. 1966-Jun 1971.

9. President, Russell M. Nelson - Jun 1971-Oct 1979. See photo, current QUORUM OF THE TWELVE. (Note: titles changed from superintendent to president, and from assistants to counselors on June 25, 1972.)

First Counselors, Joseph B. Wirthlin - Jun 1971-Apr 1975, B. Lloyd Poelman - Apr 1975-Mar 1978; Joe J. Christensen - Mar 1978-Aug 1979; William D. Oswald - Aug 1979-Oct 1979.

Second Counselors, Richard L. Warner - Jun 1971-Apr 1975; Joe J. Christensen - Apr 1975-Mar 1978; William D. Oswald - May 1978-Aug 1979; J. Hugh Baird - Aug 1979-Oct 1979.

(From Oct. 6, 1979, to April 3, 2004, the general presidency of the Sunday School was composed of members of the Seventy.)

10. **President**, Hugh W. Pinnock - Oct 1979-Aug 1986. See photo, PRESIDENCY OF THE SEVENTY, No. 20.

First Counselors, Ronald E. Poelman - Oct 1979-Jul 1981; Robert D. Hales - Jul 1981-Jul 1985; Adney Y. Komatsu - Jul 1985-Aug 1986.

Second Counselors, Jack H Goaslind Jr. - Oct 1979-Jul 1981; James M. Paramore - Jul 1981-Jan 1983; Loren C. Dunn - Jan 1983-Jul 1985; Ronald E. Poelman - Jul 1985-Aug 1986.

11. **President**, Robert L. Simpson - Aug 1986-30 Sep 1989. See photo, FIRST QUORUM OF THE SEVENTY, No. 18.

First Counselors, Adney Y. Komatsu - Aug 1986-Aug. 1987; Devere Harris - Aug 1987-30 Sep 1989.

Second Counselors, A. Theodore Tuttle - Aug 1986-Nov 1986; Devere Harris - Jan 1987-Aug 1987; Phillip T. Sonntag - Aug 1987-Aug 1988; Derek A. Cuthbert - Aug 1988-30 Sep 1989.

12. **President**, Hugh W. Pinnock - 30 Sep 1989-15 Aug 1992. See photo, PRESIDENCY OF THE SEVENTY, No. 20.

First Counselors, Derek A. Cuthbert - 15 Aug 1988-1 Jan 1991; H. Verlan Andersen - 1 Jan 1991-5 Oct 1991; Hartman Rector Jr. - 5 Oct 1991-15 Aug 1992.

Second Counselors, Ted E. Brewerton - 30 Sep 1989-1 Oct 1990; H. Verlan Andersen - 6 Oct 1990-1 Jan 1991; Rulon G. Craven - 1 Jan 1991-5 Oct 1991; Clinton L. Cutler - 5 Oct 1991-15 Aug 1992.

13. **President**, Merlin R. Lybbert - 15 Aug 1992-15 Aug 1994. See photo, SECOND QUORUM OF THE SEVENTY, No. 35.

First Counselor, Clinton L. Cutler - 15 Aug 1992-April 9, 1994.

Second Counselor, Ronald E. Poelman - 15 Aug 1992-15 Aug 1994.

14. **President,** Charles Didier, 15 Aug 1994 – 30 Sep 1995. See photo, current FIRST QUORUM OF THE SEVENTY.

First Counselor, J Ballard Washburn - 15 Aug 1994-30 Sep 1995.

Second Counselor, F. Burton Howard - 15 Aug 1994-30 Sep 1995.

15. **President**, Harold G. Hillam, 30 Sep 1995 – 7 Oct 2000. See photo, PRESIDENCY OF THE SEVENTY, No. 31.

First Counselors, F. Burton Howard, 30 Sep 1995 - 4 Oct 1997; Glenn L. Pace, 4 Oct 1997 - 3 Oct 1998; Neil L. Andersen, 3 Oct 1998 - 7 Oct 2000.

Second Counselors, Glenn L. Pace, 30 Sep 1995 - 4 Oct 1997; Neil L. Andersen, 4 Oct 1997 - 3 Oct 1998; John H. Groberg, 3 Oct 1998 - 7 Oct 2000.

16. **President,** Marlin K. Jensen - 7 Oct 2000-6 Oct 2001. See photo, current FIRST QUORUM OF THE SEVENTY.

First Counselor, Neil L. Andersen - 7 Oct 2000-6 Oct 2001.

Second Counselor, John H. Groberg - 7 Oct 2000-6 Oct 2001.

17. **President,** Cecil O. Samuelson - 6 Oct 2001-5 Apr 2003. See photo, current FIRST QUORUM OF THE SEVENTY.

First Counselor, John H. Groberg - 6 Oct 2001 - 5 Apr 2003.

Second Counselor, Richard J. Maynes - 6 Oct 2001 - 5 Oct 2002; Val R. Christensen - 5 Oct 2002 - 5 Apr 2003.

18. **President**, Merrill J. Bateman - 5 Apr 2003-3 Apr 2004. See photo, PRESIDENCY OF THE SEVENTY, NO. 41.

First Counselor, John H. Groberg - 5 Apr 2003 - 3 Apr 2004.

Second Counselor, Val R. Christensen, 5 Apr 2003 - 3 Apr 2004.

YOUNG MEN

The Young Men organization has been significantly streamlined and simplified since its inception in 1875 as the Young Men's Mutual Improvement Association. The YMMIA was established by President Brigham Young, who called Junius F. Wells to organize Mutual Improvement Associations in wards throughout the Church, under the direction of ward superintendencies. It was intended that the YMMIA help young men develop spiritually and intellectually and provide supervised recreational opportunities. Today, its primary purpose is furthering the work of the Aaronic Priesthood.

On June 10, 1875, Brother Wells called a meeting in the 13th Ward chapel in Salt Lake City and the first ward YMMIA was organized.

In the fall of 1875, John Henry Smith, Milton H. Hardy, and B. Morris Young were called by the First Presidency to assist Brother Wells in visiting the settlements of the Saints and promoting the YMMIA. By April 1876, there were 57 ward YMMIAs in existence with a membership of about 1,200 youth. That same year, a YMMIA central committee was formed with Brother Wells as president. The committee later became the General Board of the YMMIA, which has continued through the years and is now known as the Young Men General Board.

From 1876 to 1905, young men were called to serve YMMIA missions to increase membership and assist local superintendencies. Initially, all of the young men met together regardless of age. Later, the YMMIA adopted four grades or classes: Scouts (ages 12-14), Vanguards (15-16), M Men (17-23), and Adults. As the programs developed and as needs of the youth changed, further refinements were made to the class structure. Today, Young Men classes correspond with the deacons, teachers, and priests quorums in the Aaronic Priesthood.

In October 1879, the monthly *Contributor* was launched with Brother Wells as editor. It served as the publication of the YMMIA until October 1899, at which time the publication of the *Improvement Era* was begun by the General Board.

The YMMIA met separately from the Young Women's Mutual Improvement Association (YWMIA) until around 1900 when the two joined to form the Mutual Improvement Association (called MIA or Mutual).

In 1913, the Church formed a formal partnership with Boy Scouts of America and was granted a national charter on May 21 of that year. Scouting exists today as a major component of the Young Men organization to help accomplish the purposes of the Aaronic Priesthood and to complement Sunday quorum instruction. Besides its partnership with BSA, the Church has established affiliations with other national Scouting organizations throughout the world whose programs, values, goals, and ideals are compatible with those of the Church.

In addition to Scouting, YMMIA activities in the early and mid-1900s included sports, dance, drama, and music. Athletics became a major part of the program, and stake tournament winners progressed to the All-Church tournaments in Salt Lake City, which were discontinued in the early 1970s.

In the mid-1900s, the general-level organization consisted of a superintendency of five men and a general board of 60 to 70 men. The general level was supported by a general fund, paid into by stakes based on YMMIA membership, sale of YMMIA materials, and investments. Besides planning and organizing major sports and cultural events, general board members would regularly travel with General Authorities and provide training for local YMMIA leaders.

In the 1960s under priesthood correlation, responsibility for training shifted to local priesthood leaders, the general fund was discontinued, production and sale of materials were centralized, and the size and scope of the general superintendency and board were greatly reduced.

On June 25, 1972, the title of the presiding officers of the YMMIA and Sunday School were changed from superintendent to president, and the title of assistants to counselors "to more closely define the relationship between the two auxiliaries with the functions of the priesthood," according to President Harold B. Lee, then first counselor in the First Presidency.

The Aaronic Priesthood-MIA was organized Nov. 9, 1972, with efforts centering more fully around the Aaronic Priesthood quorums. In June 1974, the name Aaronic Priesthood-MIA was shortened to Aaronic Priesthood and conducted under the direction of the Presiding Bishopric. In May 1977, the name was changed to Young Men and a general presidency was reinstated. In October 1979, it was announced that the Young Men general presidency would be comprised of three members of the Seventy. Since 1989, the general board has been comprised of less than a dozen men who continue to assist the presidency with curriculum development and Aaronic Priesthood and Scouting training.

On Sept. 28, 2001, the First Presidency announced a new program, "Aaronic Priesthood: Fulfilling Our Duty to God," for which were introduced three guidebooks, one each for deacons, teachers and priests, that explain the program and outline steps to earning the Duty to God Award. The Aaronic Priesthood Duty to God program, implemented in the United States and Canada in January 2002, is designed to help young men prepare for the Melchizedek Priesthood, the temple endowment, a full-time mission, marriage and fatherhood. At the same time, the First Presidency also announced an updated, simplified Young Women Personal Progress Program, which mirrors the values of the new Duty to God program. Both programs are based on standards set forth in an updated For the Strength of Youth guidebook.

An administrative change in the general presidency of the Young Men was announced at general conference April 3, 2004. Members of the Seventy were relieved from the responsibility of serving in auxiliary presidencies, and a new Young Men general presidency, composed of non-General Authorities, was called. Members of the Seventy had served in the Young Men general presidency since Oct. 6, 1979.

Sources: *Encyclopedia of Mormonism; Encyclopedic History of the Church* by Andrew Jenson, p. 969; *Church News*, July 1, 1972, May 3, 1997; "Program will improve their lives," by Jason Swensen, *Church News*, Oct. 27, 2001.

YOUNG MEN OFFICERS
(As of October 2008)

| **Dean R. Burgess** | **Charles W. Dahlquist II** | **Michael A. Neider** |
| First Counselor | President | Second Counselor |

President – Charles W. Dahlquist II, 3 Apr 2004 – present. Born in Provo, Utah, to C. Winston and Afton Ahlander Dahlquist, spent his childhood in Boise, Idaho; served as president of the Germany Hamburg Mission, stake president and counselor, high councilor, Young Single Adult branch president, ward Young Men president and Scoutmaster; attorney; received bachelor's degree from BYU and juris doctorate from University of Utah; wife, Zella Darley Dahlquist; parents of five daughters.

First Counselor – Dean R. Burgess, 3 Apr 2004 - present. Born in Alpine, Utah, to Reid and Ethel King Burgess, spent his early years in Alpine, Utah; served as president of the Brazil Belo Horizonte East Mission, counselor in stake presidency, stake Young Men presidency, bishop and high councilor; construction supervisor and home builder; received degree in business management from BYU; wife, Annette Christensen Burgess; parents of five children.

Second Counselor – Michael A. Neider, 3 Apr 2004 - present. Born in Pocatello, Idaho, to H. Boyd and Donna Hansen Neider, grew up in Tyhee, Idaho; served as counselor in Utah Salt Lake City South Mission presidency, stake president, stake Young Men president, bishop, ward mission leader and Scoutmaster; attorney and owner of construction-materials manufacturing business; received bachelor's and law degrees from BYU; wife, Rosemary Curtis Neider; parents of eight children.

HISTORICAL LISTING OF GENERAL SUPERINTENDENCIES AND PRESIDENCIES OF THE YOUNG MEN'S MUTUAL IMPROVEMENT ASSOCIATION AND YOUNG MEN

(Presidents, superintendents pictured)

1. **Superintendent**, Junius F. Wells - 1876-1880.

First Counselor, M. H. Hardy.

Second Counselor, Rodney C. Badger.

2. **Superintendent**, Wilford Woodruff (as apostle, president of the Church) - 1880-1898. See photo, PRESIDENTS OF THE CHURCH, No. 4.

First Assistant, Joseph F. Smith.

Second Assistant, Moses Thatcher.

3. **Superintendent**, Lorenzo Snow (as president of the Church) - 1898-1901. See photo, PRESIDENTS OF THE CHURCH, No. 5.

First Assistant, Joseph F. Smith.

Second Assistant, Heber J. Grant.

Assistant, B. H. Roberts.

4. **Superintendent**, Joseph F. Smith (as president of the Church) - 1901-1918. See photo, PRESIDENTS OF THE CHURCH, No. 6.

First Assistant, Heber J. Grant.

Second Assistant, B. H. Roberts.

5. **Superintendent**, Anthony W. Ivins (as apostle) - 1918-1921. See photo, FIRST COUNSELORS IN THE FIRST PRESIDENCY, No. 10.

First Assistant, B. H. Roberts

Second Assistant, Richard R. Lyman.

6. **Superintendent**, George Albert Smith (as apostle — 1921-1935. See photo, PRESIDENTS OF THE CHURCH, No. 8.

First Assistant, B. H. Roberts.

Second Assistants, Richard R. Lyman; Melvin J. Ballard.

7. **Superintendent**, Albert E. Bowen - 1935-1937. See photo, QUORUM OF THE TWELVE, No. 59.

First Assistant, George Q. Morris.

Second Assistant, Franklin West.

8. **Superintendent**, George Q. Morris - 1937-1948. See photo, QUORUM OF THE TWELVE, No. 72.

First Assistants, Joseph J. Cannon; John D. Giles.

Second Assistants, Burton K. Farnsworth; Lorenzo H. Hatch.

9. **Superintendent**, Elbert R. Curtis - 1948-1958.

First Assistant, A. Walter Stevenson.

Second Assistants, Ralph W. Hardy; David S. King.

10. **Superintendent**, Joseph T. Bentley - 2 Jul 1958-6 Oct 1962.

First Assistants, Alvin R. Dyer - 2 Jul 1958-6 Dec 1958; G. Carlos Smith - 6 Dec 1958-9 Jun 1961; Marvin J. Ashton, 9 Jun 1961-6 Oct 1962.

Second Assistants, Marvin J. Ashton - 6 Dec 1958-9 Jun 1961; Verl F. Scott, 9 Jun 1961-4 Oct 1961; Carl W. Buehner, 25 Oct 1961-Oct 1962.

11. **Superintendent**, G. Carlos Smith - 6 Oct 1962-17 Sep 1969.

First Assistant, Marvin J. Ashton - 6 Oct 1962-17 Sep 1969.

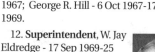

Second Assistants, Carl W. Beuhner - 6 Oct 1962-Oct 1967; George R. Hill - 6 Oct 1967-17 Sep 1969.

12. **Superintendent**, W. Jay Eldredge - 17 Sep 1969-25 Jun 1972.

First Assistants, George R. Hill - 17 Sep 1969-24 Jun 1972.

Second Assistant, George I. Cannon - 17 Sep 1969-25 Jun 1972.

13. **President**, W. Jay Eldredge - 25 Jun 1972-9 Nov 1972 (see photo above).

First Counselor, George I. Cannon - 25 Jun 1972-9 Nov 1972.

Second Counselor, Robert L. Backman, 25 Jun 1972-9 Nov 1972.

AARONIC PRIESTHOOD MIA

14. President, Robert L. Backman - 9 Nov 1972-23 Jun 1974. See photo, PRESIDENCY OF THE SEVENTY, No. 18.

First Counselor, LeGrand R. Curtis - 9 Nov 1972-23 Jun 1974.

Second Counselor, Jack H Goaslind Jr. - 9 Nov 1972-23 Jun 1974.

Note: On June 23, 1974, the Aaronic Priesthood MIA was dissolved and was replaced by the Aaronic Priesthood and the Young Women directly under the stewardship of the Presiding Bishop. In April 1977, it was renamed the Young Men, and both it and the Young Women came under the direction of the Priesthood Department.

YOUNG MEN

15. President, Neil D. Schaerrer - 7 Apr 1977-Oct 1979.

First Counselor, Graham W. Doxey - 7 Apr 1977-Oct 1979.

Second Counselor, Quinn G. McKay - 7 Apr 1977-Oct 1979

From Oct. 6, 1979, to April 3, 2004, the general presidency of the Young Men was composed of members of the Seventy.

16. President, Robert L. Backman Oct 1979-Nov 1985. See photo, PRESIDENCY OF THE SEVENTY, No. 18.

First Counselor, Vaughn J Featherstone - Oct 1979-Nov 1985.

Second Counselor, Rex D. Pinegar - Oct 1979-Nov 1985.

17. President, Vaughn J Featherstone - Nov 1985-6 Oct 1990. See photo, FIRST QUORUM OF THE SEVENTY, No. 36.

First Counselors, Rex D. Pinegar - Nov 1985-30 Sep 1989; Jeffrey R. Holland - 30 Sep 1989-6 Oct 1990.

Second Counselors, Robert L. Simpson - Nov 1985-15 Aug 1986; Hartman Rector Jr. - 15 Aug 1986-Oct 1988; Robert B Harbertson, Oct 1988-30 Sep 1989; Monte J. Brough, 30 Sep 1989-6 Oct 1990.

18. President, Jack H Goaslind - 6 Oct 1990-3 Oct 1998. See photo, PRESIDENCY OF THE SEVENTY, No. 17.

First Counselors, LeGrand R. Curtis -6 Oct 1990-5 Oct 1991; Robert K. Dellenbach - 5 Oct 1991-3 Oct 1992; Stephen D. Nadauld - 3 Oct 1992-5 Oct 1996; Vaughn J Featherstone - 5 Oct 1996-17 May 1997; F. David Stanley - 17 May 1997-4 Oct 1997; Robert K. Dellenbach - 4 Oct 1997-3 Oct 1998.

Second Counselors, Robert K. Dellenbach, 6 Oct 1990-5 Oct 1991; Stephen D. Nadauld - 5 Oct 1991-30 Oct 1992; L. Lionel Kendrick - 3 Oct 1992-15 Aug 1993; Vaughn J Featherstone -15 Aug 1993-5 Oct 1996; F. David Stanley - 5 Oct 1996-17 May 1997; Robert K. Dellenbach - 17 May 1997-4 Oct 1997; F. Melvin Hammond - 4 Oct 1997-3 Oct 1998.

19. President, Robert K. Dellenbach – 3 Oct 1998 – 6 Oct 2001. See photo, FIRST QUORUM OF THE SEVENTY, No. 96.

First Counselor, F. Melvin Hammond - 3 Oct 1998-6 Oct 2001.

Second Counselor, John M. Madsen - 3 Oct 1998-6 Oct 2001.

20. President, F. Melvin Hammond – 6 Oct 2001 – 3 Apr 2004. See photo, FIRST QUORUM OF THE SEVENTY, No. 99.

First Counselor, Glenn L. Pace - 6 Oct 2001 - 4 Oct 2003; Lynn G. Robbins - 4 Oct 2003 - 3 Apr 2004.

Second Counselor, Spencer J. Condie - 6 Oct 2001 - 4 Oct 2003; Donald L Hallstrom - 4 Oct 2003 - 3 Apr 2004.

PRIMARY

Noting the rough and careless behavior of the boys in her Farmington, Utah, neighborhood, Aurelia Spencer Rogers asked, "What will our girls do for good husbands, if this state of things continues?" Then she asked, "Could there not be an organization for little boys, and have them trained to make better men?"

The answer was, "Yes." With the approval of President John Taylor, the encouragement of Relief Society general president Eliza R. Snow, and after receiving a calling from her bishop, Sister Rogers began planning for the first meeting of the Primary Association, and it was an overwhelming success. On Sunday, Aug. 25, 1878, she stood at the entrance to the meetinghouse and welcomed 224 boys and girls to Primary. Girls were invited because Sister Rogers thought they could help with the singing that she believed necessary. During the first meeting, Sister Rogers instructed the children to be obedient and to be kind to one another.

During the next decade, the Primary Association was organized in almost every LDS settlement. During one trip through Southern Utah, Sister Snow and her first counselor in the Relief Society presidency, Zina Young, organized 35 Primaries.

From its beginning, Primary included songs, poetry, and activities. The boys wore uniforms to the meetings. All the children met together during the first 10 years. After that, they were divided into age groups.

Sister Louie B. Felt was called as the first general president of the Primary in 1880, but the Relief Society continued to take the responsibility for organizing Primaries. Sister Felt and other general officers began taking more responsibility for Primary development after 1890.

Serving as Primary general president for 45 years, Sister Felt oversaw many developments in the organization. In 1902, publication of the *Children's Friend* magazine began. In 1913, the Primary began contributing to pediatric hospital care. That program was culminated in 1952 with the completion of the Primary Children's Hospital in Salt Lake City. Contributions from Primary children helped support the hospital.

Beginning in 1929 when the Primary took over more responsibility for the spiritual training of children, lessons were planned for three weeks of the month and an activity on the fourth week. The Cub Scout program became the responsibility of the Primary in 1952.

Primary meetings were held midweek until the Church instituted the consolidated meeting plan in 1980. Then it replaced Junior Sunday School for providing Sunday religious instruction for children ages 3 to 11. The Primary meets for one hour and forty minutes of the three-hour meeting block, dividing the time between group meetings, classroom instruction, and sharing time. Athough women continue to serve exclusively in Primary presidencies, men are also called to teach classes. Weekday activities are held on a quarterly basis.

Yearly, usually in September or October, ward and branch Primaries throughout the Church present the Children's Sacrament Meeting Presentation, during which the children share, through song and the spoken word, what they have learned during the year.

In April 2003, the First Presidency announced a new Faith in God for Girls and Faith in God for Boys program. The program, for children ages 8 through 11, was implemented in the United States and Canada July 1, 2003, and implemented internationally in 2004.

The new program replaces the Gospel in Action award and Achievement Days and alters what has been known as the Cub Scout Faith in God Award. As part of the program, the Church published Faith in God guidebooks for boys and girls, which are designed to help boys prepare for the Aaronic Priesthood and girls to become righteous young women.

Sources: *Sisters and Little Saints*, by Carol Cornwall Madsen and Susan Oman; *Encyclopedia of Mormonism*; *Church News*.

PRIMARY GENERAL PRESIDENCY
(As of October 2008)

Margaret S. Lifferth	**Cheryl C. Lant**	**Vicki F. Matsumori**
First Counselor	President	Second Counselor

President – Cheryl Clark Lant, April 2, 2005 – present. Born in Manti, Utah, to Charles Verl and Vivian Keller Clark; studied human development and family relations at BYU; served on the Primary general board and was stake and ward Primary president, counselor in stake Relief Society presidency, ward Young Women president and counselor, and ward Relief Society president and counselor; co-founder and co-owner with her husband of a private school for children and co-founder and developer of a phonics-based beginning reading program; married John Lant; parents of nine children.

First Counselor – Margaret Swensen Lifferth, April 2, 2005 – present. Born in Washington, D.C., to Albert D. and Jennie Romney Swensen; received bachelor's degree in English from BYU; former member of Primary general board, counselor in stake Relief Society presidency, ward Relief Society and Young Women president, counselor in ward Primary presidency and volunteer docent at the Museum of Church History and Art; served on elementary and high school PTA boards and on BYU Women's Conference Committee; married Dennis R. Lifferth; parents of seven children.

Second Counselor – Vicki Fujii Matsumori, April 2, 2005 – present. Born in Murray, Utah, to George Yasuyuki and Yoshie Matsumoto Fujii; received bachelor's degree in journalism with a teaching certificate from University of Utah; served on Primary general board, ward Primary, Young Women and Relief Society president, and Young Women counselor; taught junior high English and was an adjunct instructor at Salt Lake Community College; married Jim Reed Matsumori; parents of three children.

HISTORICAL LISTING OF GENERAL PRESIDENCIES
OF THE PRIMARY ASSOCIATION
(Presidents pictured)

1. **President**, Louie Bouton Felt, 19 Jun 1880-6 Oct 1925.

First Counselors, Matilda Morehouse W. Barratt - 19 Jun 1880-Oct 1888; Lillie Tuckett Freeze - Oct 1888-8 Dec 1905; May Anderson - 29 Dec 1905-6 Oct 1925.

Second Counselors, Clare Cordelia Moses Cannon - 19 Jun 1880-4 Oct 1895; Josephine Richards West - 15 Dec 1896-24 Nov 1905; Clara Woodruff Beebe - 29 Dec 1905-6 Oct 1925.

2. **President**, May Anderson - 6 Oct 1925-31 Dec 1939.

First Counselors, Sadie Grant Pack - 6 Oct 1925-11 Sep 1929; Isabelle Salmon Ross - 11 Sep 1929-31 Dec 1939.

Second Counselors, Isabelle Salmon Ross - 6 Oct 1925-11 Sep 1929; Edna Harker Thomas - 11 Sep 1929-11 Dec 1933; Edith Hunter Lambert - 11 Dec 1933-31 Dec 1939.

3. **President**, May Green Hinckley - 1 Jan 1940-2 May 1943.

First Counselor, Adele Cannon Howells - 1 Jan 1940-2 May 1943.

Second Counselors, Janet Murdock Thompson - 1 Jan 1940-May 1942; LaVern Watts Parmley - May 1942-2 May 1943.

4. **President**, Adele Cannon Howells - 20 Jul 1943-14 Apr 1951.

First Counselor, La-Vern Watts Parmley - 20 Jul 1943-14 Apr 1951.

Second Counselor, Dessie Grant Boyle - 20 Jul 1943-14 Apr 1951.

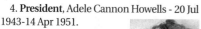

5. **President**, LaVern Watts Parmley - 16 May 1951-5 Oct 1974.

First Counselors, Arta Matthews Hale - 16 May 1951-6 Apr 1962; Leone Watson Doxey - 6 Apr 1962-23 Oct 1969; Lucile Cardon Reading - 8 Jan 1970-6 Aug 1970; Naomi Ward Randall - 4 Oct 1970-5 Oct 1974.

Second Counselors, Florence Holbrook Richards - 15 May 1951-11 Jun 1953; Leone Watson Doxey - 10 Sep 1953-6 Apr 1962; Eileen Robinson Dunyon - 6 Apr 1962-3 Jun 1963; Lucile Cardon Reading - 23 Jul 1963-8 Jan 1970; Florence Reece Lane - 8 Jan 1970-5 Oct 1974.

6. **President**, Naomi Maxfield Shumway - 5 Oct 1974-5 Apr 1980.

First Counselors, Sarah Broadbent Paulsen - 5 Oct 1974-2 Apr 1977; Colleen Bushman Lemmon - 2 Apr 1977-5 Apr 1980.

Second Counselors, Colleen Bushman Lemmon - 5 Oct 1974-2 Apr 1977; Dorthea Christiansen Murdock - 2 Apr 1977-5 Apr 1980.

7. **President**, Dwan Jacobsen Young - 5 Apr 1980-2 Apr 1988.

First Counselor, Virginia Beesley Cannon - 5 Apr 1980-2 Apr 1988.

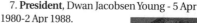

Second Counselor, Michaelene Packer Grassli - 5 Apr 1980-2 Apr 1988.

8. **President**, Michaelene Packer Grassli - 2 Apr 1988-1 Oct 1994.

First Counselor, Betty Jo Nelson Jepsen - 2 Apr 1988-1 Oct 1994.

Second Counselor, Ruth Broadbent Wright - 2 Apr 1988-1 Oct 1994.

9. **President**, Patricia P. Pinegar - 1 Oct 1994 - 2 Oct 1999.

First Counselor, Anne G. Wirthlin, 1 Oct 1994-2 Oct 1999.

Second Counselor, Susan L. Warner, 10 Oct 1994-2 Oct 1999.

10. **President,** Coleen K. Menlove – 2 Oct 1999 – 2 April 2005.

First Counselor, Sydney S. Reynolds – 2 Oct 1999 – 2 April 2005.

Second Counselor, Gayle M. Clegg – 2 Oct 1999 – 2 April 2005.

YOUNG WOMEN

President Brigham Young organized the Young Ladies Department of the Cooperative Retrenchment Association — predecessor to the Young Women program — on the evening of Nov. 28, 1869, in the parlor of the Lion House in Salt Lake City. He encouraged his older daughters, who were the charter members, to "retrench in your dress, in your tables, in your speech, wherein you have been guilty of silly, extravagant speeches and light-mindedness of thought. Retrench in everything that is bad and worthless, and improve in everything that is good and beautiful."

Thus, the Retrenchment Association was organized. Relief Society Gen. Pres. Eliza R. Snow supervised the association; Ella Young Empey was named as president.

News of the organization spread quickly. By the end of 1870, retrenchment associations had been established in several Mormon settlements. In addition, the organization had divided into senior and junior associations.

Not long after the creation of the Young Men's Mutual Improvement Association in 1875, President Young approved a name change to "Young Ladies National Mutual Improvement Association" to correspond to the young men's organization. The two organizations began holding monthly meetings together. In 1904, the word "National" was dropped since the Young Ladies' organization had become international in scope. Throughout the early years of the association's existence, the YLNMIA was directed through local ward efforts. The first stake board was organized in 1878 in the Salt Lake Stake, antedating the appointment of a general board. In 1880, Elmina S. Taylor was called as the first general president. She called as her counselors Margaret (Maggie) Y. Taylor and Martha (Mattie) Horne, with Louie Wells as secretary and Fanny Y. Thatcher as treasurer. That same year, Pres. Taylor presided over the first general conference of the YLNMIA.

New Young Women presidency sustained

A new Young Women general presidency was sustained in general conference on April 5, 2008. Elaine S. Dalton, who previously served as first and second counselor in the general presidency was called as Young Women president, succeeding Susan W. Tanner, who was released. Called as first counselor in the Young Women general presidency was Mary N. Cook, who previously served as second counselor. Ann M. Dibb, who was serving on the Young Women general board, was called as second counselor.

Under the new general presidency's direction, the association encouraged the study of gospel principles, development of individual talents, and service to those in need. General, stake, and ward boards were subsequently appointed, lesson manuals were produced, and joint activities were established with the YMMIA. The *Young Woman's Journal* began in 1889 and began printing a series of lessons.

In 1888, the first annual June Conference for young women and young men was held. Leaders provided special training in physical activity, story-telling, and music and class instruction.

Four decades later, in 1929, a new summer camping program was announced at June Conference, and the *Young Woman's Journal* and *The Improvement Era* merged with the November issue. During the 1930s, MIA leaders gave new emphasis to music, dance, and the performing arts, with an annual June Conference dance festival being held.

In the late 1940s and the 1950s, the First Presidency turned over to the YWMIA leaders a girls enrollment incentive program, previously administered by the Presiding Bishopric. It was designed to increase attendance at Church meetings.

In the early 1970s, President Harold B. Lee introduced a correlation program designed to integrate Church programs for youth. From this effort eventually came the Personal Progress program and the Young Womanhood Achievement Awards. During the 1980s, Sunday Young Women classes began meeting at the same time as priesthood meeting for Young Men.

During the tenure of general Pres. Ardeth G. Kapp, who served from 1984-1992, the Young Women motto, "Stand for Truth and Righteousness," was introduced, along with the Young Women logo, represented by a torch with the profile of the face of a young woman. The torch represents the light of Christ.

During Pres. Kapp's administration, the Young Women theme and values were also introduced. The values are faith, divine nature, individual worth, knowledge, choice and accountability, good works, and integrity.

A memorable event for the program is the Young Women Worldwide Celebration, held every three years. Another Young Women Worldwide Celebration was held in the year 2000, two years after the 1998 celebration, rather than the usual three years between celebrations. An exception was made for 2000 because it was the bimillennial commemoration of the Savior's birth.

An updated, simplified Young Women Personal Progress Program, which mirrors the values of the new Aaronic Priesthood Duty to God program, was implemented in the United States and Canada in January 2002. On Sept. 28, 2001, the First Presidency announced the updated Personal Progress Program, along with the new Duty to God program. Both programs are based on standards set forth in an updated For the Strength of Youth guidebook. The Young Women Personal Progress Program is designed to help girls prepare for the Young Womanhood Recognition Award. The Young Womanhood Recognition medallion was also updated to feature spires of the Salt Lake Temple in gold or silver.

Sources: *Encyclopedia of Mormonism*, vols. 3-4; *A Century of Sisterhood; History of the YWMIA*, by Marba C. Josephson; *Deseret News 1993-1994 Church Almanac; Church News*, Jan. 24, 1998, April 4, 1998;; "Stand as a witness," by Julie Dockstader Heaps, Church News, Dec. 2, 2000; "Personal Progress: temple preparation," by Julie Dockstader Heaps, *Church News*, Oct. 27, 2001.

YOUNG WOMEN GENERAL PRESIDENCY
(As of October 2008)

Mary N. Cook	Elaine S. Dalton	Ann M. Dibb
First Counselor	President	Second Counselor

President – Elaine S. Dalton, April 5, 2008 – present; previously served as first counselor from March 31, 2007, to April 5, 2008, and second counselor from Oct. 5, 2002, to March 31, 2007. Born in Ogden, Utah, to Melvin L. and Emma Martin Schwartz; received bachelor's degree in English from BYU; served as second counselor in Young Women general presidency until being sustained as first counselor March 31, 2007; former Young Women general board member, stake Young Women president, counselor and adviser; Young Single Adult Relief Society adviser and Relief Society instructor; married Stephen E. Dalton; parents of six children.

First Counselor – Mary N. Cook, April 5, 2008 – present; previously served as second counselor from March 31, 2007, to April 5, 2008. Born in Salt Lake City, Utah, to Kenneth N. and Fern Swan Nielsen; received bachelor's and master's degree in speech pathology and audiology, and Ed.S. degree from BYU; former member of Young Women general board, Relief Society president, Primary counselor, and served with her husband when he was in the Asia Area presidency as a member of the Second Quorum of the Seventy and when he presided over the Mongolia Ulaanbaatar Mission; former special education teacher, administrator and elementary school principal in Jordan (Utah) School District; married Richard E. Cook; he and his first wife, Clea, who died in 1984, had four children.

Second Counselor – Ann M. Dibb, April 5, 2008 – present. Born in Salt Lake City, Utah, to Thomas S. and Frances Johnson Monson; received bachelor's degree from BYU in elementary education; former Young Women general board member, Primary president, Young Women president, Relief Society counselor, and counselor in stake Young Women presidency; married Roger A. Dibb; parents of four children.

HISTORICAL LISTING OF GENERAL PRESIDENCIES OF YOUNG WOMEN'S MUTUAL IMPROVEMENT ASSOCIATION AND YOUNG WOMEN

(Presidents pictured)

1. **President**, Elmina Shepherd Taylor - 19 Jun 1880-6 Dec 1904.

First Counselors, Margaret Young Taylor - 19 Jun 1880-1887; Maria Young Dougall - 1887-6 Dec 1904.

Second Counselor, Martha Horne Tingey - 19 Jun 1880-6 Dec 1904.

2. **President**, Martha Horne Tingey - 5 Apr 1905-28 Mar 1929.

First Counselor, Ruth May Fox - 5 Apr 1905-28 Mar 1929.

Second Counselors, Mae Taylor Nystrom - 5 Apr 1905-15 Jul 1923; Lucy Grant Cannon, 15 Jul 1923-28 Mar 1929.

3. **President**, Ruth May Fox - 28 Mar 1929-Oct 1937.

First Counselor, Lucy Grant Cannon - 28 Mar 1929-Oct 1937.

Second Counselor, Clarissa A. Beesley - 30 Mar 1929-Oct 1937.

4. **President**, Lucy Grant Cannon - Nov 1937-6 Apr 1948.

First Counselors, Helen Spencer Williams - Nov 1937-17 May 1944; Verna Wright Goddard - Jul 1944-6 Apr 1948.

Second Counselors, Verna Wright Goddard - Nov 1937-Jul 1944; Lucy T. Anderson - 6 Jul 1944-6 Apr 1948.

5. **President**, Bertha Stone Reeder - 6 Apr 1948-30 Sep 1961.

First Counselor, Emily Higgs Bennett - 13 Jun 1948-30 Sep 1961.

Second Counselor, LaRue Carr Longden - 13 Jun 1948-30 Sep 1961.

6. **President**, Florence Smith Jacobsen - 30 Sep 1961-9 Nov 1972.

First Counselor, Margaret R. Jackson - 30 Sep 1961-9 Nov 1972.

Second Counselor, Dorothy Porter Holt - 30 Sep 1961-9 Nov 1972.

AARONIC PRIESTHOOD MIA
(YOUNG WOMEN)

7. **President**, Ruth Hardy Funk - 9 Nov 1972-23 Jun 1974.

First Counselor, Hortense Hogan Child - 9 Nov 1972-23 Jun 1974.

Second Counselor, Ardeth Greene Kapp - 9 Nov 1972-23 Jun 1974.

YOUNG WOMEN

8. **President**, Ruth Hardy Funk - 23 Jun 1974-12 Jul 1978.

First Counselor, Hortense Hogan Child - 23 Jun 1974-12 Jul 1978.

Second Counselor, Ardeth Greene Kapp - 23 Jun 1974-12 Jul 1978.

9. **President**, Elaine Anderson Cannon - 12 Jul 1978-7 Apr 1984.

First Counselor, Arlene Barlow Darger - 12 Jul 1978-7 Apr 1984.

Second Counselor, Norma Broadbent Smith - 12 Jul 1978-7 Apr 1984.

10. **President**, Ardeth Greene Kapp - 7 Apr 1984-4 Apr 1992.

First Counselors, Patricia Terry Holland - 11 May 1984-6 Apr 1986; Maurine Johnson Turley - 6 Apr 1986-4 Apr 1987; Jayne Broadbent Malan - 4 Apr 1987-4 Apr 1992.

Second Counselors, Maurine Johnson Tur-

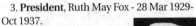

ley - 11 May 1984-6 Apr 1986; Jayne Broad-
bent Malan - 6 Apr 1986-4 Apr 1987; Elaine
Low Jack - 4 Apr 1987-31 Mar 1990; Janette
Callister Hales - 31 Mar 1990-4 Apr 1992.

11. President, Janette Hales Beckham - 4
Apr 1992-4 Oct 1997.

First Counselor, Virginia
Hinckley Pearce - 4 Apr
1992-4 Oct 1997.

Second Counselors, Patricia Peterson Pinegar - 4
Apr 1992-1 Oct 1994; Bon-
nie Dansie Parkin - 1 Oct
1994-5 Apr 1997; Carol Burdett Thomas - 5
Apr 1997-4 Oct 1997.

12. President, Margaret Dyreng Nadauld -
4 Oct 1997- 5 Oct 2002.

First Counselor, Carol
Burdett Thomas - 4 Oct
1997- 5 Oct 2002.

Second Counselor,
Sharon Greene Larson, - 4
Oct 1997- 5 Oct 2002.

13. President, Susan Winder Tanner – 5 Oct
2002 – 5 Apr 2008.

First Counselor, Julie
Bangerter Beck – 5 Oct 2002
– 31 Mar 2007; Elaine
Schwartz Dalton – 31 Mar
2007 – 5 Apr 2008.

Second Counselor, Elaine
Schwartz Dalton – 5 Oct
2002 – 31 Mar 2007; Mary Nielsen Cook – 31
Mar 2007 – 5 Apr 2008.

RELIEF SOCIETY

In 1842, a small group of women met at the home of Sarah M. Kimball in Nauvoo, Ill., to organize a sewing society to aid Nauvoo Temple workmen. They sought the endorsement of
the Prophet Joseph Smith, who praised their efforts but said the Lord had something better
in mind for them. It would be an organization under the priesthood after the pattern of the
priesthood. He organized the Female Relief Society on March 17, 1842. The Prophet said that
the restored Church could not be perfect or complete without it. He charged members with
the responsibility to save souls and taught them principles of the gospel. The women elected
Emma Smith as their president, and she selected two counselors.

From that original organization stemmed what is now the Relief Society, the official adult
women's organization of the Church. Its motto, "Charity Never Faileth," states what has been
the objective of society members from the first: to love and nurture one another and minister
to the needs of Church members and others. The Female Relief Society of Nauvoo contributed
to the Nauvoo Temple and supported moral reform. Members were primarily concerned with
helping the poor. In July 1843, a visiting committee of four was appointed in each ward to as-
sess needs and distribute necessities, the beginning of the visiting teaching effort that has
been a part of Relief Society since then. By 1844, the society had 1,341 members. The Female
Relief Society of Nauvoo ceased to function after March 1844 amid increasing tension.

Although women carried out charitable works and a few meetings were conducted at Winter
Quarters, Neb., there was no formal Relief Society during the Saints' westward trek or for several years thereafter.

In February 1854, 16 women responded to an exhortation of President Brigham Young to
form a society of females to make clothing for Indian women and children. This "Indian Relief
Society" met until June 1854, when President Young encouraged such organizations in individual wards. In 1866, President Young reorganized the Relief Society Churchwide, appointing
Eliza R. Snow to assist bishops in establishing the organization in each ward. By 1880, there
was a local unit of the Relief Society in each of 300 wards, caring for the needy within its ward
boundaries and using visiting teachers to collect and distribute donations. Ward Relief Soci-

eties managed their own finances and many built their own meeting halls. In line with the Church's move for self-sufficiency, the Relief Society sponsored cooperative economic enterprises in the late 1800s, such as making and marketing homemade goods, raising silk worms, storing grain, and financing the medical training of midwives and female doctors. The Relief Society also promoted women's right to vote and helped organize and nurture the Young Ladies' Retrenchment Association (forerunner to the Young Women) and the Primary.

By the turn of the 20th century, needs of women were changing, and the format of lessons was adapted and standardized to meet the needs. The *Relief Society Magazine*, introduced in 1915, contained lessons for each month on theological, cultural, and homemaking topics. The monthly format of rotating topics has remained since then, with various subject matter.

Beginning in 1921, concern over high maternal and infant mortality led to the establishment of health clinics and two stake Relief Society maternity hospitals, one operated in the Snowflake (Arizona) Stake and another in the Cottonwood (Utah) Stake. In 1944, visiting teachers ceased collecting charitable funds. After September 1971, all LDS women were automatically included as members of the Relief Society, rather than paying dues.

In 1956, the Relief Society Building in Salt Lake City, built from contributions from LDS women and funds from the Church, was dedicated. In the latter 20th Century, Relief Society became more fully coordinated under the larger Church structure.

The ward Relief Society president, under the direction of the bishop, has been responsible since 1921 for assessing needs and distributing relief to the needy. Ward Relief Society presidents supervise other charitable work such as caring for the sick, called "compassionate service" to distinguish it from "welfare service."

The Relief Society promoted scholarly study of women's concerns by helping establish the Women's Research Center at BYU, rallied members to contribute to the Monument to Women at Nauvoo, Ill., in 1978, and celebrated its sesquicentennial in 1992. A literacy effort, implemented in January 1993, was to teach basic gospel literacy skills.

Sources: *Encyclopedia of Mormonism*; *Women of Covenant: The Story of Relief Society*, by Jill Mulvay Derr, Janath Russell Cannon, and Maureen Ursenbach Beecher, Deseret Book, 1992; *Church News*, Jan. 30, 1993; "Strengthening the Work of Melchizedek Priesthood Quorums and Relief Society," *Church News*, Nov. 1, 1997; *Church News*, Oct. 1, 1999.

The First Relief Society Meeting

a painting by Lynde Mott, one of a series of paintings of women in Nauvoo.

RELIEF SOCIETY GENERAL PRESIDENCY
(As of October 2008)

Silvia H. Allred	**Julie B. Beck**	**Barbara Thompson**
First Counselor	President	Second Counselor

President — Julie B. Beck, March 31, 2007-present. Born in Salt Lake City, Utah, to Wm. Grant and Geraldine Hamblin Bangerter. Received bachelor's degree in family science from BYU; former first counselor in the Young Women general presidency; Young Women general board member; ward Young Women president, counselor and adviser; Primary president, counselor and teacher; stake Relief Society president's counselor; ward Relief Society teacher; PTA president and officer. Married Ramon P. Beck; parents of three children.

First counselor — Silvia Henriquez Allred, March 31, 2007-present. Born in San Salvador, El Salvador, to Carlos Florentino and Hilda Alvarenga Henriquez. Received teaching certificate in El Salvador, attended BYU and University of Arizona. Served with husband when he was president of the Dominican Republic Missionary Training Center and president of the Paraguay Asuncion Mission; former member of Young Women general board, stake Relief Society president and stake Primary president; PTA president in Argentina. Married Jeffry A. Allred; parents of eight children.

Second counselor — Barbara Thompson, March 31, 2007-present. Born in San Luis Obispo, Calif., to Wesley Peter and Fern Rymer Thompson. Received bachelor's degree in social work from BYU; master's degree from the University of Utah; former member of Relief Society general board, ward Young Women president, Relief Society counselor, Laurel and Beehive adviser, gospel doctrine teacher, and ward activities committee chairwoman. Serves as an official with Christmas Box International, a charity focused on abused and neglected children; executive director of an international assessment center for abused and neglected children.

HISTORICAL LISTING OF GENERAL PRESIDENCIES OF THE RELIEF SOCIETY
(Presidents pictured)

1. **President**, Emma Hale Smith - 17 Mar 1842-16 Mar 1844.

First Counselor, Sarah Marietta Kingsley Cleveland - 17 Mar 1842-16 Mar 1844.

Second Counselor, Elizabeth Ann Smith Whitney - 17 Mar 1842-16 Mar 1844.

2. **President**, Eliza Roxcy Snow - 1866-5 Dec 1887.

First Counselor, Zina Diantha Huntington Young - 19 Jun 1880-8 Apr 1888.

Second Counselor, Elizabeth Ann Smith Whitney - 19 Jun 1880-15 Feb 1882.

3. **President,** Zina Diantha Huntington Young - 8 Apr 1888-28 Aug 1901.

First Counselor, Jane Snyder Richards - 11 Oct 1888-10 Nov 1901.

Second Counselor, Bathsheba Wilson Smith - 11 Oct 1888-10 Nov 1901.

4. **President**, Bathsheba Wilson Smith - 10 Nov 1901-20 Sep 1910.

First Counselor, Annie Taylor Hyde - 10 Nov 1901-2 Mar 1909.

Second Counselor, Ida Smoot Dusenberry, 10 Nov 1901-20 Sep 1910.

5. **President**, Emmeline Woodward B. Wells - 3 Oct 1910-2 Apr 1921.

First Counselor, Clarissa Smith Williams - 3 Oct 1910-2 Apr 1921.

Second Counselor, Julina Lambson Smith - 3 Oct 1910-2 Apr 1921.

6. **President**, Clarissa Smith Williams - 2 Apr 1921-7 Oct 1928.

First Counselor, Jennie Brimhall Knight - 2 Apr 1921-7 Oct 1928.

Second Counselor, Louise Yates Robison - 2 Apr 1921-7 Oct 1928.

7. **President**, Louise Yates Robison - 7 Oct 1928-Dec 1939.

First Counselor, Amy Brown Lyman - 7 Oct 1928-Dec 1939.

Second Counselors, Julia Alleman Child - 7 Oct 1928-23 Jan 1935; Kate Montgomery Barker - 3 Apr 1935-31 Dec 1939.

8. **President**, Amy Brown Lyman - 1 Jan 1940-6 Apr 1945.

First Counselor, Marcia Knowlton Howells - Apr 1940-6 Apr 1945.

Second Counselors, Donna Durrant Sorensen, Apr 1940-12 Oct 1942; Belle Smith Spafford, 12 Oct 1942-6 Apr 1945.

9. **President**, Belle Smith Spafford - 6 Apr 1945-3 Oct 1974.

First Counselor, Marianne Clark Sharp - 6 Apr 1945-3 Oct 1974.

Second Counselor, Gertrude Ryberg Garff - 6 Apr 1945-30 Sep 1947; Velma Nebeker Simonsen - 3 Oct 1947-17 Dec 1956; Helen Woodruff Anderson - Jan 1957-Aug 1958; Louise Wallace Madsen - Aug 1958-3 Oct 1974.

10. **President**, Barbara Bradshaw Smith - 3 Oct 1974-7 Apr 1984.

First Counselors, Janath Russell Cannon - 3 Oct 1974-28 Nov 1978; Marian Richards Boyer - 28 Nov 1978-7 Apr 1984.

Second Counselors, Marian Richards Boyer - 3 Oct 1974-28 Nov 1978; Shirley Wilkes Thomas - 28 Nov 1978-24 Jun 1983; Ann Stoddard Reese, 1 Oct 1983-7 Apr 1984.

11. **President**, Barbara Woodhead Winder - 7 Apr 1984-31 Mar 1990.

First Counselor, Joy Frewin Evans - 21 May 1984-31 Mar 1990.

Second Counselor, Joanne Bushman Doxey - 21 May 1984-31 Mar 1990.

12. **President**, Elaine Low Jack - 31 Mar 1990-5 Apr 1997.

First Counselor, Chieko Nishimura Okazaki - 31 Mar 1990-5 Apr 1997.

Second Counselor, Aileen Hales Clyde - 31 Mar 1990-5 Apr 1997.

13. **President**, Mary Ellen Wood Smoot - 5 Apr 1997-6 Apr 2002.

First Counselor, Virginia Urry Jensen - 5 Apr 1997-6 Apr 2002.

Second Counselor, Sheri L. Dew - 5 Apr 1997-6 Apr 2002.

14. **President,** Bonnie Dansie Parkin - 6 Apr 2002-31 Mar 2007.

First Counselor, Kathleen Hurst Hughes, 6 Apr 2002-31 Mar 2007.

Second Counselor, Anne Clark Pingree, 6 Apr 2002-31 Mar 2007

WORLDWIDE CHURCH

AREAS OF THE WORLD

(Temples depictedl)

Africa Southeast Area

As of December 31, 2007

Membership: 118,312; Stakes: 20; Wards: 148; Missions: 9; Districts: 15; Branches: 226; Temples: 1; Headquarters: Johannesburg, South Africa.

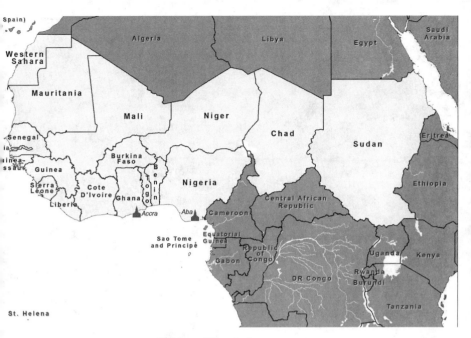

Africa West Area

As of December 31, 2007

Membership: 146,290; Stakes: 26; Wards: 188; Missions: 9; Districts: 23;
Branches: 220; Temples: 2; Headquarters: Accra, Ghana.

The Africa West Area is organized with boundaries of stakes and districts designed to bring the Church closer to the members and allow missionaries to baptize new converts who live within walking distance of the meetinghouse.

In 2008, two new stake centers were dedicated in Ghana: the Tema Ghana Stake and the Accra Ghana Stake; a new stake center was dedicated for the Abobo Cote D'Ivoire Stake; and the Accra Ghana McCarthy Hill Stake held it's second annual youth conference centered on the theme "succeeding in life."

The All-frica Service Project is a unique activity for members wherever the Church exists in Africa. Members contribute time, skill, and effort to improve their communities. In 2008, members in the Africa West Area provided service to orphanages, health clinics, hospitals, marketplaces, libraries, and senior citizen's residences, and at parks and on roadways. Caring for children, sweeping, mopping, painting, cleaning up litter, dusting, weeding, mowing, repairing, and in some cases building were among services preformed. It is evidence that "when we are in the service of our fellowmen, we are only in the service of our God."

The temples in Ghana and Nigeria have blessed the lives of many people. Twice a year, hundreds of adults and youth of the Ivory Coast Stakes attend the Ghana Accra Temple. They bring thousands of family names with them in order to perform proxy ordinances for their deceased family members. When the youth are not in the temple, they participate in seminary, basketball, dances and firesides.

Six Area Seventies are serving in the Africa West Area: Adesina J. Olukanni, David Eka, Alexander A. Odume, Richard K Ahadjie, Declan O. Madu, and Norbert K. Ounleu. These men provide excellent leadership and direction for the Stakes and Districts in Cote D'Ivoire, Sierra Leone, Liberia, Ghana, Togo, Benin and Nigeria.

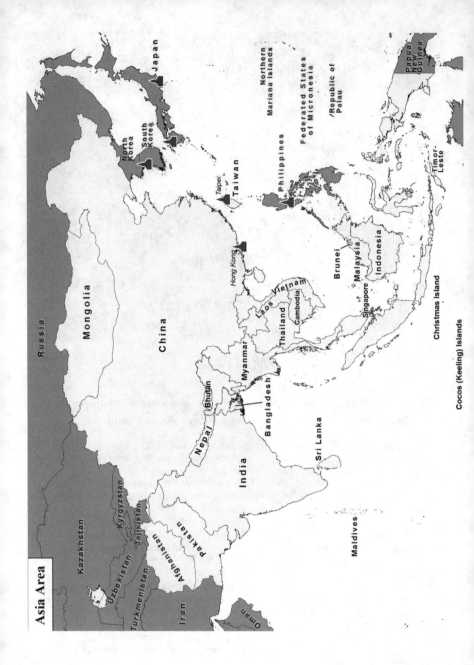

Asia Area

Asia Area

As of December 31, 2007

Membership: 133,593; Stakes: 16; Wards: 115; Missions: 11; Districts: 27; Branches: 231; Temples: 2; Headquarters: Hong Kong, China.

The Church continues to grow in numbers and faithfulness among the 3.4 billion people spread across the 24 countries and territories of the Asia Area.

Late in 2007, the India New Delhi Mission was created to provide a greater focus on the 1.1 billion people who live in northern India, Pakistan, Bangladesh, Nepal, and Bhutan. In its first year of operation, the number of branches in New Delhi increased dramatically, a second district was created in the country of Pakistan, and LDS Charities was officially registered in Nepal to better support humanitarian efforts. The first translation of the Book of Mormon in Urdu, the language of Pakistan, was published in late 2007.

As a result of the creation of the India New Delhi Mission, the Singapore Mission was restructured to focus only on the countries of Singapore and Malaysia. The East Malaysia island previously referred to as Borneo has yielded a rich harvest of souls. In 2008, the Miri District was created, the third district in East Malaysia and the fifth district in the entire country. For the first time in this nation of many people and languages, all missionaries called to serve in the Singapore Mission are being taught the Bahasa Malay language at the Missionary Training Center.

For many members in the Asia Area who live far from a temple, the sacrifice to receive their temple blessings is worth the sacrifice of significant time and expense. The members in Mongolia save their money, then board trains for the 36-hour journey across China to arrive in Hong Kong for a week of temple work before making the long trek home again. Although the Saints in India must make the long flight to Hong Kong, they value their temple recommend as a symbol of their membership. One district in the India Bangalore Mission reports 90 percent of those who have been endowed hold a current temple recommend.

The deeply respected and beloved translator of the first Chinese Book of Mormon, Hu WeiYi, died in June 2008 in Taipei, Taiwan, at the age of 94. In 1963, as a relatively new member of the Church employed by an airline, he was set apart by then-Elder Gordon B. Hinckley to complete this important scripture translation. He later translated many other Church books, including Jesus the Christ. In 1976 when the first Chinese stake of this dispensation was formed in Taipei, Elder Hinckley ordained Brother Hu both as a high priest and as the first patriarch in Taiwan. In 1984 after the dedication of the Taipei Taiwan temple, President Hinckley, as a counselor in the First Presidency, conferred on Brother Hu the sealing power. When President Hinckley came to dedicate a new building in Taipei in 2005, he looked into the congregation and spotted the then-91-year-old Brother Hu. The prophet asked him to stand and told a powerful story about Brother Hu's faith as a new Church member to pay a full tithing. Brother Hu's translation of the Book of Mormon was used by Chinese people worldwide for 42 years until an updated translation was published in late 2007. Hu WeiYi's life of faithful service illustrates that pioneers are in every land, not just on the plains of Nebraska and Wyoming.

Brazil Area

As of December 31, 2007

Membership: 1,018,901; Stakes: 218; Wards: 1,329; Missions: 27; Districts: 53; Branches: 486; Temples: 5, Manaus announced; Headquarters: Sao Paulo, Brazil.

To increase ordinances, the São Paulo Temple Presidency asked the 33 remaining stakes in the temple district to try an experiment. Every morning various groups of temple patrons were carpooled to the temple and carpooled back to their respective stakes at night. Retired persons, seniors and those not occupied during the day were invited. It was very successful. The dedicated attendance of these members resulted in an increase of about 30 percent in temple ordinances performed monthly.

Humanitarian Project, Helping Hands – On Sept. 6th, 2008, the day before Brazil´s National Independence Day, 90,000 members and friends of the Church paid homage to their nation by spending the day volunteering to paint, clean and improve 350 lower income public schools throughout the country.

Working from 8 a.m.-5 p.m., in more than 150 Brazilian cities including all 26 states and the federal district, the volunteers applied thousands of liters of paint and white wash. They replaced sinks, changed doors, painted walls and windows, cleared school yards, and made plumbing and electrical repairs. The initiative was accomplished with help from the National Council of State Secretaries of Education, Parent-Teacher-Student Associations, School Directors, Communication Departments and with support from private initiatives. About 220,000 students were blessed through these efforts.

On Aug. 5, 2007, Brazil reached a membership of one million. Only 70 years ago, Elder Melvin J. Ballard dedicated the land of South America for the preaching of the Gospel of Jesus Christ. He said thousands would join the church. Today, there are five temples in operation, and one in Manaus under construction, 27 missions, 218 stakes, 53 districts with more than 1,021 functioning chapels and 1,040,377 members of the Church in Brazil.

The LDS Church was recognized by the Brazilian National Senate. Senator Edison Lobão related some of the history of the Church in Brazil and discussed its present growth.

He said, "The Church is now functioning in every part of Brazil, to our honor and happiness." Senator Àlvaro Dias praised the humanitarian help given by the Church throughout the world and especially in Brazil.

Senator Romeu Tuma, with tears in his eyes, added "That which was described here brings enormous satisfaction because we can still believe in God and Jesus Christ and that we are our neighbor´s keeper." Senator Mão Santa praised this type of religious action as contributing to the reduction of violence.

In November 2007, **the Planalto Ward, São Bernardo Brazil Stake began a missionary program called, "I Will Go."** The objective was to involve the entire ward in full-time missionary service and to do what has been revealed in D&C 88:81 "All those who have been warned should warn their neighbor."

All ward leaders were involved. Seventy percent of the members participated. Some 1,600 pass-along cards were distributed. Baptisms doubled. Thirty people were baptized with 80 percent remaining active. Leaders challenged the members in a 12-step program to do activities as families to increase missionary work, which included fellowshipping, holding family home evenings with investigators and friends, handing out pass-along cards, visiting the less-active, providing references, and missionary-focused ward activities which involved all members, including the Primary and youth organizations.

A spectacular musical production centered on "The Family – A Proclamation to the World" with beautiful music composed by Steven Kapp Perry and Marvin Payne was presented six times by members of the Brazil South Area. Beautiful choirs sang, dancers dressed in traditional, colorful costumes performed and actors portrayed the pain and preoccupation by and between dear ones who challenge the way, the happiness and love for those who return, the certainty that good will prevail over evil, and the reality of a Savior who says "Come Unto Me." Audiences comprised of members and non-

members were touched by the presentation. The hope of eternity was shared with families in need, parents became more aware of their responsibility in their homes and children reconciled with their parents. Many felt miracles were happening. Baptisms resulted from attendance at the presentations.

The musical demonstrated the quality, professionalism, excellent abilities and talents of the participants in every aspect. More than 200 volunteers, including choir members, children, dancers, soloists and stage hands dedicated themselves for one year. About 10,000 people, including the mayor of São Bernardo do Campo, attended the presentations and stood applauding, wanting more.

Senator Romeu Tuma, with tears in his eyes, added "That which was described here brings enormous satisfaction because we can still believe in God and Jesus Christ and that we are our neighbor´s keeper."

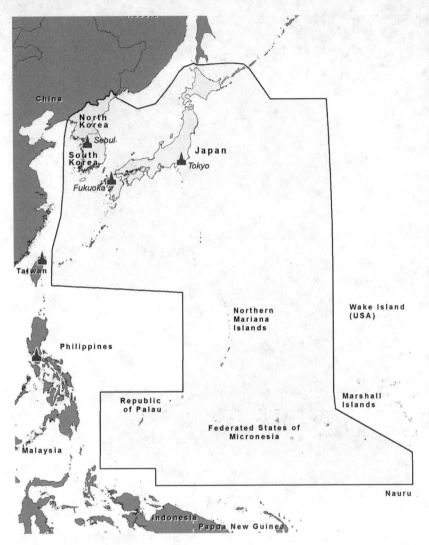

Asia North Area

As of December 31, 2007

Membership: 209,510; Stakes: 46; Wards: 259; Missions: 12; Districts: 25; Branches: 202; Temples: 3; Headquarters: Tokyo, Japan.

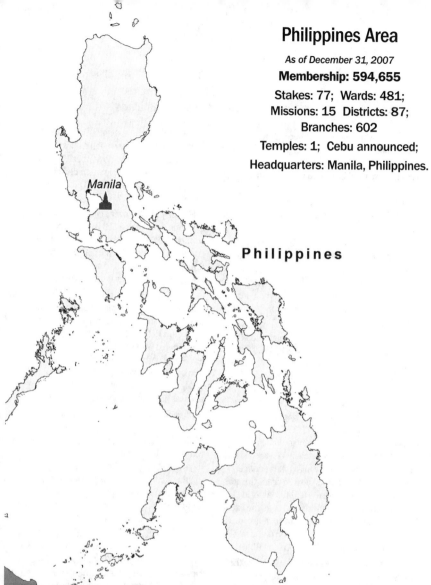

As of December 31, 2007

Membership: 594,655

Stakes: 77; Wards: 481;
Missions: 15 Districts: 87;
Branches: 602

Temples: 1; Cebu announced;

Headquarters: Manila, Philippines.

Philippines

Manila

While there were some attempts to establish the Church as a result of the presence of military personnel as early as 1898 during the the Spanish American War, it was not until the 1960s that the work began to flourish under the direction of Elder Gordon B. Hinckley, an Assistant to the Twelve.

Manila is the headquarters for the Philippines Area. There have been two native Filipino General Authorities, Augusto A. Lim (1992-97), and Michael J. Teh (2007-present). Elder Lim was the first stake president in the Philippines with the creation of the Manila stake in 1973.

Fundamental to the success of the Church in the Philippines is the nurture and care of the rising generation. At the end of May and the first of June 2008, about 30,000 youth and leaders from 80 stakes and districts participated in 80 multistake youth conferences. Activities were held in different locations and were spread over three days, allowing youth to become better acquainted and form friendships.

Pacific Area

As of December 31, 2007

Membership: 429,294; Stakes: 107; Wards: 706; Missions: 15; Districts: 34; Branches: 376; Temples: 10; Headquarters: Auckland, New Zealand.

The Pacific Area was created on August 1, 2008, by the consolidation of the New Zealand/Pacific Islands Area and the Australia Area and is headquartered in Auckland, New Zealand. The Area has a population of more than 27 million across 22 nations and territories with 433,591, about 1.5 percent, who are members of the Church.

There are 16 Church schools in the Pacific Area with 5,455 students. The Church College of New Zealand (CCNZ) located in Hamilton, New Zealand will close in November, 2009 having served the area exceptionally well for more than 50 years. The Perpetual Education Fund operates in Fiji, Samoa and Tonga.

The members in **New Zealand celebrated the Hamilton Temple 50-year Jubilee** in April 2008 with special commemoration programs in each of the 25 stakes. The construction of the Hamilton Temple and the CCNZ was a "labor of love," built by labor missionaries. The temple was the first in the southern hemisphere and was dedicated in April 1958 by President David O. McKay. The dedication followed significant growth in the South Pacific that was spurred by 17-year-old Matthew Cowley's historic missionary service beginning in 1914. For the next 25 years, this was the only temple to serve the faithful Saints in Australia and New Zealand as well as all the Pacific Islands, south of the equator. The increase in membership led to the organization of the first stake outside the United States on May 18, 1958.

The Hamilton Visitors Center adjacent to the temple has undergone major renovation and re-opened to the public on March 15, 2008. The renovation includes a magnificent Christus statue and a new exhibit in the lobby area describing the history of the Church in New Zealand. The historical exhibit is a guided pictorial tour using records gathered by local Church historian, Rangi Parker, who has spent more than 20 years collecting 30,000 photographs and related journals. In recognition of her contribution she received the "Queen's Service Medal" in The Queen's Birthday Honours 2008.

Three temples in the area have been rebuilt, renovated or expanded and then rededicated during the past three years: Apia Samoa, September 2005; Papeete Tahiti, November 2006; and Nuku'alofa Tonga, November 2007. The Nuku'alofa Tonga Temple was rededicated by Elder Russell M. Nelson of the Quorum of the Twelve on Nov. 4, 2007.

He also presided over a cultural extravaganza featuring more than 2,500 young men and young women. The program highlighted the Polynesian culture of the South Pacific and was attended by King George Tupou V and other members of the Royal Family as well as most VIPs in the nation.

The events leading up to the rededication of the Nuku'alofa Tonga Temple brought a spirit of peace to Tonga. The most significant event was a **"Mormon Helping Hands"** project that was coordinated with the Royal Family, the highest levels of government beginning with Prime Minister Feleti Sevele, local businessmen, academics, leaders of all churches in the nation and was liberally promoted by local media.

More than 25 service projects were completed on the four major islands, including the painting of 28 school buildings on five different campuses. More than 13,200 volunteers participated in the day's activities and more than 1,500 were friends of other faiths. Thousands of volunteers have participated in "Mormon Helping Hands" nationwide projects in each of the major Pacific Islands and in Australia and New Zealand.

The Church is recognized and well respected at the highest levels of government throughout the Area. The President of Kiribati attended the creation of the second stake in Tarawa, the prime ministers of Tonga and Samoa have participated in many Church events, as have the recent presidential leaders in French Polynesia.

In New Zealand, both Prime Minister Helen Clark, and John Key, leader of the Opposition (National Party), have spoken to large gatherings of more than 1,200 youth and young adults. Both Helen Clark and the Prime Minister of Australia, Kevin Rudd, have received their personal family histories during official presentations by the Church. Prime Minister Rudd's history has been lodged in the National Library of Australia.

The Church co-hosted a Pacific Futures Trade

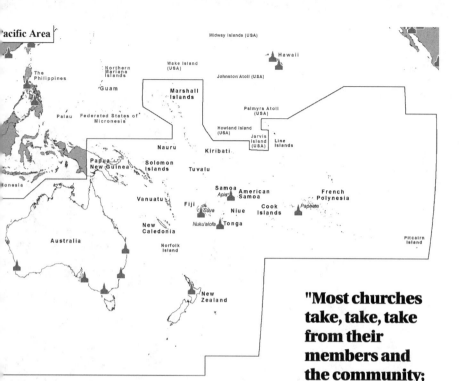

Pacific Area

Midway Islands (USA)

Hawaii

The Philippines

Wake Island (USA)

Johnston Atoll (USA)

Northern Mariana Islands

Guam

Marshall Islands

Palmyra Atoll (USA)

Palau

Federated States of Micronesia

Howland Island (USA)

Jarvis Island (USA)

Line Islands

Nauru

Kiribati

Papua New Guinea

Solomon Islands

Tuvalu

Vanuatu

Fiji

Samoa

Apia

American Samoa

French Polynesia

Papeete

Suva

Niue

Cook Islands

Nuku'alofa

Tonga

New Caledonia

Australia

Norfolk Island

Pitcairn Island

New Zealand

> **"Most churches take, take, take from their members and the community; but The Church of Jesus Christ of Latter-day Saints gives, gives, gives."**

Conference with the University of Auckland and the New Zealand Business Council that was attended by more than 150 leaders of government and business executives from the South Pacific. Misa Telefoni, Deputy Prime Minister of Samoa expressed his appreciation for the Church at this conference by saying: "Most churches take, take, take from their members and the community; but The Church of Jesus Christ of Latter-day Saints gives, gives, gives."

Humanitarian aid donations and welfare projects have blessed the lives of many across the Pacific. Elder Dirk Smibert, Area Seventy, presented a $200,000 donation from the Church to the Queensland Deputy Premier Paul Lucas for humanitarian assistance to deal with a flood. Donations of wheelchairs have been presented in Tonga, Samoa, American Samoa, Fiji and Papua New Guinea.

National Young Single Adult conferences were held in Australia, New Zealand, Tahiti, Fiji, Samoa and Tonga. Several members of the Church represented New Zealand in the 2008 Beijing Olympics in netball and swimming. A group of YSAs attended a session of the Federal Parliament in Canberra. Similar events were held at other state capitals throughout Australia.

Numerous favorable articles were printed in the Australian media about LDS rugby players, including returned missionaries, concerning their excellence both "on and off the field."

Elder Paul Sybrowsky of the Seventy visited with Western Australia Gov. Dr. Ken Michaels in Perth. Derek Robson, Australia National Secretary for the Return and Service League, was presented a "Standing for Something Award." Elder Sybrowsky met with Israeli Ambassador Yuval Rotem in Canberra. This was the first of many favorable interactions with Ambassador Rotem. U.S. Ambassador David McCallum spoke at a Church fireside in Canberra.

The BYU Young Ambassadors gave performances and firesides to thousands in attendance in Newcastle, Sydney, Canberra, Albury, Launceston, Hobart, and Melbourne. In Brisbane their performance was at the State Parliament.

Caribbean

As of December 31, 2007
Membership: 157,373; Stakes: 23; Wards: 155; Missions: 8; Districts: 27;
Branches: 202; Temples: 1;
Headquarters: Santo Domingo, Dominican Republic

Humanitarian Services in the Dominican Republic are in the process of supplying 500 hand pumps for water wells. Citizens of each town have the responsibility of pouring concrete pads at the top of the wells. The end result is that many people throughout the DR will have access to safe, clean water.

At the National Conference of the National Association of Amas de Cases (Homemakers) in the Dominincan Republic, Jose Castro taught participants about family home evening. Three hundred copies of the non-denominational family home evening manuals were distributed.

Guyana has a small farm organization for women. Each member was provided the necessary materials to build a 12-foot x 10-foot mesh pen with roof and water cans, food for 50 chicks and ducklings. After raising them for 8 to 12 weeks they marketed the birds. They then buy an even-greater number of chicks and ducklings, thus slowly increasing their numbers and income.

A new mission. The Puerto Rico San Juan East Mission was approved by the First Presidency and the Quorum of the Twelve, effective July 1, 2007. This second mission in Puerto Rico was created by taking part of the Puerto Rico San Juan Mission and combining it with part of the West Indies Mission.

The Area Presidency visited every stake and district in the area. They conducted priesthood and auxiliary training, firesides and home visits of less-active members. Many less-active members were reactivated.

The BYU Dance Company Caribbean Tour. This group performed in Puerto Rico, Dominican Republic, and Jamaica. In Jamaica, this was the first time the members interacted with the community in this way. A major breakthrough in media relations was achieved. With the publicity of the coming of this tour group, considerable enthusiasm was seen among the people.

Hurricane Dean, Tornado in Dajabon and Tropical Storms Olga and Noel left many people homeless while crops and bridges were destroyed. These storms killed 117 people and many more were missing. Mormon "helping hands" delivered hygiene kits, food, water and bedding to the victims.

Senior Missionary, Elder Rick Graff, with the help of full-time missionaries, Elders Rasmussen and Washburn, visited less-active members in the village of Taranes. Through their efforts there and in the village of Gonzalo, a new branch was created. On Mother's Day, they held the first Church service in an open field with 70 people attending. On the second Sunday, sacrament meeting was attended by 87 people, approximately 80 of those were investigators.

The first chapel in Freeport, Grand Bahamas, was dedicated May 13, 2007, by Elder Clate W. Mask, president of the Caribbean Area. Also attending were President David Gingery, president of the Jamaica Mission, and Branch President Michael Brown. President Brown was the first member and was instrumental in bringing the gospel to the island.

The first Jamaica Young Adult Conference was held July 11, 2007. Young men and women gathered from 22 branches with 110 young adults in attendance. These young adults donned "Helping Hands" t-shirts and went to work cleaning and polishing the chapel of the former military camp that is now used as a boarding school.

Puerto Rico youth to the temple. Ten youth and their leaders from the Trujillo Alto Ward, San Juan Puerto Rico Stake, spent two years earning money to attend the temple in the Dominican Republic. While in the DR, they dedicated their time to the vicarious work of the temple, studying scriptures and writing in their journals.

Record keeping has greatly improved. Most of the units are fully staffed with competent clerks. Promptness, accuracy, completeness and timely deposits of funds were stressed in classes taught by Elder Lavar Skousen, Area auditor/trainer.

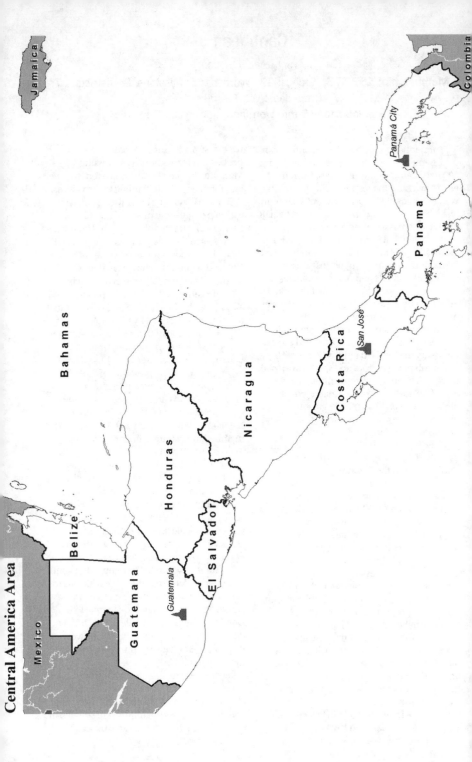

Central America Area

Jamaica

Colombia

Panamá City

Panama

Bahamas

San José

Costa Rica

Nicaragua

Honduras

Belize

El Salvador

Guatemala

Guatemala

Mexico

Central America Area

As of December 31, 2007

Membership: 575,727; Stakes: 97; Wards: 614; Missions: 12; Districts: 55; Branches: 465; Temples: 3; three announced, Quetzaltenango Guatemala, Tegucigalpa Honduras and San Salvador, El Salvador; Headquarters: Guatemala City, Guatemala.

1. Church Growth

The first members of the Church arrived in Panama in 1940 as part of the North American troops stationed in this country. One of them, Otto Hunsaker, requested authorization from the First Presidency to form a branch, which occurred on May 18, 1941, as part of the Mexican Mission. At the end of the first year, the branch had 100 members, all of them North Americans. Subsequently, John F. O'Donnal asked that missionaries be sent to Guatemala and they arrived in 1947. Brother O'Donnal baptized the first convert in the area, his wife Carmen, on Nov. 13, 1948. Since then, the Church has grown until it now has 586,000 members, living in 95 stakes, 54 districts and 12 missions.

A total of about 20,000 youth of the Aaronic Priesthood and young women participated in national camps from countries in the area.

The Perpetual Education Fund is helping almost 2,000 young people by providing loans with a level of return above 80 percent.

A total of 1,500 missionaries from the area are serving full time missions around the world.

2. Pioneers

The Guatemala City Temple, dedicated in 1984, was the first temple constructed in Central America, with John O'Donnal as president. Alberto Vásquez, Luis Leonardo, Carlos Fuentes, Aura Castellanos, Flor Guzman, Amalia Conde, Santiago Velásquez and Faustina Alvarado all served as temple workers between 22 and 24 uninterrupted years.

One of the pioneers of the Church in Central America was Udine Falabella, who presided over the first stake in 1967 and was the first local president of the Guatemala City Temple, serving for four years. He organized the first temple trip to the Meza Arizona Temple. He evaluated several transportation possibilities, finally deciding to contract buses. A few days before the trip, during a meeting with those who were going to the temple, the mission president approached him and whispered into his ear: "President, tell the brethren that we are not going to the temple because the owner of the buses canceled the contract". Thinking for a moment Brother Falabella told the attendees: "He has just told me that we are not traveling by the Atlantic Coast but we will go by the Pacific Coast. Such was the faith and confidence that the trip would be a reality. Brother Falabella died on Sept. 7, 2007.

3. President Monson visits Panamanian President Torrijos in August 2008.

On August 11, 2008, President Thomas S. Monson had a meeting in the Government Palace with President Martin Torrijos, president of Panama. The visit came as part of President Monson's trip to Panama to dedicate the Panama City temple. During the meeting, President Torrijos and First Lady Vivian Torrijos expressed their gratitude to the Church for the humanitarian help and the work that has been done in the country. This was the first time that the president of the Church had met with a representative of Panama.

Mexico Area

As of December 31, 2007

Membership: 1,121,933; Stakes: 210; Wards: 1,459; Missions: 21; Districts: 40; Branches: 504; Temples: 12; Headquarters: Mexico City, Mexico.

The history of the Church in Mexico goes back to 1875, when Brigham Young sent Daniel Jones with a group of missionaries to Mexico City to distribute pamphlets to Mexican leaders. One of those pamphlets regarding the Book of Mormon fell into the hands of Plotino C. Rhodacanaty, who after reading the pamphlet wrote President John Taylor, requesting more information.

In October General Conference in 1879, President John Taylor called Elder Moses Thatcher of the Twelve to initiate missionary work in Mexico City. The following month on Nov. 13, 1879, Elder Thatcher organized the first branch of the Church with Plotino C. Rhodacanaty as branch president and first member of the Church.

The gospel began to spread slowly among the Mexican people. On April 6, 1881, Elder Thatcher, Feramorz Young and Ventura Páez climbed the Popocatépetl Volcano and dedicated the country for the preaching of the gospel. In 1885, Meliton G. Trejo and James Z. Stewart completed the translation of the Book of Mormon in Spanish.

The constant migration of people to Utah caused Brigham Young to find new places to colonize. In 1885, a group of 400 saints from Utah and Arizona formed small colonies in: Juárez, Dublán, Díaz, Pacheco, García, and Chuichupa in Chihuahua, as well as the colonies in Oaxaca and Morelos in the State of Sonora.

Since that time, the growth of the Church in Mexico has been constant, although not without its challenges. During the Mexican Revolution of 1910, the saints in the Mormon colonies in Chihuahua had to leave the country. Two faithful leaders in the State of

BYU scientists unearth clues about Mayan marketplace

Using improved methods of chemical analysis, BYU environmental scientists have unearthed clues that may prove the existence of a marketplace economy among the ancient Maya civilizations of the Yucatan

peninsula and not a tax and redistribution system, as is the widely-held belief.

As reported in the December issue of Latin American Antiquity, a quarterly journal published by the Society for American Archeology, BYU professor of environmental science Richard Terry and his team of students have confirmed that a large open area surrounded by thoroughfares located in the northwestern region of Mexico's Yucatan peninsula was actually an ancient marketplace. This provides powerful new evidence for understanding the advanced civilization's economy. — *Church News* Jan. 26, 2008

Hidalgo, Rafael Monroy and Vicente Morales became martyrs in 1915, when they were shot for not denying their faith. Also during this time, however, there were interesting events, as when Andrés Carlos González Rodríguez, the first full-time local missionary, gave President Francisco I. Madero a Book of Mormon.

The first stake was organized in 1895 in Colonia Juárez for English-speaking members, and on Dec. 3, 1961, the first Spanish-speaking stake was created in Mexico City.

The Juarez Academy founded in 1897 meets the educational needs of the Mormon colonies in Chihuahua, as the Benemérito de las Américas High School has done in Mexico City since 1963. The greatest impact in education, however, has been in seminary and institutes, which in 2007 had an

enrollment of 19,195 young people between 14 and 17 years of age, and 21,799 single adults in institute.

On April 3, 1976, under the direction of President Spencer W. Kimball, the construction of the Mexico City Temple was announced and dedicated on Dec. 2, 1983, by President Gordon B. Hinckley, who left a deep influence in the country when he received the revelation to build smaller temples as he concluded his visit to the Juarez Academy for the celebration of their one hundred years since founded. The era of small temples started when President Hinckley announced them on Oct. 4, 1997, during general conference. Currently Mexico has twelve temples operating.

The Mexico City Temple was closed for remodeling on March 31, 2007 and will be rededicated on Nov. 16, 2008.

Chile Area

As of December 31, 2007

Membership: 548,726; Stakes: 74;
Wards: 419; Missions: 9; Districts: 24; Branches: 192; Temples: 1;
Headquarters: Santiago, Chile.

ORIGINS OF THE CHURCH IN CHILE

The first meeting of the Church in Chile took place in July 1956 in Santiago in the home of Billy F. Fotheringham, an executive of Eastman Kodak. A short time later the Saints – of the very recent organized small branch of Santiago – rented a house in the Ñuñoa Community.

In those days Chile was a district of the Argentine Mission and President Lorin N. Pace traveled from Buenos Aires to Chile to train the leadership and look for other places to establish the Church. In 1957, President Pace bought the first property for the Church in Chile. It was a house located on 547 El Bosque Avenue and served as headquarters for the Providencia Branch and later as the Chilean headquarters for the Andes Mission, located in Lima, Peru.

On July 8, 1962, the Church purchased the second piece of property in Chile. This was a house on 360 Alcántara Av. This house served as the residence for President A. Delbert Palmer and his family and as the headquarters for the Chilean Mission, organized in 1961. It was still being used in 2008 by mission presidents.

One of the first announcements of the recently organized Chilean Mission was plans to construct the first LDS meetinghouse in Chile at 401 Manuel de Salas Street in the Ñuñoa Community. On April 8, 1962, the groundbreaking ceremony for the meetinghouse was held. This ceremony was repeated in Concepción and Viña del Mar during the presidency of Elder Palmer.

In 1963, another piece of property was bought in the República section of Santiago that had been headquarters for the Peruvian Embassy. Later the house was demolished and the stake center for the República Stake was built on the site.

As the church organized new branches, homes were rented until the 1980s when an extensive program for building chapels began.

CASABLANCA RECREATION CAMP

This 903-acre property was purchased in December 2005 as a recreational facility, primarily for the Chile Area Young Women and Young Men activities.

Church use began in 2007 with one camping module to house 200 people. Currently, there are six modules with capacity for 600 people and the final planned capacity is 12 modules to house 1,200 people. The coverage of this property is up to 53 stakes/districts. During the summer of 2008, 2,504 young people attended the camp.

SANTIAGO TEMPLE

In the year 2000 just 17 percent of the ordinances performed in the Santiago Chile Temple were from local family group sheets. Since then, that percentage has grown continuously each year so that in 2007, 52 percent of all ordinances originated from names that Chilean members had submitted. With the beginning of the well-received "New Family Search" program in 2008, it appears that percentage will grow even higher, as members work diligently to find and redeem their ancestors. The joy and pride on the faces of members who have found scores of names after long searching is only exceeded by their visible happiness when they personally perform the basic ordinances for these departed kindred.

CHAITEN VOLCANO

The volcano Chaiten is a type of boiler Chilean volcano, located 10 km northeast of the town of Chaiten, capital of the province of Palena, in the Lakes Region.

During the first week of May 2008 it began to erupt after centuries without activity, resulting in 100 percent of the people being evacuated from Chaiten, where a branch of the Church is located. Ricardo Gonzalez, counselor to President Carl Falkner in the Osorno Mission, personally contacted every active member of the Chaiten Branch, most of whom went to Puerto Montt. Fifteen were placed in the homes of members. One couple went to the home of their daughter, and another opted to take shelter provided by a Health System because the wife was employed by the local hospital. The Puerto Montt Stake received the members from Chaiten into their homes and cared for them until more permanent arrangements could be made. Their faith and service were evident during this disaster.

Once the government declared Chaiten a disaster area, those living with members, decided that they would look for houses to rent and the local leaders helped them in this project. The government paid the rent. The local leaders solicited help from the Welfare Department of the area to help the member families cover some of the necessary expenses. All the members were cared for.

South America South Area

As of December 31, 2007

Membership: 525,830; Stakes: 96;
Wards: 636; Missions: 14; Districts: 54; Branches: 536; Temples: 3;
Cordoba, Argentina announced; Headquarters: Buenos Aires, Argentina.

The South America South Area, then presided over by Elder Theodore A. Tuttle, was organized in 1984 and included the countries of Argentina, Chile, Paraguay and Uruguay. In 1996 Chile, was organized as a new Area.

In the beginning, the countries that are now a part of the South America South Area had a membership of 165,561, living in 45 stakes and seven missions. No temples had been built in any of the three countries. Today, the membership is 525,830, with 96 stakes, 14 missions and a temple in each country.

The first meetinghouse in Argentina was built in 1938 in Liniers, a suburb of Buenos Aires; in Uruguay the first meetinghouse was built in 1954 and in Paraguay in 1962, which started a constant program of construction. Today, there are 753 meetinghouses in the Area, which indicate the strong roots and strength of the Church in a physical and tangible way.

The presence of the Church in the community has become more known with the construction of temples: in 1985 in Buenos Aires, Argentina; in 2001 in Montevideo, Uruguay; and in 2002 in Asunción, Paraguay. More recently, the bonds with the community and the governments have grown mainly due to the public-service activities and the outreach of Church Welfare programs.

In 1995, Elder John B. Dickson, a member of the Area Presidency, encouraged the leaders of the Church to perform community-service activities. It was then that an annual day was established in which all the stakes and units of the area gave service by cleaning streets, parks and other public spaces and painting and repairing schools and hospitals. In 1998, this annual activity was named "Helping Hands," with more than 34,000 participating members. In the following years "Helping Hands" was taken to Brazil, where it was a big success, and later it extended throughout the Church.

The growing respect and consideration toward the Church have made possible an approach to the political leaders: Uruguayan President Jorge Batlle visited the open house of the Montevideo temple, and the First Lady of Paraguay Susana Galli Gonzalez Macchi attended the open house of the Asunción temple.

In March 2007, the First Lady of Paraguay, Mrs. María Gloria Penayo Duarte, visited Salt Lake City and met with the First Presidency. Also, former Uruguayan President Luis Alberto Lacalle visited Brigham Young University and gave a talk.

In Argentina, the Humanitarian Services have worked with the National Government and the Provincial Governments in the program of wheel-chair delivery and other humanitarian projects for more than five years.

In July 24, 2008, Elder Ernersto Da Silva, an Area Seventy, met with the elect-president of Paraguay, Fernando Lugo, and had the opportunity of explaining the activities and purposes of the Church.

Regarding Latter-day Saints' contribution to society, Dr. Williams Sill's work stands out. Dr. Sill dedicated himself for more than 30 years to paleontology research in the valley of Ischigualasto in Argentina, one of the most important dinosaur fossil deposits in the world. After Brother Sill's death in March 2008, the government of the province of San Juan rendered tribute to him, acknowledging the scientific work and the three-decade effort for the Valley of Ischigualasto to be named World Heritage.

In 2007, there was a special training for priesthood leaders to strengthen the Aaronic Priesthood and the Young Women. In 2008, the training was focused on "making the temple the center of our lives."

Today the Area is presided over by Elder Shayne M. Bowen with Elders Claudio D. Zivic and Marcos A. Aidukaitis as counselors. The efforts of the work are aimed at blessing the lives of the Saints by inviting them to prepare to and attend the temple more often and to share the gospel using the manual "Preach My Gospel."

In August 2008, Elder Richard G. Scott of the Quorum of the Twelve visited the Area and held some meetings with leaders in which he emphasized the need to strengthen the stakes. He highlighted the importance of trusting the promptings of the Spirit and exercising the active part of faith.

Guadeloupe

Dominica

Martinique

St. Lucia

Aruba   Netherlands
          Antilles   Barbados

                                      Grenada

ama   Caracas   Trinidad
                                               and
                                               Tobago

                    Venezuela

                                               Guyana

        Bogotá

        Colombia

Ecuador

    Guayaquil

                                      Brazil

    Peru

South America North Area

As of December 31, 2007

Membership: 481,980; Stakes: 87; Wards: 563; Missions: 11; Districts: 34; Branches: 270; Temples: 3; Headquarters: Bogota, Colombia.

The South America North Area is presided over by President Elder Carl B. Pratt, and his counselors, Elder Benjamin De Hoyos, first counselor, and Elder Rafael E. Pino, second counselor. The South America North Area includes the countries of Colombia, Ecuador, and Venezuela. As of September 2008, the South America North Area had 333,019 members, 87 stakes, 33 districts, 562 wards, 270 branches, and 11 missions. There is a temple for each country in the cities of Bogota, Colombia; Guayaquil, Ecuador; and Caracas, Venezuela.

In recent years, the South America North Area has faced many challenges. Church members have responded to these challenges through much prayer, fasting, and service. As a result, many members and non-member lives have been blessed.

Many Church humanitarian projects have been implemented in the area. In Popayan, Colombia, a pilot garden project was established to teach self-sufficiency. Under the guidance of Alfonso Tenorio, district president of Popayan, and with the collaboration of the University of Cauca, the community became highly involved. Many members and non-members, including the governor of Popayan, have now started their own gardens.

In the cities of Cartagena and Barranquilla, Colombia, many uninsured children and adults received free eyeglasses. This vision project is still ongoing. Cartagena and Barranquilla also benefited from a Neonatal Resuscitation Project in which a team of doctors from Salt Lake City, Utah, provided hands-on training to approximately 50 Colombian doctors to help decrease infant mortality rates. Kits were donated which included mannequins and resuscitating equipment to be used in various hospitals. Also, in 2006, vision projects and neonatal resuscitation projects were carried out in Ecuador, and there is a neonatal resuscitation project planned for Venezuela in December 2008.

In 2008, the Church held its second annual blood drive. With the help of the Red Cross and local community organizations, 16 blood banks throughout Bogota, Colombia, were set up in various meetinghouses. A total of 1,136 people participated in the event. The number of participants doubled from the previous year.

Major flooding affected the lives of thousands of people who live along the coastline of Ecuador. The Church and the Red Cross helped many members and non-members by donating hygiene kits to those affected.

The Perpetual Education Fund has positively affected the lives of faithful young adults. For example, Elizabeth Rondùn, a Church member from Popayan, Colombia, was a recipient of the fund. Through her faithfulness and hard work, she has now been given a teaching position in gardening at a secondary school. Through repaying her loan, Sister Rondùn has been blessed and she is now blessing the lives of others. Presently, there are 2,400 participants in the area. Eighty percent of all Perpetual Education Fund participants have graduated, and 82 percent have a better job.

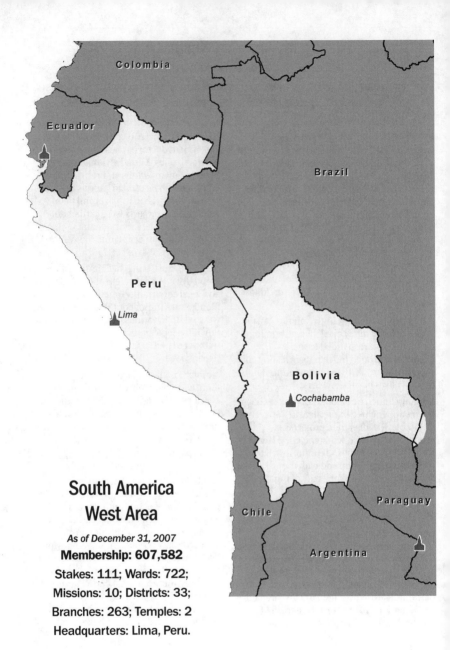

South America
West Area

As of December 31, 2007
Membership: 607,582
Stakes: 111; Wards: 722;
Missions: 10; Districts: 33;
Branches: 263; Temples: 2
Headquarters: Lima, Peru.

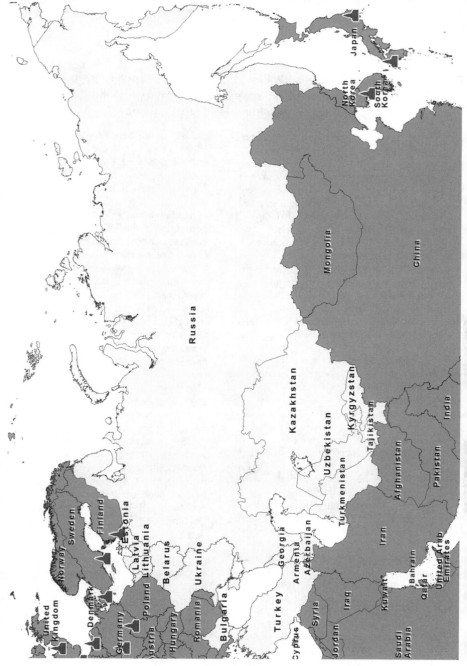

Europe East Area

As of December 31, 2007

Membership: 38,459; Stakes: 1; Wards; 8; Missions: 14; Districts: 26;
Branches: 242; Temples: Kiev/Kyiv, Ukraine announced;
Headquarters: Moscow, Russia.

Europe Area

As of December 31, 2007

Membership: 431,380; Stakes: 111; Wards: 695; Missions: 37; Districts: 45; Branches: 623; Temples: 10; Rome, Italy announced; Headquarters: Frankfurt, Germany.

The Europe Area, with headquarters in Frankfurt, Germany, was created August 1, 2008, in a consolidation of the Europe West and Europe Central Areas.

The Church has had a continual presence in Europe since 1837. By September 2008, there were 433,196 members, 10 temples, 111 stakes, 45 districts, 1,316 wards and branches, 576 family research locations, 37 missions, 4,180 missionaries, 23 languages, and 47 countries in the Europe Area. New chapels were built in Offenbach and Augsburg, Germany; Elbasan, Albania; and Ljubljana, Slovenia. The European distribution operation ships 550,000 tons of Church materials annually to 73 countries in 104 languages.

Elder Robert C. Oaks, formerly of the Presidency of the Seventy, is president of the Europe Area, with Elder Erich W. Kopischke of the First Quorum of Seventy as first counselor, and Elder Gérald J. Caussé, also, of the First Quorum of Seventy, as second counselor. Elder Caussé is the first person from France to become a General Authority in the history of the Church.

There has been a renewed emphasis on missionary work in the Europe Area, especially among Young Single Adults, resulting in a 5.5 percent increase in convert baptisms during the period from January – June 2008. An "Outreach Program" to strengthen Young Single Adults, originating in the Europe Central Area and being implemented only in Europe, has been highly successful. Before the "Outreach Program," 80 percent of YSA converts became less-active, now 80 percent of YSA converts are retained. Senior missionaries provide institute classes and varied activities throughout the week for young single adults in parts of Europe. There are various "Outreach Centers" in Europe where Young Single Adults congregate.

The goal is to help missionaries teach Young Single Adult investigators; strengthen Young Single Adult members who have become less-active (Search and Rescue;) and build the testimonies of active Young Single Adults by encouraging them to attend institute classes, serve missions, and marry worthy companions in the temple. The "Outreach Program" is accomplishing its goals.

In Croatia a young single adult sister had been studying with the missionaries for more than a year. After attending a YSA Conference, she returned enthusiastic about the gospel and began keeping her commitments with the missionaries and was baptized.

The Church Website, available in some parts of Europe, is now available for the first time in other European countries. Translations for the Website are being done in 23 different languages, in 26 European countries.

The Mormon Helping Hands program was used with great success in some European countries. During 2008, for the first time, it was used in Switzerland for a tri-stake youth conference. An historic youth conference was held in Hungary where youth from Albania, Croatia, Slovakia, Poland, Serbia, Romania, Moldova, Slovenia and Czech Republic participated in the conference and in a Mormon Helping Hands activity for the first time.

Also during 2008 was the 60th anniversary of the Berlin Airlift. Retired Air Force Colonel, Gail S. Halvorsen, a member of the Church who received fame as the "Candy Bomber" during the airlift, returned to Germany where about 10,000 people, including U.S. soldiers attended an open house at Wiesbadern Garrison to commemorate one of the largest humanitarian undertakings of all time. American, British, Canadian, Australian, New Zealand and South African pilots flew some 278,000 missions and carried some 23 million tons of supplies into Berlin. The Weisbaden mayor said that the Berlin Airlift was about more than humanitarianism, calling it a fight for freedom overall.

An inspirational story of a conversion in Spain: Carlos Fernández González approached the branch president of the tiny Algeciras branch, with just 10 faithful members, and asked to be baptized. He had never met the missionaries nor heard the discussions. Some time before, in Madrid, he had known some members who shared their testimonies with him of the joy and peace they found in the gospel. Carlos wasn't interested. He had a successful business, owned several ships, had a girlfriend and a little girl, and felt no need for religion.

Then his life drastically changed. His business partner died; his girlfriend and daughter left him and went to Australia. He was devastated and depressed. He thought about the things his friends had told him about the gospel. He remembered they had mentioned a book. Searching the Internet, he found the name of the book and acquired a used copy of the Book of Mormon. hrough his study, he gained a testimony of the Book of Mormon and wanted to be baptized. Searching the Internet again, he found a branch close to his home, attended, and surprised the branch president by requesting baptism.

The branch president arranged for missionaries to teach Carlos. They would go to his home, a luxury yacht; and he would be waiting, his used copy of the Book of Mormon open on the table. He was soon baptized. He remembered a young woman in Madrid, who had tried to teach him about the gospel. He discovered she had gone to Mexico. He located her and were later married, and are living in Spain. He now has the Melchizedek Priesthood, and they are preparing to be sealed in the temple. They are a great strength to the tiny Algeciras Branch.

Middle East/Africa North Area

As of December 31, 2007

Membership: 2,813; Stakes: 1; Wards; 6; Missions: 0; Districts: 2;
Branches: 19; Headquarters: Salt Lake City, Utah.

North America Northwest Area

As of December 31, 2007

Membership: 465,769; Stakes: 107; Wards: 802; Missions: 9; Districts: 2;
Branches: 168; Temples: 6; Vancouver, British Columbia announced;
Headquarters: Salt Lake City, Utah.

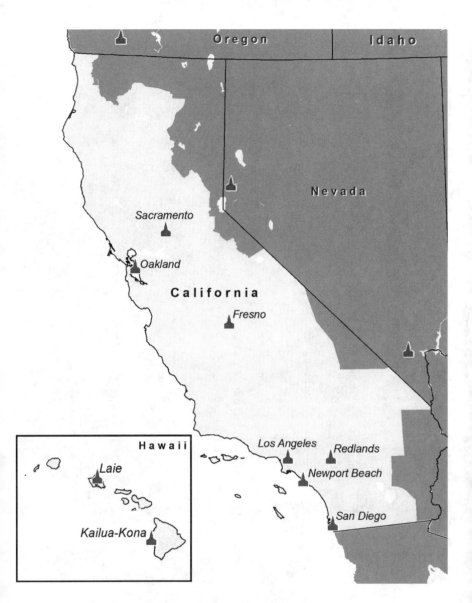

North America West Area

As of December 31, 2007

Membership: 809,171; Stakes: 173; Wards: 1,303; Missions: 18; Branches: 176; Temples: 9; Headquarters: Salt Lake City, Utah.

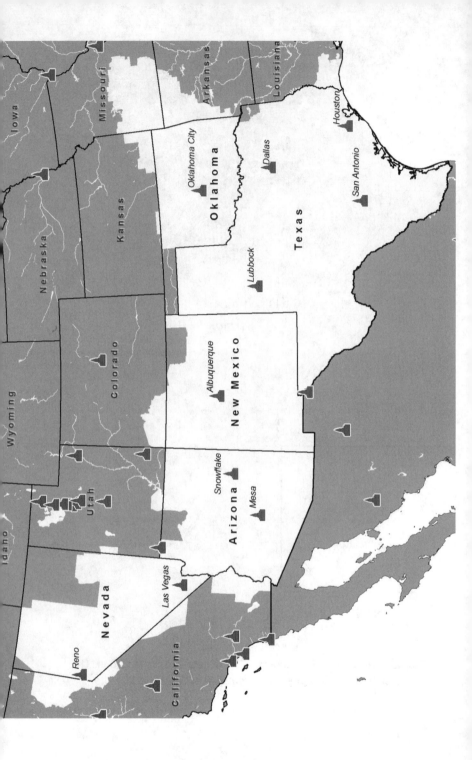

North America Southwest Area

As of December 31, 2007

Membership: 953,013; Stakes: 198; Wards: 1,590; Missions: 17; Districts: 3; Branches: 299; Temples: 10; three announced, Gilbert, Gila Valley and Phoenix; Headquarters: Salt Lake City, Utah.

The North America Southwest Area comprises a large geographic area of the United States comprising 17 missions – Arizona Mesa, Arizona Phoenix, Arizona Tempe, Arizona Tucson, Nevada Las Vegas, Nevada Las Vegas West, New Mexico Albuquerque, Oklahoma Oklahoma City, Oklahoma Tulsa, Texas Dallas, Texas Fort Worth, Texas Houston, Texas Houston East, Texas Houston South, Texas Lubbock, Texas McAllen, and Texas San Antonio Missions. There are 205 stakes and three mission districts in the Area covering the states of Nevada, Arizona, New Mexico, Texas, and Oklahoma and parts of California, Utah, Colorado, Kansas, Missouri, Arkansas, and Louisiana. Elder Neil L. Andersen of the Presidency of the Seventy supervises the Area with the assistance of nine Area Seventies.

The Church members are strong and active throughout the Area. There were 726,928 members assigned to units in the Area on Dec. 31, 2007. Sacrament meeting attendance has been at 45 percent for the past five years. Activity of Young Women and Young Men continues to increase a little each year – 71 percent of Young Women and 68 percent of Young Men are attending Sunday meetings.

Missionary work is strong and the Church continues to grow at a steady rate in the Area. In 2007, there were 9,976 convert baptisms (ages 9 and above). In addition, 8,702 8-year-old children were baptized during the year. Approximately 5,000 members are moving into the Area each year which is also adding to Church growth. This sustained growth has enabled 12 new stakes to be created in the Area between Jan. 1, 2007 and Sept. 15, 2008. The greatest growth was in Queen Creek, Ariz., where five stakes were created out of three stakes in early 2008. At the end of 2007, 4,819 missionaries were serving from the North America Southwest Area and 5,246 missionaries were serving in the 17 missions in the Area.

Currently 10 temples are operating in the Area – the Reno Nevada, Las Vegas Nevada, Snowflake Arizona, Mesa Arizona, Albuquerque New Mexico, Oklahoma City Oklahoma, Dallas Texas, Houston Texas, Lubbock Texas, and San Antonio Texas temples; and in 2008, three new temples were announced for the Area – the Gila Valley Arizona, Gilbert Arizona, and Phoenix Arizona temples. Temple attendance and family history work have remained strong, and members are excited and engaged in the roll-out of the New FamilySearch program which is now nearing completion for the 10 temples in the Area.

Significant Church-provided-humanitarian assistance continues to be rendered in areas devastated by earthquakes, wildfires, ice storms, hurricanes, tornados, and floods. In 2007, over $4 million of humanitarian relief was provided in the Area with increasing amounts being provided in 2008 because of Hurricanes Gustav and Ike and large wildfires. Many hours of volunteer labor have also been provided by Church members to assist with relief and clean-up efforts following these natural disasters.

A remarkable effort has been made to carry the gospel blessings to those of the Hispanic community and to strengthen the Church among Spanish-speaking members in the Southwest United States. In the first eight months of 2008, 22 new Spanish-speaking branches were approved throughout the Area with another nine applications are in process of approval. Twenty percent of the convert baptisms of the Area are Hispanic.

Much has been taught throughout the Area at all levels to support strong marriages, families, and homes. In the past three years, there has been a 10 percent increase in the number of endowed adults holding temple recommends. A major effort in 2008, by Church members as citizens in Arizona, has been 1.) their rally in support of getting the Arizona Marriage Amendment on the Arizona November 2008 general election ballot and 2.) their strong participation in a Christian coalition to get citizens to vote in support of the amendment, which states, "Only a union of one man and one woman shall be valid or recognized as a marriage in this state."

North America Central Area

As of December 31, 2007

Membership: 538,233; Stakes: 132; Wards: 987; Missions: 18; Districts: 2; Branches: 375; Temples: 11; two announced, Calgary, Alberta, and Kansas City, Mo.; Headquarters: Salt Lake City, Utah.

North America Northeast Area

As of December 31, 2007

Membership: 559,491; Stakes: 119; Wards: 847; Missions: 27; Districts: 9; Branches: 418; Temples: 9, Philadelphia, Pa., announced; Headquarters: Salt Lake City, Utah.

North America Southeast Area

As of December 31, 2007
Membership: 481,114;
Stakes: 97; Wards: 664; Missions: 18;
Districts: 0; Branches: 287; Temples: 9;
Headquarters: Salt Lake City, Utah.

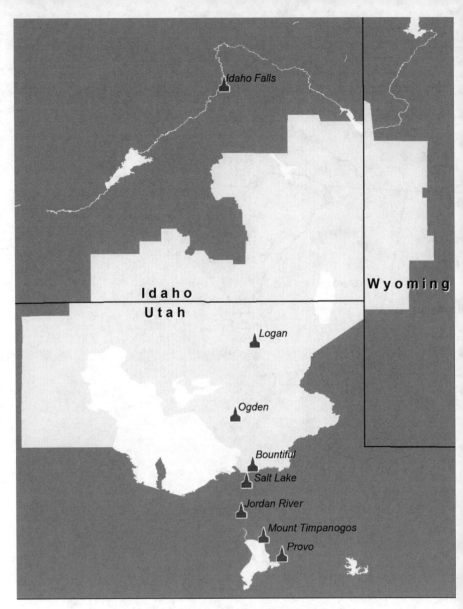

Utah North Area

As of December 31, 2007

Membership: 517,664; Stakes: 144; Wards: 1,223; Missions: 1;
Branches: 100; Temples: 3; Headquarters: Salt Lake City, Utah

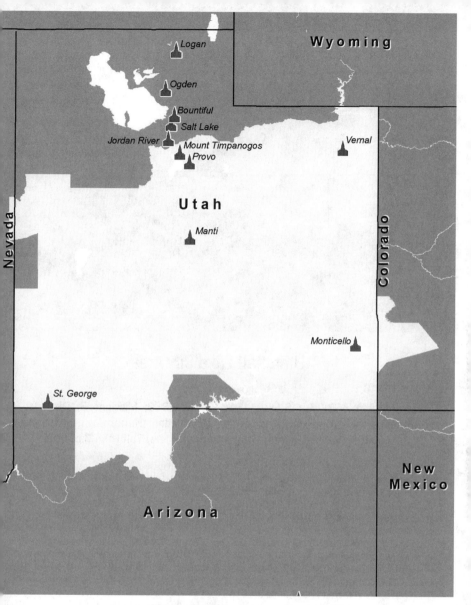

Utah South Area

As of December 31, 2007

Membership: 693,868; Stakes: 210; Wards: 1,819; Missions: 1;
Branches: 138; Temples: 6; Headquarters: Salt Lake City, Utah.

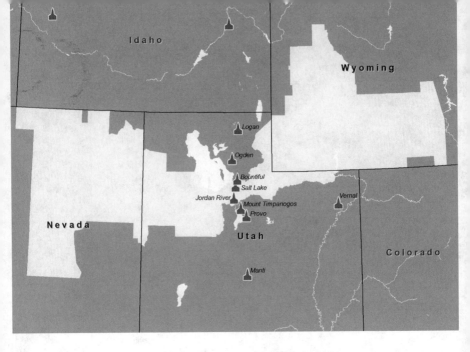

Utah Salt Lake City Area

As of December 31, 2007

Membership: 667,264; Stakes: 186; Wards: 1,386; Missions: 3; Districts: 1; Branches: 143; Temples: 2; two under construction; Draper, Utah, and Oquirrh Mountain in South Jordan, Utah; Headquarters: Salt Lake City, Utah.

The Church in Utah grew in numbers of members and meetinghouses in 2008. Seven stakes were created, 27 meetinghouses were built.

The most rapid growth occurred in:
• Utah County in the Eagle Mountain and Saratoga Springs cities;
• Salt Lake County in the southwestern area of the county in the Herriman area;
• Davis and Weber Counties along the I-15 corridor in the cities of Farmington, North Salt Lake, Hooper, Kanesville, Kaysville, Syracuse and West Point.

During the year 2008, extensive efforts were organized to assist diverse families from around the world and U.S. relocating in Utah. Members of the Church, along with non-members neighbors, voluntarily provided services such as:
• Aiding the homeless
• Attending to spiritual and emotional welfare of the refugees
• Providing legal aid
• Dispensing free medical care at newly established clinics
• Offering English language instruction
• Tutoring school-age youth

Major events witnessed in 2008 include:
• Assisting in relief efforts following the mine cave-in disaster in Price, Utah.
• Suffering the loss of community leaders in Blanding and Cedar City caused by separate plane crashes.

Idaho Area

As of December 31, 2007

Membership: 366,054; Stakes: 103; Wards: 854; Missions: 2;
Branches: 104; Temples: 4; Headquarters: Salt Lake City, Utah.

The two major events to take place in the Idaho Area during 2008 were the dedication of temples in Rexburg and Twin Falls.

The Rexburg Idaho Temple was dedicated on Feb. 10, by President Thomas S. Monson in what he called his "first official act" since becoming president of the Church. The temple serves 47,000 members in 17 stakes in the communities of Ashton, Driggs, Rexburg, St Anthony, and Sugar City. Over 200,000 toured the temple during the open house period. The Twin Falls Idaho Temple was dedicated on Aug. 24, by President Monson. This temple serves 42,000 members in 14 stakes in the communities of Burley, Hailey, Jerome, Ketchum, Rupert and Twin Falls. More than 159,000 toured the temple during the open-house period. A total of 815 referrals came from the two open houses. The cultural events accompanying each of the temple dedications featured thousands of youth from stakes within the temple districts.

Four new stakes were created in the Idaho Area during the year—BYU-Idaho 9th Stake, Twin Falls Idaho South Stake, Rexburg Idaho Henry's Fork Stake and the Ammon Idaho North Stake bringing the total number of stakes in Idaho to 107.

In addition, 13 new wards were created as of Sept. 1, 2008.

The boundaries of the Idaho Boise Mission and the Idaho Pocatello Mission were realigned as of July 1, 2008. Seven stakes were moved from the Pocatello Mission to the Boise Mission. Those stakes include: Burley, Burley West, Rupert, Rupert West, Paul, Oakley and Declo.

During the period Feb. 22-25, Church members in the Boise/Meridian area hosted 104 International delegates from nine countries for the Special Olympics. The local Saints organized and coordinated with local community officials including the Idaho State governor to provide a wonderful

Continued on next page

experience for these international athletes, leaders and officials. Those countries represented include the following: Austria (12 delegates), China (30 delegates), Czech Republic (4 delegates), Denmark (7 delegates), Germany (8 delegates), Kuwait (15 delegates), Lebanon (4 delegates), Libya (4 delegates), Romania (9 delegates), and Sweden (15 delegates).

In August 2008 a wildfire ripped through the hills east of Boise threatening several neighborhoods and ultimately destroying ten homes along Boise's east bench. Local Church members immediately organized and provided temporary shelter, food and support and later worked hand in hand with local emergency response agencies and community leaders to assist those families displaced by the fire.

Leon Parson is a local artist who was responsible for painting the murals for the Rexburg and Twin Falls Temples. With 30-years of oil-based art experience, Brother Parson has been working for the past 8-years in the Idaho Falls Temple helping to preserve and at times modify the murals there.

In the Rexburg Temple, Brother Parson shaped the mural concepts by sorting through more than 20,000 existing and new photographs of various scenes around Rexburg. After renovating a farm shed to serve as his studio, he went to work. Each mural is approximately 10 feet high and 27 feet wide. The 90-pound canvases were hoisted onto large wood panels serving as easels and placed according to each mural's actual location in the ordinance rooms.

The murals in the Rexburg Temple reflect the natural beauty of eastern Idaho. Plant life such as aspens, cottonwoods, pines, and sage are depicted. Deer, elk, and the mountain bluebird are among the wildlife represented. He went through the same painstaking process to select subjects for the Twin Falls Temple. Brother Parson said he hoped that when people came to the temples and saw the murals they would think, "Oh! I'm home. This is where I have chosen to live."

Then, he noted, "I hope they recognize the beauty of the Savior's creation and gift to us." He worked six days a week for almost two years, with some days lasting 16-hours. Even with the painstaking work and grueling schedule, Brother Parson felt blessed.

2007 MEMBERSHIP STATISTICS

MEMBERSHIP AND UNITS BY CHURCH AREA

As of 31 Dec. 2007; area boundaries do not necessarily follow country, state or province boundaries.

Country	Membership	Stakes	Wards	Branches in stakes	Missions	Districts	Branches in missions	Total wards, branches
AFRICA SOUTHEAST	118,312	20	148	78	9	15	148	374
AFRICA WEST	146,290	26	188	47	9	23	173	408
ASIA	133,593	16	115	18	11	27	213	346
ASIA NORTH	209,510	46	259	83	12	25	119	461
BRAZIL	1,018,901	218	1,329	200	27	50	266	1,795
CARIBBEAN	157,373	23	155	41	8	27	161	357
CENTRAL AMERICA	575,727	97	614	197	12	55	268	1,079
CHILE	548,726	74	419	66	9	24	128	613
EUROPE	431,380	111	695	312	37	45	311	1,318
EUROPE EAST	38,459	1	8	3	14	26	239	250
IDAHO	368,054	103	854	104	2	0	0	958
MEXICO	1,121,933	210	1,459	239	21	40	265	1,963
MIDDLE EAST/ NORTH AFRICA	2,813	1	6	10	0	2	9	25
NORTH AMERICA CENTRAL	538,233	132	987	358	18	2	17	1,362
NORTH AMERICA NORTHEAST	559,491	119	847	353	27	9	65	1,265
NORTH AMERICA NORTHWEST	465,769	107	802	157	9	2	11	970
NORTH AMERICA SOUTHEAST	481,114	97	664	287	18	0	0	951
NORTH AMERICA SOUTHWEST	953,013	198	1,590	285	17	3	14	1,889
NORTH AMERICA WEST	809,171	173	1,303	176	18	0	0	1,479
PACIFIC	429,294	107	706	145	15	34	231	1,082
PHILIPPINES	594,655	77	481	127	15	87	475	1,083
SOUTH AMERICA NORTH	481,980	87	563	92	11	34	178	833
SOUTH AMERICA SOUTH	525,830	96	636	244	14	54	292	1,172
SOUTH AMERICA WEST	607,582	111	722	100	10	33	163	985
UTAH NORTH	517,664	144	1,223	100	1	0	0	1,323
UTAH SALT LAKE CITY	667,264	186	1,386	138	3	1	5	1,529
UTAH SOUTH	693,868	210	1,819	138	1	0	0	1,957
TOTALS	**13,193,999**	**2,790**	**19,978**	**4,098**	**348**	**618**	**3,751**	**27,827**

2007 Membership by Countries

Country	Membership	Stakes	Wards	Branches in stakes	Missions	Districts	Branches in missions	Total wards, branches
AFRICA								
ANGOLA	759	0	0	0	0	0	1	1
BENIN	216	0	0	0	0	0	1	1
BOTSWANA	1,302	0	2	1	0	0	1	4
CAMEROON	639	0	0	0	0	0	3	3
CAPE VERDE	6,709	0	0	0	1	3	18	18
CENTRAL AFRICAN REPUBLIC	396	0	0	0	0	0	1	1
COTE D'IVOIRE / IVORY COAST	12,463	3	23	1	1	0	5	29
DEMOCRATIC REPUBLIC OF CONGO	19,313	4	43	5	1	4	17	65
ETHIOPIA	784	0	0	0	0	0	3	3
GHANA	36,242	7	45	14	2	5	34	93
KENYA	8,124	1	5	3	1	1	23	31
LESOTHO	576	0	0	0	0	0	1	1
LIBERIA	4,910	0	0	0	0	2	9	9
MADAGASCAR	4,160	1	6	4	1	0	5	15
MALAWI	705	0	0	0	0	0	4	4
MAURITIUS	368	0	0	0	0	0	2	2
MAYOTTE	7	0	0	0	0	0	1	1
MOZAMBIQUE	4,216	0	0	0	1	2	15	15
NAMIBIA	506	0	0	0	0	0	2	2
NIGERIA	83,919	16	120	32	5	14	104	256
REPUBLIC OF CONGO	3,974	1	8	4	0	0	2	14
REUNION	773	0	0	0	0	1	5	5
SIERRA LEONE	7,657	0	0	0	1	2	18	18
SOUTH AFRICA	45,981	11	65	55	3	0	10	130
SWAZILAND	1,049	0	1	2	0	0	0	3
TANZANIA	879	0	0	0	0	1	4	4
TOGO	733	0	0	0	0	0	2	2
UGANDA	4,701	0	0	0	1	2	14	14
ZAMBIA	2,095	0	0	0	0	2	11	11
ZIMBABWE	16,969	2	18	4	1	2	23	45
AFRICA TOTALS	**271,537**	**46**	**336**	**125**	**19**	**41**	**341**	**802**
ASIA								
ARMENIA	2,650	0	0	0	1	1	14	14
BAHRAIN	76	0	0	1	0	0	0	1
CAMBODIA	8,188	0	0	0	1	4	22	22
CHINA, HONG KONG	22,939	4	23	1	1	1	9	33
CYPRUS	303	0	0	0	0	1	4	4
GEORGIA	153	0	0	0	0	0	2	2
INDIA	7,008	0	0	0	2	3	26	26
INDONESIA	6,256	0	0	0	1	3	24	24

Country	Membership	Stakes	Wards	Branches in stakes	Missions	Districts	Branches in missions	Total wards, branches
ISRAEL	246	0	0	0	0	1	3	3
JAPAN	122,442	29	165	61	7	14	68	294
KAZAKHSTAN	125	0	0	0	0	0	1	1
MACAU	1,191	0	0	0	0	0	2	2
MALAYSIA	4,626	0	0	1	0	4	18	19
MONGOLIA	7,721	0	0	0	1	2	21	21
PAPUA NEW GUINEA	16,060	1	5	3	1	7	45	53
PHILIPPINES	594,655	77	481	127	15	87	475	1,083
SINGAPORE	2,723	1	8	0	1	0	1	9
SOUTH KOREA	80,421	17	94	22	4	6	27	143
SRI LANKA	1,228	0	0	0	0	1	4	4
TAIWAN	47,034	10	77	10	3	2	10	97
THAILAND	15,457	1	7	6	1	5	26	39
TURKEY	198	0	0	0	0	0	4	4
ASIA TOTALS	**957,154**	**141**	**866**	**241**	**42**	**147**	**886**	**1,993**

NORTH AMERICA

Country	Membership	Stakes	Wards	Branches in stakes	Missions	Districts	Branches in missions	Total wards, branches
ANTIGUA AND BARBUDA	161	0	0	0	0	0	1	1
ARUBA	416	0	0	0	0	1	3	3
BAHAMAS	774	0	0	0	0	1	3	3
BARBADOS	669	0	0	0	0	1	4	4
BELIZE	3,306	0	0	0	0	3	12	12
BERMUDA	131	0	0	0	0	0	1	1
CANADA								
ALBERTA	73,630	22	173	32	2	0	0	205
BRITISH COLUMBIA	28,915	8	47	26	1	1	4	77
MANITOBA	4,465	1	7	5	1	0	0	12
NEW BRUNSWICK	3,065	1	5	2	0	0	0	7
NEWFOUNDLAND	695	0	0	0	0	0	5	5
NORTHWEST TERRITORIES	192	0	0	0	0	0	1	1
NOVA SCOTIA	4,772	1	6	7	1	1	7	20
NUNAVUT	13	0	0	0	0	0	1	1
ONTARIO	46,105	9	61	29	2	2	12	102
PRINCE EDWARD ISLAND	391	0	0	0	0	0	3	3
QUEBEC	10,096	3	17	12	1	1	3	32
SASKATCHEWAN	5,501	2	8	7	0	0	0	15
YUKON	262	0	0	1	0	0	0	1
CANADA TOTALS	**178,102**	**47**	**324**	**121**	**8**	**5**	**36**	**481**
CAYMAN ISLAND	118	0	0	0	0	0	1	1
COSTA RICA	35,647	5	43	11	1	6	22	76
DOMINICA	77	0	0	0	0	0	3	3
DOMINICAN REPUBLIC	106,243	16	115	32	3	8	47	194
EL SALVADOR	98,575	16	105	33	2	2	18	156
GRENADA	176	0	0	0	0	0	1	1

Country	Membership	Stakes	Wards	Branches in stakes	Missions	Districts	Branches in missions	Total wards, branches
GUADELOUPE	356	0	0	0	0	1	5	5
GUATEMALA	210,101	40	241	79	4	21	110	430
HAITI	14,493	2	14	0	1	2	15	29
HONDURAS	125,606	20	129	42	3	11	49	220
JAMAICA	5,811	0	0	0	1	4	21	21
MARTINIQUE	156	0	0	0	0	0	2	2
MEXICO	1,121,893	210	1,459	239	21	40	264	1,962
NETHERLANDS ANTILLES								
BONAIRE	105	0	0	0	0	0	1	1
CURACAO	485	0	0	0	0	1	2	2
SAINT MAARTEN	260	0	0	0	0	0	2	2
TOTALS	850	0	0	0	0	1	5	5
NICARAGUA	59,886	8	54	10	1	6	28	92
PANAMA	42,606	8	42	22	1	6	29	93
PUERTO RICO	19,808	5	26	9	2	2	8	43
SAINT KITTS-NEVIS	120	0	0	0	0	1	2	2
SAINT LUCIA	113	0	0	0	0	0	2	2
SAINT VINCENT / GRENADINES	384	0	0	0	0	0	2	2
TRINIDAD & TOBAGO	2,271	0	0	0	1	2	11	11
UNITED STATES								
ALABAMA	33,404	6	41	30	1	0	0	71
ALASKA	29,460	7	48	24	1	1	7	79
ARIZONA	368,417	86	677	85	4	0	0	762
ARKANSAS	25,296	5	32	24	1	0	0	56
CALIFORNIA	749,490	159	1,195	172	17	0	0	1,367
COLORADO	133,727	30	253	32	3	0	0	285
CONNECTICUT	14,338	4	27	5	1	0	0	32
DELAWARE	4,585	1	8	2	0	0	0	10
DISTRICT OF COLUMBIA	2,166	0	2	1	0	0	0	3
FLORIDA	129,238	25	183	57	5	0	0	240
GEORGIA	72,760	16	105	35	3	0	0	140
HAWAII	67,106	15	120	11	1	0	0	131
IDAHO	399,427	115	936	111	2	0	0	1,047
ILLINOIS	54,424	12	91	38	4	0	0	129
INDIANA	40,139	11	68	28	1	0	0	96
IOWA	23,301	7	36	33	1	0	0	69
KANSAS	32,116	7	52	22	0	0	0	74
KENTUCKY	30,498	6	40	32	1	0	0	72
LOUISIANA	27,119	6	31	18	1	0	0	49
MAINE	10,160	2	14	18	0	0	0	32
MARYLAND	38,850	8	66	14	2	0	0	80
MASSACHUSETTS	24,114	4	38	13	1	0	0	51
MICHIGAN	42,422	8	65	33	2	1	10	108
MINNESOTA	29,550	7	52	23	1	0	1	76

Country	Membership	Stakes	Wards	Branches in stakes	Missions	Districts	Branches in missions	Total wards, branches
MISSISSIPPI	20,377	4	28	16	1	0	0	44
MISSOURI	62,217	14	104	39	2	0	0	143
MONTANA	44,976	11	77	42	1	0	0	119
NEBRASKA	21,890	4	40	20	1	0	1	61
NEVADA	172,330	33	291	26	2	0	0	317
NEW HAMPSHIRE	8,091	3	16	4	1	0	0	20
NEW JERSEY	30,280	5	35	20	2	1	3	58
NEW MEXICO	63,987	14	89	39	1	0	0	128
NEW YORK	74,004	14	83	52	4	3	17	152
NORTH CAROLINA	71,737	15	102	42	2	0	0	144
NORTH DAKOTA	6,005	2	7	9	0	0	0	16
OHIO	56,492	13	91	33	3	0	0	124
OKLAHOMA	40,683	7	57	25	2	0	0	82
OREGON	144,808	36	255	50	2	0	0	305
PENNSYLVANIA	47,832	10	74	30	3	1	7	111
RHODE ISLAND	3,608	0	6	0	0	0	0	6
SOUTH CAROLINA	36,141	6	46	14	1	0	0	60
SOUTH DAKOTA	9,397	2	9	14	1	1	10	33
TENNESSEE	42,102	10	65	23	2	0	0	88
TEXAS	269,670	49	413	91	8	3	14	518
UTAH	1,823,613	523	4,296	365	5	1	5	4,666
VERMONT	4,302	1	7	5	0	0	0	12
VIRGINIA	83,225	19	144	39	2	0	0	183
WASHINGTON	253,166	54	440	55	5	0	0	495
WEST VIRGINIA	16,491	4	24	14	1	0	0	38
WISCONSIN	23,907	6	41	27	1	0	0	68
WYOMING	59,970	16	131	20	0	0	0	151
U. S. TOTALS	5,873,408	1,422	11,151	1,975	106	12	75	13,201
VIRGIN ISLANDS	530	0	0	0	0	0	2	2
VIRGIN ISLANDS, British	75	0	0	0	0	0	2	2
NORTH AMERICA TOTALS	7,902,968	1,799	13,703	2,573	155	136	786	17,062
EUROPE								
ALBANIA	1,730	0	0	0	1	1	10	10
ANDORRA	89	0	0	0	0	0	1	1
AUSTRIA	4,176	2	13	5	0	0	0	18
BELGIUM	6,029	2	10	8	1	0	0	18
BULGARIA	2,142	0	0	0	1	2	21	21
CROATIA	503	0	0	0	0	1	6	6
CZECH REPUBLIC	2,028	0	0	0	1	2	14	14
DENMARK	4,343	2	13	9	1	0	1	23
ESTONIA	927	0	0	0	0	1	4	4
FINLAND	4,533	2	15	4	1	2	11	30

Country	Membership	Stakes	Wards	Branches in stakes	Missions	Districts	Branches in missions	Total wards, branches
FRANCE (includes Corsica)	34,638	9	59	43	2	2	15	117
GERMANY	37,159	14	92	65	4	3	18	175
GREECE	661	0	0	0	1	0	5	5
GREENLAND	23	0	0	0	0	0	1	1
GUERNSEY	43	0	0	1	0	0	0	1
HUNGARY	4,380	1	5	5	1	0	9	19
ICELAND	250	0	0	0	0	0	2	2
IRELAND	2,805	1	4	4	1	1	5	13
ISLE OF MAN	283	0	1	0	0	0	0	1
ITALY	22,633	5	31	22	3	9	49	102
JERSEY	286	0	1	0	0	0	0	1
LATVIA	966	0	0	0	1	1	7	7
LITHUANIA	833	0	0	0	0	1	5	5
LUXEMBOURG	285	0	1	0	0	0	0	1
MALTA	139	0	0	0	0	0	1	1
MOLDOVA	264	0	0	0	0	0	2	2
NETHERLANDS	8,548	3	18	16	0	0	0	34
NORWAY	4,126	1	7	2	1	0	13	22
POLAND	1,527	0	0	0	1	2	12	12
PORTUGAL	38,100	6	35	16	2	4	24	75
ROMANIA	2,672	0	0	0	1	2	19	19
RUSSIA	15,615	0	0	0	5	13	102	102
SERBIA	275	0	0	0	0	1	3	3
SLOVAKIA	124	0	0	0	0	0	4	4
SLOVENIA	352	0	0	0	1	1	4	4
SPAIN	42,873	9	61	23	4	9	49	133
SWEDEN	8,830	4	24	13	1	1	5	42
SWITZERLAND	7,875	5	23	15	2	0	1	39
UKRAINE	10,394	1	8	3	3	4	48	59
UNITED KINGDOM								
ENGLAND	140,994	36	227	37	5	0	0	264
NORTHERN IRELAND	5,316	1	8	5	0	0	0	13
SCOTLAND	26,336	5	29	10	1	0	4	43
WALES	9,110	3	18	9	0	0	0	27
TOTALS	181,756	45	282	61	6	0	4	347
EUROPE TOTALS	**455,730**	**112**	**703**	**315**	**46**	**64**	**480**	**1,498**
SOUTH AMERICA								
ARGENTINA	363,990	70	467	187	10	39	209	863
BOLIVIA	158,427	24	165	24	3	10	56	245
BRAZIL	1,019,153	218	1,329	200	27	50	267	1,796
CHILE	548,743	74	419	66	9	24	129	614
COLOMBIA	158,954	28	170	24	4	14	75	269
ECUADOR	181,463	33	212	32	3	10	49	293

Country	Membership	Stakes	Wards	Branches in stakes	Missions	Districts	Branches in missions	Total wards, branches
FALKLAND ISLAND	4	0	0	0	0	0	1	1
FRENCH GUIANA	287	0	0	0	0	0	2	2
GUYANA	2,572	0	0	0	0	2	12	12
PARAGUAY	71,531	10	62	29	2	11	55	146
PERU	448,903	87	557	76	7	23	106	739
SURINAME	847	0	0	0	0	1	6	6
URUGUAY	90,292	16	107	28	2	4	27	162
VENEZUELA	141,563	26	181	36	4	10	54	271
S. AMERICA TOTALS	**3,186,729**	**586**	**3,669**	**702**	**71**	**198**	**1,048**	**5,419**
PACIFIC								
AMERICAN SAMOA	14,514	4	30	5	0	0	1	36
AUSTRALIA	119,975	33	195	31	7	11	62	288
COOK ISLANDS	1,803	0	0	0	0	1	5	5
FIJI	14,866	4	25	9	1	2	10	44
FRENCH POLYNESIA	19,711	6	51	6	1	3	25	82
GUAM	1,690	0	0	0	1	1	3	3
KIRIBATI	12,446	2	11	6	0	0	11	28
MARSHALL ISLANDS	4,623	0	0	0	1	2	11	11
MICRONESIA	3,754	0	0	0	0	4	19	19
NAURU	110	0	0	0	0	0	1	1
NEW CALEDONIA	1,828	0	0	0	0	1	8	8
NEW ZEALAND	98,710	25	148	39	2	3	15	202
NIUE	253	0	0	0	0	0	3	3
NORTHERN MARIANA ISLANDS	777	0	0	0	0	0	1	1
PALAU	426	0	0	0	0	0	1	1
SAMOA	66,249	16	116	17	1	0	1	134
SOLOMON ISLANDS	231	0	0	0	0	0	1	1
TONGA	54,281	16	125	29	1	2	10	164
TUVALU ISLANDS	113	0	0	0	0	0	1	1
VANUATU	3,521	0	0	0	0	2	21	21
PACIFIC TOTALS	**419,881**	**106**	**701**	**142**	**15**	**32**	**210**	**1053**

MISSIONARY STATISTICS

Year	Missionaries called	Year	Missionaries called	Year	Missionaries called	Year	Missionaries called
1830	16	1875	197	1920	889	1965	7,139
1831	58	1876	211	1921	880	1966	7,021
1832	72	1877	154	1922	886	1967	6,475
1833	41	1878	152	1923	812	1968	7,178
1834	111	1879	179	1924	867	1969	6,967
1835	84	1880	219	1925	1,131	1970	7,590
1836	80	1881	199	1926	1,236	1971	8,344
1837	52	1882	237	1927	1,017	1972	7,874
1838	16	1883	248	1928	1,193	1973	9,471
1839	67	1884	205	1929	1,058	1974	9,811
1840	80	1885	235	1930	896	1975	14,446
1841	100	1886	209	1931	678	1976	13,928
1842	45	1887	282	1932	399	1977	14,561
1843	374	1888	242	1933	525	1978	15,860
1844	586	1889	249	1934	843	1979	16,590
1845	84	1890	283	1935	960	1980	16,600
1846	32	1891	331	1936	899	1981	17,800
1847	40	1892	324	1937	1,079	1982	18,260
1848	55	1893	317	1938	1,146	1983	19,450
1849	58	1894	162	1939	1,088	1984	19,720
1850	50	1895	526	1940	1,194	1985	19,890
1851	44	1896	746	1941	1,257	1986	20,798
1852	158	1897	922	1942	629	1987	21,001
1853	33	1898	943	1943	261	1988	22,619
1854	119	1899	1,059	1944	427	1989	25,609
1855	65	1900	796	1945	400	1990	26,255
1856	130	1901	522	1946	2,297	1991	24,861
1857	88	1902	848	1947	2,132	1992	28,716
1858	0	1903	658	1948	2,161	1993	28,774
1859	18	1904	699	1949	2,363	1994	27,912
1860	96	1905	716	1950	3,015	1995	29,015
1861	19	1906	1,015	1951	1,801	1996	31,227
1862	27	1907	930	1952	872	1997	33,726
1863	50	1908	919	1953	1,750	1998	33,229
1864	52	1909	1,014	1954	2,022	1999	33,915
1865	71	1910	933	1955	2,414	2000	34,503
1866	32	1911	822	1956	2,572	2001	34,684
1867	133	1912	769	1957	2,518	2002	36,196
1868	32	1913	858	1958	2,778	2003	30,467
1869	250	1914	684	1959	2,847	2004	29,548
1870	46	1915	621	1960	4,706	2005	30,587
1871	167	1916	722	1961	5,793	2006	30,653
1872	132	1917	543	1962	5,630	2007	30,384
1873	35	1918	245	1963	5,781		
1874	98	1919	1,211	1964	5,886		

CHURCH STATISTICS

As of Dec. 2007	Total Members	Stakes	Stake wards & branches	Missions	Mission branches	Total wards & branches
Apr. 6, 1830	6	0	0	0	0	0
Dec. 31	280	0	0	0	0	4
1831	680	0	0	0	0	6
1832	2,661	0	0	0	0	33
1833	3,140	0	0	0	0	40
1834	4,372	2	22	0	18	40
1835	8,835	2	22	0	26	48
1836	13,293	2	25	0	29	54
1837	16,282	2	25	1	42	67
1838	17,881	2	26	1	65	91
1839	16,460	3	16	2	70	86
1840	16,865	10	18	2	69	87
1841	19,856	2	19	2	84	103
1842	23,564	2	26	2	199	225
1843	25,980	2	31	2	238	269
1844	26,146	2	33	3	239	272
1845	30,332	1	34	4	277	311
1846	33,993	0	30	5	311	341
1847	34,694	1	48	5	357	405
1848	40,477	1	55	5	426	481
1849	48,160	1	75	5	515	590
1850	51,839	1	61	9	637	698
1851	52,165	4	60	11	717	777
1852	52,640	5	65	13	795	860
1853	64,154	5	75	14	885	960
1854	68,429	6	79	13	859	938
1855	63,974	6	99	14	858	957
1856	63,881	7	124	12	841	965
1857	55,236	6	77	12	742	819
1858	55,755	4	81	9	661	742
1859	57,038	4	98	9	635	733
1860	61,082	4	110	8	611	721
1861	66,211	4	126	7	588	714
1862	68,780	4	135	7	563	698
1863	71,770	4	143	7	524	667
1864	74,348	4	161	8	471	632
1865	76,771	4	164	8	436	600
1866	77,884	4	167	8	420	587
1867	81,124	4	175	8	407	582
1868	84,622	5	178	8	385	563
1869	88,432	9	187	7	383	570
1870	90,130	9	195	7	363	558
1871	95,596	9	200	7	342	542
1872	98,152	9	206	7	347	553
1873	101,538	9	213	7	348	561
1874	103,916	10	216	7	309	525
1875	107,167	10	222	7	302	524
1876	111,111	10	230	8	307	537
1877	115,065	20	252	8	285	537
1878	125,046	21	254	9	272	526
1879	128,386	22	263	10	289	552
1880	133,628	23	272	10	287	559
1881	140,733	23	283	10	293	576
1882	145,604	24	292	10	291	583
1883	151,593	27	317	11	292	609
1884	158,242	29	340	13	296	636

As of Dec. 2007	Total Members	Stakes	Stake wards & branches	Missions	Mission branches	Total wards & branches
1885	164,130	29	348	12	311	659
1886	166,653	30	342	12	315	657
1887	173,029	31	360	12	326	686
1888	180,294	32	373	13	336	709
1889	183,144	32	388	12	339	727
1890	188,263	32	395	12	330	725
1891	195,445	32	409	12	332	741
1892	200,961	33	439	14	350	789
1893	214,534	34	451	15	356	807
1894	222,369	34	457	15	356	813
1895	231,116	37	479	15	356	835
1896	241,427	37	489	17	348	837
1897	255,736	37	493	18	374	867
1898	267,251	40	516	20	401	917
1899	271,681	40	506	20	412	918
1900	283,765	43	529	20	438	967
1901	292,931	50	577	21	442	1,019
1902	299,105	50	595	22	481	1,076
1903	304,901	51	612	23	477	1,089
1904	324,289	55	619	21	475	1,094
1905	332,048	55	627	22	514	1,141
1906	345,014	55	636	22	541	1,177
1907	357,913	55	634	22	558	1,192
1908	371,472	59	666	22	595	1,261
1909	377,279	60	684	21	590	1,274
1910	398,478	62	699	21	611	1,310
1911	407,291	62	706	21	632	1,338
1912	417,555	65	716	22	647	1,363
1913	431,607	66	749	22	650	1,399
1914	454,718	68	772	21	601	1,373
1915	466,238	72	783	21	608	1,391
1916	477,321	73	808	22	559	1,367
1917	488,038	75	875	22	578	1,453
1918	495,962	75	893	22	559	1,452
1919	507,961	79	888	23	554	1,442
1920	525,987	83	904	24	623	1,527
1921	548,803	86	933	25	665	1,598
1922	566,358	87	946	25	661	1,607
1923	575,896	90	962	26	697	1,659
1924	597.861	94	969	25	716	1,685
1925	613,572	94	985	28	720	1,705
1926	623,909	96	992	28	739	1,731
1927	644,745	99	1,005	28	758	1,763
1928	655,686	101	1,004	29	813	1,817
1929	663,652	104	1,004	30	823	1,827
1930	670,017	104	1,000	30	868	1,868
1931	688,435	104	1,004	31	861	1,865
1932	703,949	104	1,012	31	867	1,879
1933	717,619	105	1,014	31	875	1,889
1934	730,738	110	1,035	31	892	1,927
1935	746,384	115	1,064	32	900	1,964
1936	760,690	118	1,081	33	933	2,014
1937	767,752	118	1,101	35	951	2,052
1938	784,764	126	1,137	36	947	2,084
1939	803,528	129	1,154	35	1,002	2,156
1940	862,664	134	1,191	35	728	1,919
1941	892,080	139	1,224	36	757	1,981
1942	917,715	143	1,242	37	776	2,018

As of Dec. 2007	Total Members	Stakes	Stake wards & branches	Missions	Mission branches	Total wards & branches
1943	937,050	146	1,261	38	807	2,068
1944	954,004	148	1,273	38	773	2,046
1945	979,454	153	1,295	38	909	2,204
1946	996,505	161	1,340	39	959	2,299
1947	1,016,170	169	1,425	43	1,149	2,574
1948	1,041,970	172	1,451	44	1,323	2,774
1949	1,078,671	175	1,501	46	1,327	2,828
1950	1,111,314	180	1,541	43	1,370	2,911
1951	1,147,157	191	1,666	42	1,414	3,080
1952	1,189,053	202	1,767	43	1,551	3,318
1953	1,246,362	211	1,884	42	1,399	3,283
1954	1,302,240	219	1,993	42	1,476	3,469
1955	1,357,274	224	2,082	44	1,471	3,553
1956	1,416,731	239	2,210	45	1,854	4,064
1957	1,488,314	251	2,362	45	1,740	4,102
1958	1,555,799	273	2,513	47	1,757	4,270
1959	1,616,088	290	2,614	50	1,895	4,509
1960	1,693,180	319	2,882	58	1,811	4,693
1961	1,823,661	345	3,143	67	1,872	5,015
1962	1,965,786	364	3,423	74	1,802	5,225
1963	2,117,451	389	3,615	77	1,782	5,397
1964	2,234,916	400	3,749	79	2,016	5,765
1965	2,395,932	412	3,897	76	2,137	6,034
1966	2,480,899	425	4,022	75	2,053	6,075
1967	2,614,340	448	4,166	77	1,987	6,153
1968	2,684,073	473	4,385	83	2,112	6,497
1969	2,807,456	496	4,592	88	2,016	6,608
1970	2,930,810	537	4,922	92	1,943	6,865
1971	3,090,953	562	5,135	98	1,942	7,077
1972	3,218,908	592	5,394	101	1,891	7,285
1973	3,306,658	630	5,707	108	1,817	7,524
1974	3,409,987	675	5,951	113	1,822	7,773
1975	3,572,202	737	6,390	134	1,761	8,151
1976	3,742,749	798	6,903	148	1,422	8,325
1977	3,969,220	885	7,466	157	1,694	9,180
1978	4,166,854	990	8,064	166	1,790	9,854
1979	4,404,121	1,092	9,365	175	1,121	10,486
1980	4,639,822	1,218	10,324	188	2,267	12,591
1981	4,920,449	1,321	11,063	186	2,030	13,093
1982	5,162,619	1,392	11,492	180	1,979	13,471
1983	5,351,724	1,458	11,953	177	1,991	13,943
1984	5,641,054	1,507	12,422	180	2,046	14,468
1985	5,919,483	1,582	12,939	188	2,068	15,007
1986	6,166,974	1,622	13,318	193	2,064	15,382
1987	6,394,314	1,666	13,727	205	2,307	16,034
1988	6,721,210	1,707	14,069	222	2,470	16,539
1989	7,308,444	1,739	14,533	228	2,751	17,284
1990	7,761,207	1,784	15,003	256	3,079	18,082
1991	8,089,848	1,837	15,513	267	3,325	18,838
1992	8,404,087	1,919	16,292	276	3,819	20,112
1993	8,689,168	1,968	17,048	295	4,051	21,099
1994	9,024,368	2,008	17,521	303	4,311	21,832
1995	9,338,397	2,150	18,396	307	4,277	22,673
1996	9,692,441	2,296	19,522	309	3,994	23,516
1997	10,071,783	2,424	20,776	318	3,923	24,697
1998	10,404,448	2,505	21,649	331	3,904	25,553
1999	10,752,984	2,542	21,897	333	3,896	25,793
2000	11,068,861	2,581	22,071	334	3,844	25,915

As of Dec. 2007	Total Members	Stakes	Stake wards & branches	Missions	Mission branches	Total wards & branches
2001	11,394,518	2,607	22,249	333	3,835	26,084
2002	11,721,548	2,602	22,231	335	3,912	26,143
2003	11,985,254	2,624	22,418	337	3,819	26,237
2004	12,275,822	2,665	22,886	338	3,784	26,670
2005	12,560,869	2,701	23,307	341	3,780	27,087
2006	12,868,606	2,745	23,703	344	3,772	27,475
2007	13,193,999	2,790	24,076	348	3,751	27,827

TEMPLES

Draper Utah Temple

TEMPLES OF THE CHURCH

Listed in order of completion

	TEMPLE	LOCATION	DEDICATED	BY WHOM
	Kirtland*	Kirtland, Ohio	27 Mar 1836	Joseph Smith
	Nauvoo**	Nauvoo, Ill.	30 Apr 1846	Joseph Young (private)
			1 May 1846	Orson Hyde (public)
1	St. George Utah	St. George, Utah	6 Apr 1877	Daniel H. Wells
	Rededicated after remodeling		11 Nov 1975	Spencer W. Kimball
2	Logan Utah	Logan, Utah	17 May 1884	John Taylor
	Rededicated after remodeling		13 Mar 1979	Spencer W. Kimball
3	Manti Utah	Manti, Utah	17 May 1888	Wilford Woodruff (private)
			21 May 1888	(His prayer read by
				Lorenzo Snow; public)
	Rededicated after remodeling		14 Jun 1985	Gordon B. Hinckley
4	Salt Lake	Salt Lake City, Utah	6 Apr 1893	Wilford Woodruff
5	Laie Hawaii	Laie, Oahu, Hawaii	27 Nov 1919	Heber J. Grant
	Rededicated after remodeling		13 Jun 1978	Spencer W. Kimball
6	Cardston Alberta	Cardston, Alberta	26 Aug 1923	Heber J. Grant
	Rededicated after remodeling		2 Jul 1962	Hugh B. Brown
	Rededication after remodeling		22 Jun 1991	Gordon B. Hinckley
7	Mesa Arizona	Mesa, Ariz.	23 Oct 1927	Heber J. Grant
	Rededicated after remodeling		15 Apr 1975	Spencer W. Kimball
8	Idaho Falls Idaho	Idaho Falls, Idaho	23 Sep 1945	George Albert Smith
9	Bern Switzerland	Zollikofen, Switzerland	11 Sep 1955	David O. McKay
	Rededicated after remodeling		23 Oct 1992	Gordon B. Hinckley
10	Los Angeles California	Los Angeles, Calif.	11 Mar 1956	David O. McKay
11	Hamilton New Zealand	Hamilton, New Zealand	20 Apr 1958	David O. McKay
12	London England	Newchapel, Surrey,	7 Sep 1958	David O. McKay
	Rededicated after remodeling		18 Oct 1992	Gordon B. Hinckley
13	Oakland California	Oakland, Calif.	17 Nov 1964	David O. McKay
14	Ogden Utah	Ogden, Utah	18 Jan 1972	Joseph Fielding Smith
15	Provo Utah	Provo, Utah	9 Feb 1972	Joseph Fielding Smith
				(Prayer read by Harold B. Lee)
16	Washington D.C.	Kensington, Md.	19 Nov 1974	Spencer W. Kimball
17	Sao Paulo Brazil	Sao Paulo, Brazil	30 Oct 1978	Spencer W. Kimball
	Rededicated after remodeling		22 Feb 2004	Gordon B. Hinckley
18	Tokyo Japan	Tokyo, Japan	27 Oct 1980	Spencer W. Kimball
19	Seattle Washington	Bellevue, Wash.	17 Nov 1980	Spencer W. Kimball
20	Jordan River Utah	South Jordan, Utah	16 Nov 1981	Marion G. Romney
21	Atlanta Georgia	Sandy Springs, Ga.	1 Jun 1983	Gordon B. Hinckley
22	Apia Samoa	Apia, Western Samoa	5 Aug 1983	Gordon B. Hinckley
	Destroyed by fire July 9, 2003.			
	Dedicated after rebuilding		4 Sep 2005	Gordon B. Hinckley
23	Nuku'alofa Tonga	Nuku'alofa, Tonga	9 Aug 1983	Gordon B. Hinckley
	Rededicated after remodeling		4 Nov 2007	Russell M. Nelson
24	Santiago Chile	Santiago, Chile	15 Sep 1983	Gordon B. Hinckley
	Rededicated after remodeling		12 Mar 2006	Gordon B. Hinckley
25	Papeete Tahiti	Pirae, Tahiti	27 Oct 1983	Gordon B. Hinckley
	Rededicated after remodeling		12 Nov 2006	L. Tom Perry
26	Mexico City D.F. Mexico	Mexico City, Mexico	2 Dec 1983	Gordon B. Hinckley
	Rededicated after remodeling		16 Nov 2008	

27	Boise Idaho	Boise, Idaho	25 May 1984	Gordon B. Hinckley
28	Sydney Australia	Carlingford, Australia	20 Sep 1984	Gordon B. Hinckley
29	Manila Philippines	Quezon City, Philippines	25 Sep 1984	Gordon B. Hinckley
30	Dallas Texas	Dallas, Texas	19 Oct 1984	Gordon B. Hinckley
31	Taipei Taiwan	Taipei, Taiwan	17 Nov 1984	Gordon B. Hinckley
32	Guatemala City Guatemala	Guatemala City, Guat.	14 Dec 1984	Gordon B. Hinckley
33	Freiberg Germany	Freiberg, Germany	29 Jun 1985	Gordon B. Hinckley
	Rededicated after remodeling		7 Sep 2002	Gordon B. Hinckley
34	Stockholm Sweden	Västerhaninge, Sweden	2 Jul 1985	Gordon B. Hinckley
35	Chicago Illinois	Glenview, Ill.	9 Aug 1985	Gordon B. Hinckley
36	Johannesburg South Africa	Johannesburg, SA	24 Aug 1985	Gordon B. Hinckley
37	Seoul Korea	Seoul, Korea	14 Dec 1985	Gordon B. Hinckley
38	Lima Peru	Lima, Peru	10 Jan 1986	Gordon B. Hinckley
39	Buenos Aires Argentina	Buenos Aires, Argentina	17 Jan 1986	Thomas S. Monson
40	Denver Colorado	Littleton, Colo.	24 Oct 1986	Ezra Taft Benson
41	Frankfurt Germany	Friedrichsdorf, Germany	28 Aug 1987	Ezra Taft Benson
42	Portland Oregon	Lake Oswego, Ore.	19 Aug, 1989	Gordon B. Hinckley
43	Las Vegas Nevada	Las Vegas, Nev.	16 Dec 1989	Gordon B. Hinckley
44	Toronto Ontario	Brampton, Ontario,	25 Aug 1990	Gordon B. Hinckley
45	San Diego California	San Diego, Calif.	25 Apr 1993	Gordon B. Hinckley
46	Orlando Florida	Windermere, Fla.	9 Oct 1994	Howard W. Hunter
47	Bountiful Utah	Bountiful, Utah	8 Jan 1995	Howard W. Hunter
48	Hong Kong China	Hong Kong	26 May 1996	Gordon B. Hinckley
49	Mount Timpanogos Utah	American Fork, Utah	13 Oct 1996	Gordon B. Hinckley
50	St. Louis Missouri	Town and Country, Mo.	1 Jun 1997	Gordon B. Hinckley
51	Vernal Utah	Vernal, Utah	2 Nov 1997	Gordon B. Hinckley
52	Preston England	Chorley, England	7 Jun 1998	Gordon B. Hinckley
53	Monticello Utah	Monticello, Utah	26 Jul 1998	Gordon B. Hinckley
	Rededicated after remodeling		17 Nov 2002	Gordon B. Hinckley
54	Anchorage Alaska	Anchorage, Alaska	9 Jan 1999	Gordon B. Hinckley
	Rededicated after remodeling		8 Feb 2004	Gordon B. Hinckley
55	Colonia Juarez Chihuahua Mexico	Colonia Juarez, Mexico	6 Mar 1999	Gordon B. Hinckley
56	Madrid Spain	Moratalaz, Spain	19 Mar 1999	Gordon B. Hinckley
57	Bogota Colombia	Bogota, Colombia	24 Apr 1999	Gordon B. Hinckley
58	Guayaquil Ecuador	Guayaquil, Ecuador	1 Aug 1999	Gordon B. Hinckley
59	Spokane Washington	Spokane, Wash.	21 Aug 1999	Gordon B. Hinckley
60	Columbus Ohio	Columbus, Ohio	4 Sept 1999	Gordon B. Hinckley
61	Bismarck North Dakota	Bismarck, N.D.	19 Sep 1999	Gordon B. Hinckley
62	Columbia South Carolina	Columbia, S.C.	16 Oct. 1999	Gordon B. Hinckley
63	Detroit Michigan	Bloomfield Hills, Mich.	23 Oct 1999	Gordon B. Hinckley
64	Halifax Nova Scotia	Dartmouth, Nova Scotia	14 Nov 1999	Gordon B. Hinckley
65	Regina Saskatchewan	Regina, Saskatchewan	14 Nov 1999	Boyd K. Packer
66	Billings Montana	Billings, Mont.	20 Nov 1999	Gordon B. Hinckley
67	Edmonton Alberta	Edmonton, Alberta	11 Dec 1999	Gordon B. Hinckley
68	Raleigh North Carolina	Apex, N.C.	18 Dec 1999	Gordon B. Hinckley
69	St. Paul Minnesota	Oakdale, Minn.	9 Jan 2000	Gordon B. Hinckley
70	Kona Hawaii	Kailua-Kona, Hawaii	23 Jan 2000	Gordon B. Hinckley
71	Ciudad Juarez Mexico	Ciudad Juarez, Mexico	26 Feb 2000	Gordon B. Hinckley
72	Hermosillo Sonora Mexico	Hermosillo, Mexico	27 Feb 2000	Gordon B. Hinckley
73	Albuquerque New Mexico	Albuquerque, N. M.	5 Mar 2000	Gordon B. Hinckley
74	Oaxaca Mexico	Oaxaca, Mexico	11 Mar 2000	James E. Faust
75	Tuxtla Gutierrez Mexico	Tuxtla Gutierrez, Mexico	12 Mar 2000	James E. Faust
76	Louisville Kentucky	Crestwood, Ky.	19 Mar 2000	Thomas S. Monson

77	Palmyra New York	Palmyra Village, N. Y.	6 Apr 2000	Gordon B. Hinckley
78	Fresno California	Fresno, Calif.	9 Apr 2000	Gordon B. Hinckley
79	Medford Oregon	Central Point, Ore.	16 Apr 2000	James E. Faust
80	Memphis Tennessee	Bartlett, Tenn.	23 Apr 2000	James E. Faust
81	Reno Nevada	Reno, Nev.	23 Apr 2000	Thomas S. Monson
82	Cochabamba Bolivia	Cochabamba, Bolivia	30 Apr 2000	Gordon B. Hinckley
83	Tampico Mexico	Ciudad Madero, Mexico	20 May 2000	Thomas S. Monson
84	Nashville Tennessee	Franklin, Tenn.	21 May 2000	James E. Faust
85	Villahermosa Mexico	Villahermosa, Mexico	21 May 2000	Thomas S. Monson
86	Montreal Quebec	Longueuil, Quebec	4 Jun 2000	Gordon B. Hinckley
87	San Jose Costa Rica	San Antonio, Costa Rica	4 Jun 2000	James E. Faust
88	Fukuoka Japan	Fukuoka, Japan	11 Jun 2000	Gordon B. Hinckley
89	Adelaide Australia	Marden, South Australia	15 Jun 2000	Gordon B. Hinckley
90	Melbourne Australia	Wantirna, Victoria, Aus.	16 Jun 2000	Gordon B. Hinckley
91	Suva Fiji	Suva, Fiji	18 Jun 2000	Gordon B. Hinckley
92	Merida Yucatan Mexico	Merida, Mexico	8 Jul 2000	Thomas S. Monson
93	Veracruz Mexico	Veracruz, Mexico	9 Jul 2000	Thomas S. Monson
94	Baton Rouge Louisiana	Baton Rouge, La.	16 Jul 2000	Gordon B. Hinckley
95	Oklahoma City Oklahoma	Yukon, Okla.	30 Jul 2000	James E. Faust
96	Caracas Venezuela	Caracas, Venezuela	20 Aug 2000	Gordon B. Hinckley
97	Houston Texas	Klein, Texas	26 Aug 2000	Gordon B. Hinckley
98	Birmingham Alabama	Gardendale, Ala.	3 Sep 2000	Gordon B. Hinckley
99	Santo Domingo Dominican Republic	Santo Domingo, Dominican Republic	17 Sep 2000	Gordon B. Hinckley
100	Boston Massachusetts	Belmont, Mass.	1 Oct 2000	Gordon B. Hinckley
101	Recife Brazil	Recife, Brazil	15 Dec 2000	Gordon B. Hinckley
102	Porto Alegre Brazil	Porto Alegre, Brazil	17 Dec 2000	Gordon B. Hinckley
103	Montevideo Uruguay	Montevideo, Uruguay	18 Mar 2001	Gordon B. Hinckley
104	Winter Quarters Nebraska	Omaha, Neb.	22 Apr 2001	Gordon B. Hinckley
105	Guadalajara Mexico	Guadalajara, Mexico	29 Apr 2001	Gordon B. Hinckley
106	Perth Australia	Yokine, Australia	20 May 2001	Gordon B. Hinckley
107	Columbia River Washington	Richland, Wash.	18 Nov 2001	Gordon B. Hinckley
108	Snowflake Arizona	Snowflake, Ariz.	3 Mar 2002	Gordon B. Hinckley
109	Lubbock Texas	Lubbock, Texas	21 Apr 2002	Gordon B. Hinckley
110	Monterrey Mexico	Monterrey, Mexico	28 Apr 2002	Gordon B. Hinckley
111	Campinas Brazil	Campinas, Brazil	17 May 2002	Gordon B. Hinckley
112	Asuncion Paraguay	Asuncion, Paraguay	19 May 2002	Gordon B. Hinckley
113	Nauvoo Illinois	Nauvoo, Ill.	27 Jun 2002	Gordon B. Hinckley
114	The Hague Netherlands	Zoetermeer, Netherlands	8 Sept. 2002	Gordon B. Hinckley
115	Brisbane Australia	Kangaroo Point, Queensland	15 Jun 2003	Gordon B. Hinckley
116	Redlands California	Redlands, Calif.	14 Sep 2003	Gordon B. Hinckley
117	Accra Ghana	Accra, Ghana	11 Jan. 2004	Gordon B. Hinckley
118	Copenhagen Denmark	Copenhagen, Denmark	23 May 2004	Gordon B. Hinckley
119	Manhattan New York	Manhattan, New York	13 June 2004	Gordon B. Hinckley
120	San Antonio Texas	San Antonio, Texas	22 May 2005	Gordon B. Hinckley
121	Aba Nigeria	Aba, Nigeria	7 Aug 2005	Gordon B. Hinckley
122	Newport Beach California	Newport, California	28 Aug 2005	Gordon B. Hinckley
123	Sacramento California	Sacramento, California	3 Sept 2006	Gordon B. Hinckley
124	Helsinki Finland	Helsinki, Finland	22 Oct 2006	Gordon B. Hinckley
125	Rexburg Idaho	Rexburg, Idaho	10 Feb 2008	Thomas S. Monson
126	Curitba Brazil	Curitaba, Brazil	1 June 2008	Thomas S. Monson
127	Panama City Panama	Panama City, Panama	10 August 2008	Thomas S. Monson
128	Twin Falls Idaho	Twin Falls, Idaho	24 August 2008	Thomas S. Monson

* No longer in use by the Church   **Original destroyed; rebuilt in 2002, see No. 113

Temples announced or under construction

Calgary Alberta
Cebu Philippines
Cordoba Argentina
Draper Utah
Gila Valley Arizona
Gilbert Arizona

Kansas City, Missouri
Kyiv/Kiev Ukraine
Manaus Brazil
Oquirrh Mountain Utah
Philadelphia Pennsylvania
Phoenix Arizona

Quetzaltenango Guatemala
Rome Italy
San Salvador El Salvador
Tegucigalpa Honduras
Vancouver British Columbia

TEMPLES OF THE CHURCH

(Listed alphabetically as of Oct. 1, 2008)

Aba Nigeria

Announced: April 2, 2000.

Location: Okup-Umodba Road, off Aba-Owerri Road at Union Bank, Aba. Abia State, Nigeria; phone (234) 82-239-010.

Site: 6.3 acres.

Exterior finish: Namibian pearl granite.

Temple design: Classic modern.

Architects and contractors: Adeniyi Coker Architects Ltd., Marlum Nigeria Ltd.

Project manager: Russell S. Tanner.

Rooms: Celestial room, two endowment rooms, two sealing rooms and baptistry.

Total Floor area: 11,500 square feet.

Dimensions: About 147-feet by 77-feet.

District: 15 stakes, 11 districts in Nigeria, and 2 branches in Cameroon.

Groundbreaking: Feb. 23, 2002, by Elder H. Bruce Stucki.

Dedication: Aug. 7, 2005, by President Gordon B. Hinkley; four sessions.

Dedicatory prayer excerpt: *Bless this nation that it may rise in strength and freedom among the nations of Africa. Bless its leaders that they may look with favor upon Thy Saints and safeguard their rights, property, and privileges.*

Accra Ghana

Announced: Feb. 16, 1998.

Location: 57 Independence Ave., North Ridge, Accra, Ghana

Site: 6 acres.

Exterior finish: Granite quarried in Namibia, Africa, called Namibia Pearl.

Temple design: Traditional, built in third generation of small temples.

Architects: ARUP

Project manager: Russ Tanner.

Contractor: Taysec Construction Limited

Rooms: Celestial room, two endowment rooms, two sealing rooms and baptristy.

Total floor area: 17,500 square feet.

Dimensions: 190 feet by 147 feet.

District: Countries in western Africa, including Nigeria, Ghana, Ivory Coast, Sierra Leone, Liberia, Benin, Togo.

Groundbreaking: Nov. 16, 2001, by Elder Russell M. Nelson.

Dedication: Jan. 11, 2004, by President Gordon B. Hinckley; three sessions.

Dedicatory prayer excerpt: *We thank Thee for the brotherhood that exists among us, that neither color of skin nor land of birth can separate us as Thy sons and daughters who have taken upon us sacred and binding covenants.*

Adelaide Australia

Announced: March 17, 1999.

Location: 53-59 Lower Portrush Road, Marden, South Australia 5070,

Phone: (61) 8-8363-8000; no clothing rental.

Site: 6.94 acres.

Exterior finish: Snow white granite

Temple design: Traditional.

Architects: Simon Drew.

Project manager: Graham Sully.

Contractor: Balderstone-Hornibrook.

Rooms: Celestial room, two endowment rooms, two sealing rooms and baptistry.

Total floor area: 10,700 square feet.

Dimensions: 149 feet by 77 feet.

District: Three stakes and three districts in south Australia.

Groundbreaking, site dedication: May 29, 1999, by Elder Vaughn J. Featherstone of the Seventy and president of the Australia/New Zealand Area.

Dedication: June 15, 2000, by President Gordon B. Hinckley; 4 sessions.

Dedicatory prayer excerpt: *We are grateful for this nation of Australia, where there is freedom of worship, freedom of assembly, and freedom to take upon ourselves the name of our Divine Redeemer and to keep sacred the covenants which we make with Him.*

Albuquerque New Mexico

Announced: April 4, 1997.

Location: 10301 San Francisco Dr. NE, Albuquerque, N.M. 87122-3437; phone (505) 822-5110.

Site: 8.5 acres.

Exterior finish: Cast stone/granite.

Temple design: Classic modern.

Architects: Fanning Bard & Tatum.

Project manager: James Aulestia and Lloyd Hess.

Contractor: Okland Construction Co.

Rooms: Celestial room, baptistry, three sealing rooms, two ordinance rooms.

Total floor area: 34,000 square feet.

Dimensions of building: 145 feet by 134 feet.

District: 14 stakes and one district in New Mexico, part of Arizona and Colorado.

Groundbreaking, site dedication: June 20, 1998, by Elder Lynn A. Mickelsen of the Seventy and president of the North America Southwest Area.

Dedication: March 5, 2000, by President Gordon B. Hinckley; 4 sessions.

Dedicatory prayer excerpt: *Let it be a sanctuary of peace, a refuge from the noise of the world. May it be a house of quiet contemplation concerning the eternal nature of life and of Thy divine plan for Thy sons and daughters as they walk the road of immortality and eternal life.*

Anchorage Alaska

Announced: Oct. 4, 1997.

Location: 13161 Brayton Drive, Anchorage, AK 99516; phone: (907) 348-7890; no clothing rental.

Site: 5.54 acres, including adjoining meetinghouse.

Exterior finish: Granite.

Temple design: Classic modern.

Architects: McCool, Carlson & Green Architects and Church A&E Services.

Project manager: Cory Karl.

Contractor: H. Watt & Scott.

Rooms: Baptistry, celestial room, one ordinance room, one sealing room.

Total floor area: Originally 6,800 square feet; 11,937 square feet after remodeling.

Dimensions: 79 feet by 108 feet.

District: Six stakes, one district in Alaska and Yukon.

Groundbreaking, site dedication: April 17, 1998, by Elder F. Melvin Hammond of the Seventy and president of the North America Northwest Area.

Dedication: Jan. 9, 1999, by President Gordon B. Hinckley; 7 sessions. Rededicated after remodeling Feb. 8, 2004, by President Hinckley; one session,

Dedicatory prayer excerpt: *May this great work of temple building go forward across the earth to bless Thy people wherever they may be found. May all who come with hope and high expectation, leave with satisfaction and gratitude.*

Apia Samoa (rebuilt)

Announced: The First Presidency announced on July 16, 2003, that the Apia Samoa Temple, which was destroyed by fire on July 9, 2003, would be rebuilt.

Location: On site of original temple, near the school and mission home in Pesega.

Site: 2 acres.

Exterior finish: Granite.

Temple design: Reflects original design.

Architect: Naylor, Wentworth, Lund.

Project manager: William Naylor.

Contractor: Bud Bailey Construction/Jacobsen Construction.

Rooms: Celestial room, baptistry, two ordinance rooms, two sealing rooms.

Total floor area: 18,691 square feet.

Dimensions: 108 feet by 197 feet.

District: 20 stakes in Samoa and American Samoa.

Groundbreaking, site dedication: Oct. 19, 2003, by Elder Dennis E. Simmons of the Seventy.

Dedication: Sept. 4, 2005, by President Gordon B. Hinckley; two sessions.

Dedicatory prayer excerpt: *We pray that Thou wilt watch over this sacred structure and preserve it from the kind of destructve force which destroyed its predecessor building.*

Apia Samoa (original)

Destroyed by fire July 9, 2003.

Announced: Oct. 15, 1977; plans revised April 2, 1980.

Location: Near the school and mission home in Pesega.

Site: 1.7 acres.

Exterior finish: "R-wall" exterior finish and insulation system on concrete block; split cedar shake shingles on roof.

Temple design: Modern.

Architect: Emil B. Fetzer, Church architect.

Construction advisers: Dale Cook and Richard Rowley.

Contractor: Utah Construction and Development.

Rooms: Baptistry, celestial room, three sealing rooms, two ordinance rooms.

Total floor area: 14,560 square feet.

Dimensions: 142.88 feet by 115.32 feet; statue of Angel Moroni on top spire, 78 feet high.

District: 20 stakes and one district in Western Samoa and American Samoa.

Groundbreaking, site dedication: Feb. 19, 1981, by President Spencer W. Kimball, assisted by the head of state, Malieotoa Tanumafil II. Nearly 4,000 people attended.

Dedication: Aug. 5-7, 1983, by President Gordon B. Hinckley; 7 sessions.

Dedicatory prayer excerpt: *We pray for Thy blessings upon those who govern these islands and the people who dwell here that principles of peace and equity may prevail and that the citizens of these islands may have cause to rejoice in the liberty that is theirs.*

Asuncion Paraguay

Announced: April 2, 2000.

Location: Esquina Espana y Brasilia streets, Asuncion, Paraguay; phone: (595) 21-230-035. No clothing rental.

Site: 7 acres including stake center.

Exterior finish: Light gray Asa Branca Brazilian granite.

Temple design: Traditional

Architect: Eduardo Signorelli.

Project manager: Javier Mendieta.

Contractor: Temple Construction Department, with Gonzalez, Acosta & Wood S.A. as construction managers.

Rooms: Celestial room, two ordinance rooms, two sealing rooms, baptistry.

Total floor area: 10,700 square feet.

Dimensions: 149 feet by 77 feet.

District: 10 stakes and 19 districts in Paraguay and several Argentine provinces.

Groundbreaking, site dedication: Feb. 3, 2001, by Elder Jay E. Jensen of the Seventy.

Dedication: May 19, 2002, by President Gordon B. Hinckley, 4 sessions.

Dedicatory prayer excerpts: *We are grateful that this Thy house has been constructed in this nation of Paraguay. Marvelous has been the growth of Thy work in this part of Thy vineyard. . . . May this temple stand as a crowning jewel to Thy work in this nation. May Thy Saints throughout the land look to this Thy holy house as a sanctuary to which they may come to make sacred covenants with Thee and partake of the great blessings which Thou hast prepared for Thy faithful children.*

Atlanta Georgia

Announced: April 2, 1980.

Location: In Sandy Springs, on the northeastern outskirts of Atlanta; 6450 Barfield Rd., Atlanta, GA 30328-4283; phone, (770) 393-3698.

Site: 13.33 acres.

Exterior finish: Pre-cast stone walls, built-up roof.

Temple design: Modern.

Architect: Emil B. Fetzer, Church architect.

Construction adviser: Michael Enfield and Ronald Prince.

Contractor: Cube Construction Company.

Rooms: Baptistry, celestial room, five sealing rooms, four ordinance rooms.

Total floor area: 37,000 square feet.

Dimensions: 198 feet by 212 feet; statue of Angel Moroni on top spire, 92 feet high.

District: 13 stakes in Georgia, and a small part of Tennessee and Alabama.

Groundbreaking, site dedication: March 7, 1981, by President Spencer W. Kimball.

Dedication: June 1-4, 1983, by President Gordon B. Hinckley; 11 sessions.

Dedicatory prayer excerpt: *May the very presence of this temple in the midst of Thy people become a reminder of the sacred and eternal covenants made with Thee. May they strive more diligently to banish from their lives those elements which are inconsistent with the covenants they have made with Thee.*

Baton Rouge Louisiana

Announced: Oct. 14, 1998.

Location: 10339 Highland Road, Baton Rouge, LA. 70810; phone, (225) 769-1197; no clothing rental.

Site: 6.3 acres, including adjoining meetinghouse.

Exterior finish: Imperial Danby White marble.

Temple design: Classic modern.

Architect: Paul Tessier of Paul Tessier & Associates, and Church A&E Services.

Project manager: Leon Rowley.

Contractor: Layton Construction Co., Construction Management Co.; Cangelosi Ward, general contractor.

Rooms: Celestial room, baptistry, two ordinance rooms, two sealing rooms.

Total floor area: 10,700 square feet.

Dimensions: 149 feet by 77 feet.

District: Nine stakes in Louisiana and Mississippi.

Groundbreaking, site dedication: May 8, 1999, by Elder Monte J. Brough of the Seventy and president of the North America Southeast Area.

Dedication: July 16, 2000, by President Gordon B. Hinckley; 4 sessions.

Dedicatory prayer excerpt: *We thank Thee for this nation in which this temple stands. It was established by men whom Thou didst raise up unto this very purpose. Thou hast spoken concerning the Constitution of its government. Surely it is a choice land and a favored nation.*

Bern Switzerland Temple

Location: In a northern suburb of Bern in a setting with the Alps on the south, and the Jura Mountains on the west and north; Tempelstrasse 2, CH - 3052, Zollikofen, Switzerland; phone: (41) 31-915-5252.

Site: 7 acres, selected July 1952, by President David O. McKay and President Samuel E. Bringhurst of the Swiss-Austrian Mission.

Exterior finish: Reinforced concrete with a creamish gray terra cotta facing trimmed in white. Tower is white base and spire is gold-colored.

Temple design: Modern-contemporary, but similar to lines of early Church temples.

Architect: Edward O. Anderson, Church architect. Re-drawn into German specifications by Wilhelm Zimmer of Bercher and Zimmer Architects.

Contractor: Hans Jordi of Bern.

Rooms: Baptistry, celestial room, four ordinance rooms, seven sealing rooms.

Total floor area: 39,457 square feet; after remodeling, 39,063 square feet.

Dimensions: 152 feet by 84 feet; top of tower rises 140 feet.

District: 10 stakes and 21 districts in Switzerland, Austria, France, Italy, Albania and Israel (for expatriates).

Groundbreaking, site dedication: Aug. 5, 1953, by President David O. McKay.

Dedication: Sept. 11-15, 1955, by President David O. McKay; 10 sessions. Rededicated Oct. 23-25, 1992, by President Gordon B. Hinckley; 10 sessions.

Dedicatory prayer excerpt: *Increase our desire, O Father, to put forth even greater effort towards the consummation of Thy purpose to bring to pass the immortality and eternal life of all thy children.*

Billings Montana Temple

Announced: Aug. 16, 1996.

Location: 3100 Rim Point Drive, Billings, MT, 59106; phone: (406) 655-0607.

Site: 10 acres.

Exterior finish: Wyoming white dolomite precast concrete.

Temple design: Classic modern.

Architects: CTA Architects Engineers.

Project manager: Cory Karl.

Contractor: Jacobson Construction Inc.

Rooms: Baptistry, celestial room, two ordinance rooms, three sealing rooms.

Total floor area: 33,800 square feet.

Dimensions: 183 feet by 212 feet.

District: 13 stakes in Montana and Wyoming.

Groundbreaking, site dedication: March 28, 1998, by Elder Hugh W. Pinnock of the Seventy and president of the North America Central Area.

Dedication: Nov. 20, 1999, by President Gordon B. Hinckley; 8 sessions.

Dedicatory prayer excerpt: *Those of this area who are called to teach the gospel to the world will first come here to be endowed with power from on high. Lead them in their ministry to those who will accept their testimony of the divinity of Thy restored work.*

Birmingham Alabama

Announced: Sept. 11. 1998.

Location: 1927 Mount Olive Blvd., Gardendale, AL 35071; phone: (205) 631-3444; no clothing rental.

Site: 5.6 acres, including adjoining meetinghouse.

Exterior finish: Imperial Danby White Marble.

Temple design: Classic modern

Architects: Robert Waldrip of Joyce, Prout and Associates, and Church A&E Services.

Project manager: Leon Rowley.

Contractor: Layton Construction Co., Construction Management Co., Gary C. Wyatt, Inc., general contractor.

Rooms: Celestial room, baptistry, two ordinance rooms; two sealing rooms.

Total floor area: 10,700 square feet.

Dimensions: 149 feet by 77 feet.

District: Seven stakes in Alabama, Florida.

Groundbreaking, site dedication: Oct. 9, 1999, by Elder Stephen A. West of the Seventy and second counselor in the North America Southeast Area presidency.

Dedication: Sept. 3, 2000, by President Gordon B. Hinckley: 4 sessions.

Dedicatory prayer excerpt: *May the influence of this Thy house be felt throughout this great temple district. May the Church grow and prosper here. May those in government be friendly to Thy people.*

Bismarck North Dakota

Announced: July 29, 1998.

Location: 2930 Cody Drive in northwest Bismarck, ND 58503-0116; phone (701)258-9590; no clothing rental.

Site: 1.6 acres.

Exterior finish: White marble.

Temple design: Classic modern.

Architects: Ritterbush-Ellig-Hulsing and Church A&E Services.

Project manager: Cory Karl.

Contractor: Capital City Construction.

Rooms: Celestial room, two ordinance rooms, two sealing rooms, baptistry.

Total floor area: 10,700 square feet.

Dimensions: 149 feet by 77 feet.

District: Three stakes and one district in North Dakota and South Dakota.

Groundbreaking, site dedication: Oct. 17, 1998; Elder Kenneth Johnson of the Seventy and first counselor in the North America Central Area.

Dedication: Sept. 19, 1999, by President Gordon B. Hinckley; 3 sessions.

Dedicatory prayer excerpt: *We thank Thee for the faith of Thy sons and daughters in the vast area of this temple district, men and women who love Thee and love their Redeemer, and have stood steadfast as Thy people. They have felt much alone. They are out on the frontier of the Church. Their numbers are still not large. But they are entitled to every blessing which the Church has to offer.*

Bogata D.C. Colombia

Announced: April 7, 1984.

Location: Carrera 37 No. 125A-65, Bogota D.C., Colombia; phone: (57) 1-625-8000.

Site: 3.71 acres.

Exterior finish: granite, Asa Branca.

Temple design: Classic modern.

Architects: Cuellar, Cerrano y Gomez, S.A. and Church A&E Services.

Project manager: Cesar Davila.

Contractor: Cuellar, Cerrano y Gomez, S.A.

Rooms: Celestial room, baptistry, four ordinance rooms and three sealing rooms.

Total floor area: 53,500 square feet.

Dimensions: 76 feet by 186 feet.; spire, 124 feet high.

District: 44 stakes and districts in Colombia.

Groundbreaking, site dedication: June 26, 1993, by Elder William R. Bradford of the Seventy and president South America North Area.

Dedication: April 24, 1999, by President Gordon B. Hinckley; 11 sessions.

Dedicatory prayer excerpt: *The faithful saints of Colombia have given generously of their means to this cause.*

Boise Idaho

Announced: March 31, 1982.

Location: Just off Interstate 84 at 1211 S. Cole Road, Boise, ID 83709-1871; phone: (208) 322-4422.

Site: 4.83 acres.

Exterior finish: Faced with light colored marble with a slate roof. It is surrounded by three detached towers on each end; 8-foot statue of the Angel Moroni tops highest spire.

Temple design: Modern adaptation of six-spire design.

Architects: Church architectural staff, with assistance from Ron Thurber & Associates of Boise.

Construction adviser: Jerry Sears.

Contractor: Comtrol Inc. of Midvale, Utah.

Rooms: Baptistry, celestial room, four ordinance rooms, three sealing rooms.

Total floor area: 35,868 square feet after 1987 addition.

Dimensions: 236 feet by 78 feet; statue of Angel Moroni 112 feet high.

District: 35 stakes in western Idaho and two in eastern Oregon.

Groundbreaking, site dedication: Dec. 18, 1982, by Elder Mark E. Petersen of the Quorum of the Twelve.

Dedication: May 25-30, 1984, by President Gordon B. Hinckley; 24 sessions. Remodeled facilities dedicated by Elder James E. Faust Feb. 14, 1987; new baptistry dedicated by Elder Faust May 29, 1987.

Dedicatory prayer excerpt: *May Thy faithful Saints of this and future generations look to this beautiful structure as a house to which they will be made welcome . . . for the making of eternal covenants with Thee, for inspiration and sanctification, as they serve unselfishly.*

Boston Massachusetts

Announced: Sept. 30, 1995.

Location: 86 Frontage Rd., Belmont, MA 02478-2135; phone: (617) 993-9993.

Site: 8 acres.

Exterior finish: Granite.

Temple design: Classic Modern.

Architect: Tsoi/Kobus & Associates and Church A&E Services.

Project manager: William Treu.

Contractor: Barr & Barr.

Rooms: Baptistry, celestial room, four sealing rooms, four ordinance rooms.

Total floor area: 69,000 square feet.

Dimensions: 90 feet by 190 feet.

District: 19 stakes, 3 districts in Connecticut, Maine, New Hampshire, Rhode Island, Massachusetts, Maine, and New York.

Groundbreaking, site dedication: June 13, 1997, by Elder Richard G. Scott of the Quorum of the Twelve.

Dedication: Oct. 1, 2000, by President Gordon B. Hinckley, 4 sessions.

Dedicatory prayer excerpt: *We are assembled to dedicate this Thy holy house. It is a special occasion. This temple becomes the 100th operating temple of Thy Church.*

We have looked forward to this occasion. We have prayed for this day....

To us it is indeed a miracle. The ground on which it stands, the circumstances of its preservation for this use, and the decision to build it here — all are miracles unto those who have been a part of this process.

Bountiful Utah

Announced: May 28, 1988.

Location: In the Bountiful foothills on east bench (at 1650 East), 640 S. Bountiful Blvd, Bountiful, UT 84010-1394; phone: (801) 296-2100.

Site: 11 acres.

Exterior finish: Bethel white granite.

Temple design: Modern, with single spire.

Architect: Allen Ereckson, architect of record; Keith Stepan, project architect; and Church architectural staff.

Contractor: Okland Construction Co.

Project manager: Jerry Sears.

Construction adviser: Michael Enfield.

Rooms: Baptistry, celestial room, four endowment rooms, eight sealing rooms.

Total floor area: 104,000 square feet.

Dimensions: 145 feet by 198 feet; statue of Angel Moroni on top spire; 176 feet high.

District: 30 stakes in Central and south Davis County, Utah.

Groundbreaking, site dedication: May 2, 1992, by President Ezra Taft Benson.

Dedication: Jan. 8-14, 1995, by President Howard W. Hunter; 28 sessions.

Dedicatory prayer excerpt: *May this house provide a spirit of peace to all who observe its majesty, and especially to those who enter for their own sacred ordinances and to perform the work for their loved ones beyond the veil. Let them feel of Thy divine love and mercy. May they be privileged to say, as did the Psalmist of old, 'We took sweet counsel together, and walked unto the house of God in company.'*

Brisbane Australia

Announced: July 20, 1998.

Location: 200 River Terrace; Kangaroo Point, QLD 4169, Australia; phone: (01161) 73 240-3600; no clothing rental.

Site: .86 acres

Exterior finish: Light gray granite.

Temple design: Traditional.

Architects: Phillips, Smith, Conwell Architects.

Project manager: Graham Sully

Contractor: John Holland Pty., Ltd.

Rooms: Celestial room, two ordinances rooms, two sealing rooms, baptistry.

Total floor area: 10,700 square feet.

Dimensions: 149 feet by 72 feet; statue of Angel Moroni on top spire; 71feet high.

District: Queensland and northern areas of New South Wales.

Groundbreaking: May 26, 2001, by Elder Kenneth Johnson of the Seventy and president of the Australia/New Zealand Area,

Dedication: June 15, 2003, by President Gordon B. Hinckley in 4 sessions.

Dedicatory prayer excerpt: *We thank Thee for the strength of Thy work in this good land. We thank Thee for other houses of the Lord on the soil of this nation and are grateful to now have this beautiful structure in this great city of Brisbane together with the accompanying chapel and other facilities. On this Sabbath morning our hearts reach up to Thee in gratitude and love.*

Buenos Aires Argentina

Announced: April 2, 1980.

Location: On southwest outskirts of Buenos Aires; Autopista Richieri y Puente 13, B1778 dua Ciudad Evita, Buenos Aires, Argentina. Telephone: (54) 11-4 487-1520.

Site: 3.73 acres.

Exterior finish: Light gray native granite.

Temple design: Modern adaptation of earlier six-spire design.

Architects: Church architectural staff; local architect Ramon Paez.

Construction adviser: Gary Holland.

Contractor: Benito Roggio and Sons.

Rooms: Baptistry, celestial room, four ordinance rooms, three sealing rooms.

Total floor area: 17,687 square feet.

Dimensions: 178 feet by 71 feet. Angel Moroni statue is atop tallest spire, 112 feet.

District: 65 stakes, 36 districts in Argentina.

Groundbreaking, site dedication: April 20, 1983, by Elder Bruce R. McConkie of the Quorum of the Twelve.

Dedication: Jan. 17-19, 1986, by President Thomas S. Monson of the First Presidency; 11 sessions.

Dedicatory prayer excerpt: *We remember that it was in this very city of Buenos Aires, on Christmas Day in the year 1925, just 60 years ago, that Elder Melvin J. Ballard, an apostle of the Lord, dedicated all of South America for the preaching of the gospel.*

Calgary Alberta

Announced: Oct. 4, 2008.

Status: In planning stages. The Calgary temple will be built on Church-owned land next to an existing chapel at Rocky Ridge Road and Royal Oak Road.

Campinas Brazil

Announced: April 3, 1997.

Location: Rodovia Heitor Penteado Kn 4,3 Distrito Souzas, Campinas, SP 13092-543 Brazil; phone: ((55) 19-3258-5470.

Site: 6.18 acres.

Exterior finish: Light gray Asa Branca granite from the state of Ceara.

Temple design: Classic modern.

Architect: JCL Arquitetos Ltd., and Church A&E Services.

Project manager: Raul Lins.

Contractor: Ernesto Woebcke.

Rooms: Four ordinance rooms, three sealing rooms, celestial room, baptistry.

Total floor area: 49,100 square feet.

Dimensions: 142 feet by 163 feet.

District: 36 stakes and six districts in the states of Sao Paulo, Rio de Janeiro and Minas Gerais.

Groundbreaking, site dedication: May 1, 1998, by President James E. Faust, second counselor in the First Presidency.

Dedication: May 17, 2002, by President Gordon B. Hinckley in 4 sessions.

Dedicatory prayer excerpt: *Here will occur a great and dedicated service in behalf of those who have passed beyond the veil of death that they might be freed from the prison-house in which they have been held, many of them for centuries. Here a selfless work of love will take place. We thank Thee for every blessing, for every opportunity which will be offered here.*

Caracas D.F. Venezuela

Announced: Sept. 30, 1995.

Location: Avenida C Con Calle C-1, Urb. Caurimare, Caracas D.F. 1062-A, Venezuela; phone: (58) 212-985-9123; no clothing rental.

Site: .5 acre.

Exterior finish: Granite.

Temple design: Classic modern.

Architect: Taller de Arquitectura and Church A&E Services.

Project manager: Duane Cheney.

Contractor: Jahn

Rooms: Two ordinance rooms, two sealing rooms, celestial room, baptistry.

Total floor area: 15,332 square feet.

Dimensions: 78 feet by 115 feet.

District: Venezuela, Trinidad and Tabago.

Groundbreaking, site dedication: Jan. 10, 1999, by Elder Francisco J. Viñas of the Seventy and president of the South America North Area.

Dedication: Aug. 20, 2000, by President Gordon B. Hinckley; 4 sessions.

Dedicatory prayer excerpt: *We pray for this great nation of Venezuela. May it hold its place among the sovereign nations of the earth. May its people be blessed and prospered. May they enjoy freedom to worship Thee without molestation of any kind. Bless the leaders of the nation with wisdom and understanding, and a great desire to serve the needs of the people.*

Cardston Alberta

Location: Cardston, about 140 miles south of Calgary in southern Alberta; 348 3rd St. West, Cardston, AB TOK OKO ; phone: (403) 653-3552.

Site: In 1887, eight-acre site laid out and given to the Church by Charles Ora Card. It was then called the Tabernacle Block.

Exterior finish: White granite quarried near Kootenai Lakes in Nelson, B. C. Each stone was hand-hewn at the quarry or temple site. Additions of artificial precast granite.

Temple design: Octagonal design has Grecian massiveness and a Peruvian touch of Aztec influence in pyramid silhouette.

Architects: Hyrum C. Pope and Harold W. Burton of Salt Lake City.

Rooms: Approximately 40 in original structure; now 80, including baptistry, celestial, four ordinance, five sealing.

Total floor area: Originally 29,471 square feet, 81,700 square feet after remodeling.

Dimensions: 118 feet square, height, 85 feet; footprint 165 feet by 311 feet.

District: 21 stakes in Central and southern Alberta, southeastern British Columbia, northern Montana.

Groundbreaking, site dedication: July 27, 1913, President Joseph F. Smith dedicated site . Ground broken Nov. 9, 1913, by Daniel Kent Greene of Glenwood, Alberta.

Dedication: Aug. 26-29, 1923, by President Heber J. Grant; 11 sessions. Rededicated after remodeling July 2, 1962, by President Hugh B. Brown of the First Presidency; Rededicated after additional remodeling by President Gordon B. Hinckley June 22-24, 1991; 12 sessions.

Rededicatory prayer excerpt: *Bless the Latter-day Saints of Canada that they may be*

good citizens of the nation, men and women of integrity worthy of the respect of the people of this nation, and contributing of their talents and strength to its well-being.

Chicago Illinois

Announced: April 1, 1981.

Location: 20 miles north of Chicago; 4151 West Lake Ave., Glenview, IL 60025-1240; phone: (847) 299-6500.

Site: 13 acres.

Exterior finish: Gray buff marble, gray slate roof.

Temple design: Modern adaptation of earlier six-spire design.

Architects: Church architectural staff; local architect, Wight & Co.

Construction adviser: Virgil Roberts.

Contractor: Pora Construction Co., Des Plaines, Ill., with Utah Construction and Development Co.

Rooms: Baptistry, celestial room, five ordinance rooms, three sealing rooms.

Total floor area: Originally 17,850 square feet; 37,062 square feet following addition.

Dimensions: 236 feet by 78 feet; seven-foot-tall Angel Moroni statue is 112 feet high.

District: 20 stakes in Illnois, Iowa, Wisconsin, Indiana, Michigan.

Groundbreaking, site dedication: Aug. 13, 1983, by President Gordon B. Hinckley.

Dedication: Aug. 9-13, 1985, by President Gordon B. Hinckley; 19 sessions. Addition dedicated by Pres. Hinckley Oct. 8, 1989.

Dedicatory prayer excerpt: *We are mindful that Thy Prophet Joseph and his brother Hyrum were martyred in Carthage, Ill., at a time of terrible conflict and persecution.*

Cebu Philippines

Announced: April 18, 2006.

Groundbreaking, site dedication: Nov. 14, 2007, by Elder Dallin H. Oaks of the Quorum of the Twelve. **Status:** Under construction.

Ciudad Juarez Mexico

Announced: May 7, 1998.

Location: Calle Paraguay 290, Esq Jose Borunda, Col. Partido Romero, Ciudad Juarez, Mexico; phone:(52) 656-611-5146; ; no clothing rental.

Site: 1.63 acres.

Exterior finish: White marble veneer.

Temple design: Traditional Spanish.

Architect: Alvaro Iñigo and Church A&E Services.

Project manager: David Wills.

Contractor: Granay Montero/Jacobsen Construction.

Rooms: Two ordinance rooms, two sealing rooms, celestial room, baptistry.

Total floor area: 10,700 square feet.

Dimensions: 77 feet by 149 feet.

District: 10 stakes, one district in northern Chihuahua, El Paso, Texas.

Groundbreaking, site dedication: Jan. 9, 1999, by Elder Eran A. Call of the Seventy and president of the Mexico North Area.

Dedication: Feb. 26-27, 2000, by President Gordon B. Hinckley; 6 sessions.

Dedicatory prayer excerpt: *Bless this great nation of Mexico that it may rise and shine among the nations of the earth. Lift the burden of poverty from the backs of the people. Bless the leaders of government that they may welcome Thy servants, and may the message brought by Thy servants take root in the hearts of many souls.*

Cochabamba Bolivia

Announced: Jan. 13, 1995.

Location: northern side of Cochabamba at Av. Melchor Urquidi, 1500, Alto Queru Quero, Cochabamba, Bolivia; phone: (591) 4-42-93161.

Site: 6.51 acres.

Exterior finish: Blend of hand-hewn Comanche granite and plaster.

Temple design: Classic modern.

Architects: BSW and Church A&E Services.

Project manager: Javier Mendieta.

Contractor: CBI.

Rooms: Two ordinance rooms, three sealing rooms, celestial room, baptistry.

Total floor area: 33,000 square feet.

Dimensions: 128 feet by 145 feet.

District: 21 stakes, 9 districts in Bolivia.

Groundbreaking, site dedication: Nov. 10, 1996, by President Gordon B. Hinckley.

Dedication: April 30, 2000, by President Gordon B. Hinckley; 4 sessions.

Dedicatory prayer excerpt: *Our hearts are filled with thanksgiving on this historic day when we meet to dedicate this Thy holy house in Bolivia. How thankful we are for it. It is the fulfillment of our dreams, our hopes, our prayers, our faith.*

Colonia Juarez
Chihuahua Mexico

Announced: Oct. 4, 1997.

Location: Calle Chihuahua y Diaz, Colonia Juarez, Chihuahua 31857, Mexico; phone: (52) -636-695-0144; no clothing rental.

Site: 1 acre.

Exterior finish: White marble.

Temple design: Classic modern.

Architects: Alvaro Iñigo and Church A&E Services.

Project manager: David Wills.

Contractor: Jacobsen Construction Co.

Rooms: Baptistry, celestial room, one ordinance room, one sealing room.

Total floor area: 6,800 square feet.

Dimensions: 102 feet by 76 feet.

District: Two stakes, two districts.

Groundbreaking, site dedication: March 7, 1998, by Elder Eran A. Call of the Seventy and president of the Mexico North Area.

Dedication: March 6, 1999, by President Gordon B. Hinckley; 4 sessions.

Dedicatory prayer excerpt: *It was here in Northern Mexico that Thou didst reveal the idea and the plan of a smaller temple, complete in every necessary detail, but suited in size to the needs and circumstances of the Church membership in this area of Thy vineyard. That revelation came of a desire and a prayer to help Thy people of these colonies who have been true and loyal during the century and more that they have lived here. They are deserving of this sacred edifice in which to labor for themselves and their forebears.*

Columbia River Washington

Announced: April 2, 2000.

Location: 969 Gage Blvd., Richland, WA 99352; phone: (509) 628-0990; no clothing rental

Site: 2.88 acres.

Exterior finish: Bethel white granite from Vermont and Italy.

Temple design: Traditional.

Architect: Architectural & Engineering Services/Temple Construction Dept.

Project manager: Bill Naylor

Contractor: Vitus Construction, Medford, Ore.

Rooms: Celestial room, two ordinance rooms, two sealing rooms, baptistry and eating area.

Total floor area: 16,880 square feet.

Dimensions: 196 feet by 106 feet.

District: 12 stakes in southeast Washington and one stake in Oregon.

Groundbreaking, site dedication: Oct. 28, 2000, by Elder Stephen A. West of the Seventy and second counselor in the North America Northwest Area Presidency.

Dedication: Nov. 18, 2001, by President Gordon B. Hinckley; 4 sessions.

Dedicatory excerpt: *We pray that Thou wilt smile upon Thy people and their families. Open the windows of heaven and shower down blessings upon the faithful who contribute of their time and resources according to Thy will and law. May the whole earth become as Zion as Thy work spreads among the nations.*

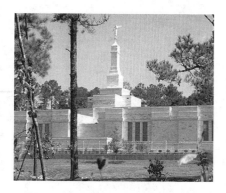

Columbia South Carolina

Announced: Sept. 11, 1998.

Location: Corner of Trotter Road and Caughman Road in Hopkins, SC 29061-9573; phone: (803) 647-9472; no clothing rental.

Site: 3.6 acres.

Exterior finish: Imperial Danby Vermont marble.

Temple design: Traditional.

Architects: Mike Watson of Watson-Tate Architects Inc.

Project manager: Bruce Catanzaro.

Contractor: Walbridge Aldinger.

Rooms: Celestial room, two ordinance rooms, two sealing rooms and baptistry.

Total floor area: 10,700 square feet.

Dimensions: 149 feet by 77 feet.

District: 11 stakes in South Carolina, North Carolina, Georgia and Tennessee.

Groundbreaking, site dedication: Dec. 5, 1998, by Elder Gordon T. Watts of the Seventy and first counselor in the North America Southeast Area presidency.

Dedication: Oct. 16-17, 1999, by President Gordon B. Hinckley; 6 sessions.

Dedicatory prayer excerpt: *We rejoice in the presence of this house in this great state of South Carolina which has hosted Thy messengers of eternal truth. They have been coming here for generations, and there has been established a great body of faithful Latter-day Saints. We pray that the very presence of this Thy house will have a sanctifying influence upon the people of this area, and particularly upon those who enter its portals.*

Columbus Ohio

Announced: April 25, 1998.

Location: 3870 Gateway Blvd., Columbus, OH 43228; phone: (614) 351-5001; no clothing rental.

Site: 2.2 acres.

Exterior finish: Imperial Danby Vermont marble.

Temple design: Traditional.

Architects: Firestone Jaros Mullin.

Project manager: Bruce Catanzaro.

Contractor: Corna/Kokosing Construction Co.

Rooms: Celestial room, baptistry, two ordinance rooms, two sealing rooms.

Total floor area: 10,700 square feet.

Dimensions: 149 feet by 77 feet.

District: 11 stakes in northern and central Ohio, western West Virginia.

Groundbreaking, site dedication: Sept. 12, 1998, by Elder John K. Carmack of the Seventy and president of North America East Area.

Dedication: Sept. 4, 1999, by President Gordon B. Hinckley; 6 sessions.

Dedicatory prayer excerpt: *We are assembled to dedicate this Thy house. It is now 163 years since a temple was dedicated in the State of Ohio. We are reminded today of the dedication of the Kirtland Temple and of the prayer given on that occasion which Thy prophet declared was revealed unto him.*

We, too, as Saints of this day, seek Thine inspiration in the words which we direct in prayer to Thee, our Father and our God.

No artist rendering available

Copenhagen Denmark

Announced: March 17, 1999.

Location: Priorvej 12, 2000 Frederiksberg, Denmark; near "Old Copenhagen."

Site: Less than one acre.

Exterior finish: Original brick and columns.

Temple design: Neo-classical style of original meetinghouse.

Architects and contractors: Arcito.

Project manager: Carl Champagnie.

Rooms: Celestial room, two endowment rooms, two sealing rooms and baptistry with font resting on 12 fiberglass oxen.

Total floor area: Approximately 25,000 square feet.

Dimensions: 45 feet by 120 feet.

District: Stakes in Aarhus and Copenhagen, Denmark; Goteborg and Malmo, Sweden; and Iceland District.

Groundbreaking, site dedicated: Priorvej Chapel originally dedicated June 14, 1931. Later remodeled to become the Copenhagen Denmark Temple. Temple site dedicated April 24, 1999, by Elder Spencer J. Condie of the Seventy and president of the Europe North Area.

Dedication: May 23, 2004, by President Gordon B. Hinckley in four sessions.

Dedicatory prayer excerpt: *We thank Thee for this land, where the restored gospel was first preached more than a century and a half ago. We thank Thee for Thy faithful servants who have come here as teachers of Thy divine truth. We express our gratitude for the many thousands who have responded to their message over the years.*

Cordoba Argentina

Announced: Oct. 4, 2008.

Status: In planning stages.

The temple in Córdoba, Argentina, will be situated on the Belgrano meetinghouse site, next to the present mission home of the Church.

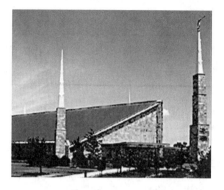

Curitiba Brazil

Announced: Aug. 23, 2002

Location: Rua Deputado Heitor Alencar Furtado, 3641 — Massungue suburb, Curitiba, Parana, Brazil.

Site: 8.15 acres

Exterior features: Reinforced concrete cast onsite, with facade of sienna white granite native to the state of Espirito Santo, Brazil. Thirty art-glass window panes complete the facade exterior.

Architects: Jeronimo da Cunha Lima, Brazil; GSBS, United States.

Contractor: LDS Church Temple Construction Department of Brazil.

Rooms: Baptistry, celestial room, two ordinance rooms, two sealing rooms.

Total floor area: 27,850 square feet

Dimensions: 125 feet, 2 inches to the top of the Angel Moroni statue (the statue is 14 feet, 2 inches tall).

District: Stakes and mission districts in the Brazilian state of Parana and a portion of the state of Santa Catarina.

Groundbreaking: March 10, 2005

Dedication: June 1, 2008, by President Thomas S. Monson; four sessions.

Dedicatory prayer excerpt: *The Atonement wrought by Thy Son gives purpose to our being and turns our thoughts heavenward.*

Dallas Texas

Announced: April 1, 1981.

Location: 12 miles north of the downtown area, at 6363 Willow Lane, Dallas, TX 75230-2227; phone: (972) 991-1273.

Site: 6 acres.

Exterior finish: Light-colored marble tile walls, dark gray slate roof.

Temple design: Modern adaptation of earlier six-spire design.

Architects: Church architectural staff, with assistance from West & Humphries of Dallas.

Construction adviser: Virgil Roberts.

Contractor: Comtrol Inc. of Midvale, Utah.

Rooms: Baptistry, celestial room, five ordinance rooms, three sealing rooms.

Total floor area: Originally 17,850 square feet; 44,207 square feet following addition.

Dimensions: 236 feet by 78 feet; tower, 95 feet; statue of Angel Moroni on top spire.

District: 16 east Texas stakes and one Louisiana stake.

Groundbreaking, site dedication: Jan. 22, 1983, by President Gordon B. Hinckley.

Dedication: Oct. 19-24, 1984, by President Gordon B. Hinckley; 23 sessions. Rededicated March 5, 1989 by President Gordon B. Hinckley.

Dedicatory prayer excerpt: May this beautiful temple, standing in this community, become a declaration to all who shall look upon it of the faith of thy Saints in the revealed things of eternity, and may they be led to respect that which is sacred unto us.

Denver Colorado

Announced: March 31, 1982.

Location: In Littleton, about 20 miles south of Denver, at County Line Road and South University Boulevard; 2001 E. Phillips Circle, Littleton, CO (303) 730-0220.

Site: 7.56 acres.

Exterior finish: Modern design; precast stone walls and built-up roof.

Temple design: Modern.

Architects: Church architectural staff.

Supervising architect: Local architect, Bobby R. Thomas.

Construction adviser: Michael Enfield.

Contractor: Langley Constructors.

Rooms: Baptistry, celestial room, four ordinance rooms, six sealing rooms.

Total floor area: 27,006 square feet.

Dimensions: 184 feet by 192 feet; single 90-foot spire capped with statue of Angel Moroni.

District: 25 stakes, one district in Colorado, eastern Wyoming, western Kansas.

Groundbreaking, site dedication: May 19, 1984, by President Gordon B. Hinckley.

Dedication: Oct. 24-28, 1986, by President Ezra Taft Benson; 19 sessions.

Dedicatory prayer excerpt: *Touch the hearts of Thy people that they may look to this temple as a refuge from the evil and turmoil of the world. May they ever live worthy of the blessings here to be found. May they be prompted to seek the records of their forebears and to serve here in their behalf, under that plan which Thou hast revealed for the salvation and exaltation of Thy children of all generations.*

Detroit Michigan

Announced: Aug. 10, 1998.

Location: 37425 N. Woodward Ave., in Bloomfield Hills, MI 48304; phone (248) 593-0690; no clothing rental.

Site: 3.1 acres.

Exterior finish: Imperial Danby Vermont marble.

Temple design: Traditional.

Architect: John Coakley of Bernath-Bernath-Coakley Associates.

Project manager: Bruce Catanzaro.

Contractor: Walbridge-Aldinger.

Rooms: Celestial room, baptistry, two ordinance rooms, two sealing rooms.

Total floor area: 10,700 square feet.

Dimensions: 149 feet by 77 feet.

District: Seven stakes, two districts in Michigan.

Groundbreaking, site dedication: Oct. 10, 1998, by Elder Jay E. Jensen of the First Quorum of the Seventy and president of the North America Northeast Area.

Dedication: Oct. 23, 1999, by President Gordon B. Hinckley; 6 sessions.

Dedicatory prayer excerpt: *May the work that will go forward in this sacred edifice please Thee and bring untold blessings to Thy sons and daughters on both sides of the veil.*

Draper Utah

Announced: A third temple to be built in Salt Lake Valley announced Oct. 2, 2004; city announced Nov. 21, 2004.

Location: Approximately 1900 East and 14000 South, Draper, Utah.

Site: 12 acres.

Total floor area: 57,000 square feet.

Groundbreaking, site dedication: Aug. 5, 2006, by President Gordon B. Hinckley.

Edmonton Alberta

Announced: Aug. 11, 1998.

Location: 14325 53rd Ave. NW, Edmonton, Alberta T6H 5G6; phone: (780) 434-7436; no clothing rental.

Site: 1 acre.

Exterior finish: Light gray granite quarried in Quebec.

Temple design: Classic modern.

Architect: Robert Bennett of Bennett Architect, Inc. and Church A&E Services.

Project manager: Cory Karl.

Contractor: Binder Construction Limited.

Rooms: Baptistry, celestial room, two ordinance rooms, two sealing rooms.

Total floor area: 10,700 square feet.

Dimensions: 149 by 77 feet.

District: Six Edmonton area stakes.

Groundbreaking, site dedication: Feb. 27, 1999, by Elder Yoshihiko Kikuchi of the Seventy and second counselor in the North America Central Area presidency.

Dedication: Dec. 11-12, 1999, by President Gordon B. Hinckley; 7 sessions.

Dedicatory prayer excerpt: *Let Thy providence be felt in this great nation of Canada that it shall continue to be a land where Thy sons and daughters enjoy the precious boon of freedom of assembly and worship. Bless those who govern that they shall look with favor upon Thy people, and may Thy work grow in numbers, in majesty, and in strength in this good land.*

Frankfurt Germany

Announced: April 1, 1981.

Location: In the center of Friedrichsdorf, a small town nine miles north of Frankfurt; Talstrasse #10, D-61381 Friedrichsdorf/TS, Germany; phone (49) 6172-59000.

Site: 5.2 acres.

Exterior finish: White granite, copper roof.

Architects: Church architectural staff; local architect, Borchers-Metzner-Kramer; project architect, Hanno Luschin.

Construction adviser: Henry Haurand.

Contractor: Hochtief AG.

Rooms: Baptistry, celestial room, four ordinance rooms, five sealing rooms.

Total floor area: 24,170 square feet.

Dimensions: 93 feet by 232 feet; statue of Angel Moroni on top spire, 82 feet high.

District: 10 stakes, 4 districts in Luxembourg, northern France, Germany, Yugoslavia, Slovenia.

Groundbreaking, site dedication: July 1, 1985, by President Gordon B. Hinckley.

Dedication: Aug. 28-30, 1987, by President Ezra Taft Benson; 11 sessions.

Dedicatory prayer excerpt: *The presence of this house, on the soil of this nation, is an answer to the prayers of Thy people, and a fulfillment of the words of Thy prophets.*

Freiberg Germany

Announced: Oct. 9, 1982.

Location: In Freiberg, Hainichener Strasse 64, D09599 Freiberg, Germany; phone: (49) 3731-35960.

Site: 1 acre.

Exterior finish: Exterior white German stucco over 24-inch thick brick walls, blue gray slate stone slab roof.

Temple design: Modern design with German influence; two high arches, reminicent of Gothic style, are parallel with front of building and bisected by two similar arches to form a single spire.

Architect: Emil B. Fetzer, original; Rolf Metzner, contractor/architect of addition.

Government construction adviser: Dr. Dieter Hantzche, architect director of Bauakademie of Dresden.

Rooms: Celestial room, one ordinance room, two sealing rooms, baptistry.

Total floor area: originally 7,840 square feet; 13,500 square feet after remodeling.

Dimensions: Originally 94 feet by 75 feet; 94 feet by 112 feet after remodeling.

District: Three stakes, 15 districts in Eastern Germany, Czech Republic, Romania, Hungary, Ukraine, Bulgaria.

Groundbreaking, site dedication: April 23, 1983, by Elder Thomas S. Monson of the Quorum of the Twelve.

Dedication: June 29, 1985, by President Gordon B. Hinckley; 7 sessions.

Rededication: Sept. 7, 2002, by President Gordon B. Hinckley, in one session.

Dedicatory prayer excerpt: *We thank Thee for all who have made possible its building and all who have made possible this glorious day of dedication.*

Fresno California

Announced: Jan. 8, 1999.

Location: Northwest Fresno near intersection of Valentine and Sierra avenues, 6290 N. Valentine, Fresno, CA 93711; phone: (559) 437-9451; no clothing rental.

Site: 2.2 acres.

Exterior finish: Sierra white granite

Temple design: Traditional.

Architects: Paul Stommel.

Project manager: Amos and Gloria Wright.

Contractor: Jacobsen Construction Co.

Rooms: Celestial room, baptistry, two ordinance rooms, two sealing rooms.

Total floor area: 10,700 square feet.

Dimensions: 149 feet by 77 feet.

District: Eight stakes in central California.

Groundbreaking, site dedication: March 20, 1999, by Elder John B. Dickson of the Seventy and president of the North America West Area.

Dedication: April 9, 2000, by President Gordon B. Hinckley; 4 sessions.

Dedicatory prayer excerpt: *May the work in this house unlock the prison doors beyond the veil that those who there receive the gospel may rejoice in the vicarious work performed here in their behalf.*

Fukuoka Japan

Announced: May 7, 1998.

Location: 46 Hirao Josui-Machi, Chuo-Ku, Fukuoka-shi, Fukuoka-ken 810-0029, Japan; phone: (81) 92-525-8255.

Site: .5 acres.

Exterior finish: Two granites: Empress White and Majesty Grey granite from China.

Temple design: Traditional.

Architect: Kanji Moriya and Church A&E Services.

Project manager: Jerry Sears.

Contractor: Taisei Construction Co.

Rooms: Celestial room, two endowment rooms, two sealing rooms and a baptistry.

Total floor area: 10,700 square feet.

Dimensions: 149 feet by 77 feet.

District: Four stakes, five districts in southern Japan.

Groundbreaking, site dedication: March 20, 1999, by Elder L. Lionel Kendrick of the Seventy, president of the Asia North Area.

Dedication: June 11, 2000, by President Gordon B. Hinckley; 4 sessions.

Dedicatory prayer excerpt: *Bless Thy Saints of this great nation. Magnify them, inspire them, bless them among the millions of this land that by the virtue of their lives they may stand as a city upon a hill whose light cannot be hid. Prosper them in their labors. May they never lack for food upon their tables or clothing on their backs or a shelter over their heads.*

No artist rendering available

Gila Valley Arizona

Announced: April 26, 2008.
Status: In planning stages.

No artist rendering available

Gilbert Arizona

Announced: April 26, 2008.
Status: In planning stages.

Guadalajara Mexico

Announced: April 14, 1999.

Location: Avenida Patria 879; Fraccionamiento Jardines Tepeyac, Zapopan, Jalisco 45030, Mexico; phone: 52 - 333-125- 1283; no clothing rental.

Site: 2.69 acres

Exterior finish: Blanco Guardiano white marble from Torreon, Mexico.

Temple design: Traditional.

Architect: Alvaro Iñigo.

Project manager: John Webster

Contractor: Impulsa Construction.

Rooms: Celestial room, two ordinances rooms, two sealing rooms, baptistry.

Total floor area: 10,700 square feet.

Dimensions: 77 feet x 149 feet.

District: 18 stakes and eight districts in Durango, Guadalajara, Aguascalientes, Irapuato, Leon, Mazatlan, Tepic, Xamora and Zacatecas.

Groundbreaking, site dedication: June 12, 1999, by Elder Eran A. Call of the Seventy and president of the Mexico North Area.

Dedication: April 29, 2001, by President Gordon B. Hinckley, 4 sessions.

Dedicatory prayer excerpt: *We thank Thee for the progress of Thy work in this great nation of Mexico. Move it forward, dear Father. Touch the lives and hearts of great numbers of people who will hearken to the message of truth and come into the fold of Christ. Bring about the miracle of conversion among the great and good people of this land.*

Guatemala City Guatemala

Announced: April 1, 1981.

Location: At the base of hills in southeastern Guatemala City; 24 Avenida 2-20, Zona 15, Vista Hermosa 1, Guatemala City, Guatemala; phone: (502)369-3426.

Site: 1.43 acres.

Exterior finish: Natural white Guatemala marble.

Temple design: Modern adaptation of earlier six-spire design.

Architects: Church archectural staff, assisted by Jose Asturias, Guatemala City.

Construction adviser: David Judd.

Contractor: Isa Constructors Aires Y Cia Ltd.

Rooms: Baptistry, celestial room, four ordinance rooms, three sealing rooms.

Total floor area: 17,609 square feet.

Dimensions: 178 feet by 72 feet, six spires; statue of Angel Moroni tops 126-foot spire.

District: 124 stakes and districts in Guatemala, Nicaragua, El Salvador, Honduras, Belize.

Groundbreaking, site dedication: Sept. 12, 1982, by Elder Richard G. Scott of the First Quorum of the Seventy.

Dedication: Dec. 14-16, 1984, by President Gordon B. Hinckley; 10 sessions.

Dedicatory prayer excerpt: *Bless our land, O Father, this nation of Guatemala where now stands Thy holy house. May those who govern do so in righteousness. Bless them as they act to preserve the liberties ... and enhance the prosperity of the people. May there be peace in the land.*

Guayaquil Ecuador

Announced: March 31, 1982.

Location: El Principado de Las Lomas de Urdesa North in Guayaquil; Calle 6ta y Av Rodrigo Chavez Gonzalez, Principado de Las Lomas, Urdessa Norte, Guayaquil, Ecuador; phone: (593) 42-889-388.

Site: 6.25 acres.

Exterior finish: Granite (Asa Branca).

Temple design: Classic modern.

Architects: Rafael Velez Calisto, Architects & Consultants and Church A&E Services.

Project manager: Roger Sears.

Contractor: Inmomariuxi.

Rooms: Celestial room, baptistry, four ordinance rooms, three sealing rooms.

Total floor area: 70,884 square feet.

Dimensions: 154 feet by 76 feet.

District: 50 stakes and districts in Ecuador.

Groundbreaking, site dedication: Aug. 10, 1996, by Elder Richard G. Scott of the Quorum of the Twelve.

Dedication: Aug. 1, 1999, by President Gordon B. Hinckley; 8 sessions.

Dedicatory prayer excerpt: *We thank Thee for the inspiration given Thy servant in selecting this property on which to construct this sacred building. Thy guiding hand was evident in the circumstances when this site was found and determined upon.*

Halifax Nova Scotia

Announced: May 7, 1998.

Location: 44 Cumberland Drive, Dartmouth, Nova Scotia B2V 2C7; phone: (902) 434-6920; no clothing rental.

Site: 1 acre.

Exterior finish: White Bethel Granite.

Temple design: Classic modern.

Architects: L.A. Beaubien and Associates, and Church A&E Services.

Project manager: William Treu.

Contractor: Dineen Construction.

Rooms: Two ordinance rooms, two sealing rooms; celestial room, baptistry.

Total floor area: 10,700 square feet.

Dimensions: 149 feet by 77 feet.

District: Two stakes, one district in Nova Scotia, New Brunswick.

Groundbreaking, site dedication: Oct. 12, 1998, by Elder Jay E. Jensen of the Seventy.

Dedication: Nov. 14, 1999, by President Gordon B. Hinckley; 3 sessions.

Dedicatory prayer excerpt: *We dedicate the ground which surrounds this temple and upon which it stands. In the season of summer it will be beautiful with Thy wondrous creations.*

Hamilton New Zealand

Announced: Feb. 17, 1955.

Location: At site of Church College of New Zealand in Temple View, outside of Hamilton; 509 Tuhikaramea Rd., Temple View, New Zealand; phone: (64) 7-846-2750.

Site: 35 acres.

Exterior finish: Reinforced concrete block, manufactured at site, structural steel; painted white.

Temple design: Modern-contemporary.

Architect: Edward O. Anderson, Church architect.

Construction chairman: Wendell B. Mendenhall.

Construction supervisor: E. Albert Rosenvall and George R. Biesinger.

Rooms: Baptistry, celestial room, one ordinance room, three sealing rooms.

Total floor area: 42,304 square feet.

Dimensions: 159 feet by 84 feet; height of tower, 157 feet.

District: 25 stakes, 7 districts in New Zealand, Cook Islands.

Groundbreaking, site dedication: Dec. 21, 1955. First sod turned by Ariel Balliff, Wendell B. Mendenhall, and George R. Biesinger.

Dedication: April 20, 1958, by President David O. McKay; eight sessions.

Dedicatory prayer excerpt: *We invoke Thy blessing particularly upon the men and women who have so willingly and generously contributed their means, time and effort to the completion of this imposing and impressive structure. Especially we mention all those who have accepted calls as labor missionaries and literally consecrated their all upon the altar of service.*

Helsinki Finland

Announced: April 2, 2000.

Location: Leppäsillantie 3, 02620 Espoo, Finland.

Exterior finish: Light gray Italian granite; stone walls surrounding temple made of Finnish brown granite.

Temple design: classic elegance

Site: 7.4 acres

Architects: Evata Architects, Helsinki, Finland.

Project manager: Hanno Luschin.

Contractor: NCC Rakennus OY, Helsinki, Finland.

Rooms: Celestial room, baptistry, two ordinance rooms, two sealing rooms.

Total floor area: 16,350 square feet.

Dimensions: 212-feet by 103-feet by 139-feet

District: Members in Finland and Eastern Europe countries of Russia and Baltic countries.

Groundbreaking, site dedication: March 29, 2003, by Elder D. Lee Tobler.

Dedication: Oct. 22, 2006, by President Gordon B. Hinckley; four sessions.

Dedicatory prayer excerpt: *O God, we are so deeply grateful to those who have come to this land as Thy servants to preach the everlasting gospel.... We pray for this great nation of Finland. May it ever be respected and honored among the nations of the earth.*

Hermosillo Sonora Mexico

Announced: July 20, 1998.

Location: General Pedro Garcia Conde No. 303; Esq. con Juan Jose Rios, Colonia Pitic, Hermosillo, Sonora CP 83150, Mexico; phone (52) 662-210-5660; no clothing rental.

Site: 2.07 acres.

Exterior finish: White marble veneer.

Temple design: Classic modern.

Architect: Alvaro Iñigo and Church A&E Services.

Project manager: David Wills.

Contractor: Grana y Montero / Jacobsen Construction Co.

Rooms: Two ordinance rooms, two sealing rooms, celestial room, baptistry.

Total floor area: 10,700 square feet.

Dimensions: 77 feet by 149 feet.

District: 11 stakes and six districts in surrounding area.

Groundbreaking, site dedication: Dec. 5, 1998, by Elder Eran A. Call of the Seventy and counselor in the Mexico South Area presidency.

Dedication: Feb. 27, 2000, by President Gordon B. Hinckley, 4 sessions.

Dedicatory prayer excerpt: *May [this temple] be a structure of beauty, a crowning gem in this great city. We are grateful that the officials of government have permitted its construction and that it is now completed.*

Hong Kong China

Announced: Oct. 3, 1992.

Location: 2 Cornwall Street, Kowloon Tong Kowloon, Hong Kong; phone: (852) 2339-8100. First temple from existing building, comprising basement and upper floors.

Site: .3 acres.

Exterior finish: Polished granite.

Temple design: Hong Kong colonial.

Architects: Liang Peddle Thorpe Architects.

Rooms: Baptistry, celestial room, two ordinance rooms, two sealing rooms.

Total floor area: 21,744 square feet.

Dimensions of building: 70 feet by 92 feet; Angel statue is 135 feet above main floor.

District: Six stakes, four districts in China, Singapore, Mongolia.

Groundbreaking, site dedication: Jan. 22, 1994, by Elder John K. Carmack of the First Quorum of the Seventy and Asia Area president.

Dedication: May 26-27, 1996; by President Gordon B. Hinckley; 7 sessions.

Dedicatory prayer excerpt: *Thy Church in this area now comes to full maturity with the dedication of this sacred temple. We pray that this harvest of souls may continue, that in the future as in the present, Thy people may be free and secure in their worship and that none shall hinder the service of missionaries called to this area. We pray that Thy work may grow and prosper in the great Chinese realm, and may those who govern be ever receptive to those called and sent as messengers of revealed truth.*

Houston Texas

Announced: Sept. 30, 1997.

Location: 15725 Champion Forest Drive, Klein, TX 77379-7036; phone (281) 376-6804.

Site: 10.35 acres.

Exterior finish: Cast stone/granite.

Temple design: Classic modern.

Architect: Spencer Partnership Architects and Church A&E Services.

Project manager: Leon Rowley.

Contractor: SpawGlass Const.

Rooms: Two ordinance rooms, three sealing rooms, celestial room, baptistry.

Total floor area: 33,970 square feet.

Dimensions of building: 145 feet by 136 feet; spire 159 feet high.

District: 22 area stakes and two districts in Texas.

Groundbreaking, site dedication: June 13, 1998, by Elder Lynn A. Mickelsen of the Seventy and president of the North America Southwest Area.

Dedication: Aug. 26-27, 2000, by President Gordon B. Hinckley; 8 sessions.

Dedicatory prayer excerpt: *How glorious and complete is Thy plan for the salvation and exaltation of Thy children of all generations. How tremendous is our obligation to carry forward this great vicarious work in their behalf.*

Idaho Falls Idaho

Announced: March 3, 1937.

Location: In northwestern Idaho Falls on the banks of the Snake River; 1000 Memorial Drive, Idaho Falls, ID 83402-3497; phone: (208) 522-7669.

Site: 7 acres.

Exterior finish: Built of reinforced concrete. A mixture of white quartz aggregate and white cement called cast stone covers the 16-inch thick exterior walls in slabs two inches thick.

Temple design: Modern-contemporary.

Architects: Church board of temple architects: Edward O. Anderson, Georgius Y. Cannon, Ramm Hansen, John Fetzer, Hyrum C. Pope, Lorenzo S. Young.

Construction adviser: Arthur Price.

Contractor: Birdwell Finlayson of Pocatello, Idaho.

Rooms: Baptistry, celestial room, four ordinance rooms, nine sealing rooms.

Total floor area: 92,177 square feet.

Dimensions: 192 feet by 234 feet; tower 148 feet high. Two annexes added 7,700 square feet. A 12-foot statue of Angel Moroni was added to the tower Sept. 5, 1983.

District: 58 stakes in eastern Idaho, western Wyoming.

Groundbreaking, site dedication: Dec. 19, 1939, ground broken by David Smith, North Idaho Falls Stake president. Site dedicated Oct. 19, 1940, by President David O. McKay of the First Presidency.

Dedication: Sept. 23, 1945, by President George Albert Smith, 8 dedicatory sessions.

Dedicatory prayer excerpt: *We pray that Thou wilt accept this temple as a freewill offering from Thy children, that it will be sacred unto Thee.*

Johannesburg South Africa

Announced: April 1, 1981.

Location: 2 miles north of city center; 7 Jubilee Rd., Parktown, Johannesburg 2193, South Africa; phone, (27) 11-645-1540.

Site: One acre.

Exterior finish: Masonry exterior.

Temple design: Modern adaptation of earlier six-spire design.

Architects: Church architectural staff; local architect, Halford & Halford.

Construction adviser: Stanley G. Smith.

Contractor: Tiber Bonvac.

Rooms: Baptistry, celestial room, four ordinance rooms, three sealing rooms.

Total floor area: 19,184 square feet.

Dimensions: 178 feet by 71 feet; Angel Moroni statue is atop tallest spire at 112 feet.

District: 29 stakes and districts in southern Africa.

Groundbreaking, site dedication: Nov. 27, 1982, by Elder Marvin J. Ashton of the Quorum of the Twelve.

Dedication: Aug. 24-25, 1985, by President Gordon B. Hinckley; 4 sessions.

Dedicatory prayer excerpt: *Almighty God, wilt Thou overrule for the blessing and safety of Thy faithful Saints. We pray for peace in this troubled land. Bless this nation which has befriended Thy servants. May those who rule in the offices of government be inspired to find a basis for reconciliation among those who now are in conflict one with another. May the presence of Thy house on the soil of this land bring blessings to the entire nation.*

No artist rendering available

Jordan River

Announced: Feb. 3, 1978.

Location: About 15 miles south of Salt Lake City in South Jordan; 10200 South 1300 West, South Jordan, UT 84095-8814; phone: (801) 254-3003.

Site: 15 acres.

Exterior finish: Cast stone containing white marble chips. Tower appears same as the rest of the building, but in order to reduce weight it contains fiberglass in a product called cemlite.

Temple design: Modern.

Architect: Emil B. Fetzer, Church architect.

Resident project inspector: Jerry Sears.

Construction superintendent: Lawrence O. Dansie for Layton Construction Co.

Rooms: Baptistry, celestial room, six ordinance rooms, 17 sealing rooms.

Total floor area: 148,236 square feet.

Dimensions: Basement and main floor, 211 feet by 218 feet; two upper levels, 140 by 166 feet. Height to square is 58 feet, to top of tower, 219 feet, including a 20-foot statue of the Angel Moroni.

District: Southern Salt Lake County, Utah.

Groundbreaking, site dedication: June 9, 1979, by President Spencer W. Kimball.

Dedication: Nov. 16-20, 1981, by President Marion G. Romney; 15 sessions.

Dedicatory prayer excerpt: *May all who enter have clean hands and pure hearts, and may they participate with faith in the ordinances to be given herein.*

Kansas City Missouri

Announced: Oct. 4, 2008.

Status: In Planning stages.

For the temple serving the greater Kansas City area, the site will be in Clay County, Missouri, on residential land within the Kansas City limits that is already being developed by the Church. The development is known as Shoal Creek.

Artist rendering

Kyiv/Kiev Ukraine

Announced: July 20, 1998.

Ground breaking, site dedication: June 23, 2007, by Elder Paul B. Pieper of the Seventy and president of the Europe East Area.

Status: Under construction.

Kirtland

*No longer owned by the Church.

Location: Kirtland, Ohio, 25 miles east of Cleveland, on a hill west of Chagrin River.

Site: Selected March 1833; deed recorded Aug. 4, 1834.

Exterior finish: Sandstone covered with stuccoed plaster.

Temple design: Adaptation of Federal Georgian and New England Colonial.

Architect: Joseph Smith.

Building committee: Hyrum Smith, Reynolds Cahoon and Jared Carter.

Master builder: Artemis Millett.

Rooms: Originally 15.

Total floor area: Approximately 15,000 square feet.

Dimensions: 79 feet by 59 feet; walls 50 feet high; tower height above ground, 110 feet.

Start of work: Hauling of sandstone to site began June 5, 1833.

Cornerstones: July 23, 1833.

Dedication: March 27 and 31, 1836, by President Joseph Smith. *(DHC II:433)*

Dedicatory prayer excerpt: *And we ask Thee, Holy Father, that Thy servants may go forth from this house, armed with Thy power and that Thy name may be upon them.*

Kona Hawaii

Announced: May 7, 1998.

Location: 75-230 Kalani Street; Kailua-Kona, HI 96740-1833; phone: (808) 331-8504; no clothing rental.

Site: 4 acres.

Exterior finish: White marble veneer.

Temple design: Traditional.

Architect: Jon Pharis of Pharis & Associates.

Project manager: Jerry Sears.

Contractor: Bud Bailey Construction.

Rooms: Celestial room, baptistry, two ordinance rooms, two sealing rooms.

Total floor area: 10,700 square feet.

Dimensions: 149 feet by 77 feet.

District: Kona, Hilo and Kahului Hawaii stakes on the islands of Maui, Molokai and Lanai.

Groundbreaking, site dedication: March 13, 1999, by Elder John B. Dickson of the Seventy and president of the North America West Area.

Dedication: Jan. 23, 2000, by President Gordon B. Hinckley; 4 sessions.

Dedicatory prayer excerpt: *Now we have this second temple here on the big island. May the work increase. May there come into the hearts of the people a growing desire to come to the House of the Lord, here to taste the sweet refreshment of the Holy Spirit.*

Laie Hawaii

Announced: Oct. 3, 1915.

Location: In Laie, on the northeast side of the island of Oahu, 32 miles from Honolulu.

Site: 11.4 acres, a portion of original property purchased by Church.

Exterior finish: Concrete made of the crushed lava rock of the area and tooled to a white cream finish.

Temple design: Suggestive of the ancient temples found in South America.

Architects: Hyrum C. Pope and Harold W. Burton.

General superintendent: Samuel E. Woolley. Polynesian Saints did much of the work.

Rooms: Baptistry, celestial room, three ordinance rooms, six sealing rooms.

Total floor area: 10,500 square feet originally; approximately 47,224 square feet after remodeling.

Dimensions of building: 157 feet by 283 feet.

District: 11 stakes in Oahu and central islands.

Site dedication: June 1, 1915, site dedicated by Pres. Joseph F. Smith.

Dedication: Thanksgiving Day, Nov. 27, 1919, by President Heber J. Grant; five sessions.

Rededicated June 13-15, 1978, by President Spencer W. Kimball after extensive remodeling; nine sessions.

Dedicatory prayer excerpt: *May all who come upon the grounds which surround this temple, in the years to come, whether members of the Church or not, feel the sweet and peaceful influence of this blessed hallowed spot.*

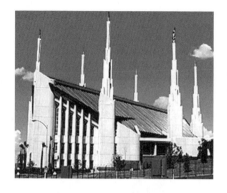

Las Vegas Nevada

Announced: April 7, 1984.

Location: On the east side of Las Vegas on the slope of Frenchman Mountain, 827 Temple View Drive; Las Vegas, NV 89110-2920; phone: (702) 452-5011.

Temple design: Six spires

Site: 10.3 acres.

Exterior finish: White precast stone walls and copper roof and detailing.

Architects: Tate & Snyder.

Construction adviser: Gary Holland

Contractor: Hogan & Tingey.

Rooms: Baptistry, celestial room, four ordinance rooms, six sealing rooms.

Total floor area: 80,350 square feet.

Dimensions: 195 feet by 260 feet; statue of Angel Moroni on top spire 137 feet high.

District: 19 southern Nevada stakes, two Arizona and one California stakes.

Groundbreaking, site dedication: Nov. 30, 1985, by President Gordon B. Hinckley.

Dedication: Dec. 16-18, 1989, by President Gordon B. Hinckley; 11 sessions.

Dedicatory prayer excerpt: *Within its walls are to be tasted the refreshing waters of living and eternal truth. For all who enter the portals of Thy house may this be an oasis of peace and life and light, in contrast with the clamor and evil and darkness of the world.*

Lima Peru

Announced: April 1, 1981.

Location: Southwest part of Lima, in the Molina district; Prolg. Av. Javier Prado Este 6420, La Molina, Lima 12, Peru; phone: (51) 1 348-0418.

Site: 4.5 acres.

Exterior finish: Local granite, Oriental design.

Temple design: Modern adaptation of earlier six-spire design.

Architects: Church architectural staff; local architect Jose Asturias.

Construction adviser: Sergio Gomez.

Rooms: Baptistry, celestial room, four ordinance rooms, three sealing rooms.

Total floor area: 9,600 square feet.

Dimensions: 178 feet by 71 feet. Angel Moroni statue is atop tallest spire at 112 feet.

District: 80 stakes and 32 districts in Peru.

Groundbreaking, site dedication: Sept. 11, 1982, by Elder Boyd K. Packer of the Quorum of the Twelve.

Dedication: Jan. 10-12, 1986, by President Gordon B. Hinckley; 11 sessions.

Dedicatory prayer excerpt: *We are particularly mindful this day of the sons and daughters of Lehi. They have known so much of suffering and sorrow in their many generations. They have walked in darkness and in servitude. Now thou hast touched them by the light of the everlasting gospel. The shackles of darkness are falling from their eyes as they embrace the truths of thy great work.*

Logan Utah

Location: On eastern bench overlooking Cache Valley; 175 N. 300 East, Logan, UT.

Site: 9 acres, selected by Brigham Young, May 18, 1877.

Exterior finish: Dark-colored, siliceous limestone used for the major portion of the temple. Buff-colored limestone, more easily carved, used for intricate shaping.

Temple design: Castellated style.

Architect: Truman O. Angell.

Construction heads: Superintendent of construction, Charles O. Card; master mason, John Parry; plastering foreman, William Davis. More than 25,000 people worked on temple.

Rooms: Baptistry, celestial room, four ordinance rooms, 11 sealing rooms; five stories.

Total floor area: Originally 59,130 square feet; 115,507 square feet after remodeling.

Dimensions: 168 feet by 224 feet; 86 feet high. The east tower is 170 feet high; west tower, 165 feet high; four octagonal towers, each 100 feet high.

District: 44 stakes in northern Utah, southeastern Idaho.

Groundbreaking, site dedication: May 17, 1877; site dedicated by Elder Orson Pratt, ground broken by President John W. Young of the First Presidency.

Dedication: May 17-19, 1884, by President John Taylor; 3 sessions.

On March 13-15, 1979, after extensive remodeling, the temple was rededicated by President Spencer W. Kimball; 9 sessions.

Dedicatory prayer excerpt: *And, as all wisdom dwells with Thee, and, as all light, truth and intelligence. . . . We ask that in this house a more full knowledge of Thee and Thy laws may be developed.*

London England

Location: 25 miles south of London, formerly an Elizabethan farm at Newchapel near Lingfield; Surrey RH7 6HW, United Kingdom; phone: (44) 1342-832759.

Site: Selected in June 1952 by President David O. McKay and Elder Stayner Richards. Purchased in 1953; 32 acres.

Exterior finish: Concrete and steel structure, brick masonry walls faced with cut Portland limestone. Spire sheathed in copper.

Temple design: Modern-contemporary.

Architect: Edward O. Anderson.

Supervising architects: T.T. Bennett and Son, London.

Contractor: Kirk and Kirk, Ltd., London.

Rooms: Baptistry, celestial room, four ordinance rooms, seven sealing rooms.

Total floor area: Originally 34,000 square feet; 42,775 square feet after remodeling.

Dimensions: 84 feet wide, 159 feet long, 56 feet to the square. The tower rises 156 feet inches from ground level, spire 33 feet above that.

District: 20 stakes in England and two in Wales.

Groundbreaking, site dedication: Aug. 10, 1953; site dedicated by David O. McKay, who broke ground on Aug. 27, 1955.

Dedication: Sept. 7-9, 1958, by President David O. McKay; 6 sessions. Rededicated Oct. 18-20, 1992, by President Gordon B. Hinckley; 10 sessions.

Dedicatory prayer excerpt: *With humility and deep gratitude we acknowledge Thy nearness, Thy divine guidance and inspiration. Help us, we pray Thee, to become even more susceptible in our spiritual response to Thee.*

Los Angeles California

Location: Atop a hill near Westwood Village, two miles west of Beverly Hills,10777 Santa Monica Blvd.; Los Angeles, CA 90025-4718; phone: (310) 474-5569.

Site: On 13 of the original 24.23 acres purchased from the Harold Lloyd Motion Picture Company on March 23, 1937, by President Heber J. Grant.

Exterior finish: The exterior is covered with 146,000 square feet of Mo-Sai stone facing, a mixture of crushed quartz and white Portland cement quarried in Utah and Nevada. Wainscot around exterior is Rockville granite from Minnesota.

Temple design: Modern.

Architect: Edward O. Anderson, Church architect. (Millard F. Malin, sculptor of 15-foot statue of Angel Moroni on spire.)

Superintendent: Vern Loder.

Contractor: Soren N. Jacobsen.

Rooms: Baptistry, celestial room, four ordinance rooms, 10 sealing rooms.

Total floor area: 190,614 square feet, or approximately 4.5 acres.

Dimensions: 269 feet by 369 feet; overall height is 257 feet .

District: 44 stakes in Southern California.

Groundbreaking, site dedication: Sept. 22, 1951, by President David O. McKay.

Dedication: March 11-14, 1956, by President David O. McKay; 8 sessions.

Dedicatory prayer excerpt: *May all who come within these sacred walls feel a peaceful, hallowed influence. Cause, O Lord, that even people who pass the grounds, or view the temple from afar, may lift their eyes from the groveling things of sordid life and look up to Thee and Thy providence.*

Louisville Kentucky

Announced: March 17, 1999.

Location: 7116 W. Highway 22, Crestwood, KY 40014; phone: (502) 241-4115; no clothing rental.

Site: 1.1 acres.

Exterior finish: Danby Vermont marble.

Temple design: Traditional.

Architects: Firestone Jaros Mullin — Mike Karpinski Architect.

Project manager: Bruce Catanzaro.

Contractor: Corna/Kokosing Construction Co.

Rooms: Celestial room, baptistry, two ordinance rooms, two sealing rooms.

Total floor area: 10,700 square feet.

Dimensions: 149 feet by 77 feet.

District: 10 stakes in Kentucky, Indiana and Ohio.

Groundbreaking, site dedication: May 29, 1999, by Elder John K. Carmack of the Seventy and president of the North America East Area.

Dedication: March 19, 2000, by President Thomas S. Monson first counselor in the First Presidency; 4 sessions.

Dedicatory prayer excerpt: *May those in the life beyond who are helpless to move forward rejoice in the completion of this sacred building.*

Lubbock Texas

Announced: April 2, 2000.

Location: 7016 Frankford Ave., Lubbock, TX 79424; phone: (806) 794-0774; no clothing rental.

Site: 2.67-acre site shared with a stake center.

Exterior finish: Light colored granite.

Temple design: Traditional.

Architect: Tisdel Minckler and Associates.

Project manager: Leon Rowley.

Contractor: SpawGlass Construction.

Rooms: Celestial room, two ordinance rooms, two sealing rooms, baptistry, chapel, offices and waiting area.

Total floor area: 16,498 square feet.

Dimensions: 188 feet x 98 feet.

District: Five stakes in west Texas and one district in eastern New Mexico.

Groundbreaking, site dedication: Nov. 4, 2000, by Elder Rex D. Pinegar of the Seventy;

Dedication: April 21, 2002, by President Gordon B. Hinckley, 4 sessions.

Dedicatory prayer excerpt: *Bless all who serve in Thy work throughout the earth. Grant unto them great joy. May the assurance of Thy love crown their lives and bring into their hearts peace and gladness. . . . We invoke Thy blessings upon this community, upon this state, upon this nation. Bless this chosen land that it may remain forever free, that peace and liberty may bless the lives of its people, and that righteousness may reign in the land.*

Madrid Spain

Announced: Country announced April 4, 1993, city announced Oct. 9, 1994.

Location: Barrio of Moratalaz, corner of Hacienda de Pavones and Valdebernando, Calle del Temple No. 2; E-28030 Madrid, Spain; phone: (34) 913-017-607.

Site: 3.5 acres.

Exterior finish: Camaro Marble from Italy.

Temple design: Modern Classic.

Architects: Arquitechior Langdon, SA.

Project manager: Ralph Cluff.

Contractor: JOSTSA Construction Co.

Rooms: Baptistry, celestial room, four ordinance rooms, four sealing rooms.

Total floor area: 45,800 square feet.

Dimensions: 116 feet by 138 feet.

District: 49 stakes and districts in Spain, Portugal, Canary Islands, Cape Verde, France.

Groundbreaking, site dedication: June 11, 1996, by President Gordon B. Hinckley.

Dedication: March 19-21, 1999, by President Gordon B. Hinckley; 10 sessions.

Dedicatory prayer excerpt: *We thank Thee for this great kingdom of Spain which has been hospitable to Thy Saints. Bless this land. We are mindful that it was from these shores that Columbus sailed to discover America as foretold in the Book of Mormon.*

Artist rendering

Manaus Brazil

Announced: May 23, 2007.

Groundbreaking, site dedication: June 20, 2008, by Elder Charles Didier of the Seventy and president of the Brazil Area.

Status: Under construction.

Manhattan New York

Announced: Aug. 7, 2002.

Location: Near Lincoln Center, 125 Columbus Ave., New York City, N.Y. 10023; between 65th and 66th. Temple comprises first, second, fifth and sixth floors; meetinghouse comprises third and fourth floors.

Site: Area occupied by former stake center.

Exterior finish: Light, variegated granite.

Architects: Frank Fernandez.

Contractors: East Coast Construction Group.

Project manager: Cory Karl.

Rooms: Two ordinance rooms, two sealing rooms, celestial room and baptistry.

Total floor area: 20,630 square feet.

District: Parts of New York, New Jersey and Connecticut.

Groundbreaking and site dedication: Building originally dedicated in 1975 by Elder Spencer W. Kimball.

Dedication: June 13, 2004, by President Gordon B. Hinckley; four sessions.

Dedicatory prayer excerpt: *"May this temple be a place of quiet refuge in the midst of this great and noisy metropolis. May all who enter its portals feel they have stepped from the world into a place of thy divine presence."*

Manila Philippines

Announced: April 1, 1981.

Location: In Quezon City; 13 Temple Drive, Greenmeadows Subdivision, 1110 Quezon City, Metro Manila, Philippines.

Site: About 3.5 acres.

Exterior finish: Ceramic tile.

Temple design: Six-spire design.

Architect: Church staff, with assistance from Felipe M. Mendoza & Partners, Manila.

Construction adviser: Wayne Tuttle.

Contractor: A. C. K. Construction.

Rooms: Baptistry, celestial room, four ordinance rooms, three sealing rooms.

Total floor area: 26,683 square feet.

Dimensions: 200 feet by 75 feet, six spires; statue of Angel Moroni is 115 feet high.

District: Stakes and districts in Philippines, Indonesia, Singapore, Thailand, India, Sri Lanka, Malaysia, Cambodia, Burma and Micronesia: Majuro, Kosrae, Chuuk, Phonpei, Yap, Guam, Kwajalein.

Groundbreaking, site dedication: Aug. 25, 1982, by President Gordon B. Hinckley.

Dedication: Sept. 25-27, 1984, by President Gordon B. Hinckley; 9 sessions.

Dedicatory prayer excerpt: *Lift the blight of poverty from which so many suffer. Particularly bless Thy faithful Saints who live honestly with Thee in the payment of their tithes and offerings. Bless them that neither they nor their generations after them will go hungry, nor naked, nor without shelter from the storms that beat about them.*

Manti Utah

Location: Hill above U.S. Highway 89 in Sanpete Valley in Manti, Utah.

Site: 27 acres. "Manti Stone Quarry" had been prophesied as site for a temple since area's settlement in 1849.

Exterior finish: Cream-colored oolite limestone from quarries on which temple is built.

Temple design: The castellated style reflecting influence of Gothic Revival, French Renaissance Revival, French Second Empire and colonial architecture.

Architect: William H. Folsom.

Construction heads: William H. Folsom from Oct. 15, 1877, to Aug. 7, 1888, when Daniel H. Wells took his place as supervisor; master mason, Edward L. Parry.

Rooms: Four ordinance rooms and eight sealing rooms; baptistry, celestial room.

Total floor area: 74,792 square feet.

Dimensions of building: 178 feet by 244 feet; 86 feet high. East tower is 179 feet high, west tower 169 feet high, building at ground level is 60 feet above highway below.

District: 26 stakes in Central Utah.

Groundbreaking, site dedication: April 25, 1877, by President Brigham Young.

Dedication: May 17, 1888, private dedication held; dedicated by President Wilford Woodruff of the Quorum of the Twelve. Three public dedicatory services held May 21-23, 1888; Elder Lorenzo Snow read the prayer.

Rededicated June 14-16, 1985, by President Gordon B. Hinckley; 9 sessions.

Dedicatory prayer excerpt: *May this holy temple be to them as one of the gates of heaven, opening into the straight and narrow path that leads to endless lives and eternal dominion.*

Medford Oregon

Announced: March 17, 1999.

Location: 3900 Grant Road, in Central Point, OR 97502; phone: (541) 664-2050; no clothing rental.

Site: 2 acres.

Exterior finish: Granite.

Temple design: Traditional.

Architects: Dan Park and Church A&E Services.

Project manager: Amos and Gloria Wright.

Contractor: Corey Vitas Construction.

Rooms: Celestial room, baptistry, two ordinance rooms, two sealing rooms.

Total floor area: 10,700 square feet.

Dimensions: 149 feet by 77 feet.

District: Nine stakes in southern Oregon and northern California.

Groundbreaking, site dedication: May 20, 1999, by Elder D. Lee Tobler of the Seventy and first counselor in the North America Northwest Area presidency.

Dedication: April 16, 2000, by President James E. Faust, second counselor in the First Presidency; 4 sessions.

Dedicatory prayer excerpt: *Bless the youth of the Church, dear Father. Lead them in paths of righteousness and truth. Protect them from the alluring and seductive calls of the adversary.*

Melbourne Australia

Announced: Oct. 30, 1998.

Location: Corner of Cathies Lane and Pumps Lane; 76 Cathies Lane, Wantirna South, VIC 3152, Australia; phone: (61) 3-9881-9700; no clothing rental.

Site: 5.98 acres, including adjoining meetinghouse.

Exterior finish: Snow white granite.

Temple design: Traditional.

Architect: Warwick Tempany and Church A&E Services.

Project manager: Graham Sully.

Contractor: Probuild.

Rooms: Celestial room, two ordinance rooms, two sealing rooms and a baptistry.

Total floor area: 10,700 square feet.

Dimensions: 149 feet by 77 feet.

District: Melbourne, Hobart, Devonport stakes and Albury districts.

Groundbreaking, site dedication: March 20, 1999, by Elder P. Bruce Mitchell, Area Authority Seventy and second counselor in the Austrialia/New Zealand Area presidency.

Dedication: June 16, 2000, by President Gordon B. Hinckley; 4 sessions.

Dedicatory prayer excerpt: *We are grateful for this nation of Australia, where we may worship Thee in peace, without molestation or fear or threat. Bless this land that it may remain ever strong, a nation of peace and progress among the nations of the earth.*

Memphis Tennessee

Announced: Sept. 17, 1998.

Location: 4199 Kirby-Whitten Parkway, Bartlett, TN 38135; phone: (901) 379-0202; no clothing rental.

Site: 6.35 acres, including adjoining meetinghouse.

Exterior finish: Imperial Danby White marble.

Temple design: Classic modern.

Architect: Dusty Driver of Bounds & Gillespie Architects and Church A&E Services.

Project manager: Leon Rowley.

Contractor: Layton Construction Co., Construction Management Company; Rentenbach Construction, general contractor.

Rooms: Celestial room, baptistry, two ordinance rooms, two sealing rooms.

Total floor area: 10,700 square feet.

Dimensions: 149 feet by 77 feet.

District: Five stakes in Memphis, Tenn., and Little Rock, Ark., and Tupelo, Miss.

Groundbreaking, site dedication: Jan. 16, 1999, by Elder Gordon T. Watts of the Seventy and first counselor in the North America Southeast Area presidency.

Dedication: April 23, 2000, by President James E. Faust, second counselor in First Presidency; 4 sessions.

Dedicatory prayer excerpt: *We are grateful for this nation whose Constitution and laws protect us in our worship. May these precious liberties never be lost to the people. May they be safeguarded and kept secure from those who would destroy the precious boon of freedom of worship.*

Merida Yucatan Mexico

Announced: Sept. 25, 1998.

Location: Calle 70 #527, Esq. 65 y 67; Col. Centro, Merida, Yucatan CP 97000, Mexico; phone: (52) 999-928-1643; no clothing rental.

Site: 1.31 acres.

Exterior finish: Guardiano white marble.

Temple design: Classic modern.

Architect: Alvaro Iñigo and Church A&E Services.

Project manager: Dean Fife.

Contractor: PyCSA / Okland Construction Co.

Rooms: Celestial room, baptistry, two ordinance rooms, two sealing rooms.

Total floor area: 10,700 square feet.

Dimensions: 77 feet by 149 feet.

District: Nine stakes, two districts and three branches on Yucatan Peninsula.

Groundbreaking, site dedication: Jan. 16, 1999, by Carl B. Pratt of the Seventy and president of the Mexico South Area.

Dedication: July 8, 2000, by Thomas S. Monson, first counselor in the First Presidency; 4 sessions.

Dedicatory prayer excerpt: *Help us this day to rededicate our lives to the advancement of Thy cause and kingdom.*

Mesa Arizona

Location: In Mesa, 16 miles east of Phoenix, in central Arizona's Valley of the Sun.

Site: 20-acre site selected Feb. 1, 1920, by President Heber J. Grant, Apostles David O. McKay and George F. Richards. Purchased in 1921.

Exterior finish: Concrete reinforced with steel. Exterior is faced with a terra cotta glaze that is egg-shell in color and tile-like in finish.

Temple design: Modification of the classic style, suggestive of pre-Columbian temples and even the Temple of Herod.

Architects: Don C. Young and Ramm Hansen.

Construction supervisor: Arthur Price.

Construction chairman: J.W. LeSueur, O.S. Stapley, John Cummard, Andrew Kimball.

Rooms: Baptistry, celestial room, four ordinance, nine sealing rooms.

Total floor area: 113,916 square feet.

Dimensions: 220 feet by 243 feet, and 50 feet in height above the foundation.

District: Stakes in southern Arizona.

Site dedication, groundbreaking: Site dedicated Nov. 28, 1921; ground broken April 25, 1922, by President Heber J. Grant.

Dedication: Oct. 23, 1927, by President Heber J. Grant, broadcast by radio. Rededicated after extensive remodeling April 15-16, 1975, by President Spencer W. Kimball; 7 sessions.

Dedicatory prayer excerpt: *Accept the dedication of this house and these grounds, which we have dedicated unto thee by virtue of the Priesthood of the Living God which we hold.*

Mexico City D.F. Mexico

Announced: April 3, 1976.

Location: Near Aragon public park and zoological gardens, bounded by Calle Ignacio Allende and Calle Emiliano Zapata; Avenida 510 #90, Col. San Juan de Aragon, Mexico D.F. 07950; phone: (52) 555-747-4861.

Site: 7 acres.

Exterior finish: White cast stone, ornate with adaptations of ancient Mayan designs, especially on upper portion of the structure.

Temple design: Modern adaptation of ancient Mayan architecture.

Architect: Emil B. Fetzer, Church architect.

Resident inspector: Ricardo Espiriti.

Construction superintendent: Jose Ortiz for Urbec Construction Co.

Rooms: Baptistry, celestial room, four ordinance rooms, 11 sealing rooms.

Total floor area: 116,642 square feet.

Dimensions: 178 feet by 214.5 feet; two upper levels, 119.5 feet by 157 feet. Height to square, 70 feet; to top of tower with Statue of Angel Moroni, 152 feet.

District: 109 Stakes, districts in central Mexico.

Groundbreaking, site dedication: Nov. 25, 1979, by Elder Boyd K. Packer of the Quorum of the Twelve.

Dedication: Dec. 2-4, 1983, by President Gordon B. Hinckley; 9 sessions. Rededicated Nov. 16, 2008.

Dedicatory prayer excerpt: *Bless Thy Saints in this great land and those from other lands who will use this temple. Most have in their veins the blood of Father Lehi. Thou hast kept Thine ancient promise.*

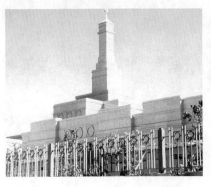

Monterrey Mexico

Announced: Dec. 27, 1995.

Location: Avenida Eugenio Garza Sada, Esq. Privada Valle de la Estansuela Colonia Valle Alto, Monterrey, Nuevo Leon 64989, Mexico; phone: (52) 806-794-0774; no clothing rental.

Site: 8.2 acres on site shared with a stake center.

Exterior finish: White marble.

Temple design: Traditional.

Architect: Alvaro Iñigo.

Project manager: William Treu.

Contractor: Okland Constructcion Co. Impulsa.

Rooms: Celestial room, two ordinance rooms, two sealing rooms, baptistry.

Total floor area: 16,017 square feet.

Dimensions: 98 feet by 188 feet.

District: 25 stakes and 7 districts in Monterrey area of northern central Mexico.

Groundbreaking, site dedication: Nov. 4, 2000, by Elder Lynn A. Mickelsen.

Dedication: April 28, 2002, by President Gordon B. Hinckley; 4 sessions.

Dedicatory prayer excerpt: *We express appreciation for the many missionaries who have labored in this great nation in teaching the eternal truths of Thy gospel. They have served with such devotion that today hundreds of thousands of Thy sons and daughters have entered the waters of baptism and have thereafter walked in faith before Thee.*

Montevideo Uruguay

Announced: Nov. 2, 1998.

Location: Calle San Carlos de Bolivar, entre Horacio Quiroga; Bolonia 1722, entre Horacio Quiroga y Bologna, Montevideo, Uruguay; phone: (598) 2-604-2212; no clothing rental.

Site: 1.59 acres.

Exterior finish: Granite.

Temple design: Classic modern.

Architect: Edvardo Signorelli.

Project manager: Javier Mendieta.

Contractor: Luis Maranges S.A.

Rooms: Two ordinance, two sealing, celestial room, baptistry.

Total floor area: 10,700 square feet.

Dimensions of building: 149 feet by 77 feet.

District: 15 Stakes and 6 districts in Uruguay.

Groundbreaking, site dedication: April 27, 1999, by Elder Richard G. Scott of the Quorum of the Twelve.

Dedication: March 18, 2001, by President Gordon B. Hinckley; 4 sessions.

Dedicatory prayer excerpt: *Dear Father, wilt Thou accept this temple as the gift of Thy sons and daughters. It has come through the faithful payment of tithing by Thy Saints across the world. May it grace this land. May the nation of Uruguay be blessed because of its presence on this soil.*

Monticello Utah

Announced: Oct. 4, 1997.

Location: 397 No. 200 West, Monticello, UT 84535; phone: (435) 587-3500; no rental clothng..

Site: 1.33 acres.

Exterior finish: White marble.

Temple design: Classic modern.

Architects: Church Architectural Services.

Construction advisers: Bob Dewey, Ron Prince.

Contractor: Jacobsen Construction Co.

Rooms: Celestial room, baptistry; originally one ordinance room, one sealing room; one ordinance room and one sealing room added in remodeling.

Size: Originally 7,000 square fee; increased to 11,225 square feet in remodeling.

Dimensions: 79 feet by 108 feet, 66 feet high to statue of Angel Moroni.

District: Five stakes in southeastern Utah and southwestern Colorado.

Groundbreaking, site dedication: Nov. 17, 1997, by Elder Ben B. Banks of the Seventy and president of the Utah South Area.

Dedication: July 26-27, 1998, by President Gordon B. Hinckley; 8 sessions; rededicated Nov. 17, 2002, one session by President Gordon B. Hinckley.

Dedicatory prayer excerpt: *Bless the children that there may grow in their hearts a desire to serve Thee all the days of their lives.*

Montreal Quebec

Announced: Aug. 6, 1998.

Location: on the south shore of the St. Lawrence River across from Montreal; 1450 Boulevard Marie-Victorin, Longueuil, Quebec J4G 1A4; phone: (450) 646-5775; no clothing rental.

Site: .75 acres.

Exterior finish: Bethel white granite.

Temple design: Classic modern.

Architect: Andrij Serbyn, Sichten Soiferman and Church A&E Services.

Project manager: William Treu.

Contractor: Opron Inc.

Rooms: Celestial room, baptistry, two ordinance rooms, two sealing rooms.

Total floor area: 10,700 square feet.

Dimensions: 149 feet by 77 feet.

District: Five stakes and a district in Quebec , Ontario and Vermont.

Groundbreaking, site dedication: April 9, 1999, by Elder Gary J. Coleman of the Seventy.

Dedication: June 4, 2000, by President Gordon B. Hinckley; 4 sessions.

Dedicatory prayer excerpt: *On this historic day we sing Thy praises, dear Father. We speak words of thanksgiving.... May all who enter the portals of Thy house be worthy to come as Thy guests and enjoy Thy rich and bounteous blessings. This is a house of salvation and exaltation for the living and the dead, made possible through the Atonement of the Savior of the world. Every ordinance performed herein, every blessing granted will be eternal in its consequences.*

Mount Timpanogos

Announced: Oct. 3, 1992.

Location: 742 North 900 East, American Fork, UT 84003-9124; phone: (801) 763-4540.

Site: 16.7 acres, part of a larger parcel of land that was once a welfare farm.

Exterior finish: Sierra white granite, art glass windows and bronze doors.

Temple design: Traditional, with a single spire.

Architects: Allen Erekson, architect of record; Keith Stepan, project architect; and Church architectural staff.

Contractor: Okland Construction Co.

Project manager: Jerry Sears.

Operation adviser: Michael Enfield.

Rooms: Celestial room, baptistry, four ordinance rooms, eight sealing rooms.

Total floor area: 104,000 square feet.

Dimensions: 145 feet by 198 feet; 190 foot spire, including statue of Angel Moroni.

District: 49 stakes in northern Utah County and Wasatch County.

Groundbreaking, site dedication: Oct. 9, 1993, by President Gordon B. Hinckley.

Dedication: Oct. 13-19 1996, by President Gordon B. Hinckley; 27 sessions.

Dedicatory prayer excerpt: *May it be a beacon of peace and a refuge to the troubled. May it be an holy sanctuary to those whose burdens are heavy and who seek Thy consoling comfort.*

Nashville Tennessee

Announced: Originally announced Nov. 9, 1994. Revised plans announced April 25, 1998.

Location: Franklin, about 15 miles south of Nashville, at 1100 Gray Fox Lane near Mack Hatcher Parkway; Franklin TN 37069-6501; phone: (615) 791-8668.

Site: 6.86 acres, including adjoining meetinghouse.

Exterior finish: White Imperial Danby marble.

Temple design: Classic modern.

Architect: Robert Waldrip of Joyce Prout & Associates and Church A&E Services.

Project manager: Leon Rowley.

Contractor: Layton Construction Co., construction management company; MPact Construction Group, general contractor.

Rooms: Celestial room, baptistry, two ordinance rooms, two sealing rooms.

Total floor area: 10,700 square feet.

Dimensions: 149 feet by 77 feet.

District: Seven stakes in Kentucky and Tennessee.

Groundbreaking, site dedication: March 13, 1999, by Elder John K. Carmack of the Seventy and president of the North America East Area.

Dedication: May 21, 2000, by President James E. Faust, second counselor in the First Presidency; 4 sessions.

Dedicatory prayer excerpt: *Bless all who come into the Church that they may look forward with eagerness to the day when they may enter this Thy holy house and receive the higher ordinances of the gospel.*

Nauvoo

Original no longer stands; burned by arson fire in 1848. Rebuilt 2002; see Nauvoo Illinois Temple.

Announced: Aug. 1, 1840.

Location: In Nauvoo, Ill., on a high bluff on the east side of the Mississippi River. Temple block bounded by Woodruff, Mulholland, Knight and Wells streets.

Site: Selected in October 1840 by Joseph Smith on property known as the Wells addition, slightly less than four acres.

Exterior finish: Light gray limestone quarried to the north and south of the city.

Temple design: Incorporated several types of architecture, no single style dominating.

Architect: William Weeks.

Temple building committee: Alpheus Cutler, Elias Higbee and Reynolds Cahoon. After the death of Elias Higbee in 1843, Hyrum Smith replaced him until his own death.

Rooms: Approximately 60.

Total floor area: Approximately 50,000 square feet.

Dimensions: Approximately 128 feet by 88 feet; 65 feet high, with the tower and spire reaching to 165 feet.

Groundbreaking: Feb. 18, 1841.

Cornerstones: April 6, 1841, President Joseph Smith presiding.

Dedication: Portions of the temple were dedicated and used as soon as completed. To avoid possible violence, a private dedication was held April 30, 1846, with Orson Hyde and Joseph Young officiating. The temple was dedicated publicly May 1-3, 1846; dedicatory prayer was given by Orson Hyde.

Dedicatory prayer excerpt: *We thank Thee that Thou hast given us strength to accomplish the charges delivered by Thee. Thou hast seen our labors and exertions to accomplish this purpose. By the authority of the Holy Priesthood now we offer this building as a sanctuary to Thy worthy name.*

Nauvoo Illinois

Announced: April 4, 1999.

Location: 50 North Wells, Nauvoo, Ill. 62354-0310; (217) 453-6252.

Site: About 4 acres.

Exterior finish: Limestone quarried in Alabama, a near duplicate of the original stone.

Temple design: Several styles.

Architect: FFKR Architecture of Salt Lake City, Utah.

Project director: Stephen Jacobsen.

Project manager: Gale Mair.

Project superintendent: Richard Holbrook.

Contractor: Legacy Constructors of Salt Lake City, Utah.

Rooms: Assembly room, baptistry, chapel, five progressive instruction rooms and celestial room, and six sealing rooms.

Total floor area: 47,000 square feet.

Dimensions: 128 feet by 88 feet; 150 feet high.

District: Five stakes in western Illinois and eastern Iowa.

Groundbreaking, site dedication: Oct. 24, 1999, by President Gordon B. Hinckley; cornerstone laying Nov. 5, 2000.

Dedication: June 27-30, 2002, by President Gordon B. Hinckley in 13 sessions transmitted by satellite to members around the world, including Europe East and Asia areas.

Dedicatory prayer excerpts: *On this same site in the year 1841, Thy people, under the direction of the Prophet Joseph Smith, and in obedience to revelation from Thee, began construction of a temple to the Most High.*

May this sacred house stand as a memorial to him who lived here and was buried here, Joseph Smith, the great prophet of this dispensation, and his brother Hyrum, whom he loved.

Newport Beach California

Announced: April 20, 2001.

Location: 2300 Bonita Canyon Drive, Newport Beach, Calif. (949) 729-9148.

Site: 8.8 acres.

Exterior finish: Salisbury pink granite.

Temple design: Southern California traditional.

Architects: Lloyd Platt & Associates, Lloyd Platt architect of record, Allen Erekson, project architect.

Project manager: Vern Hancock.

Contractor: Jacobsen Construction.

Rooms: Celestial room, baptistry, two ordinance rooms, three sealing rooms.

Total floor area: 17,800 square feet.

Dimensions: 200-feet by 98-feet.

District: Nearly 50,000 members from 16 stakes in Orange County, Calif.

Groundbreaking, site dedication: Aug. 15, 2003, by Elder Duane B. Gerrard.

Dedication: Aug. 28, 2005, by President Gordon B. Hinckley; four sessions.

Dedicatory prayer excerpt: *We thank Thee that Thy Church has come out of obscurity and darkness and now shines forth before the world.... May it continue to roll forth in majesty and power to fill the whole earth.*

Nuku'Alofa Tonga

Announced: April 2, 1980.

Location: At site of Church's Liahona College; Loto Rd., Tongatapu, Nuku'alofa, Tonga.

Site: 1.2 acres.

Exterior finish: "R-wall" exterior finish and insulation system on concrete block.

Temple design: Modern.

Architect: Emil B. Fetzer, Church architect. Renovation Architect; Naylor Whenton Lund Architects.

Construction adviser: Richard Westover and Richard Rowley. Renovation adviser: Alan Rudolf.

Contractor: Utah Construction & Development. Renovation contractor: Cabella Construction, John Cabella.

Rooms: Baptistry, celestial room, three sealing rooms, two ordinance rooms.

Floor area: 14,572 square feet. Renovated floor area: 21,184 square feet.

Dimensions: 142 feet by 115 feet. Renovated dimensions: 200 feet by 115 feet.

District: 16 stakes, two districts in Tongan islands.

Groundbreaking, site dedication: Feb. 18, 1981, by President Spencer W. Kimball with Tonga's King Taufa'ahau Tupou IV.

Original dedication: Aug. 9-11, 1983, by President Gordon B. Hinckley; seven sessions. Rededicated Nov. 4, 2007, by Elder Russell M. Nelson, two sessions.

Dedicatory prayer excerpt: *We ask that Thou wilt accept this temple as the gift of Thy people presented unto Thee with love for the accomplishments of Thy holy purposes with reference to Thy children. It is Thy house. It is the house of Thy Son.*

Oakland California

Location: On hill overlooking San Francisco Bay, near intersection of Lincoln Avenue and Monterey Blvd.; 4770 Lincoln Ave., Oakland, CA 94602-2535; phone: (510) 531-3200.

Site: Inspected and approved by President David O. McKay in 1942; 14.5 acres purchased Jan. 28, 1943; additional land acquired later to make 18.3 acres.

Exterior finish: Reinforced concrete faced with Sierra white granite from Raymond, Calif.

Temple design: Modern, with an Oriental motif.

Architect: Harold W. Burton. Resident architect supervisor, Arthur Price.

Construction chairman: W. B. Mendenhall.

Construction supervisor: Robert C. Loder.

Contractors: Leon M. Wheatley Co., Palo Alto, Calif., and Jacobsen Construction Co., Salt Lake City.

Rooms: Baptistry, celestial room, four ordinance rooms, 7 sealing rooms.

Total floor area: 95,000 square feet.

Dimensions: Temple proper, 210 feet by 302 feet with a central tower rising 170 feet.

District: 31 stakes in northern California.

Groundbreaking, site dedication: May 26, 1962, by President David O. McKay.

Dedication: Nov. 17-19, 1964, by President David O. McKay, 6 sessions.

Dedicatory prayer excerpt: *This temple is a monument testifying to the faith and loyalty of the members of thy Church in the payment of their tithes and offerings. We thank Thee for every effort that has been put forth by the members.*

Oaxaca Mexico

Announced: Feb. 23, 1999.

Location: Avenida Universidad and Esq. Hacienda de Candiani; Fraccionamiento Real de Candiani, Oaxaca, Oaxaca 68130, Mexico; phone: (52) 951-516-9588; no clothing rental.

Site: 1.87 acres, including adjoining meetinghouse.

Exterior finish: White marble.

Temple design: Classic modern.

Architects: Alvaro Iñigo and Church A&E Services.

Project manager: Jay Erekson.

Contractor: Impulsa/Okland Construction Co.

Rooms: Celestial room, baptistry, two ordinance rooms, two sealing rooms.

Total floor area: 10,700 square feet.

Dimensions: 77 feet by 149 feet.

District: 10 stakes, one district, four branches in southern Mexico.

Groundbreaking, site dedication: March 13, 1999, by Elder Carl B. Pratt of the Seventy and president of the Mexico South Area.

Dedication: March 11, 2000, by President James E. Faust, second counselor in the First Presidency; 4 sessions.

Dedicatory prayer excerpt: *We pray for this nation of Mexico that its people may be blessed of Thee, that the poverty of the past may be lifted from their shoulders, that freedom and peace and prosperity might be enjoyed.*

Artist rendering

Oquirrh Mountain Utah

Announced: On Oct. 1, 2005, President Gordon B. Hinckley announced plans for a fourth temple in the southwest area of the Salt Lake Valley. The site was later announced at 11022 S. 4000 West in South Jordan, Utah. Originally, named the South Jordan Utah Temple, it was changed on Dec. 16, 2006, to avoid confusion with the Jordan River Utah Temple, also in South Jordan.

Groundbreaking, site dedication: Dec. 16, 2006, by President Gordon B. Hinckley.

Status: Under construction.

Ogden Utah

Announced: Aug. 24, 1967.

Location: In downtown Ogden, between Grant Avenue and Washington Boulevard; 350 22nd Street, Ogden, UT 84401-1487; phone: (801) 621-6880.

Site: 10 acres.

Exterior finish: White cast stone with a fluted appearance, gold anodized aluminum grillwork, gold directional glass windows.

Temple design: Modern and functional.

Architect: Emil B. Fetzer, Church architect.

Construction chairman: Mark B. Garff, with Fred A. Baker, vice chairman.

Contractor: Okland Construction Co.

Rooms: Baptistry, celestial room, six ordinance rooms, 11 sealing rooms, four floors.

Total floor area: 131,000 square feet.

Dimensions: 200 feet by 184 feet; tower 180 feet above ground level; single tower of 180 feet.

District: 71 Stakes in northeastern Utah, southwestern Wyoming.

Groundbreaking, site dedication: Sept. 8, 1969, President N. Eldon Tanner conducted; prayers given by President Alvin R. Dyer and President Joseph Fielding Smith; ground broken by President Hugh B. Brown.

Dedication: Jan. 18-20, 1972, by President Joseph Fielding Smith; 6 sessions.

Dedicatory prayer excerpt: *It has been our privilege, as guided by the whisperings of Thy Spirit, to build unto Thee this temple, which we now present unto Thee as another of Thy holy houses.*

Oklahoma City Oklahoma

Announced: March 14, 1999.

Location: 12030 North Mustang Road, Yukon, OK 73099-9801; phone: (405) 373-2309; no clothing rental.

Site: 1.05 acres.

Exterior finish: Imperial Danby White Marble.

Temple design: Classic modern.

Architects: Richard Lueb of the Architectural Partnership and Church A&E Services.

Project manager: Leon Rowley.

Contractor: Arnell-West Inc.

Rooms: Celestial room, baptistry, two ordinance rooms, two sealing rooms.

Total floor area: 10,769 square feet.

Dimensions: 149 feet by 77 feet.

District: 12 stakes Oklahoma, Kansas, Arkansas and Missouri.

Groundbreaking, site dedication: July 3, 1999, by Elder Rex D. Pinegar of the Seventy and president of the North America Southwest Area.

Dedication: July 30, 2000, by President James E. Faust, second counselor in the First Presidency; 4 sessions.

Dedicatory prayer excerpt: *We pray for Thy cause and kingdom, that it may grow ever stronger in this community. May all who have favored Thy cause be blessed for that which they have done. May many continue to seek for knowledge concerning Thy work until they have embraced Thy restored gospel.*

Orlando Florida

Announced: Feb. 17, 1990.

Location: On a knoll overlooking Butler chain of lakes at Apopka-Vineland Road on the edge of Orlando suburb of Windermere, five miles southwest of Orlando near Florida Turnpike and Interstate 4; 9000 Windy Ridge Road, Windermere, FL 34786-8347; phone: (407) 876-0022.

Site: 13 acres.

Exterior finish: White precast concrete with marble chips.

Temple design: Classic modern with one spire.

Architects: Scott Partnership Architects.

Church project manager: Ralph Cluff.

Contractor: Brice Building Company.

Rooms: Baptistry, celestial room, four ordinance rooms, five sealing rooms.

Total floor area: 69,000 square feet.

Dimensions: 216 feet by 252 feet; tower with statue of Angel Moroni is 165 feet high.

District: 23 stakes, 3 districts in Florida, Georgia, Jamaica, Puerto Rico.

Groundbreaking, site dedication: June 20, 1992, by Elder James E. Faust of the Quorum of the Twelve.

Dedication: Oct. 9-11, 1994, by President Howard W. Hunter; 12 sessions.

Dedicatory prayer excerpt: *To all who look upon it, including those who reside in this area, may it ever present a picture of peace and beauty, a structure partaking of Thy divine nature.*

Palmyra New York

Announced: Feb. 9, 1999, the 100th temple to be announced.

Location: 2720 Temple Road, Palmyra, NY 14522; phone: (315) 597-6001; no clothing rental.

Site: 5 acres; 48.7 combined with meeting-house.

Exterior finish: Bethel White granite.

Temple design: Classic modern.

Architects: Dave A. Richards and Church A&E Services.

Project manager: William Treu.

Contractor: Okland Construction Co.

Rooms: Celestial room, baptistry, two ordinance rooms, two sealing rooms.

Total floor area: 10,700 square feet.

Dimensions: 149 feet by 77 feet.

District: Seven stakes and one district in upper New York.

Groundbreaking, site dedication: May 25, 1999, by President Gordon B. Hinckley.

Dedication: April 6, 2000, by President Gordon B. Hinckley, exactly 170 years after the organization of the Church by Joseph Smith in nearby Fayette, N. Y.; 4 sessions. First session transmitted by satellite to members around the world.

Dedicatory prayer excerpts: *It was here, on this land which the Smiths once farmed, it was here in the Grove below and to the west that Thou, the Almighty God of the universe, and Thy Beloved Son, the resurrected Lord, appeared to the boy Joseph Smith. This wondrous event parted the curtain that had been closed for centuries.*

Panama City Panama

Announced: Aug. 23, 2002

Location: Cardenas, Corozal, Corregimiento de Ancon, entering through the Ministerio De Education, Panama City, Panama

Site: 6.96 acres

Exterior finish: China stone and art-glass windows

Temple design: Classical

Architect: Mallol & Mallol of Panama City and Naylor Wentworth Lund of Salt Lake City

Construction adviser: Duane Cheney

Contractor: Diaz and Guardia Panama

Rooms: Celestial room, baptistry, two ordinance rooms, two sealing rooms

Total floor area: 18,943 square feet

Dimensions: 90-feet by 103-feet, height of spire 111 feet

District: Eight stakes and six districts in Panama

Groundbreaking, site dedication: Oct. 20, 2005, by Elder Spencer V. Jones of the Seventy.

Dedication: August 10, 2008, by President Thomas S. Monson; 4 sessions.

Dedicatory prayer excerpts: *We are grateful for the completion of this, Thy Holy House. We ask that Thou wilt bless those faithful members here and throughout the world who have contributed their tithes, making possible this magnificent edifice for the blessing of all who enter herein.*

Papeete Tahiti

Announced: April 2, 1980.

Location: Route de Fautaua; Pateete, Tahiti; French Polynesia; phone: (689) 503-939.

Site: 1.7; 5 acres with meetinghouse.

Exterior finish: Stucco, using imported white sand.

Temple design: Shows some European elements of French influence as well as Polynesian culture.

Architect: Emil B. Fetzer, Church architect; upgrade, Naylor Wentworth Lund Architects.

Construction adviser: George Bonnet; upgrade, Alan Rudolph.

Contractor: Comtrol Inc., a Midvale, Utah, construction firm.

Rooms: Baptistry, celestial room, two ordinance rooms, two sealing rooms; upgrade, enlarged baptistry, additional sealing room.

Total floor area: 9,936 square feet; after remodeling, 12,150 square feet.

Dimensions: 125 feet by 105 feet, with an eight-foot statue of Angel Moroni on a 66-foot spire.

District: Six stakes and three districts in French Polynesia and the Cook Islands.

Groundbreaking, site dedication: Feb. 13, 1981, by President Spencer W. Kimball.

Dedication: Oct. 27-29, 1983, by President Gordon B. Hinckley; 6 sessions. Rededicated Nov. 12, 2006, by Elder L. Tom Perry of the Quorum of the Twelve.

Dedicatory prayer excerpt: *We ask that Thou wilt preserve [the temple] as Thy house. May it be protected by Thy power from any who would defile it. May it stand against the winds and the rains.*

Perth Australia

Announced: June 11, 1999.

Location: 163-173 Wordsworth Ave., Yokine, W.A. 6080, Australia; phone: (61) 89 276-0000; no clothing rental.

Site: 2.76 with meetinghouse.

Exterior finish: Olympic White Granite.

Temple design: Classic modern

Architect: Christou Cassella & JEC.

Contractor: Doric Building PTY LTD.

Rooms: Celestial room, two ordinances rooms, two sealing rooms, baptistry.

Total floor area: 10,700 square feet.

Dimensions: 149 feet by 77 feet.

District: Four Perth stakes.

Groundbreaking, site dedication: Nov. 20, 1999, by Elder Kenneth Johnson of the Seventy and first counselor in the Australia/New Zealand Area Presidency.

Dedication: May 20, 2001, by President Gordon B. Hinckley; 4 sessions.

Dedicatory prayer excerpt: *Thou hast made us partakers of Thy divine love that we may reap wondrous blessings in our own behalf and also in behalf of those who have gone before us.*

Thou hast commanded us to build sacred temples wherein these holy ordinances may be administered. In obedience to that command, we present to Thee this day another house of the Lord and dedicate it to Thy holy purposes.

No artist rendering available

Philadelphia Pennsylvania

Announced: Oct. 4, 2008.

Status: In planning stages.

The Philadelphia temple will be built in downtown Philadelphia, at North Broad Street between Hamilton Street and Noble Street. Several other temples occupy urban sites, including those in Manhattan and Hong Kong.

No artist rendering available

Phoenix Arizona

Announced: May 24, 2008.

Status: In planning stages.

Portland Oregon

Announced: April 7, 1984.

Location: In a wooded suburb about 10 miles southwest of downtown Portland, in the northwest corner of Oswego, adjacent to Interstate 5, 13600 SW Kruse Oaks Blvd.; Lake Oswego, OR 97035-8602; phone: (503) 639-7066.

Site: The land was purchased by the Church in mid-1960s for a junior college, but 7.3 acres was later chosen as a temple site.

Exterior finish: White marble walls and slate roof.

Temple design: Six spires.

Architects: Leland A. Gray, architect; Lee/Ruff/Waddle, site and local architects.

Construction adviser: Michael Enfield.

Contractor: Zwick Construction Co.

Rooms: Baptistry, celestial room, four ordinance, fourteen sealing rooms.

Total floor area: 80,500 square feet.

Dimensions: 267 feet by 180 feet, four towers 124 feet tall; statue of Angel Moroni on east spire, 181 feet tall.

District: 30 stakes in Oregon and parts of Washington.

Groundbreaking, site dedication: Sept. 20, 1986, by President Gordon B. Hinckley.

Dedication: Aug. 19-21, 1989, by President Gordon B. Hinckley; 11 sessions.

Dedicatory prayer excerpt: *May a spirit of solemnity rest upon all who enter herein. Open to their vision a glimpse of Thy great and everlasting designs.*

Porto Alegre Brazil

Announced: Oct 4, 1997.

Location: Northern zone of Porto Alegre, Chacara das Pedras, Rua General Salvador Pinheiro, 50-Vila Jardim, Porto Alegre RS CEP 91320-240, Brazil; phone: (55) 51-3338-0400; no clothing rental.

Site: 2 acres.

Exterior finish: Cotton white granite from Ceara State of Brazil.

Temple design: Classic modern.

Architects: Andre Belo de Faria and Church A&E Services.

Project manager: Raul Lins.

Contractor: Ernesto Woebcke.

Rooms: Two ordinance rooms, two sealing rooms, celestial room, baptistry.

Total floor area: 10,700 square feet.

Dimensions: 149 feet by 77 feet.

District: 27 stakes and four districts in southern Brazil.

Groundbreaking, site dedication: May 2, 1998, by President James E. Faust, second counselor in the First Presidency.

Dedication: Dec. 17, 2000 by President Gordon B. Hinckley; 4 sessions.

Dedicatory prayer excerpt: *We invoke Thy blessings on this great nation of Brazil that it may always be hospitable toward the missionaries who are assigned here. May the people reach out with friendly hands and have ears to listen, that Thy work may continue to grow in this part of the earth.*

Preston England

Announced: Oct. 19,1992.

Location: A6/M61 Link road, Hartwood Green; Chorley, Lancashire PR6 7EQ United Kingdom; Phone (44) 1257-226100.

Site: 15 acres (6 hectares).

Exterior finish: Olympia white granite from Sardinia.

Temple design: Modern.

Architects: Church physical facilities staff.

Project manager: Hanno Luschin.

Contractor: John Laing Construction, Ltd.

Rooms: Baptistry, celestial room, four ordinance rooms; four sealing rooms.

Total floor area: 60,000 square feet (6482.53 square meters).

Dimensions: 102 feet by 174 feet (31 meters by 53 meters); 155 foot high spire (47 meters), including statue of Angel Moroni 159 feet high.

District: 23 stakes, one district in Northern England, Scotland, Ireland, and Northern Ireland.

Groundbreaking, site dedication: June 12, 1994, by President Gordon B. Hinckley.

Dedication: June 7-10, 1998, by President Gordon B. Hinckley; 15 sessions.

Dedicatory prayer excerpt: *This magnificent temple has been reared in this beautiful area where Thy chosen servants, in the days of their deep poverty and great sacrifice, first preached the restored gospel. Through 161 years of history this land of England, together with Scotland, Wales, and Ireland, has yielded a harvest of converts who have blessed and strengthened Thy Church.*

No artist rendering available

Provo Utah

Quetzaltenango Guatemala

Announced: Aug. 14, 1967.

Location: At the entrance of Rock Canyon on the east bench of Provo; 2200 Temple Hill Drive, Provo, UT 84604; phone; (801) 375-5775.

Site: 17 acres.

Exterior finish: White cast stone, gold anodized aluminum grills, bronze glass panels, and single spire finished in gold and anodized aluminum; similar to Ogden Temple.

Temple design: Modern and functional.

Architect: Emil B. Fetzer, Church architect.

Construction chairman: Mark B. Garff, with Fred A. Baker, vice chairman.

Construction supervisor: Hogan and Tingey, general contractors.

Rooms: Baptistry, celestial room, six ordinance rooms, 12 sealing rooms.

Total floor area: 130,825 square feet.

Dimensions: 200 feet by 184 feet; 175 feet high with a 118-foot spire on top of the building.

District: 64 stakes in Central, eastern Utah.

Groundbreaking, site dedication: Sept. 15, 1969, ground broken by President Hugh B. Brown.

Dedication: Feb. 9, 1972; dedicatory prayer written by President Joseph Fielding Smith and read by President Harold B. Lee; 2 sessions.

Dedicatory prayer excerpt: *We dedicate this temple to Thee, the Lord. We dedicate it as a house of baptism, a house of endowment, a house of marriage, a house of righteousness for the living and the dead.*

Announced: Dec. 16, 2006.

Status: In planning stages.

Raleigh North Carolina

Announced: Sept. 3, 1998.

Location: Off State Highway 55 about 10 miles SW of Raleigh; 574 Bryan Dr., Apex, NC 27502; phone: (919) 362-4135; no clothing rental.

Site: 3.4 acres.

Exterior finish: Danby white marble with art glass windows.

Temple design: Traditional.

Architects: Dan Dills of Dills and Ainscuff.

Project manager: Bruce Catanzaro.

Contractor: Walbridge Aldinger.

Rooms: Celestial room, baptistry, two ordinance rooms, two sealing rooms.

Total floor area: 10,700 square feet

Dimensions: 149 feet by 77 feet.

District: Eight stakes in North Carolina.

Groundbreaking, site dedication: Feb. 6, 1999, by Elder Loren C. Dunn of the Seventy, first counselor in the North America East Area.

Dedication: Dec. 18, 1999, by President Gordon B. Hinckley; 7 sessions.

Dedicatory prayer excerpt: *May all who come as patrons to this temple know that they are dealing with the things of eternity, and that the relationships here entered into are everlasting.*

Recife Brazil

Announced: Jan. 13, 1995.

Location: Rua Dr. Jose de Goes 284; Parnamirim 52.060- 380 Recife - PE, Brazil; phone: (55) 81-3267 4300.

Site: 5.59 acres.

Exterior finish: Asa Branca granite from state of Ceara.

Temple design: Classic modern.

Architects: J&P Arquitetos Ltd. and Church A&E Services.

Project manager: Raul Lins.

Contractor: Hochtief do Brasil SA.

Rooms: Celestial room, baptistry, two ordinance rooms and three sealing rooms.

Total floor area: 37,200 square feet.

Dimensions: 114 feet by 158 feet.

District: 39 stakes and five districts in northern Brazil.

Groundbreaking, site dedication: Nov. 15, 1996, by President Gordon B. Hinckley.

Dedication: Dec. 15, 2000, by President Gordon B. Hinckley, 4 sessions.

Dedicatory prayer excerpts: *We are met to dedicate this beautiful temple which has been erected in honor to Thee and Thy Beloved Son, our Redeemer. Our hearts are full on this occasion for which we have longed and prayed.*

We are grateful to have in our midst a House of the Lord to which we may come frequently and with convenience. We thank Thee, Father, for this wonderful blessing.

Redlands California

Announced: April 20, 2001.

Location: Corner of Wabash and Fifth Ave., (1761 Fifth Ave.) Redlands, CA.

Site: 4.55 acres.

Exterior finish: Light gray granite.

Temple design: Southern California traditional.

Architects: Lloyd Platt & Associates, with associate firm of Higginson & Cartozian.

Project manager: Jerry Sears.

Contractor: Layton Construction Co.

Rooms: Celestial room, baptistry, two ordinance rooms, three sealing rooms.

Total floor area: 17,279 square feet.

Dimensions: 200 feet by 98 feet.

District: 21 stakes in San Bernardino and Riverside counties.

Groundbreaking, site dedication: Dec. 1, 2001 by Elder Dieter F. Uchtdorf.

Dedication: Sept. 14, 2003, by President Gordon B. Hinckley; 4 sessions

Dedicatory prayer excerpt: *Father, our people are not strangers to this area. Not long after settling the Salt Lake Valley, some of them came to this region to establish an outpost of Thy Church. Thy work has more recently been firmly planted here. Wilt Thou cause it to grow and flourish and touch many hearts that they may turn to Thee and learn of Thy ways and do Thy will and bidding.*

Regina Saskatchewan

Announced: Aug. 3, 1998.

Location: 111 Wascana Gate North; Regina, Saskatchewan S4V 2J6, Canada; phone: (306) 545-8194; no clothing rental.

Site: 1 acre.

Exterior finish: Light gray granite.

Temple design: Classic modern.

Architect: Roger B. Mitchell of Banadyga Mitchell Partnership and Church A&E Services.

Project manager: Cory Karl.

Contractor: Graham Construction and Engineering, Ltd.

Rooms: Celestial room, baptistry, two ordinance rooms, two sealing rooms.

Total floor area: 10,700 square feet.

Dimensions: 149 feet by 77 feet.

District: Two stakes and one district in Saskatchewan and Manitoba.

Groundbreaking, site dedication: Nov. 14, 1998, by Elder Hugh W. Pinnock of the Seventy and president of the North America Central Area.

Dedication: Nov. 14, 1999, by President Boyd K. Packer, acting president of the Quorum of the Twelve; 3 sessions.

Dedicatory prayer excerpt: *May all who come within these walls be clean of hands and pure of mind as they engage in Thy sacred work. Bless them with joy in this service.*

Reno Nevada

Announced: April 12, 1999.

Location: 2000 Beaumont Parkway, Reno, NV 89503; phone: (775) 747-6688; no clothing rental.

Site: 1.2 acres.

Exterior finish: Granite.

Temple design: Traditional.

Architects: Church A&E Services.

Project manager: Amos and Gloria Wright

Contractor: Jacobsen Construction Co.

Rooms: Celestial room, baptistry, two ordinance rooms, two sealing rooms.

Total floor area: 10,700 square feet.

Dimensions: 149 feet by 77 feet.

District: Eight stakes in western Nevada and eastern California.

Groundbreaking, site dedication: July 24, 1999, by Elder Rex D. Pinegar of the Seventy and president of the North America Southwest Area.

Dedication: April 23, 2000, by President Thomas S. Monson, first counselor in the First Presidency; four sessions.

Dedicatory prayer excerpt: *Bless all who enter the portals of this structure that they may be worthy to come here as Thy Saints. May they do so with reverence and with a desire to promote Thy work in behalf of Thy children of all generations.*

Rexburg Idaho

Announced: Dec. 12, 2003

Location: 750 South 2nd East, Rexburg, Idaho

Site: 10 acres

Exterior finish: Precast concrete with a quartz rock finish, 700 art-glass windowpanes

Temple design: Classic modern.

Architects: Architectural Nexus; Bob Petroff

Project manager: Vern Martindale.

Contractor: Jacobsen Construction Co.

Rooms: Baptistry, celestial room, four ordinance rooms, five sealing rooms.

Total floor area: 57,504 square feet

Dimensions: 85-feet wide by 190-feet long by 169 feet high.

District: Stakes in eastern Idaho, including BYU-Idaho stakes.

Groundbreaking: July 30, 2005, by Elder John H. Groberg, of the Presidency of the Seventy.

Dedication: Feb. 10, 2008, by President Thomas S. Monson; four sessions.

Dedicatory prayer excerpt: *May Thy faithful saints of this and future generations look to this temple as a sanctuary and a place of service to Thee and to Thy children.*

No artist rendering available

Rome Italy

Announced: Oct. 4, 2008.

Status: In planning stages.

In Rome, the temple will occupy part of a 15-acre Church-owned site near the ring road skirting the northeast section of Rome.

Sacramento California

Announced: April 20, 2001.

Location: 2110 California Circle, Rancho Cordova, CA 95742-6402. (916) 357-5870.

Exterior finish: Temple white granite from Fuzhou, China.

Temple design: Classic elegance

Site: 47 acres.

Architects: Brian Everett and Maury Maher of Nichols, Melburg & Rossetto of Fair Oaks, Calif.

Project manager: Vern Hancock.

Contractor: Okland Construction of Salt Lake City, Utah.

Rooms: Celestial room, baptistry, two ordinance rooms, four sealing rooms.

Total floor area: 19,500 square feet.

Dimensions: 220-feet by 120-feet by 131-feet.

District: 21 stakes in northern California.

Groundbreaking, site dedication: Aug. 22, 2004, by President Gordon B. Hinckley.

Dedication: Sept. 3, 2006, by President Gordon B. Hinckley; four sessions.

Dedicatory prayer excerpt: *We pray for this nation of which we are citizens, that the liberties and freedoms of the people may be preserved, that righteousness may reign, and peace may prevail. Take from our hearts all bitterness and hatred, and end the conflicts which rage in many quarters.*

St. George Utah

Announced: May 1861.

Location: near the center of St. George; 250 E. 400 South, St. George, UT 84770-3699; phone: (435) 673-3533.

Site: 6 acres, selected by Brigham Young in 1871.

Exterior finish: Native red sandstone quarried north of the city; then plastered white.

Temple design: Castellated Gothic style.

Architect: Truman O. Angell.

Construction superintendent: Miles P. Romney; Edward L. Parry, head stone mason.

Rooms: Baptistry, celestial room, three ordinance rooms; eight sealing rooms, 64 rooms in original structure.

Total floor area: 56,062 square feet in original building; 108,536 square feet after remodeling completed in 1975.

Dimensions: 142 feet by 96 feet; to top of buttresses, 80 feet; after remodeling 249 feet by 282 feet.

District: Stakes in southwestern Utah, small part of Nevada and Arizona.

Groundbreaking, site dedication: Nov. 9, 1871, by President Brigham Young; site dedication prayer by George A. Smith.

Dedication: Jan. 1, 1877, completed portions were dedicated. Final dedication, April 6-8, 1877, President Brigham Young presiding, and Daniel H. Wells offered prayer.

On Nov. 11-12, 1975, after extensive remodeling, the temple was rededicated by President Spencer W. Kimball; 5 sessions.

Dedicatory prayer excerpt: *We implore Thy blessings upon the various congregations of Thy people who may assemble in this house from time to time.'*

St. Louis Missouri

Announced: Dec. 18, 1990.

Location: 12555 North Outer Forty Drive, Town and Country, MO 63141-8620; phone: (314) 514-1122.

Exterior finish: Cast stone and Bethal white granite with thermal finish.

Temple design: Modern.

Site: 13 acres.

Architects: Chiodini Associates.

Project manager: Gary Holland.

Contractor: BSI Constructors Inc.

Rooms: Baptistry, celestial room, four ordinance rooms, four sealing rooms.

Total floor area: 60,085 square feet.

Dimensions: 88 feet by 190 feet; angel statue, 150 feet high.

District: 17 Stakes in Missouri, Illinois, Iowa, Kansas.

Groundbreaking, site dedication: Oct. 30, 1993, by President Gordon B. Hinckley.

Dedication: June 1-5, 1997, by President Gordon B. Hinckley; 19 sessions.

Dedicatory prayer excerpt: *Today Thy Church basks in the sunlight of good will. Hundreds of thousands of visitors have come to view this Thy holy house. They have left with respect and appreciation.*

St. Paul Minnesota

Announced: July 29, 1998.

Location: 2150 N. Hadley Ave., Oakdale, MN 55128; phone: (651) 748-5910; no clothing rental.

Site: 7.5 acres, including adjoining meetinghouse.

Exterior finish: Light gray granite veneer.

Temple design: Classic modern.

Architect: Ed Kodet, Jr. of Kodet Architect Group Ltd., and Church A&E Services.

Project manager: Cory Karl.

Contractor: Walbridge Aldinger.

Rooms: Celestial room, baptistry, two ordinance rooms, two sealing rooms.

Total floor area: 10,700 square feet.

Dimensions: 149 feet by 77 feet.

District: Nine stakes in Minnesota, parts of Wisconson and Manitoba.

Groundbreaking, site dedication: Sept. 26, 1998, by Elder Hugh W. Pinnock of the Seventy and president of the North America Central Area.

Dedication: Jan. 9, 2000, by President Gordon B. Hinckley; 4 sessions.

Dedicatory prayer excerpt: *And that all people who should enter upon the threshold of the Lord's house may feel Thy power, and feel constrained to acknowledge that Thou hast sanctified it, and that it is Thy house.*

Salt Lake

Announced: July 28, 1847.

Location: On Temple Square in the center of Salt Lake City; 50 W. North Temple St., Salt Lake City, UT 84150; phone: (801) 240-2640.

Site: 10 acres. Selected by Brigham Young.

Exterior finish: Granite from Little Cottonwood Canyon, 20 miles southeast.

Temple design: Suggestive of Gothic and other classical styles.

Architect: Truman O. Angell, Church architect, worked out plans under direction of Brigham Young. During Angell's illness, William Folsom temporarily filled his post. After Angell's death in 1887, Don Carlos Young completed work on the temple.

Construction supervisor: Daniel H. Wells supervised construction.

Rooms: Baptistry, celestial room, four progressive instruction rooms, eight sealing rooms.

Total floor area: 253,015 square feet in the temple, including the annex.

Dimensions: 117 feet by 184 feet. At east end of the building, the height of the center pinnacle is 210 feet. The center of the three towers on the west end is 204 feet high.

District: Stakes in Salt Lake, Tooele and eastern Nevada.

Groundbreaking, site dedication: Feb. 14, 1853, President Brigham Young broke ground and Heber C. Kimball dedicated the site.

Dedication: April 6-24, 1893, by President Wilford Woodruff; 31 sessions.

Dedicatory prayer excerpt: *When Thy people... are oppressed and in trouble ... we beseech Thee to look down from Thy holy habitation in mercy and tender compassion.*

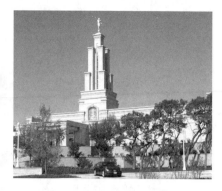

San Antonio Texas

Announced: June 24, 2001; site announced Aug. 19, 2002.

Location: 20080 Stone Oak Parkway at Hardy Oak Boulevard, San Antonio, Texas 78258.

Site: About 5.5 acres

Exterior finish: Granite.

Temple design: Traditional.

Architects: Rehler, Vaughn & Koone

Project manager: Vern Martindale.

Contractor: Jacobsen Construction.

Rooms: Celestial room, two endowment rooms, two sealing rooms and baptistry.

Total floor area: Approximately 16,800 square feet.

Dimensions: 97-feet by 191-feet; height to top of statue is 115 feet.

District: Southwest Texas.

Groundbreaking, site dedication: March 29, 2003, by Elder J. Bruce Stucki of the Seventy.

Dedication: May 22, 2005, by President Gordon B. Hinckley; four sessions.

Dedicatory prayer excerpt: *We invoke Thy blessings upon the citizens of this community and state and pray that Thou wilt bless this nation of which we are all a part. May it ever remain free from bondage and be recognized as an ensign of peace and strength before the entire world. Prosper its people as they walk in righteousness before Thee.*

San Diego California

Announced: Apr. 7, 1984.

Location: In the northern part of city of San Diego near the suburb of La Jolla on a ridge above the San Diego Freeway; 7474 Charmant Dr., San Diego, CA 92122-5000.

Site: 7.2 acres.

Exterior finish: Marble chips in plaster.

Temple design: Modern, with two major towers.

Architects: Deems, Lewis & McKinnley-William Lewis, and Hyndman & Hyndman.

Project representative: Stanley G. Smith.

Contractor: Okland Construction Co.

Rooms: Baptistry, celestial room, four ordinance and eight sealing rooms.

Total floor area: 72,000 square feet.

Dimensions: 165 feet by 194 feet; roof 62 feet high; statue of Angel Moroni on top spire, 200 feet high.

Groundbreaking, site dedication: Ground broken Feb. 27, 1988, by President Ezra Taft Benson; site dedicated the same day by President Thomas S. Monson.

District: Stakes in San Diego area and northwestern Mexico.

Dedicated: April 25-30, 1993, by President Gordon B. Hinckley; 23 sessions.

Dedicatory prayer excerpt: *We thank Thee that hundreds of thousands of men and women of various faiths and philosophies have had the opportunity of walking through this sacred house prior to this time of dedication. May an attitude of respect and reverence grow within them. May very many of them be stirred to seek and learn the truths of Thy restored work.*

Artist rendering

No artist rendering available

San Jose Costa Rica

Announced: March 17, 1999.

Location: Del Hotel Marriott, 600 metros oeste, Ribera de Belen, San Jose, Costa Rica.

Site: 2 acres.

Exterior finish: Blanco Guardiano white marble.

Temple design: Classic modern.

Architect: Alvaro Iñigo and Church A&E Services.

Project manager: Duane Cheney.

Contractor: Galvez y Volio.

Rooms: Celestial room, two endowment rooms, two sealing rooms, baptistry.

Total floor area: 10,700 square feet.

Dimensions: 149 feet by 77 feet.

District: 5 stakes and 6 districts in Costa Rica and Nicaragua.

Groundbreaking, site dedication: April 24, 1999, by Elder Lynn G. Robbins of the Seventy and first counselor in the Central America Area presidency.

Dedication: June 4, 2000, by President James E. Faust, second counselor in the First Presidency; 3 sessions.

Dedicatory prayer excerpt: *We thank Thee for him through whom Thou hast revealed the ordinances of this house, even the Prophet Joseph Smith. May we ever hold him in sacred remembrance as Thy servant in initiating Thy work in this season when Thou hast moved again to build Thy kingdom.*

San Salvador El Salvador

Announced: Nov. 7, 2007.

Groundbreaking, site dedication: Sept. 20, 2008 by Elder Don R. Clarke of the Seventy and president of the Central America Area.

Status: Under construction.

Santiago Chile

Announced: April 2, 1980.

Location: At former Church school. Pocuro #1940 Providencia, 6641404 Santiago, Chile; phone: (56) 2 340 5070.

Site: 2.61 acres.

Exterior finish: Stucco on concrete block.

Temple design: Modern.

Architect: Emil B. Fetzer, Church architect.

Construction adviser: Gary Holland.

Contractor: H. Briones Y Cia & The Church of Jesus Christ of Latter-day Saints.

Rooms: Baptistry, celestial room, two ordinance rooms, three sealing rooms.

Total floor area: original 14,572 square feet; after remodeling, 20,831 square feet.

Dimensions: 178.6 feet by 112.5 feet; statue of Angel Moroni on top spire, 76 feet high.

District: 74 stakes and 25 districts in Chile, plus three stakes and two districts in Argentina.

Groundbreaking, site dedication: May 30, 1981, by President Spencer W. Kimball, in a cold rain, attended by 6,000 members.

Dedication: Sept. 15-17, 1983, by President Gordon B. Hinckley; 10 sessions. Rededicated after renovation and enlarging March 12, 2006, by President Hinckley; two sessions.

Dedicatory prayer excerpt: *Bless Thy work in this great nation of Chile. May its citizens enjoy the blessings of freedom and liberty. May Thy work grow in strength and power, in size and dimension. ... We remember before Thee Thy servant who is with us this day. He has grown old in years. Strengthen him in his body and in his mind.*

Santo Domingo Dominican Republic

Announced: Nov. 16, 1993.

Location: Avenida Bolivar and and Avenida Genesis; Avenida Bolivar No. 825, Los Robles, Santo Domingo, Dominican Republic; phone: (809) 731-2000.

Site: 6.42 acres.

Exterior finish: Granite, regina white.

Temple design: Classic modern.

Architects: Scott Partnership and Church A&E Services.

Project manager: Robert Prina.

Contractor: Caralva.

Rooms: Four ordinance rooms and four sealing rooms, celestial room, baptistry.

Total floor area: 67,000 square feet.

Dimensions: 88 feet by 190 feet.

District: 14 stakes and 17 districts in the Caribbean.

Groundbreaking, site dedication: Aug. 18, 1996, by Elder Richard G. Scott of the Quorum of the Twelve.

Dedication: Sept. 17, 2000, by Gordon B. Hinckley; 4 sessions.

Dedicatory prayer excerpt: *Dear Father, please look down with love upon Thy sons and daughters in this island nation and in surrounding lands. Prosper them in their labors that they may have food upon their tables and shelter over their heads. As they look to Thee, reward their faith and open Thy hand of providence toward them. May they find peace in the midst of conflict.*

Sao Paulo Brazil	Seattle Washington

Sao Paulo Brazil

Announced: March 1, 1975.

Location: In the Butanta section of Sao Paulo; Av. Prof. Francisco Morato 2390, Caxingui, 05512-300 Sao Paulo-SP, Brazil; phone, (55) 11-3721-9622.

Exterior finish: Reinforced concrete faced with quartz and marble aggregates.

Site: 1.85 acres.

Temple design: Modern design with Spanish influence.

Architect: Emil B. Fetzer, Church architect.

Construction chairman: Christiani Nielsen, general contractor.

Construction supervisor: Ross Jensen and James Magleby.

Rooms: Baptistry, celestial room, two ordinance rooms, four sealing rooms.

Total floor area: Originally 51,279 square feet; 55,000 square feet after remodeling.

Dimensions: 116 feet by 256 feet.

District: 154 stakes and districts in Brazil .

Groundbreaking, site dedication: March 20, 1976, by Elder James E. Faust, then an Assistant to the Twelve.

Dedication: Oct. 30-Nov. 2, 1978, by President Spencer W. Kimball; 10 sessions. Rededicated after remodeling Feb. 22, 2004, by President Gordon B. Hinckley; one session.

Dedicatory prayer excerpt: *Our Father, may peace abide in all the homes of Thy saints. May holy angels guard them. May prosperity shine upon them and sickness and disease be rebuked from their midst. May their land be made fruitful. May the waters be pure and the climate tempered to the comfort and well-being of Thy people.*

Seattle Washington

Announced: Nov. 15, 1975.

Location: Across from Bellevue Community College, near the Eastgate Interchange on Interstate 90 at 2808 148th Ave. SE; Bellevue, WA 98007-6453; phone: (425) 643-5144.

Site: 18.5 acres, selected June 1975.

Exterior finish: Reinforced concrete faced with white marble aggregate and cast stone.

Temple design: Modern.

Architect: Emil B. Fetzer, Church architect.

Project representative: Michael Enfield.

Construction superintendent: Kent Carter for Jacobsen Construction Co.

Rooms: Baptistry, celestial room, four ordinance rooms, 12 sealing rooms.

Total floor area: 110,000 square feet.

Dimensions: Ground level is 141 feet by 193 feet; upper levels are 117 feet by 163 feet. Height to square is 70 feet; to top of the Angel Moroni, 179 feet.

District: Stakes in western Washington, British Columbia.

Groundbreaking, site dedication: May 27, 1978, by President Marion G. Romney of the First Presidency.

Dedication: Nov. 17-21, 1980, by President Spencer W. Kimball; 13 sessions.

Dedicatory prayer excerpt: *Bless, we pray Thee, the presidency of this temple and the matron and all the officiators herein. Help them to create a sublime and holy atmosphere so that all ordinances may be performed with love and a sweet, spiritual tone that will cause the members to greatly desire to be here, and to return again and again.*

Seoul Korea

Announced: April 1, 1981.

Location: 500-23 Changcheon-dong, Seodae-mun-ku, Seoul-shi 120-836, South Korea; phone: (82) 2-334-9100

Site: 1 acre.

Exterior finish: Granite exterior.

Temple design: Modern adaptation of earlier six-spire design.

Dimensions: 178 feet by 71 feet; Angel Moroni statue is atop tallest spire at 112 feet.

Architects: Church architectural staff; local architect, Komerican Architects.

Construction adviser: Calvin Wardell.

Contractor: Woo Chang.

Rooms: Baptistry, celestial room, four ordinance rooms, three sealing rooms.

Total floor area: 28,057 square feet.

District: 16 stakes and seven districts in South Korea.

Groundbreaking, site dedication: May 9, 1983, by Elder Marvin J. Ashton of the Quorum of the Twelve.

Dedication: Dec. 14-15, 1985, by President Gordon B. Hinckley; 6 sessions.

Dedicatory prayer excerpt: *This is the first such house of the Lord ever constructed on the mainland of Asia, this vast continent where through the generations of the past have lived unnumbered hosts whose lives have not been touched by the saving principles of the gospel.*

Snowflake Arizona

Announced: April 2, 2000.

Location: About 150 miles northeast of Phoenix; 1875 West Canyon Drive, Snowflake, AZ 85937; phone, (928) 536-6626; no clothing rental.

Site: 7.5 acre site

Exterior finish: Two tones of imported polished granite.

Temple design: Traditional.

Architect: Trest Polina of Fanning Bard Tatum Architects.

Project manager: Leon Rowley.

Contractor: Okland Construction Co. of Tempe, Ariz.

Rooms: Baptistry, celestial room, two ordinance rooms, two sealing rooms.

Total floor area: 16,567 square feet.

Dimensions: 91 feet by 149 feet, two stories.

District: 11 stakes in northeastern Arizona and a small portion of western New Mexico.

Groundbreaking, site dedication: Sept. 23, 2000, by Elder Rex D. Pinegar of the Seventy,

Dedication: March 3, 2002, by President Hinckley, 4 sessions.

Dedicatory prayer excerpts: *We are grateful that this Thy house will be available to the sons and daughters of Lehi who live nearby. Let the scales of darkness fall from their eyes and bring a fulfillment of the ancient promises made concerning them. May this house become a hallowed sanctuary for many of these, our brothers and sisters.*

Spokane Washington

Announced: Aug. 13, 1998.

Location: 13710 East 40th Ave., Spokane, WA 99214-1420; phone: (509) 926-2824.

Site: 4.2 acres.

Exterior finish: Granite.

Temple design: Traditional.

Architect: Church A&E Services.

Contractor: Arnell-West Inc.

Rooms: Baptistry, celestial room, two ordinance rooms, two sealing rooms.

Total floor area: 10,700 square feet.

Dimensions: 149 feet by 77 feet

District: 12 stakes in eastern Washington and parts of northern Idaho and western Montana.

Groundbreaking, site dedication: Oct. 10, 1998, by F. Melvin Hammond of the Seventy and president of the North America Northwest Area.

Dedication: Aug. 21, 1999, by President Gordon B. Hinckley; 11 sessions.

Dedicatory prayer excerpt: *Touch the hearts of the people in this temple district that the spirit of Elijah may rest upon them, that their hearts may turn to their fathers, and that they may be motivated to search out their forebears and do a great vicarious work.*

Stockholm Sweden

Announced: April 1, 1981.

Location: Västerhaninge, 13 miles southeast of Stockholm; Tempelvägen 5, SE-137 41, Västerhaninge, Sweden; phone: (46) 8-500-65500.

Exterior finish: Masonry exterior, copper roof.

Temple design: Modern adaptation of earlier six-spire design.

Site: 4.47 acres.

Architects: Church architectural staff; local architect, John Sjöström.

Construction adviser: Henry Haurand.

Contractor: Johnson Construction Co.

Rooms: Baptistry, celestial room, four ordinance rooms; three sealing rooms.

Total floor area: 16,366 square feet.

Dimensions: 178 feet by 71 feet; Angel Moroni statue is atop tallest spire at 112 feet.

District: 38 stakes and districts in Sweden, Finland, Norway, Russia, Latvia, Lithuania, Belarus, Armenia, Ukraine and Estonia.

Groundbreaking, site dedication: March 17, 1984, by Elder Thomas S. Monson of the Quorum of the Twelve.

Dedication: July 2-4, 1985, by President Gordon B. Hinckley; 11 sessions.

Dedicatory prayer excerpt: *Bless this nation where is found Thy temple and its sister nations. . . . Save these nations from war and oppression, and may their people look to Thee and open their doors and hearts to Thy messengers of eternal truth.*

Suva Fiji

Announced: May 7, 1998.

Location: Corner of Princess Road and Lakeba Street, Suva, Fiji; phone (679) 380-565; no clothing rental.

Site: 10 acres.

Exterior finish: Granite.

Temple design: Traditional.

Architects: Conway Beg of Architects Pacific.

Project manager: Jerry Sears.

Contractor: Fletcher Construction Co.

Rooms: Celestial room, two endowment rooms, two sealing rooms, baptistry.

Total floor area: 10,700 square feet.

Dimensions: 149 feet by 77 feet.

District: Five stakes and six districts in Fiji, Kiribati, Vanuatu, New Caledonia.

Groundbreaking, site dedication: May 8, 1999, by Elder Earl M. Monson of the Seventy and second counselor in the Pacific Islands Area presidency.

Dedication: June 18, 2000, by President Gordon B. Hinckley; 1 session.

Dedicatory prayer excerpt: *We are grateful . . . that Thou hast favored us with a temple in this island nation. No longer will we have to travel far across the seas to do that work which Thou hast established as sacred and necessary.*

Sydney Australia

Announced: April 2, 1980.

Location: In suburban Carlingford, 15 miles northwest of downtown Sydney; 756 Pennant Hills Road, Carlingford, NSW 2118; Australia; phone: (61) 2-9841-5471.

Site: 3.06 acres.

Exterior finish: Precast panels, white quartz finish, terra cotta roof tiles.

Temple design: Modern.

Architect: Emil B. Fetzer, Church architect, and R. Lindsay Little.

Construction adviser: D. Crosbie and Richard Rowley.

Contractor: J.P. Cordukes Pty. Ltd.

Rooms: Baptistry, celestial room, three sealing rooms, two ordinance rooms.

Total floor area: 30,067 square feet.

Dimensions: 145 feet by 115 feet; statue of Angel Moroni added to top spire.

District: 11 stakes and 11 districts in Southern Australia and Papua New Guinea.

Groundbreaking, site dedication: Aug. 13, 1982, by Elder Bruce R. McConkie of the Quorum of the Twelve.

Dedication: Sept. 20-23, 1984, by President Gordon B. Hinckley; 14 sessions.

Dedicatory prayer excerpt: *May this temple with its grounds be a place of beauty to all who look upon it. May they be touched by Thy Spirit.*

Taipei Taiwan

Announced: March 31, 1982.

Location: In the Taipei business district; 256 Ai Kuo East Road, Taipei, Taiwan, R.O.C.; (886) 2 2351 0218

Site: 0.48 acres.

Exterior finish: White ceramic tile.

Temple design: Modern adaptation of earlier six-spire design.

Architect: Church architectural staff with assistance from Philip Fei & Associates of Taipei.

Construction adviser: Harold Smith.

Contractor: I. Cheng Construction & Development Corp.

Rooms: Baptistry, celestial room, four ordinance rooms, three sealing rooms.

Total floor area: 9,945 square feet.

Dimensions: 178 feet by 72 feet, six spires; statue of Angel Moroni rises to height of 126 feet.

District: Seven stakes, five districts in Taiwan.

Groundbreaking, site dedication: Aug. 26, 1982, by President Gordon B. Hinckley.

Dedication: Nov. 17-18, 1984, by President Gordon B. Hinckley; 5 sessions.

Dedicatory prayer excerpt: *We thank Thee for the firm foundation on which Thy Church is now established in this part of the earth. We thank Thee for this day when those who will use this temple may turn their hearts to their fathers, participating in this Thy holy house in those ordinances which will make it possible for their deceased forebears to move forward.*

Tampico Mexico

Announced: July 20, 1998.

Location: Av. Ejercito Mexicano 74, Colonia Lomas del Gallo, Ciudad Madero, Tamaulipas 89480, Mexico; phone: (52) 833-216-9660; no clothing rental.

Site: 3.73 acres, including adjoining meetinghouse.

Exterior finish: Blanco Guardiano white marble.

Temple design: Classic modern.

Architects: Alvaro Iñigo and Church A&E Services.

Project manager: Rodolfo Avalos.

Contractor: PyCSA / Okland Const. Co.

Rooms: Celestial room, baptistry, two ordinance rooms, two sealing rooms.

Total floor area: 10,700 square feet.

Dimensions: 77 feet by 149 feet.

District: Nine stakes and three districts in northeastern Mexico.

Groundbreaking, site dedication: Nov. 28, 1998, by Elder Eran A. Call of the Seventy and counselor in the Mexico South Area presidency.

Dedication: May 20, 2000, by President Thomas S. Monson, first counselor in the First Presidency; 4 sessions.

Dedicatory prayer excerpt: *On this historic day, may a new sense of dedication come into our hearts that we may serve Thee more diligently and walk before Thee more faithfully.*

No artist rendering available

Tegucigalpa Honduras

Announced: June 9, 2006.

Groundbreaking, site dedication: June 9, 2007, by Elder Spencer V. Jones of the Seventy and president of the Central American Area.

Status: Under construction.

The Hague Netherlands

Announced: Aug. 16, 1999.

Location: On the outskirts of The Hague; Osijlaan 2, 2722 CV Zoetermeer, The Netherlands; phone: (31) 79-3435-318; no clothing rental.

Exterior finish: polished granite.

Temple design: Classic design.

Architect: Albert van Eerde

Project manager: Hanno Luschin.

Contractor: H BG Construction, Holland.

Rooms: Celestial room, two ordinance rooms, two sealing rooms, baptistry.

Total floor area: 14,477 square feet.

Dimensions: 81-feet by 154-feet.

District: Five stakes and one district in The Netherlands, Belgium and part of France.

Groundbreaking, site dedication: Aug. 26, 1999, by Elder John K. Carmack of the Seventy.

Dedication: Sept. 8, 2002, by President Gordon B. Hinckley; 4 sessions.

Dedicatory prayer excerpts: *Dear Father, we plead with Thee that this day of dedication may herald a new day in this great nation. Touch the hearts and the minds of the people of the land. Lead them from the pursuit of the things of the world to a new yearning for knowledge of Thee and for things divine and eternal.... May there be a great flowering of Thy work in this nation and in all of the lands of Europe. ... May strong leaders rise up in ever increasing numbers.*

Tokyo Japan

Announced: Aug. 9, 1975.

Location: Opposite the Arisugawa Park; 5-8-10 Minami Azabu, Minato-Ku, Tokyo 106-0047, Japan; phone: (81) 3-3442-8171.

Site: 18,000 square feet (about 0.46 acres).

Exterior finish: Structural steel and reinforced concrete faced with 289 panels of pre-cast stone, having the appearance of light gray granite.

Architect: Emil B. Fetzer, Church architect. Architect's local representative, Masao Shiina.

Resident engineer: Sadao Nagata.

Construction superintendent: Yuji Morimura for the Kajima Corporation.

Rooms: Baptistry, celestial room, two ordinance rooms, five sealing rooms.

Total floor area: 52,590 square feet.

Dimensions: Ground floor is 103 feet by 134 feet; upper levels are 103 by 105 feet. Height to square is 70.5 feet, to top of tower, 178 feet.

Design: Modern, one spire.

District: 45 stakes and districts in northern Japan and Vladivostok, Russia.

Groundbreaking, site dedication: Neither was held.

Dedication: Oct. 27-29, 1980, by President Spencer W. Kimball; 7 sessions.

Dedicatory prayer excerpt: *Kind Father, bless all those who come to this temple, that they may do so with humble hearts, in cleanliness, and honor, and integrity. We are grateful for these Saints, for their devotion and their faith, for their worthiness.*

Toronto Ontario

Announced: April 7, 1984.

Location: On the outskirts of Brampton, about 20 miles west of Toronto; 10060 Bramalea Rd, Brampton, Ontario, Canada L6R 1A1; phone: (905) 799-1122.

Site: Announced April 15, 1984; 14 acres.

Exterior finish: White cast stone.

Temple design: Modern.

Architects: Allward-Gouinlock Inc.

Supervising architects: Alfred T. West Jr. and Dagmar Wertheim.

Construction adviser: Jerry Sears.

Contractor: Milne & Nicholls Ltd.

Rooms: Baptistry, celestial room, four ordinance rooms, six sealing rooms.

Total floor area: 57,982 square feet.

Dimensions: 154 feet by 208 feet; spire, 171 feet high with 11-foot statue of Angel Moroni.

District: Nine stakes in Ontario.

Groundbreaking, site dedication: Oct. 10, 1987, by President Thomas S. Monson of the First Presidency.

Dedication: Aug. 25-27, 1990, by President Gordon B. Hinckley; 11 sessions.

Dedicatory prayer excerpt: *This nation has become a gathering place for people from scores of other lands. In their veins flows the blood of Israel. Many have hearkened to the testimony of Thy servants and have been favored with a knowledge of the principles and ordinances of Thine everlasting gospel.*

Tuxtla Gutierrez Mexico

Announced: Feb. 25, 1999.

Location: Carretera a Chicoasen, km. 1,4; Esq. Paseo de la Roseta, Fraccionamiento San Jose Chapultepec, Tuxtla Guiterrez, Chiapas 29047, Mexico; phone: (52)961 615-8287; no clothing rental.

Site: 1.77 acres, including adjoining meeting-house.

Exterior finish: White marble.

Temple design: Classic modern.

Architects: Alvaro Iñigo and Church A&E Services

Project manager: Bryan Hutchings and John Webster.

Contractor: Impulsa/Okland Construction Co.

Rooms: Celestial room, baptistry, two ordinance rooms, two sealing rooms.

Total floor area: 10,700 square feet.

Dimensions: 77 feet by 149 feet.

District: Five stakes one district in Chiapas, near the border of Guatemala.

Groundbreaking, site dedication: March 20, 1999, by Elder Richard E. Turley Sr. of the Seventy.

Dedication: March 12, 2000, by President James E. Faust, second counselor in the First Presidency; 4 sessions.

Dedicatory prayer excerpt: *We invoke Thy blessings upon this nation of Mexico where so many of the sons and daughters of Father Lehi dwell. Bless these Thy children. Lift them out of the depths of poverty. Bring new light and understanding into their minds. Cause them to rejoice at Thy watchcare over them.*

Twin Falls Idaho

Announced: Oct. 2, 2004.

Location: 1405 Eastland Drive North, Twin Falls, ID 83301.

Site: 5.10 acres.

Exterior finish: Concrete panels with quartz rock finish.

Temple design: Classic modern.

Architects: MHTN Architects, Inc.

Project manager: Greg Rasmussen

Contractor: Big D Construction.

Rooms: Baptistry, celestial room, four ordinance rooms, five sealing rooms.

Total floor area: 31,245 square feet

Dimensions: 152-feet 10-inches high by 178-feet 10-inches long by 87-feet 10-inches wide.

District: Southern Idaho communities of Twin Falls, Jerome, Burley, Rupert, Ketchum and Hailey.

Groundbreaking, site dedication: April 15, 2006; by Elder Neil L. Andersen of the Presidency of the Seventy.

Dedication: August 24, 2008, by President Thomas S. Monson; 4 sessions.

Dedicatory prayer excerpt: *The Plan of Salvation, taught in the temple with simplicity, yet with power, will be as a never-failing beacon of divine light to guide our footsteps and keep them constantly on the pathway of eternal life.*

Artist rendering

Vancouver British Columbia

Announced: May 25, 2006.

Groundbreaking, site dedication: Aug. 4, 2007, by Elder Ronald A. Rasband of the Presidency of the Seventy.

Status: Under construction.

Veracruz Mexico

Announced: April 14, 1999.

Location: Av. Ejercito Mexicano, Esq. Michoacan, Boca del Rio, Veracruz 94290, Vera-cruz, Mexico; (52) 229-922-9621; no clothing rental

Site: 3.37 acres, including future meetinghouse site.

Exterior finish: Blanco Guardiano white marble.

Temple design: Classic modern.

Architect: Alvaro Iñigo and Church A&E Services.

Project manager: Rodolfo Avalvos.

Contractor: Impulsa / Okland Const. Co.

Rooms: Celestial room, baptistry, two ordinance rooms, two sealing rooms.

Total floor area: 10,700 square feet.

Dimensions: 77 feet by 149 feet.

District: Nine stakes, two districts and two unaffiliated branches in Veracruz, on eastern central coast of Mexico.

Groundbreaking: May 29, 1999, by Elder Carl B. Pratt of the Seventy and president of the Mexico South Area.

Dedication: July 9, 2000, by President Thomas S. Monson, first counselor in the First Presidency; 4 sessions.

Dedicatory prayer excerpt: *Bless the youth of the land, the young men and the young women, that they may grow up in righteousness before Thee. Bless them with love for the Savior of the world, our Lord and Master, that they may pattern their lives after [Him].*

Vernal Utah

Announced: Feb. 13, 1994.

Location: The temple is the remodeled 1905 Tabernacle at 170 So. 400 West; Vernal, UT 84078-2536; phone (435) 789-3220.

Site: 1.6 acres.

Exterior finish: Face brick.

Temple design: Adaptation of Uintah Stake Tabernacle.

Architects: FFKR Architects of Salt Lake City, Utah.

Project manager: Lloyd Hess.

Contractor: McCullough Engineering and Construction.

Rooms: Baptistry, celestial room, two ordinance rooms, three sealing rooms.

Total floor area: 33,400 square feet.

Dimensions: 175 feet by 210 feet.

District: Nine stakes in East central Utah, three in Colorado and two in Wyoming.

Groundbreaking, site dedication: May 13, 1995, by President Gordon B. Hinckley.

Dedication: Nov. 2-4, 1997, by President Gordon B. Hinckley; 11 sessions.

Dedicatory prayer excerpt: *We are grateful for this beautiful new structure which utilizes the historic tabernacle built by Thy people nearly a century ago.... Now that old and much-loved building has become the centerpiece of a new and beautiful House of the Lord. It has a quiet luster all its own. We thank Thee for the use to which it has been put.*

Villahermosa Mexico

Announced: Oct. 30, 1998.

Location: In center of Villahermosa; Av 27 de Febrero # 1802; Colonia Atasta de Serra, Villahermosa, Tabasco 86100, Mexico; phone: (52) 993-352-2028; no clothing rental.

Site: 1.73 acres.

Exterior finish: Blanco Guardiano white marble.

Temple Design: Classic modern.

Architects: Alvaro Iñigo and Church A&E Services.

Project manager: John Webster and Dean Fife.

Contractor: PyCSA / Okland Construction Co.

Rooms: Celestial room, baptistry, two ordinance rooms, two sealing rooms.

Total floor area: 10,700 square feet.

Dimensions: 77 feet by 149 feet.

District: Eight stakes and two districts in Tabasco, on the east coast before the Yucatan Peninsula.

Groundbreaking: Jan. 9, 1999, by Elder Richard E. Turley Sr. of the Seventy and first counselor in the Mexico South Area.

Dedication: May 21, 2000, by President Thomas S. Monson, first counselor in the First Presidency; 4 sessions.

Dedicatory prayer excerpt: *May Thy Holy Spirit touch the hearts of all who enter these portals. May they do so with reverence and respect. May this Thy house stand as an expression of the covenant between Thee and Thy children, and wilt Thou be constrained to look with favor upon Thy people and open the windows of heaven and shower down blessings upon them.*

Washington D.C.

Announced: Nov. 15, 1968.

Location: Wooded site in Kensington, Md., near Exit 33 of the Capital Beltway (Interstate 495); 9900 Stoneybrook Dr., Kensington, MD (301) 588-0650.

Site: Selected in 1962; 52 acres.

Exterior finish: Alabama white marble.

Temple design: Design portrays the Church as "a light to the world," with three towers to the east representing the Melchizedek Priesthood leadership, and those to the west, the Aaronic Priesthood leadership.

Architects: Fred L. Markham, Henry P. Fetzer, Harold K. Beecher, Keith W. Wilcox, under general direction of Church architect Emil B. Fetzer.

Contractor: Jacobsen, Okland, and Sidney Foulger construction companies.

Rooms: Baptistry, celestial room, six ordinance rooms, 14 sealing rooms; seven floors.

Total floor area: 160,000 square feet.

Dimensions of building: 240 feet long, 136 feet wide, not including annex or bridge to temple proper.

District: 36 stakes and districts in Washington D.C., Pensylvania, Virginia, Maryland, New Jersey, New York.

Groundbreaking, site dedication: Dec. 7, 1968, by President Hugh B. Brown.

Dedication: Nov. 19-22, 1974, by President Spencer W. Kimball; 10 sessions.

Dedicatory prayer excerpt: *We are so grateful, our Father, that Thy Son has thrown wide open the doors of the prisons for the multitudes who are waiting in the spirit world.*

Winter Quarters Nebraska

Announced: June 14, 1999.

Location: adjacent to Mormon Pioneer Cemetery and across from Mormon Trail Center; 8283 North 34th Street, Omaha, NE 68112; phone: (402) 453-3406; no clothing rental.

Site: 1.92 acre site.

Exterior finish: Bethel white granite.

Temple design: Traditional design.

Architect: Dan Reinhardt of Reinhardt & Associates.

Project manager: Bill Naylor

Contractor: Lund-Ross Constructors, Inc.

Rooms: Celestial room, two ordinances rooms, two sealing rooms, baptistry.

Total floor area: 10,700 square.

Dimensions: 149 feet by 77 feet; 86 feet high.

District: 12 stakes in Nebraska, Iowa, South Dakota and Kansas.

Groundbreaking, site dedication: Nov. 28, 1999, by Elder Hugh W. Pinnock of the Seventy and president of the North America Central Area.

Dedication: April 22, 2001, by President Gordon B. Hinckley, 4 sessions. First session transmitted by satellite worldwide.

Dedicatory prayer excerpt: *As we meet together, we envision the wagons and the boats pulling in from the East and the South, while others were leaving these grounds to make the long march up the Elk Horn, along the waters of the Platte, up the valley of the Sweet Water, over the Continental Divide, and finally to the valley of the Great Salt Lake.... There was, at times, much of levity here. There was also much of sorrow.*

FEATURE

Life of President Gordon B. Hinckley

GORDON B. HINCKLEY 1910-2008

Going forward
with the faith of his fathers
No stops, no detours in long life of gospel-centered living

The gates of life swing on small hinges, President Gordon B. Hinckley often taught the youth of the Church. Seemingly little decisions made early in life eventually chart a course for life. For President Hinckley, such a gate swung during the desperate times of 1933.

LDS Church News

President Gordon B. Hinckley acknowledges congregation following October General Conference 2006.

I t was the bottom of the Great Depression, a time when those who were once prosperous were now selling apples on the streets.

But roses were beginning to blossom across the Salt Lake Valley and Gordon Bitner Hinckley, who would turn 23 years old in a few days, was looking with optimism to furthering his education in the East. He had graduated from the University of Utah and had been working at small jobs to scrape enough money together to attend Columbia University where he planned to continue his studies in English and journalism.

Then stepped in John C. Duncan, a tall man who served as bishop of the First Ward in the (Salt Lake) Liberty Stake. A mission was discussed. Relatively few young men received mission calls in those days. Times were desperate and most parents didn't have the means.

President Hinckley discussed his missionary prospects with his father — his mother having died three years earlier from cancer. These were difficult times, financially and emotionally.

The young Gordon Hinckley had

always been faithful, and even though his gift for writing and literature had lifted his eyes toward a career in journalism, he answered the call to serve a mission.

"I remember my father saying, 'We will do all we can to see that your needs are met,'" President Hinckley said, as reported in an early Church News account. "It was at that time that we discovered a little savings account my mother had left — change saved from her grocery purchases and other shopping. With that little bit of help added, it appeared I could go on my mission."

In the next years, President Hinckley would lift his voice in testimony of the truthfulness of the gospel in many nations around the world, and become a mighty leader in the kingdom.

Early years

Gordon B. Hinckley was born June 23, 1910, eldest son of Bryant S. and Ada Bitner Hinckley. As a child he lived in a two-story gray frame home with white shutters and trim located on the southwest corner of Windsor and Seventh South in Salt Lake City.

At age 12, Gordon thrived on work, developing a determination to complete a task.

Known for his longevity, his many years of robust enthusiasm and inexhaustible vigor, President Hinckley was actually weak and frail as a child. At age 2, he was stricken with whooping cough which threatened his life. "The boy needs more fresh air and sunlight," the doctor said. So his father bought a farm in the East Mill Creek area of the Salt Lake Valley.

His earliest recollection of the farm was a stonemason laying rock for the fireplace in the Hinckley home. Each summer for the coming years, the Hinckleys would leave their home in Salt Lake City and live on the farm. This home later became the first home of the newlyweds, Gordon and Marjorie Hinckley.

President Hinckley's appetite for reading came naturally. His mother often read to her children, and his father had a spacious home library. But he did not care for school as a youngster and "kicked up a terrible fuss" when he started at Hamilton grade school.

He often wrestled with his younger brother, Sherman. One day their father tossed a pair of boxing gloves to them. "Now the next time you want to fight, put these on, move outside, and go after it in style," Bryant S. Hinckley said.

The young Gordon thrived on work, developing courage and determination to complete a task. He made stalled cars run, and while still a youth, he could handle household electric, carpentry and plumbing repairs. He later built and remodeled his own home. On the family farm he raised strawberries, corn, tomatoes, peaches, pears and cherries.

His first paying job was as carrier for the Deseret News. Years later he was named to the board of directors and executive committee of the Deseret News Publishing Company.

By the time he reached college, Gordon was developing a reputation as a gifted speaker. On one occasion, it was announced that U.S. Sen. Reed Smoot would speak during the First Ward's sacrament meeting. Sen. Smoot was also a member of the Quorum of the Twelve at the time.

On the day prior to the address, circumstances suddenly changed, preventing Sen. Smoot from attending. On Sunday, the bishop adjusted by calling two of "his boys" to speak. They had been ward teaching companions, though both were only about 20 years old. The bishop asked them to substitute for the senator that night.

Gordon had a watering turn on the family farm that required his attention most of that Sunday, but come sacrament meeting time, he was on the stand before an overflow congregation who had come to hear Sen. Smoot.

"When Gordy Hinckley finished speaking," recalled his companion, Bob (Robert F.) Sonntag, "people had forgotten all about Sen. Smoot's absence. The boy really stirred them."

Measuring up to his noble heritage of faith was a source of motivation for President Hinckley. Forebear Samuel Hinckley embraced the Puritan faith and set sail for America from England in 1635. His eldest son, Thomas, later distinguished himself as governor of Massachusetts Colony from 1681 to 1692.

His grandfather, Ira N. Hinckley, was born in Upper Canada and first heard the gospel in 1835 when he was 7 years old. In the spring of 1843 he walked 120 miles from Springfield, Ill., to Nauvoo where he heard the Prophet Joseph Smith preach in the grove west of the temple site.

Ira came west with the pioneers in 1850 and was later called by Brigham Young to build Cove Fort in central Utah. There his son, Bryant S., was born.

Articulate and practical, Bryant S. Hinckley became a leader in the Church.

Over the years, while in his youth, President Hinckley became acquainted with many of the leading brethren of the Church who were frequent visitors to his father's home.

Bryant Hinckley died just four months before President Hinckley was sustained an apostle.

Ada Bitner Hinckley, President Hinckley's mother, was a cultured woman who was Utah's first Gregg shorthand teacher at LDS (Business) College. She also taught English and, as a bride, brought a baby grand piano into their new home.

Mission experience

President Hinckley was called to serve a mission in England in 1933. He traveled by train from Salt Lake City to New York, where he boarded a ship for Plymouth, England.

While preaching to shifting, critical crowds from atop a wooden stand he would cement his testimony.

"Either Joseph talked with the Father and Son or he did not," he would say. "If he did not, we are engaged in a blasphemy. If he did, we have a duty from which none of us can shrink — to declare to the world the living reality of the God of the universe."

The young Elder Gordon B. Hinckley stands on a soap box addressing a crowd in Hyde Park.

He began his labors in Preston, a town of spires and green hedges in cloudy northern England. Converts were few in

Britain when he began knocking on doors and preaching at night in Preston's lonely market square.

"I was terrified," he said, speaking of his first street meeting. "I stepped up on that little stand and looked at that crowd of people that had gathered. They were dreadfully poor at that time in the bottom of the Depression. They looked rather menacing and mean, but I somehow stumbled through whatever I had to say."

Discouraged, he wrote his father, saying, "I am wasting my time and your money. I don't see any point in my staying here."

A gentle, but terse, reply came from his father. "Dear Gordon. I have your letter.... I have only one suggestion. Forget yourself and go to work. With love, Your Father."

President Hinckley pondered his father's response and, touched by the Lord's promise to those who lose their life in His service, he got on his knees and covenanted with the Lord to forget himself and go to work.

His mission experience to Great Britain affected everything else President Hinckley did the rest of his life. Years later, while speaking to missionaries in the Pennsylvania Philadelphia Mission on Oct. 25, 2002, President Hinckley said, "What a marvelous season that was in (my) life. Everything that (I) have done since then, that has been of any worth to (me), has come out of that experience which (I) had back in those days."

No sooner had he recommitted himself to the work than he was assigned to London where he became assistant to Elder Joseph F. Merrill of the Quorum of the Twelve, who was presiding over the European Mission.

Years later, in 1958, when called to serve as Assistant to the Quorum of the Twelve, President Hinckley opened his remarks in general conference that day in his typically humorous style.

"My dear brethren and sisters," he began, "I am reminded of a statement made by my first missionary companion when I received a letter of transfer to the European Mission office. After I had read it, I turned it over to him. He read it, and then said: 'Well, you must have helped an old lady across the street in the pre-existence. This has not come because of anything you've done here.'"

The experiences of his mission have since cast a mighty imprint on the unfolding missionary efforts of the Church. President Hinckley had been involved with missionary work for more than 70 years, stretching from his mission in 1933 when a total of 525 missionaries throughout the world brought in 7,000 converts a year.

Today, approximately 53,000 missionaries labor in 160 nations and baptize approximately 240,000 converts.

In all his labors as a General Authority, whether supervising the Northern and Southern Far East Missions and the Hawaii Mission of the Church, as they were known then, for 26 years, he kept close to the heartbeats of the missionaries themselves.

He was with them in the London fog, in the cold Swiss rain, in the Montana wind, and in the humid heat of Asia. He helped them when sick, comforted them when bereaved, encouraged them when despondent, sorrowed with them in their tragedies, and rejoiced with them in their accomplishments. And he was on his knees with many a young man in distress.

Home, family and leadership

During his remarkable career President Hinckley continually demonstrated unique abilities of mind and judgment that served him in dealing with weighty issues of the growing Church.

"But the greatest judgment he has ever shown in his entire life," said President Boyd K. Packer, Acting President of the Quorum of the Twelve, is the judgment he showed in marrying Marjorie Pay. "You cannot know him unless you know her — the tender, guiding, patient influence she has been in his life and in that of their children."

Marjorie Pay lived across the street from the Hinckley city home. She was a beautiful young woman who became attracted to this modest young man in whom she observed a keen intellect and the ability to achieve.

He married this brown-eyed, dark-haired, intelligent young woman in the Salt Lake Temple on April 29, 1937. They moved into the Hinckley farmhouse in East Mill Creek where he installed the furnace and layed the brick flue. Two years later they built the home where they raised five children, namely: Kathleen, Richard G., Virginia, Clark and Cynthia Jane.

At age 27, in 1937, President Hinckley was called to the Sunday School General Board where he served for nine years. A capable writer, he wrote Old Testament and Book of Mormon lessons that were used for many years.

He distinguished himself as an administrator and was called as counselor to the East Mill Creek Stake in 1946, and as president in 1956. He became the third-generation Hinckley to serve as stake president following his grandfather, Ira N. Hinckley, first president in the Millard Stake; and his father, Bryant S. Hinckley who presided over the Liberty Stake. In the October 1998 general priesthood meeting President Hinckley told how his father faced grave challenges as president of the "largest stake in the valley" during the Great Depression.

"It was before our present welfare program was established," he said. "He walked the floor worrying about his people. He and his associates established a great wood-chopping project designed to keep the home furnaces and stoves going and the people warm in the winter. They had no money with which to buy coal. Men who had been affluent were among those who chopped wood."

This example served President Hinckley well. Years later, while presiding over the East Mill Creek Stake, he drew on this example when faced with the challenges of residing in one of the most rapidly growing areas of the state. During his service, 15 wards were created, and the stake was divided twice to become four stakes.

During this time, he served as an assistant in the Missionary Department for many years, and as executive secretary of the Missionary Committee since 1951.

Under the direction of the First Presidency and the Missionary Committee, he shouldered responsibility in supplying more than 11,000 missionaries with necessary materials to teach the gospel. There were 30,000 converts as a result of missionary labor in 1957.

A General Authority

President Hinckley was serving as stake president when called as an Assistant to the Quorum of the Twelve on April 6, 1958. Three-and-a-half years later he was called to the Quorum of the Twelve on Oct. 6, 1961. He served as an apostle for 20 years until he was called as a counselor to President Spencer W. Kimball, at age 71, in July 1981.

For the next 14 years he served as a counselor in the First Presidency to three presidents of the Church, including second counselor to President Kimball, first counselor to President Ezra Taft Benson (Nov. 10, 1985), and first counselor to President Howard W. Hunter (June 5, 1994).

He worked with six presidents of the Church and was the longest serving of any General Authority, serving 49 years and nine months.

In his 85th year, he was ordained the 15th president of the Church on March 12, 1995.

A common comment by those who worked under his direction or who sought his advice was that President Hinckley loved people and was concerned for their welfare.

On one occasion while serving as executive secretary for the Missionary Department, he learned of a missionary who returned home because of a serious illness. Following an operation, a room near the hospital was secured where the mother of this young man could be with him during his convalescence.

The summer was hot and the room was unbearably warm. Elder Hinckley sent the electric fan from his office to the missionary to make his room more comfortable and ease his suffering.

President David O. McKay welcomes Elder Gordon B. Hinckley, 47, as the newest Assistant to the Twelve, sustained in General Conference on April 6, 1952.

Like all great leaders of the Church, President Hinckley's faith was forged in a crucible of refining fire. The day before he left for an assignment to New Zealand given to him by the First Presidency in 1958 pertaining to the temple which had just been dedicated, he said, "I have administered to my father who is lying unconscious in the hospital and not expected to live, but I am strongly impressed that he will not pass away while I am on this assignment."

His father gained strength and lived another three years until June 5, 1961, two weeks after Elder Hinckley had returned from another assignment in Asia.

President Hinckley's leadership advanced the Church on every front across the world during his nearly 13 years as president.

Close to 600 stakes were created during his leadership, an average of 85 per year. The Church would grow by more than 2.5 million members.

HISTORICAL CHRONOLOGY OF THE CHURCH

This chronology gives a selected listing of important dates in Church history. Among items excluded are many that can be found elsewhere in this Almanac, including information on General Authorities and the establishment of stakes and missions. Italicized entries are secular events that were taking place during those periods.

1820 Spring — In Joseph Smith's First Vision, in answer to his prayer that was motivated by his reading of James 1:5, Joseph was visited by the Father and the Son in what is now known as the Sacred Grove near his home in upstate New York. Jesus answered his question about which church to join, opening the door to the restoration of the gospel.

1823 Sept. 21-22 — In five visits with Joseph Smith, the resurrected Moroni revealed the existence of ancient gold plates, from which the Book of Mormon was translated, and instructed him on his role in restoring the gospel.

1827 Sept. 22 — Joseph Smith received the gold plates from the Angel Moroni at the Hill Cumorah in upstate New York. He also received the Urim and Thummim, which was used in translating the Book of Mormon.

1828 February — Martin Harris took a transcript and partial translation of the Book of Mormon to Professor Charles Anthon of Columbia College and to Dr. Samuel L. Mitchell of New York. In June, Harris borrowed and lost 116 manuscript pages.

1829 May 15 — Joseph Smith and Oliver Cowdery received the Aaronic Priesthood from John the Baptist along the banks of the Susquehanna River, near Harmony, Pa. (See D&C 13.) The two baptized one another, as instructed.

May or June — Peter, James and John conferred the Melchizedek Priesthood upon Joseph Smith and Oliver Cowdery near the Susquehanna River between Harmony, Pa., and Colesville, N.Y.

June — The Book of Mormon translation was completed, and the three witnesses — Oliver Cowdery, David Whitmer and Martin Harris — were shown the plates by a heavenly messenger. (See D&C 17). Soon afterward, the plates were shown to eight other witnesses.

1830 March 26 — Five thousand copies of the Book of Mormon were published by Joseph Smith and printed in Palmyra, N.Y., by E.B. Grandin at a cost of $3,000.

April 6 — Joseph Smith organized the "Church of Christ" at the Peter Whitmer Sr. home in Fayette, N.Y., with six incorporators as required by law — Joseph Smith, Oliver Cowdery, Hyrum Smith, Peter Whitmer Jr., David Whitmer and Samuel H. Smith.

June 30 — Samuel H. Smith left on a mission to neighboring villages, including Mendon, N.Y., where the Young and Kimball families resided.

Oct. 17 — Following a revelation received by the Prophet Joseph Smith (see D&C 32), Parley P. Pratt, Oliver Cowdery, Peter Whitmer Jr., and Ziba Peterson began a mission to the Lamanites, leaving copies of the Book of Mormon with the Cattaraugus Indians in New York, the Wyandots in Ohio, and the Shawnees and Delawares on the Missouri frontier. They stopped en route to teach and baptize Sidney Rigdon and a congregation of his followers in the Kirtland, Ohio, area.

Dec. 30 — The Saints were commanded in a revelation (see D&C 37) to gather in Ohio, the first commandment concerning a gathering in this dispensation.

1831 Feb. 4 — Edward Partridge was named "bishop unto the Church." (See D&C 41.) This was the first revelation given through the Prophet Joseph Smith at Kirtland, Ohio.

July 20 — Independence, Jackson County, Mo., was designated the center place for Zion. (See D&C 57).

Aug. 2 — During a ceremony in Kaw Township, 12 miles west of Independence in Jackson County, Mo., Sidney Rigdon dedicated the Land of Zion for the gathering of the Saints. The next day, on Aug. 3, Joseph Smith dedicated a temple site at Independence, Mo.

1832 Jan. 25 — Joseph Smith was sustained president of the high priesthood at a conference at Amherst, Ohio. Sidney Rigdon and Jesse Gause were named counselors in March 1832.

Feb. 16 — While working on the inspired revision of the Bible, Joseph Smith and Sidney Rigdon received a vision in Hiram, Ohio, of the three degrees of glory. (See D&C 76.)

May 24-25 — The Prophet Joseph Smith was residing with his family in the farm home of John Johnson in Hiram, Ohio, when a mob broke in to drag him from the side of his ailing son, Joseph. After being beaten, the Prophet regained strength and returned home to spend the night picking and scrubbing tar and feathers from his skin. On this day, he preached from the front steps of the farm home to a congregation assembled outside the door that included members of the mob that had attacked him the night before. Later that day, Joseph baptized three people.

June — Elders began teaching the restored gospel in Canada, the first missionary effort outside the United States.

1833 Jan. 22-23 — School of the Prophets began in Kirtland, Ohio.

Feb. 27 — The revelation known as the "Word of Wisdom" (D&C 89) was received by the Prophet Joseph Smith at Kirtland, Ohio.

March 18 — The First Presidency was organized when Sidney Rigdon and Frederick G. Williams were set apart by Joseph Smith to be his counselors, to which they had previously been called.

May 6 — The Saints were commanded by revelation to build a House of the Lord at Kirtland. (See D&C 94.) Further instructions were given by revelation on June 1. (See D&C 95.)

July 2 — The Prophet Joseph Smith finished the translation of the New Testament.

July 20 — A mob destroyed the *Evening and Morning Star* printing office in Independence, Mo., interrupting the printing of the Book of Commandments.

November — The Saints fled Jackson County, Mo., in response to mob threats and attacks and took refuge in neighboring counties, particularly Clay County.

1834 Feb. 17 — The first stake in the Church was created in Kirtland, Ohio, with Joseph Smith as president, and on the same day the first high council of the Church was organized. (See D&C 102). A similar organization was created in Clay-Caldwell counties in Missouri on July 3, 1834, with David Whitmer as president.

May 8 — Zion's Camp began its march from New Portage, Ohio, to Clay County, Mo., to assist the exiled Missouri Saints. The camp dispersed June 30.

1835 The Church published a collection of hymns and sacred songs selected by Emma Smith. She had been appointed to the work in July 1830 (see D&C 25), but destruction of the Independence, Mo., printing press by a mob in 1833 had delayed publication.

Feb. 14 — The Quorum of the Twelve was organized after the three witnesses to the Book of Mormon, as directed by revelation (see D&C 18), selected 12 apostles at a meeting of the members of Zion's Camp in Kirtland, Ohio.

Feb. 28 — The First Quorum of the Seventy was organized in Kirtland, and its first seven presidents, who were also selected from members of Zion's Camp, were named.

March 28 — A revelation in which various priesthood offices and powers were defined (see D&C 107) was received during a meeting of the First Presidency and Quorum of the Twelve in Kirtland.

May 4 — Members of the Quroum of the Twelve left Kirtland for the eastern states on their first mission as apostles.

1836 March 27 — The Kirtland Temple, the first temple built in this dispensation, was dedicated after being under construction for nearly three years.

April 3 — The Savior and also Moses, Elias and Elijah appeared in the Kirtland Temple and committed the keys of their respective dispensations to Joseph Smith and Oliver Cowdery. (See D&C 110.)

June 29 — A mass meeting of citizens at Liberty, Mo., passed a resolution to expel the Saints from Clay County. By December many had relocated on Shoal Creek (later known as Far West) in the newly established Caldwell County, located northeast of Clay County.

1837 July 20 — The first mission in the Church — the British Mission — was organized. Apostles Heber C. Kimball and Orson Hyde and Elders Willard Richards and Joseph Fielding had left Kirtland, Ohio, June 13 for England, opening up missionary work outside North America.

July 30 — Nine persons were baptized in the River Ribble at Preston, England, the first converts to the Church in Great Britain. By December, there were 1,000 LDS members in England.

1838 March 14 — Headquarters of the Church was established in

Far West, Caldwell County, Mo.

April 26 — Name of the Church — The Church of Jesus Christ of Latter-day Saints — was given by revelation. (See D&C 115).

May 19 — Joseph Smith and others visited a place on Grand River, in Missouri, about 25 miles north of Far West, called Spring Hill by the Saints, which by revelation was named Adam-ondi-Ahman because "it is the place where Adam shall come to visit his people, or the Ancient of Days shall sit, as spoken of by Daniel the prophet." (See D&C 116, Dan. 7:9-14.)

July 6 — The exodus from Kirtland, Ohio, began under the direction of the First Council of the Seventy as planned three months earlier.

July 8 — Revelation on the law of tithing (see D&C 119) was given at Far West, Mo.

Aug. 6 — A scuffle at the polls at Gallatin, Daviess County, Mo., intensified the mounting tension between Latter-day Saints and other area settlers.

Oct. 27 — Acting upon false reports of rebellion among the Mormons, Gov. Lilburn W. Boggs issued an order to exterminate or expel the Saints from Missouri.

Oct. 30 — Seventeen Latter-day Saints were killed and 12 severely wounded in the Haun's Mill Massacre at a small settlement on Shoal Creek, 12 miles east of Far West, Mo.

Oct. 31 — Joseph Smith and others were made prisoners of the militia. The next day a court-martial ordered the Prophet and the others shot, but Brig. Gen. A.W. Doniphan refused to carry out the order.

Nov. 9 — Joseph Smith and the other prisoners arrived in Richmond, Mo., where they were put in chains and suffered much abuse by the guards. An arraignment and a two-week trial followed, resulting in their being sent Nov. 28 to the Liberty Jail in Liberty, Mo., where they were imprisoned about Dec. 1.

1839 March 20 — While in Liberty Jail, Joseph Smith wrote an epistle to the Saints, which contained fervent pleadings with the Lord regarding the suffering of the Saints and words of prophecy. (See D&C 121.) A few days later, he continued the epistle, parts of which became Sections 122 and 123 of the Doctrine and Covenants.

April 16 — Joseph Smith and four other prisoners were allowed to escape while being transferred from Daviess to Boone counties in Missouri under a change of venue in their case.

April 20 — The last of the Saints left Far West, Mo. A whole community, numbering about 15,000, had been expelled from their homes on account of their religion.

April 25 — Commerce, Ill., was selected as a gathering place for the Church. On May 1, two farms were purchased by Joseph Smith and others, the first land purchased in what later became Nauvoo.

Summer — Members of the Quorum of the Twelve, as their circumstances permitted, departed from Nauvoo, Ill., for their missions to England. (See D&C 118).

Oct. 29 — Joseph Smith left Illinois for Washington, D.C., to seek redress from the president of the United States for wrongs suffered by the Saints in Missouri.

Nov. 29 — In a meeting with U.S. President Martin Van Buren in Washington, D.C., Joseph Smith was told by the president that he [Van Buren] could do nothing to relieve the oppressions in Missouri.

1840 June 6 — Forty-one members of the Church sailed for the United States from Liverpool, England, on the ship *Britannia*, being the first Saints to gather from a foreign land. By 1890, some 85,000 LDS emigrants had crossed the Atlantic Ocean in about 280 voyages.

1841 Jan. 19 — A revelation (see D&C 124) given at Nauvoo, Ill., outlined instructions for building a temple in Nauvoo. Baptism for the dead was introduced.

Feb. 4 — The Nauvoo Legion was organized with Joseph Smith as lieutenant general.

Oct. 24 — At a site on the Mount of Olives in Jerusalem, Orson Hyde dedicated Palestine for the gathering of the Jews.

1842 March 1 — The Articles of Faith were published for the first time in the *Times and Seasons* in Nauvoo, Ill. Joseph Smith, in response to a request from John Wentworth, editor of the *Chicago Democrat*.

March 17 — Joseph Smith organized the Female Relief Society of Nauvoo, with Emma Smith, Sarah M. Cleveland and Elizabeth Ann Whitney as its presidency, to look after the poor and sick.

Aug. 6 — Joseph Smith prophesied that the Saints would be driven to the Rocky Mountains, but that he would not go with them.

1843 June 21 — Illinois agents, armed with a warrant from Gov.

Thomas Ford, arrested Joseph Smith at Dixon, Lee County, Ill. He was released July 1, 1843.

July 12 — A revelation received in Nauvoo, Ill., on the "Eternity of the Marriage Covenant and Plural Marriage" (see D&C 132) was recorded, giving fuller meaning to the "new and everlasting covenant."

1844

Jan. 29 — A political convention in Nauvoo nominated Joseph Smith as a candidate for president of United States.

April 30 — Addison Pratt landed on Tubuai, the first missionary to begin work in the South Pacific.

June 11 — Joseph Smith and the city council were charged with riot in the destruction of the *Expositor* press. A Nauvoo court absolved them of the charge, but the complainant asked for the issue to be examined by the Carthage court.

June 27 — Joseph and Hyrum Smith were killed by a mob that rushed the Carthage Jail in Carthage, Ill. John Taylor was injured in the attack; Willard Richards escaped injury.

Aug. 8 — At a meeting designated for the appointment of a guardian, Rigdon stated his views, after which Brigham Young announced an afternoon meeting. During the latter session, Young claimed the right of the Twelve Apostles to lead the Church and was sustained by a vote of the Church.

1845

January — The Illinois Legislature repealed the city charter of Nauvoo.

May — The nine accused murderers of Joseph and Hyrum Smith were acquitted upon instructions of the court.

Sept. 22 — Citizens at a mass meeting in Quincy, Ill., endorsed a proposal requesting that the Saints leave Illinois as quickly as possible. The Twelve's reply reiterated the Latter-day Saints' intention to move to a remote area and asked for cooperation and an end of harassment in order to prepare for the move early the following summer.

Dec. 10, 1845-Feb. 7, 1846 — Some 5,000 members received their endowments in the yet-to-be-finished Nauvoo Temple prior to their exodus from Nauvoo.

1846

Feb. 4 — The Mormon migration from Nauvoo began. The same day the ship *Brooklyn* left New York for California under the direction of Samuel Brannan.

April 24 — A temporary settlement of the westward-moving Saints was established at Garden Grove, Iowa. Other camps were established at Mount Pisgah, Iowa, on May 16; at Kanesville (Council Bluffs), Iowa, on June 14; and at Winter Quarters, Neb., in September.

May 1 — The Nauvoo Temple was dedicated in public services by Apostle Orson Hyde

July 13 — The first of the volunteer companies of the Mormon Battalion was enlisted in response to a request delivered to Brigham Young two weeks earlier by Capt. James Allen of the United States Army. The battalion left Kanesville, Iowa, for Fort Leavenworth, Kan., on July 20.

July 31 — The ship *Brooklyn* arrived in Yerba Buena (now San Francisco), California.

Sept. 17 — The remaining Saints in Nauvoo were driven from the city in violation of a "treaty of surrender" worked out with a citizens' committee from Quincy, Ill. The siege became known as the Battle of Nauvoo.

1847

Jan. 14 — Brigham Young presented "the word and will of the Lord" (see D&C 136) concerning the westward trek, including the pattern for organizing the wagon companies and the conduct of the participants, based on gospel principles.

Jan. 27 — The Mormon Battalion, completing its march across the Southwest, arrived at San Luis Rey, Calif., near San Diego, within view of the Pacific Ocean.

April 5 — The first pioneer company, numbering 143 men, 3 women and 2 children, left Winter Quarters, Neb., for the West, under the leadership of Brigham Young.

July 16 — Members of the Mormon Battalion were discharged at Los Angeles, Calif.

July 22-24 — Brigham Young's pioneer company arrived in the Great Salt Lake Valley. Eleven companies arrived in the valley in 1847.

July 28 — Brigham Young selected a site for the Salt Lake Temple and instructed surveyors to lay out a city on a grid pattern aligned to the compass.

Dec. 5 — The First Presidency was reorganized by the Quorum of the Twelve in Kanesville, Iowa, with Brigham Young sustained as president, and Heber C. Kimball and Willard Richards as counselors.

1848

Jan. 24 — Nine members of the discharged Mormon Battalion

were at Sutter's Mill in California when gold was discovered. The millrace, or canal to the millwheel, was dug by members of the battalion. Battalion member Henry Bigler was given credit for recording in his journal the date of discovery .

May — Millions of crickets descended into Salt Lake Valley and devoured the crops of the pioneers. The "miracle of the sea gulls" saved what was left of the crops by devouring the crickets.

Aug. 13 — A conference in Manchester, England, was attended by more than 17,000 members of the British Mission.

1849 **Jan. 1** — The first $1 denomination of "valley currency" was issued and signed by Brigham Young, Heber C. Kimball and Thomas Bullock. It was the first printing in the Salt Lake Valley.

Feb. 14 — Great Salt Lake City was divided into 19 wards of nine blocks each.

March 5 — A provisional State of Deseret was established and appeals were made to the federal government for self-government.

October — A Perpetual Emigrating Fund to assist the poor to immigrate to the Salt Lake Valley was established during general conference. The system, which was incorporated a year later, continued until it was disincorporated by the Edmunds-Tucker Act in 1887.

Dec. 9 — The Sunday School was started by Richard Ballantyne in Salt Lake City. George Q. Cannon became the first general superintendent in November 1867.

1850 Missionary work took on a wider scope as missions were opened overseas in Scandinavia, France, Italy, Switzerland and Hawaii; most, however, were discontinued after a few years.

June 15 — The first edition of the *Deseret News* was published in Salt Lake City.

1851 **Jan. 26** — The second stake in the Church and the first outside the Salt Lake Valley — since the pioneers arrived in Utah — was the Weber Stake, created by Brigham Young with headquarters in Ogden. Within the next six months, two other stakes were created, in Provo, Utah, on March 19, and in San Bernardino, Calif., on July 6.

March 24 — A company of 500 settlers called to settle in California departed from Payson, Utah. The group settled in San Bernardino,

Calif., which became the first Mormon colony outside the Great Basin since the arrival of the pioneers in 1847.

May — The Book of Mormon was published in Copenhagen, Denmark, in Danish, the first language other than English in which the book was printed.

Nov. 11 — The University of the State of Deseret (now the University of Utah) in Salt Lake City was begun.

1852 During the year, areas that were opened up to missionary work included India, China, Siam, Cape of Good Hope, Prussia, Gilbraltar and the West Indies.

April 6 — An adobe tabernacle, built on the southwest corner of the Temple Block where the Assembly Hall now stands, was dedicated.

Aug. 28-29 — At a special conference in Salt Lake City, the doctrine of plural marriage was first publicly announced, although several of the leading brethren of the Church had been practicing the principle privately since it had been taught to them by Joseph Smith.

Oct. 9 — Members, meeting in conference in the tabernacle, unanimously voted to build the Salt Lake Temple.

1853 **Feb. 14** — President Brigham Young broke ground for the Salt Lake Temple and President Heber C. Kimball dedicated the site. Excavation began that day.

April 6 — The four cornerstones of the Salt Lake Temple were laid.

July 18 — The so-called "Walker War" began near Payson, Utah. This was one of several incidents of tension between Mormons and Indians in the Utah Territory. The war ended in May 1854.

1854 **Jan. 19** — The official announcement adopting the Deseret Alphabet was made in the *Deseret News*.

Dec. 31 — It was reported that 32,627 members lived in countries comprising the European missions, of which 29,441 were in Great Britain.

1855 **May 5** — The two-story adobe Endowment House in Salt Lake City was dedicated and remained in use until 1889, when it was torn down.

July 23 — The foundation of the Salt Lake Temple was finished.

Oct. 4 — The bark *Julia Ann* carrying 28 emigrating Church members from Australia ran aground on shoals near the Scilly Islands. Five were drowned.

Oct. 29 — In a general epistle, the First Presidency proposed that Perpetual Emigrating Fund immigrants cross the plains by handcart.

1856 During the year, a general "reformation" took place throughout the Church, in which Church members were admonished strongly from the pulpit to reform their lives and rededicate themselves to the service of the Lord. As a symbol of renewed dedication, many members renewed their covenants by rebaptism. The reformation movement continued into 1857.

June 9 — The first handcart company left Iowa City, Iowa. Later that year, two handcart companies, captained by James G. Willie and Edward Martin, suffered tragedy due to an early winter. More than 200 in the two companies died along the trail.

1857 March 30 — Territorial Judge W.W. Drummond, who had earlier left the Territory of Utah, wrote a letter to the Attorney General of the United States, charging Mormon leaders with various crimes.

May 13 — Elder Parley P. Pratt of the Quorum of the Twelve was assassinated while on a mission in Arkansas.

May 28 — Under instructions from President James Buchanan, the United States War Department issued orders for an army to assemble at Fort Leavenworth, Kan., to march to Utah. It was assumed that the people of Utah were in rebellion against the United States. This was the beginning of the so-called "Utah War."

July 24 — While participating in the 10th anniversary celebration in Big Cottonwood Canyon of the arrival of the Pioneers, Brigham Young received word that the army, under the command of Col. Albert S. Johnston, was approaching Utah.

Sept. 7-11 — The Mountain Meadows Massacre took place, in which Arkansas immigrants on their way to California were killed in Southern Utah. Twenty years later John D. Lee was executed for his part in the crime.

Sept. 15 — Brigham Young declared Utah to be under martial law and forbade the approaching troops to enter the Salt Lake Valley. An armed militia was ordered to go to various points to harass the soldiers and prevent their entry. Brigham Young also called the elders home from foreign missions and advised the Saints in many outlying settlements in the West

to return to places nearer the headquarters of the Church.

1858 Feb. 24 — Col. Thomas L. Kane, a friend of the Mormons, voluntarily arrived in Salt Lake City to try to bring about a peaceful solution to the difficulties between the federal government and the Church. After meeting with President Brigham Young, he went to Ft. Scott (near Ft. Bridger) in Wyoming and met with the incoming governor of Utah, Alfred Cummings.

June 26 — After having been stopped for the winter by the delaying tactics of the Mormons, Col. Johnston's army finally — and peacefully — entered the Salt Lake Valley. The army's encampment, until 1861, was at Camp Floyd in Cedar Valley in Utah County. Most of the Saints north of Utah County had moved south, and they only returned to their homes when peace seemed assured.

Aug. 5 — *The first transatlantic telegraph cable was completed between the United States and Great Britain.*

1859 July 13 — Horace Greeley, founder and editor of the *New York Tribune*, had a two-hour interview with President Brigham Young, covering a variety of subjects from infant baptism to plurality of wives. The substance of his interview was published a year later in Greeley's *Overland Journey from New York to San Francisco.*

1860 April 3 — The Pony Express mail service began. A number of young Mormons were among the riders.

Sept. 16 — At a meeting in the bowery on the Temple Block, President Brigham Young condemned the practice of missionaries asking members in the mission field for support and, instead, said that missionary service should be financed by members at home.

Sept. 24 — The last of 10 groups of pioneers to cross the plains by handcarts arrived in Salt Lake City.

1861 March 2 — A bill was approved by U.S. President James Buchanan that provided for the organization of the Nevada Territory out of the western portions of Utah.

April 12 — *The Civil War began as Confederate forces fired on Ft. Sumpter in South Carolina.*

April 23 — The first of several Church wagon trains left the Salt Lake Valley with provisions for incoming Saints, whom they would meet at the

Missouri River. This was the beginning of a new program to help immigrating Saints that lasted until the railroad came in 1869.

Oct. 1 — The first baptisms in the Netherlands took place near the village of Broek-Akkerwoude in the northern province of Friesland. A monument marking the site was erected in 1936.

Oct. 18 — President Brigham Young sent the first telegram over the just-completed overland telegraph line.

1862 March 6 — The Salt Lake Theater, which became an important cultural center for Mormon people in the area, was dedicated. It was opened to the public two days later.

May — The Church sent 262 wagons, 292 men, 2,880 oxen and 143,315 pounds of flour to the Missouri River to assist poor immigrants from Europe on their trek to the Great Basin.

July 8 — A federal law was passed and approved by President Abraham Lincoln, defining plural marriage as bigamy and declaring it a crime. Mormons considered the law unconstitutional and refused to honor it.

1863 March 10 — President Brigham Young was arrested on a charge of bigamy and placed under a $2,000 bond by Judge Kinney. He was never brought to trial, however.

1864 April 5 — A small group of Saints bound for Utah sailed from Port Elizabeth, South Africa. Five days later another group set sail for Utah from South Africa.

1865 A war with the Indians began in central Utah, known as the Black Hawk War. It lasted until 1867.

Jan. 18 — Orson Pratt and William W. Ritter arrived in Austria. They were soon banished.

Feb. 1 — *Abraham Lincoln signed the document abolishing slavery in the United States. After ratification by 27 states. The measure became the 13th Amendment to the Constitution on Dec. 18, 1865.*

April 10 — In a special conference, the Church agreed to build a telegraph line connecting the settlements in Utah. The line was completed in 1867.

April 14 — *U.S. President Abraham Lincoln was assassinated by John Wilkes Booth in Ford's Theatre in Washington, D.C., while watching a performance of "Our American Cousin."*

1866 Jan. 1 — The first edition of the *Juvenile Instructor*, the official organ of the Sunday School, was published. Its name was changed to the *Instructor* in 1930, and it continued publication until 1970.

1867 Oct. 6 — The first conference to be conducted in the newly completed Tabernacle on Temple Square in Salt Lake City began. The building was dedicated eight years later on Oct. 9, 1875.

Dec. 8 — Brigham Young requested that bishops reorganize Relief Societies within their wards. The societies had been disbanded during the Utah War.

1868 Jan. 29 — The name Great Salt Lake City was changed to simply Salt Lake City.

1869 March 1 — The Church-owned ZCMI opened for business. It was the forerunner of several cooperative business ventures in Utah territory.

May 10 — The transcontinental railroad was completed with the joining of the rails at Promontory Summit, Utah. The railroad had great impact on immigration policy and on the general economy of the Church in Utah.

Nov. 28 — The Young Ladies' Retrenchment Association, later renamed the Young Women's Mutual Improvement Association, was organized by Brigham Young in the Lion House in Salt Lake City. The first president, called June 19, 1880, was Elmina Shepherd Taylor. This was the forerunner of today's Young Women organization.

1870 Jan. 13 — A large mass meeting was held by the women of Salt Lake City in protest against certain anti-Mormon legislation pending in Congress. This and other such meetings demonstrated that, contrary to anti-Mormon claims, Mormon women were not antagonistic to the ecclesiastical leadership in Utah.

February — The "Liberal Party" was formed in Utah, which generally came to represent the anti-Mormon political interests, as opposed to the "People's Party," which generally represented Church interests until the end of the 19th century.

Feb. 12 — An act of the Territorial Legislature giving the elective franchise to the women of Utah was signed into law. Utah became one of the first American states or territories to grant women the right to vote.

1871 February — Judge James B. McKean, who had arrived in Utah in August 1870, made several rulings that began a bitter and antagonistic relationship between himself and Church members.

Oct. 2 — President Brigham Young was arrested on a charge of unlawful cohabitation. Various legal proceedings in the court of Judge James B. McKean lasted until April 25, 1872, during which time President Young was sometimes kept in custody in his own home. The case was dropped, however, due to a U.S. Supreme Court decision that overturned various judicial proceedings in Utah for the previous 18 months.

1872 June — The first issue of the *Woman's Exponent*, a paper owned and edited by Mormon women, was published. This periodical continued until 1914.

1873 April 8 — Due to failing health, President Brigham Young called five additional counselors in the First Presidency.

1874 May 9 — At general conference, which began on this date, the principal subject discussed was the "United Order." This resulted in the establishment of several cooperative economic ventures, the most notable of which were communities such as Orderville, Utah, where the residents owned no private property but held all property in common.

June 23 — The Poland Bill became a federal law. It had the effect of limiting the jurisdiction of probate courts in Utah. These courts had been authorized to conduct all civil and criminal cases and were generally favorable toward members of the Church, but now Mormons accused of crimes had to be tried in federal courts.

1875 March 18 — Judge James B. McKean, with whom the Mormons had been unhappy, was removed from office by U.S. President Ulysses S. Grant.

June 10 — The first Young Men's Mutual Improvement Association was organized in the Thirteenth Ward in Salt Lake City. On Dec. 8, 1876, a central committee was formed to coordinate all such associations. Junius F. Wells was the first superintendent. This was the forerunner of today's Young Men organization.

Oct. 16 — Brigham Young Academy, later to become Brigham Young University, was founded in Provo, Utah.

1876 March 7 — *The patent was issued for Alexander Graham Bell's telephone.*

March 23 — Advance companies of Saints from Utah who were called to settle in Arizona arrived at the Little Colorado. This was the beginning of Mormon colonization in Arizona.

1877 April 6 — The St. George Temple was dedicated by President Daniel H. Wells in connection with the 47th Annual Conference of the Church that was held in St. George. This was the first temple to be completed in Utah. The lower portion of the temple had been dedicated earlier, on Jan. 1, 1877, and ordinances for the dead had commenced.

Aug. 29 — President Brigham Young died at his home in Salt Lake City at age 76.

Sept. 4 — The Quorum of the Twelve, with John Taylor as president, publicly assumed its position as the head of the Church.

1878 May 19 — The Church had previously provided for the purchase of land in Conejos County, Colo., for settlements of Saints from the Southern States. On this date the first settlers arrived, thus opening Mormon settlements in Colorado.

Aug. 25 — The Primary, founded by Aurelia Rogers, held its first meeting at Farmington, Utah. The movement spread rapidly and on June 19, 1880, a Churchwide organization was established, with Louie B. Felt as the first president.

1879 Jan. 6 — The Supreme Court of the United States, in the important Reynolds case, upheld the previous conviction of George Reynolds under the 1862 anti-bigamy law. With the ruling, the court paved the way for more intense and effective prosecution of the Mormons in the 1880s.

Oct. 4 — The first edition of the *Contributor*, which became the official publication of the Young Men's Mutual Improvement Association, was issued. It was published until 1896.

Oct. 21 — *Thomas Edison tested an electric incandescent light bulb in Menlo Park, N.J., that burned for 13 1/2 hours, marking the beginning of a new era of electric lighting.*

1880 April 6 — At general conference, a special jubilee year celebration was inaugurated. Charitable actions, reminiscent of Old Testament jubilee celebrations, included rescinding half the debt owed to the Perpetual Emigrating Fund Company, distribution of cows and sheep among the needy, and advice to the Saints to forgive the worthy poor of their debts.

Oct. 10 — The First Presidency was reorganized with President John Taylor sustained as third president of the Church, with Presidents George Q. Cannon and Joseph F. Smith as counselors.

1881 Oct. 18 — Ngataki was the first Maori baptized in New Zealand.

1882 Jan. 8 — The Assembly Hall on Temple Square in Salt Lake City, completed in 1880 from left-over stones from the Salt Lake Temple construction, was dedicated.

March 22 — The Edmunds Anti-Polygamy bill became law when U.S. President Chester A. Arthur added his approval to that of the Senate and House of Representatives. Serious prosecution under this law began in 1884.

July 17 — The Deseret Hospital, the second hospital in Utah and the first Church hospital, was opened by the Relief Society in Salt Lake City.

Aug. 18 — The Utah Commission, authorized in the Edmunds law, arrived in the territory. The five members of the commission, appointed by the U.S. president, had responsibility of supervising election procedures in Utah. Since the result of its activities was to enforce the disenfranchisement of much of the Mormon population, Church members considered its work unfair.

1883 June 21 — The Council House, the first public building erected in Salt Lake City, was destroyed by fire. The structure was completed in December 1850 and was designed as a "general council house" for the Church, but was also used by the provisional State of Deseret as a statehouse. It also housed the University of Deseret for a number of years.

Aug. 26 — The first permanent branch of the Church among the Maoris in New Zealand was organized at Papawai, Wairarapa Valley, on the North Island.

Dec. 26 — Thomas L. Kane, long a friend of the Church and a champion for Mormon people, died in Philadelphia, Pa.

1884 May 17 — The Logan Temple, the second temple constructed after the Saints came west, was dedicated by President John Taylor.

June 9 — The building known as the "Cock Pit," in Preston, England, in which the first Mormon missionaries to England held meetings in 1837, tumbled down.

1885 Extensive prosecution under the Edmunds Law continued in both Utah and Idaho. Many who practiced polygamy were imprisoned, while others fled into exile, some to Mexico in 1885 and to Canada in 1887. Many Church leaders involved in plural marriage went into hiding, which was referred to as the "underground." Similar conditions continued for the next few years. These years are sometimes called the years of the "Crusade."

Feb. 1 — President John Taylor delivered his last public sermon in the Tabernacle in Salt Lake City. It was also his last appearance in public before he went to the "underground."

Feb. 3 — An Idaho law was approved by the governor that prohibited all Mormons from voting through the device of a "test oath." The Idaho "test oath" was upheld five years later by the U.S. Supreme Court on Feb. 3, 1890.

March 22 — The U.S. Supreme Court annulled the "test oath" formulated by the Utah Commission, thus restoring the right to vote to Saints in the territory.

May 13 — A delegation, appointed by a mass meeting held in the Tabernacle in Salt Lake City on May 2, met with U.S. President Grover Cleveland in the White House in Washington, D.C. They presented to the president a "Statement of Grievances and Protest" concerning injustices brought about because of the Edmunds law.

1886 Jan. 31 — The first Church meeting was held in the first meetinghouse built in Mexico on the Piedras Verdes River in the settlement of Colonia Juarez in northern Mexico.

March 6 — A mass meeting of 2,000 LDS women assembled in the Salt Lake Theater to protest the abuse heaped upon them by the federal courts and to protest the loss of their vote.

Oct. 28 — *The Statue of Liberty, a gift from the French people symbolizing the friendship between the United States and France, was dedicated in New York Harbor.*

1887 Feb. 17-18 — The Edmunds-Tucker Act passed Congress, and it became law without the signature of U.S. President Grover Cleveland. Among other stringent provisions, the law disincorporated the Church, dissolved the Perpetual Emigrating Fund Company and escheated its property to the government, abolished female suffrage, and provided for the confiscation of practically all the property of the Church.

June 3 — Charles O. Card, leading a contingent of eight families, pitched camp on Lee's Creek in southern Alberta, marking the beginning of the Mormon settlements in Canada. Under instructions from President John Taylor, a gathering place for Latter-day Saints in Canada was selected, and on June 17 a site was chosen for what later became Cardston.

July 25 — President John Taylor died while in "exile" at Kaysville, Utah, at age 78. The Quorum of Twelve Apostles assumed leadership of the Church until 1889.

July 30 — Under provisions of the Edmunds-Tucker Act, suits were filed against the Church and the Perpetual Emigrating Fund Company, and Church property was confiscated. A receiver for the property was appointed in November 1887, but the government allowed the Church to rent and occupy certain offices and the temple block.

1888 May 17 — The Manti Temple was dedicated in a private service by President Wilford Woodruff of the Quorum of the Twelve; a public service was held May 21.

June 8 — The Church General Board of Education sent a letter instructing each stake to establish an academy for secondary education. From 1888 to 1909, 35 academies were established in Utah, Idaho, Wyoming, Arizona, Mexico and Canada. The academy in Rexburg, Idaho, later became Ricks College and then BYU-Idaho.

1889 April 6 — The first Relief Society general conference was held in the Assembly Hall in Salt Lake City. Twenty stakes were represented.

April 7 — President Wilford Woodruff was sustained as fourth president of the Church, with Presidents George Q. Cannon and Joseph F. Smith as counselors.

October — The *Young Woman's Journal*, official organ of the Young Ladies' Mutual Improvement Association, began publication. It was merged with the *Improvement Era* in 1929.

November — The Endowment House in Salt Lake City was torn down.

1890 Sept. 24 — President Wilford Woodruff issued the "Manifesto," now included in the Doctrine and Covenants as Official Declaration — 1, that declared that no new plural marriages had been entered into with Church approval in the past year, denied that plural marriage had been taught during that time, declared the intent of the president of the Church to submit to the constitutional law of the land, and advised members of the Church to refrain from contracting any marriage forbidden by law.

Oct. 6 — The "Manifesto" was unanimously accepted by vote in general conference. This marked the beginning of reconciliation between the Church and the United States, which effectively paved the way to statehood for Utah a little more than five years later.

Oct. 25 — The First Presidency sent a letter to stake presidents and bishops directing that a week-day religious education program be established in every ward where there was not a Church school. It was recommended that classes be taught, under the direction of the Church's General Board of Education, after school hours or on Saturdays .

1891 March — At the first triennial meeting of the National Council of Women of the United States, the Relief Society attended and became a charter member of that council.

1892 Jan. 4 — The new Brigham Young Academy building at Provo, Utah, was dedicated.

Oct. 12 — Articles of incorporation for the Relief Society were filed, after which it became known as the National Women's Relief Society. The name was again changed in 1945 to Relief Society of The Church of Jesus Christ of Latter-day Saints.

1893 Jan. 4 — The President of the United States, Benjamin Harrison, issued a proclamation of amnesty to all polygamists who had entered into that relationship before Nov. 1, 1890. The Utah Commission soon ruled that voting restrictions in the territory should be removed.

April 6 — The Salt Lake Temple was dedicated by President Wilford Woodruff. The dedicatory services were repeated almost daily until April 24 with a total of 31 services held.

May 23 — The first ordinance work, baptisms for the dead, was performed in the Salt Lake Temple. On May 24, the first endowment work and sealings were performed.

Sept. 8 — The Salt Lake Tabernacle Choir, while competing in the choral contest at the Chicago World's Fair, won second prize ($1,000). While on this tour, the choir also held concerts at Denver, Colo.; Independence, Kansas City and St. Louis, Mo.; and Omaha, Neb. The First Presidency, consisting of Wilford Woodruff, George Q. Cannon and Joseph F. Smith, accompanied the choir.

Oct. 25 — President Grover Cleveland signed a resolution, passed by Congress, for the return of the personal property of the Church. Three years later, on March 28, 1896, a memorial passed by Congress and approved by the president provided for the restoration of the Church's real estate.

1894 **January** — *The railroad age continued with railroad building by far the nation's single largest economic enterprise.*

April — President Wilford Woodruff announced in general conference that he had received a revelation that ended the law of adoption. The law of adoption was the custom of being sealed to prominent Church leaders instead of direct ancestors. He re-emphasized the need for genealogical research and sealings along natural family lines. With the termination of this type of sealings, genealogical work to trace direct ancestry increased among the members of the Church.

July 14 — President Grover Cleveland signed an act that provided for statehood for Utah. This culminated 47 years of effort on the part of Mormons in Utah to achieve this status.

Aug. 27 — President Grover Cleveland issued a proclamation granting pardons and restoring civil rights to those who had been disfranchised under anti-polygamy laws.

Nov. 13 — The genealogical society of the Church, known as the Genealogical Society of Utah, was organized.

1895 **March 4** — The Utah Constitutional Convention met in Salt Lake City. John Henry Smith, a member of the Quorum of the Twelve, was elected president of that convention.

June 9 — The first stake outside the United States was created in Canada in Cardston, Alberta.

June 11 — Johan and Alma Lindelof were baptized in St. Petersburg, Russia.

Nov. 5 — By a vote of 31,305 to 7,687, the people of Utah ratified the constitution and approved statehood. The documents were later hand-delivered to President Grover Cleveland.

Dec. 9 — The first stake in Mexico, the Juarez Stake, was organized in the English-speaking Mormon colonies in northern Mexico.

1896 **Jan. 4** — President Grover Cleveland signed the proclamation that admitted Utah to the Union as the 45th state. Until statehood, the affairs of the Church in the Utah Territory had been closely associated with the affairs of the civil government. With statehood and the rights of self-government secured to the people, the Church could become separate from political struggles.

Nov. 5 — The First Presidency issued a formal letter of instruction directing that the first Sunday in each month be observed as fast day, rather than the first Thursday, which had been observed as fast day since the early days of the Church in the Utah Territory.

1897 **June 4** — Historian Andrew Jenson returned to Salt Lake City after circling the world obtaining information for Church history.

July 20-25 — The jubilee anniversary of the arrival of the Pioneers into the Salt Lake Valley was held in Salt Lake City for six days. The celebration began with the dedication by President Wilford Woodruff of the Brigham Young statue that would later stand at the intersection of Main and South Temple streets on July 20, and ended with a celebration for the Pioneers in the Tabernacle on July 24 and memorial services honoring all deceased Pioneers on July 25.

November — The *Improvement Era* began publication as the official organ of the Young Men's Mutual Improvement Association. Other Church organizations later joined in sponsoring the monthly magazine, which continued as the official voice of the Church until 1970. It was replaced by the *Ensign* magazine.

1898 **Jan. 24** — Four aged members of the Mormon Battalion took part in the 50th anniversary of the discovery of gold in California, which they had witnessed.

April 1 — Sisters Inez Knight and Lucy Brimhall were set apart to be missionaries in England, the first single, official, proselyting sister missionaries in the Church.

April 28 — A First Presidency statement

encouraged Latter-day Saint youth to support the American effort in the Spanish-American War. This placed the Church firmly on the side of the war declarations of constituted governments and ended a policy of selective pacifism.

Sept. 2 — President Wilford Woodruff died at age 91 in San Francisco, Calif., where he had gone to seek relief from his asthma problems.

Sept. 13 —President Lorenzo Snow became fifth president of the Church. He chose Presidents George Q. Cannon and Joseph F. Smith as counselors. Both had served as counselors to President Brigham Young, President John Taylor and President Wilford Woodruff.

Oct. 15 — President Lorenzo Snow announced that the Church would issue bonds to lighten the burden of its indebtedness.

1899 **May 8** — President Lorenzo Snow announced a renewed emphasis concerning the payment of tithing, which members had been neglecting for some time, at a conference in St. George, Utah.

July 2 — A solemn assembly was held in the Salt Lake Temple, attended by the Church's 26 General Authorities, presidencies of the 40 stakes, and bishops of the 478 wards of the Church. The assembly accepted the resolution that tithing is the "word and will of the Lord unto us."

Aug. 19 — Utah volunteers serving in the Philippines in the Spanish-American War returned to an enthusiastic reception from the citizens.

1900 **Jan. 8** — President Lorenzo Snow issued an official statement reaffirming the Church's ban on polygamy.

Jan. 21, 28 — The mammoth Salt Lake Stake, comprised of 55 wards throughout the Salt Lake Valley, was divided and the Jordan and Granite stakes were created. It was the first stake division in the valley since the stake was created in 1847.

Jan. 25 — The U.S. House of Representatives voted to deny Utahn B.H. Roberts of the First Council of the Seventy his seat in Congress, following an investigation of the right of polygamists to hold office under the Constitution.

July 24 — Final unveiling of Brigham Young Monument at South Temple and Main in Salt Lake City was held.

1901 **May 4** — Reconstruction of the Tabernacle organ was completed by the Kimball Organ Co., making the instrument one of the finest pipe organs in the world.

Aug. 12 — Elder Heber J. Grant of the Quorum of the Twelve dedicated Japan and opened a mission there as a first step in renewed emphasis on preaching the gospel in all the world.

Oct. 10 — President Lorenzo Snow died at his home in the Beehive House in Salt Lake City at age 87.

Oct. 17 — President Joseph F. Smith was ordained and set apart as the sixth president of the Church, with Presidents John R. Winder and Anthon H. Lund as counselors. They were sustained by Church members at a special conference on Nov. 10.

1902 The Church published in book form the first volume of Joseph Smith's *History of the Church,* edited by B.H. Roberts. Publication continued over the next decades, with a seventh volume added in 1932.

January — The *Children's Friend* began publication for Primary Association teachers. The magazine later widened its audience to include children, then eliminated the teachers' departments. It was published until 1970 when it was replaced by the *Friend* magazine.

Aug. 4 — The First Council of the Seventy opened a Bureau of Information and Church Literature in a small octagonal booth on Temple Square. It was replaced by a larger building in March 1904 and by the present visitors centers in 1966 and 1978.

1903 **Nov. 5** — The Carthage Jail was purchased by the Church as a historic site for $4,000.

Dec. 17 — *Orville and Wilbur Wright became the first men to fly when they managed to get their powered airplane off the ground near Kitty Hawk, N.C., for 12 seconds. They made four flights that day, the longest lasting for 59 seconds.*

1904 **April 5** — President Joseph F. Smith issued an official statement upholding provisions of the 1890 Manifesto and invoking excommunication against persons violating the "law of the land" by contracting new plural marriages.

1905 **Jan. 1** — The Dr. William H. Groves Latter-day Saints

Hospital opened in Salt Lake City and was dedicated three days later, the first in the Church hospital system. In 1975 the Church divested itself of its hospitals and turned them over to a private organization.

Oct. 28 — Elders John W. Taylor and Matthias F. Cowley, finding themselves out of harmony with Church policy on plural marriage, submitted resignations from the Quorum of the Twelve that were announced to the Church April 6, 1906.

Dec. 23 — President Joseph F. Smith dedicated the Joseph Smith Memorial Cottage and Monument at Sharon, Windsor County, Vt., the site of the Prophet's birth 100 years earlier. The property had been purchased by the Church earlier in the year.

1906 The Sunday School introduced a Churchwide parents' class as part of an increased emphasis on the importance of the home and of the parents' role in teaching their children the gospel.

Summer — President Joseph F. Smith traveled to Europe, the first such visit of a Church president to the area. President Smith also visited Hawaii, Canada and Mexico during his presidency.

1907 The Church purchased the 100-acre Smith farm near Palmyra, N.Y., including the Sacred Grove.

Jan. 10 — President Joseph F. Smith announced that the Church was entirely free of debt, with the payment of the last two $500,000 bond issues sold by President Lorenzo Snow in December 1899 to fund the debt. The first had been paid in 1903. Retiring the debt was largely due to the renewed emphasis in the Church on tithing.

February — The United States Senate agreed to seat Utah Sen. Reed Smoot, a member of the Quorum of the Twelve, who was elected and sworn in March 5, 1903. The vote culminated a three-year investigation, during which Church officials testified concerning polygamy and Church involvement in politics.

April 5 — A vote of the general conference approved the First Presidency's 16-page summary statement of the Church position in the Smoot hearings.

Dec. 14 — The First Presidency issued the first of four letters to urge European members to not immigrate to the United States, but to remain and build up the Church in their own countries. Subsequent letters urging members not to

immigrate were issued April 28, 1921, Aug. 2, 1921, and Oct. 18, 1929.

1908 Presiding Bishop Charles W. Nibley moved the Church to an all-cash basis and no longer issued tithing scrip.

April 8 — The First Presidency created a General Priesthood Committee on Outlines, which served until 1922. The committee created definite age groupings for priesthood offices (deacons at 12, teachers at 15, priests at 18, and elders at 21), provided systematic programs for year-round priesthood meetings, and in other ways reformed, reactivated and systematized priesthood work.

Oct. 1 — *Henry Ford introduced his famous Model-T Ford automobile.*

1909 **April 6** — *The North Pole was discovered by an expedition led by Robert E. Peary.*

Sept. 26 — U.S. President William Howard Taft visited Salt Lake City en route to California and spoke in the Tabernacle.

November — As the debate on Darwinism and evolution continued in the national press, the First Presidency issued an official statement on the origin of man.

1910 The Bishop's Building, an office building for the Presiding Bishopric and auxiliary organizations of the Church at 50 N. Main St., opened. It was used for more than 50 years.

January — The first issue of the *Utah Genealogical and Historical Magazine* was published. This quarterly publication served as the voice of the Genealogical Society of Utah. It was discontinued in October 1940.

1911 The Church adopted the Boy Scout program and has since become one of the leading sponsors of this organization for young men.

April 15 — *Collier's* magazine published a letter from Theodore Roosevelt refuting many charges made against Utah Sen. Reed Smoot and the Church. This action helped defuse an anti-Mormon propaganda surge of 1910-11.

1912 The Church colonists in northern Mexico exited the country due to unsettled conditions during the revolution.

September — The Church's first seminary began at Granite High School in Salt Lake City, marking the beginning of a released-time weekday education program for young Latter-day Saints. As the seminary program grew, the Church phased out its involvement in academies, which were Church-sponsored high schools or junior colleges. By 1924, only the Juarez Academy in Mexico remained.

Nov. 8 — The First Presidency created a Correlation Committee, headed by Elder David O. McKay of the Quorum of the Twelve, and asked it to coordinate scheduling and prevent unnecessary duplication in programs of Church auxiliaries.

1913 The Church established the Maori Agricultural College in New Zealand. It was destroyed by an earthquake in 1931 and was never rebuilt.

May 21 — The Boy Scout program was officially adopted by the Young Men's Mutual Improvement Association and became the activity program for boys of the Church.

1914 January — The *Relief Society Magazine* appeared as a monthly publication containing lesson material for use in the women's auxiliary of the Church. The magazine carried stories, poetry, articles, homemaking helps, news and lesson material until it ceased publication in December 1970, when the *Ensign* magazine became the magazine for adults in the Church.

Dec. 19 — Under the pall of war, missionaries were removed from France, Germany, Switzerland and Belgium, prior to World War I.

1915 April 27 — The First Presidency inaugurated the "Home Evening" program, inviting all families to participate.

September — James E. Talmage's influential book *Jesus the Christ* was published.

Fall — The first college classes were taught at Ricks College, which had been Ricks Academy.

1916 Feb. 21 — *The longest and bloodiest battle of World War I, the Battle of Verdun, began in France, resulting in the death of 1 million soldiers.*

June 30 — The First Presidency and Quorum of the Twelve issued a doctrinal exposition clarifying the use of the title "Father" as it is applied to Jesus Christ.

1917 April 6 — On the opening day of the 87th Annual General Conference of the Church, the United States entered World War I as it declared war against Germany.

Oct. 2 — The Church Administration Building at 47 E. South Temple was completed.

1918 May — To alleviate shortages during World War I, the Relief Society, which had been gathering and storing wheat since 1876, sold 205,518 bushels of wheat to the U.S. government at a government price, with approval of the First Presidency and the Presiding Bishopric.

Oct. 3 — While contemplating the meaning of Christ's atonement, President Joseph F. Smith received a manifestation on the salvation of the dead and the visit of the Savior to the spirit world after His crucifixion. A report of the experience was published in December and was added first to the Pearl of Great Price and then to the Doctrine and Covenants June 6, 1979, as Section 138.

Nov. 11 — *World War I ended, as Germany signed an armistice with the Allies.*

Nov. 19 — President Joseph F. Smith died six days after his 80th birthday. Because of an epidemic of influenza, no public funeral was held for the Church president.

Nov. 23 — President Heber J. Grant was ordained and set apart as the seventh president of the Church during a meeting of the Twelve in the Salt Lake Temple. He selected Presidents Anthon H. Lund and Charles W. Penrose as counselors.

1919 April — The April general conference of the Church was postponed due to the nationwide influenza epidemic. The conference was held June 1-3.

Oct. 10 — King Albert and Queen Elizabeth of Belgium attended a recital on Temple Square in Salt Lake City to hear the Tabernacle organ.

Nov. 27 — President Heber J. Grant dedicated the temple at Laie, Hawaii, the first temple outside the continental United States. Construction had begun soon after the site was dedicated in June 1915.

1920 In response to Church growth and need for a more cost-effective use of building funds, an "authentic form of LDS architecture" was developed. that structurally joined the previously separate chapel and classrooms with the recreational or cultural hall through a connecting foyer/office/classroom complex.

1921 Elder David O. McKay of the Quorum of the Twelve and President Hugh J. Cannon of the Liberty Stake in Salt Lake City traveled 55,896 miles in a world survey of Church missions for the First Presidency. The pair visited the Saints in the Pacific Islands, New Zealand, Australia and Asia and then made stops in India, Egypt, and Palestine before visiting the missions of Europe.

1922 May — Primary Children's Hospital opened in Salt Lake City.

1923 The Church purchased a part of the Hill Cumorah. Additional acquisitions in 1928 gave the Church possession of the entire hill and adjacent lands.

Jan. 21 — The first stake outside the traditional Mormon cultural area was created in Los Angeles, Calif.

Aug. 26 — President Heber J. Grant dedicated the Alberta Temple in Cardston, Alberta, Canada, which had been under construction for nearly a decade.

1924 March 21 — A First Presidency statement answered criticism of unauthorized plural marriages by once again confirming the Church's policy against the practice. Polygamists within the Church were excommunicated when discovered.

Oct. 3 — Radio broadcast of general conference began on KSL in Salt Lake City, the Church-owned station. Coverage was expanded into Idaho in 1941.

1925 Feb. 3 — President Heber J. Grant dedicated a remodeled home at 31 N. State St. in Salt Lake City as the Church's missionary home, offering the first organized training for missionaries in gospel topics, Church procedures, personal health and proper manners.

July 24 — *In the famous "Scopes Monkey Trial," John T. Scopes, a Tennessee school teacher, was found guilty of teaching evolution in a public school.*

September — The First Presidency issued a statement, " 'Mormon' View of Evolution," which, in part, stated: "The Church of Jesus Christ of Latter-day Saints, basing its belief on divine revelation, ancient and modern, declares man to be the direct and lineal offspring of Deity."

Dec. 6 — Elder Melvin J. Ballard of the Quorum of the Twelve established a mission in South America with headquarters in Buenos Aires, Argentina, opening the Church's official work in South America, which he dedicated for the preaching of the gospel on Dec. 25.

1927 May 21 — *Charles Lindbergh, aboard his "Spirit of St. Louis" monoplane, completed the first transatlantic solo flight from New York City to Paris, a distance of 3,610 miles, in 33 1/2 hours.*

Oct. 23 — President Heber J. Grant dedicated the Arizona Temple at Mesa, completing a project begun six years before. Dedicatory services were broadcast by radio.

1928 The Church purchased Hill Cumorah in western New York.

January — The Church published its first Melchizedek Priesthood handbook.

• The YMMIA introduced a Vanguard program for 15- and 16-year-old boys. After the National Boy Scout organization created the Explorer program in 1933, patterned in part after the Vanguards, the Church adopted Explorer Scouting.

• Priesthood quorums began meeting during the Sunday School hour for gospel instruction under a correlated experiment lasting 10 years. This priesthood Sunday School experiment included classes for all age groups, with Tuesday evening reserved as an activity night for both priesthood and young women.

1929 July 15 — The Tabernacle Choir started a weekly network radio broadcast on NBC. Richard L. Evans joined the program with his sermonettes in June 1930. "Music and the Spoken Word" eventually switched to KSL Radio on the CBS network, and has since become the longest continuing network radio broadcast in history.

Oct. 29 — *The New York Stock Market collapsed in frantic trading, a dramatic beginning of the Great Depression.*

November — The official publication of the Sunday School began publishing under the name of *The Instructor.* From 1877 until 1929, the publication was *The Juvenile Instructor.* The name change reflected the growing use of articles on teaching methods and gospel subjects to be used by the several Church organizations.

1930 April 6 — The centennial of the Church's organization was observed at general conference in the Tabernacle in Salt Lake City. B.H. Roberts prepared his *Comprehensive History of The Church of Jesus Christ of Latter-day Saints* as a centennial memorial.

1931 March 21 — A 10-reel film of the history of the Church was completed.

April 6 — The first edition of the *Church News* was printed by the Church's *Deseret News.*

1932 Jan. 10 — The first missionary training classes began, which were to be organized in every ward throughout the Church.

February — The Lion House, home of Brigham Young and a noted landmark of Salt Lake City, was turned over to the Young Ladies Mutual Improvement Association by the Church for a social center for women and young ladies. Another of Brigham Young's homes, the Beehive House, was previously placed under the direction of the YLMIA as a girls' home.

1933 Jan. 30 — *Adolf Hitler was named chancellor of Germany, capping a 10-year rise to power.*

Feb. 21 — The Church began a six-day commemoration of the 100th anniversary of the Word of Wisdom revelation with special observances in every ward.

June 1 — The Church opened a 500-foot exhibit in the Hall of Religions at the Century of Progress World's Fair in Chicago, Ill. The exhibit was prepared by famed LDS sculptor Avard Fairbanks.

July 26 — The first effort to mark the historic sites in Nauvoo, Ill., was made by the Relief Society when it placed a monument at the site of its organization in 1842 in Joseph Smith's store.

Nov. 5 — The First Presidency and four members of the Quorum of the Twelve participated in the dedication of the Washington, D.C., meetinghouse, which was adorned by a statue of the Angel Moroni atop its 165-foot spire.

1934 The general board of the Sunday School officially recognized the Junior Sunday School, which had been part of some ward programs for many years.

Jan. 17 — New headquarters of the Genealogical Society of Utah, located in the Joseph F. Smith Memorial Building on North Main Street in Salt Lake City, was formally opened. The building previously was part of the campus of the LDS College.

Aug. 2 — *Adolf Hitler took control of Germany after the death of President Paul von Hindenburg.*

1935 Jan. 10 — In a change of policy, members of the Quorum of the Twelve were released from auxiliary leadership positions as presiding officers and general board members.

July 21 — President Heber J. Grant dedicated the Hill Cumorah Monument near Palmyra, N.Y.

1936 A separate Aaronic Priesthood program for adults, recommended by the General Priesthood Committee on Outlines 20 years earlier, was introduced.

April — The Church introduced a formal welfare program to assist in emergency situations of needy Church members and those unemployed. Called the Church Security Program at first, it was renamed the Church Welfare Program in 1938. Later it expanded its services with the addition of local production programs.

1937 January — The First Presidency officially adopted the practice widely utilized over several preceding decades of ordaining worthy young men in the Aaronic Priesthood at specific ages. The recommended ages for advancement from deacon to teacher to priest to elder have changed from time to time since 1937.

Feb. 20 — A portion of the Nauvoo Temple lot in Nauvoo, Ill., returned to Church ownership when Wilford C. Wood, representing the Church, purchased the property.

July — The Hill Cumorah pageant, "America's Witness for Christ," began on an outdoor stage on the side of the Hill Cumorah in New York.

Sept. 12 — President Heber J. Grant returned to Salt Lake City after a three-month tour of Europe, where he visited with Church members and missionaries in 11 countries. He dedicated nine meetinghouses and gave some 55 addresses, including the principal address at the British Mission Centennial Conference at Rochdale, England, on Aug. 1.

1938 Aug. 14 — The first Deseret Industries store opened in Salt Lake City to provide work opportunities for the elderly and handicapped. Part of the Welfare Program, a growing network of stores still offers used furniture, clothing and other items.

November — The Genealogical Society of Utah had its own camera and began microfilming baptism and sealing records of the Salt Lake, Logan, Manti and St. George temples.

1939 June 19 — Wilford Wood purchased the Liberty Jail in Missouri on behalf of the Church.

Aug. 24 — The First Presidency directed all missionaries in Germany to move to neutral countries. Later the missionaries were instructed to leave Europe and return to the United States. The last group arrived in New York Nov. 6, 1939.

Sept. 1 — *World War II began when Nazi Germany invaded Poland. Britain and France declared war on Germany two days later.*

Oct. 6 — The First Presidency message on world peace was delivered in general conference by President Heber J. Grant.

1940 Jan. 28 — The Mormon Battalion Monument was dedicated in San Diego, Calif.

1941 The Presiding Bishopric inaugurated a new membership record system.

April 6 — In general conference, the First Presidency announced the new position of Assistant to the Twelve, and the first five Assistants were called and sustained.

Dec. 7 — *The Japanese bombed Pearl Harbor in Hawaii, killing 2,403 Americans and wounding 1,178. The next day, President Franklin D. Roosevelt asked Congress for a declaration of war against Japan. Four days later, Germany and Italy declared war on the United States, and on the same day the U.S. declared war on the European dictatorships.*

1942 Jan. 4 — The Church observed a special fast Sunday in conjunction with a national day of prayer called by President Franklin D. Roosevelt.

Feb. 28 — It was announced that due to World War II, the Relief Society general conference scheduled for April, which had been planned to commemorate the centennial anniversary of the founding of the Relief Society, along with centennial celebrations in the stakes, would not be held. Rather, celebrations were to be held on the ward and branch level.

March 23 — The First Presidency announced that for the duration of World War II it would call only older men who had been ordained high priests or seventies on full-time missions.

April 4-6 — Because of limitations on travel, the annual April general conference was closed to the general Church membership and confined to General Authorities and

presidencies of the 141 stakes. The First Presidency on April 5, 1942, closed the Tabernacle for the duration of the war. Conference sessions were held in the Assembly Hall on Temple Square and in the assembly room of the Salt Lake Temple.

April 18 — May Green Hinckley, general president of the Primary Association, announced that the presiding officers of the Primary on all levels would henceforth be known as "presidents" rather than "superintendents."

July — Church Welfare leaders urged members to plant gardens, to bottle as many fruits and vegetables as they could utilize, and to store coal.

Aug. 17 — The *USS Brigham Young,* a Liberty class ship, was christened.

1943 March 7 — The Navajo-Zuni Mission was formed, the first mission designated only for Indians.

May 22 — *USS Joseph Smith,* a Liberty class ship, was launched in Richmond, Calif. Ceremonies included a tribute to Joseph Smith and a description of the Church's part in the war effort.

July 24 — The MIA completed a war service project to purchase aircraft rescue boats by purchasing war bonds. The project began May 11 and ended with 87 stakes raising a total of $3.1 million, enough to purchase 52 boats, which cost $60,000 each.

Sept. 9 — *United States troops invaded Italy.*

1944 March — The Church announced the purchase of Spring Hill in Missouri, known in Church history as Adam-ondi-Ahman. (See D&C 116.). Final deeds for the purchase were dated June 27, 1944, the 100th anniversary of the martyrdom of the Prophet Joseph Smith. The deed to the land was passed on to the Church by Eugene Johnson, whose family had been in possession of the property for a century.

May 15 — A 12-page monthly *Church News* for the 70,000 LDS servicemen was inaugurated by the First Presidency in order to keep more closely in touch with the servicemen.

June 6 — *Allied forces, numbering 130,000 men, invaded Europe at Normandy, France, on "D-Day" breaking the Nazi stranglehold on the Continent and leading to the eventual surrender of Germany.*

June 25 — Memorial services were held in

each ward to commemorate the 100th anniversary of the martyrdom of the Prophet Joseph Smith and Hyrum Smith. Special services were also held in Carthage Jail on June 27.

July — The Church organized the Committee on Publications comprised of General Authorities to supervise the preparation and publication of all Church literature.

November — The name of the Genealogical Society of Utah was changed to the Genealogical Society of The Church of Jesus Christ of Latter-day Saints.

Nov. 28 — Young Women's Mutual Improvement Association celebrated its 75th anniversary. A plaque was dedicated by President Heber J. Grant and placed in the Lion House where the initial organization had taken place.

1945 May 14 — President Heber J. Grant died in Salt Lake City at age 88.

May 21 — At a special meeting of the Quorum of the Twelve in the Salt Lake Temple, the First Presidency was reorganized with President George Albert Smith ordained and set apart as the eighth president of the Church. Presidents J. Reuben Clark Jr. and David O. McKay, counselors to President Grant, were called also as counselors to President Smith.

July 16 — The First Presidency authorized monthly priesthood and auxiliary leadership meetings if they could be held without violating government restrictions concerning use of gas and rubber.

September — The First Presidency began calling mission presidents for areas vacated during the war. This process continued through 1946. The sending of missionaries soon followed the appointment of mission presidents. By the end of 1946, 3,000 missionaries were in the field.

Also, the Tabernacle was opened to the general public for the first time since March 1942.

Sept. 2 — *Formal ceremonies of surrender, ending World War II — history's deadliest and most far-reaching conflict — were held aboard the battleship* Missouri *in Tokyo Bay. Japan had surrendered on Aug. 14 (V-J Day); Germany on May 8 (V-E Day).*

Sept. 23 — The Idaho Falls Temple was dedicated by President George Albert Smith.

Oct. 5-7 — The first general, unrestricted conference of the Church in four years was held in the Tabernacle in Salt Lake City. (During World War II, general conferences were limited to general, stake, and ward priesthood leaders.)

Nov. 3 — President George Albert Smith met with U.S. President Harry S. Truman in the White House and presented the Church's plans to use its welfare facilities to help relieve the suffering of Latter-day Saints in Europe.

1946 January — The Church began sending supplies to the Saints in Europe. This continued for the next several years.

Feb. 4 — Elder Ezra Taft Benson of the Quorum of the Twelve, newly called as president of the European Mission, left New York for Europe to administer to the physical and spiritual needs of members there. He traveled throughout Europe for most of the year, visiting Saints who had been isolated by the war, distributing Church welfare supplies, and setting the branches of the Church in order.

May — President George Albert Smith became the first president of the Church to visit Mexico. While in the country, he met with Manuel Avila Camacho, president of Mexico.

May 2 — The First Presidency instructed local Church leaders that in meetings where the sacrament is passed, it should be passed to the presiding officer first.

1947 The Church reached the 1 million-member mark.

May — The vast project of revising early scripture translations and translating the scriptures into additional languages was begun by the Church offices.

July 22 — A caravan of wagon-canopied automobiles of the same number of people as the original pioneer company, arrived in Salt Lake City after following the Mormon Pioneer Trail.

July 24 — Church members celebrated the 100th anniversary of the Pioneers' arrival in Salt Lake Valley. The "This Is the Place" monument was dedicated by President George Albert Smith.

November — Some 75 tons of potatoes, raised and donated by Dutch members, were delivered to needy families in Germany. A year later, the German Saints harvested their own crop of potatoes.

December — Fast day was set aside for the

relief of those in need in Europe. About $210,000 was collected and then distributed to Europeans of all faiths by an agency not connected with the Church.

Also in December, more than one million people visited Temple Square in one year for the first time.

Dec. 1 — An ambitious project to microfilm European records was started by the Genealogical Society.

Dec. 20 — President George Albert Smith announced that following the end of World War II, the Church had the responsibility to carry the gospel to the people at home and abroad, a missionary posture leading to the internationalization of the Church.

1948 **April** — Mission presidents from around the world reported increasing numbers of baptisms. An expanded building program was started.

June — It was announced that Ricks College in Rexburg, Idaho, would become a four-year college in the 1949-50 school year.

Oct. 17 — The Tabernacle Choir performed its 1,000th national broadcast over radio.

December — Significant increases were made among the Indian membership in the Southwest states.

1949 **April 5** — At a special welfare meeting held in conjunction with general conference, the Welfare Program was declared a permanent program of the Church.

A film made by the Church in Hollywood, *The Lord's Way*, was introduced.

October — For the first time, general conference was broadcast publicly over KSL television in Salt Lake City, although since April 1948 it had been carried by closed-circuit television to other buildings on Temple Square.

1950 **Feb. 24** — The last two missionaries of the Czechoslovakian Mission were released from prison after 27 days and expelled from communist Czechoslovakia.

Feb. 25 — Missionaries returned to Hong Kong for the first time since 1853.

March — The Tahitian mission purchased an 81-foot yacht for mission travel.

June 1 — President George Albert Smith dedicated a statue of Brigham Young at the nation's Capitol.

July 1 — The responsibility of the LDS girls' program was transferred from the Presiding Bishopric to the Young Women's Mutual Improvement Association, where it remained until 1974.

September — Early morning seminaries were inaugurated in Southern California. This was the beginning of a movement that spread seminary throughout the Church on an early morning, nonreleased-time basis.

1951 **April 4** — President George Albert Smith died in Salt Lake City at age 81.

April 9 — President David O. McKay was sustained as ninth president of the Church, with Presidents Stephen L Richards and J. Reuben Clark Jr. as counselors.

July 20 — Because the Korean War reduced the number of young elders being called as missionaries, the First Presidency issued a call for seventies to help fill the need. Many married men subsequently served full-time missions.

1952 A Systematic Program for Teaching the Gospel was published for use by the missionaries of the Church. This inaugurated the use of a standard plan of missionary work throughout the Church, although the specific format of the various lessons was modified from time to time.

March 2 — The new Primary Children's Hospital in Salt Lake City was dedicated. Half the cost of the building had been raised by children of the Church through the continuing Primary penny drive.

April 5 — The Church began carrying the priesthood session of general conference by direct telephone wire to buildings beyond Temple Square.

June — President David O. McKay made a six-week tour of European missions and branches in Holland, Denmark, Sweden, Norway, Finland, Germany, Switzerland, Wales, Scotland and France. During this trip he announced Bern, Switzerland, as site of the first European temple.

Oct. 6 — A letter from the Presiding Bishopric introduced a new Senior Aaronic Priesthood program, with men over 21 years of age organized into separate Aaronic Priesthood quorums. Subsequently, special weekday classes were encouraged in each stake to prepare these brethren for the Melchizedek Priesthood and temple ordinances.

Nov. 25 — Elder Ezra Taft Benson of the

Quorum of the Twelve was chosen Secretary of Agriculture by Dwight D. Eisenhower, newly elected president of the United States. Elder Benson served in that capacity for eight years.

Dec. 31 — A letter from the First Presidency announced that the Primary Association had been assigned the duty of establishing the Cub Scout program of the Boy Scouts of America for boys of the Church.

1953 March 25 — The First Presidency announced that returning missionaries would no longer report directly to General Authorities but, rather, to their stake presidency and high council.

July 9 — Organization of the United Church School System, with Ernest L. Wilkinson as administrator, was publicly announced.

October — The semiannual conference of the Church was broadcast by television for the first time outside the Intermountain area.

1954 Jan. 2 — President David O. McKay left Salt Lake City on a trip to London, England; South Africa; and South and Central America. He returned in mid-February, and at that point had visited every existing mission of the Church. He was the first president of the Church to visit the South African Mission.

July — The Church announced the inauguration of the Indian Placement Program, whereby Indian students of elementary- and secondary-school age could be placed in foster homes during the school year in order for them to take advantage of better educational opportunities.

July 21 — The First Presidency announced the establishment of the Church College of Hawaii. The college commenced operation Sept. 26, 1955.

Aug. 31 — The First Presidency approved a plan to ordain young men of the Aaronic Priesthood to the office of teacher at age 14 and priest at age 16. The previous ages were 15 and 17.

1955 A special program of missionary work among the Jewish people was organized. It continued until 1959.

January-February — President David O. McKay took a trip covering more than 45,000 miles to the missions of the South Pacific, selected a site for the New Zealand Temple and discussed plans for the building of a Church college in New Zealand.

July — The Church Building Committee was organized to supervise the vast building program of the Church throughout the world.

August-September — The Tabernacle Choir made a major concert tour of Europe.

Sept. 11 — The Swiss Temple, near Bern, was dedicated by President David O. McKay.

Sept. 26 — The Church College of Hawaii, now BYU-Hawaii, was opened.

Dec. 27 — A letter from the Presiding Bishopric announced that students at BYU would be organized into campus wards and stakes beginning Jan. 8, 1956. This move set the pattern for student wards to be organized at Church colleges and institutes of religion wherever their numbers warranted it.

1956 Jan. 1 — Frederick S. Williams, former mission president in Argentina and Uruguay, moved with his family to Peru and contacted Church headquarters for permission to organize a branch and begin missionary work. First missionaries arrived Aug. 7, 1956.

Jan. 8 — The first campus wards and stakes in the Church were organized at BYU.

March 11 — President David O. McKay dedicated the Los Angeles Temple.

Oct. 3 — The new Relief Society Building in Salt Lake City was dedicated.

1957 July — The Pacific Board of Education was organized to supervise all Church schools in the Pacific area.

October — The semiannual general conference was canceled due to a flu epidemic.

1958 A new program for convert integration was adopted during the year, having been previously tried on a pilot basis in several stakes.

April 20 — The New Zealand Temple was dedicated by President David O. McKay.

Sept. 7 — The London Temple was dedicated by President David O. McKay.

Dec. 17 — The Church College of Hawaii in Laie, Hawaii, was dedicated by President David O. McKay.

1959 April 6 — President David O. McKay issued his famous "Every member a missionary" slogan.

Nov. 29 — The Tabernacle Choir received a Grammy award for its recording of the "Battle Hymn of the Republic" at the first television awards show of the National Academy of

Recording Arts and Sciences in Los Angeles, Calif.

1960 Jan. 3 — The First Presidency inaugurated a three-month series of weekly Sunday evening fireside programs for youth. President David O. McKay addressed an estimated 200,000 youth at the opening fireside, carried by direct telephone wire to 290 stake centers in the United States, western Canada, and Hawaii.

Also in January, the Church began setting up the administrative framework for a large building program in Europe. By early 1961, administrative building areas outside North America had been established for all parts of the world where the Church existed, and the labor missionary program, which originated in the South Pacific in the early 1950s, was utilized in each area.

March — The First Presidency requested the General Priesthood Committee, with Elder Harold B. Lee of the Quorum of the Twelve as chairman, to make a study of Church programs and curriculum with the object of providing for better "correlation."

July 21 — First Presidency issues statement allowing young men to serve missions at age 19, even though they had not met educational and military qualifications previously required.

1961 March 12 — The first non-English-speaking stake of the Church was organized at The Hague in The Netherlands.

June-July — A number of significant developments took place that revamped the missionary program of the Church. The first seminar for all mission presidents was held June 26-July 27 in Salt Lake City, at which new programs were outlined. Also, a new teaching plan of six lessons to be used in every mission of the Church was officially presented, as was the "every member a missionary" program. The missions of the world were divided into nine areas, and a General Authority was called to administer each area.

November — A Language Training Institute was established at Brigham Young University for missionaries called to foreign countries. In 1963, it became the Language Training Mission.

Dec. 3 — The first Spanish-speaking stake in the Church was created in Mexico City.

1962 Feb. 20 — *John Glenn became the first American to orbit the earth, a feat he accomplished in one hour and 37 minutes aboard the* Friendship 7 *space capsule.*

April — At the 132nd Annual Conference, the first seminar of General Authorities and presidents of stakes outside North America was held.

Oct. 10 — The Church purchased a shortwave radio station, WRUL, with a transmitter in Boston and studios in New York City. It was subsequently used to transmit Church broadcasts to Europe and South America.

1963 Oct. 12 — The Polynesian Cultural Center, located near the Church College of Hawaii and the temple in Laie, Hawaii, was dedicated.

December — Church storage vaults for records in Little Cottonwood Canyon were completed. They were dedicated on June 22, 1966.

1964 January — A new program of home teaching, replacing ward teaching, was officially inaugurated throughout the Church after having been presented in stake conferences during the last half of 1963.

Jan. 28 — Temple Square and the Lion House in Salt Lake City were recognized as National Historic Landmarks by the federal government.

March — Two LDS schools were opened in Chile, one in Santiago and the other in Vina del Mar. During the early 1970s, the Church opened an elementary school in Paraguay, one in Bolivia and one in Peru.

April — The Mormon Pavilion opened at the New York World's Fair. The Church also built elaborate pavilions for subsequent expositions in San Antonio, Texas (1968); Japan (1970); and Spokane, Wash. (1974).

April 26 — The first meetinghouse in Asia was dedicated for the Tokyo North Branch in Japan.

Nov. 17 — The Oakland Temple was dedicated by President David O. McKay.

1965 January — The family home evening program was inaugurated and wards had a choice of which night in the week to hold home evenings. A weekly home evening had been encouraged before by Church leaders, but now the Church published a formal family home evening manual, which was placed in every LDS home.

Jan. 18 — The Tabernacle Choir sang at the inauguration of U.S. President Lyndon B. Johnson in Washington, D.C.

February — The Italian government gave

permission for LDS missionaries to proselyte in the country. No missionary work had been done there since 1862.

September — Because of the war in Vietnam, a missionary quota of two per ward was established within the United States to comply with Selective Service requests.

October — With the appointment of President Joseph Fielding Smith and Elder Thorpe B. Isaacson as counselors, President David O. McKay announced that the First Presidency would be increased to five, instead of three members.

1966
May 1 — The first stake in South America was organized at Sao Paulo, Brazil.

August — A new visitors center on Temple Square was opened to tourists. While this would be the most elaborate center, it represented a trend of building visitors centers at historic sites and temples and at various other locations during the 1960s and 1970s.

1967
April — For the first time, seven Mexican television and radio stations carried a session of general conference.

June 10 — *The Six-Day War in the Middle East ended with Israel holding conquered Arab territory four times its own size.*

Sept. 29 — The new administrative position of regional representative of the Twelve was announced, and the first 69 regional representatives were called and given their initial training.

1968
Feb. 2 — Six missionaries from the Taiwan and Hong Kong zones of the Southern Far East Mission were transferred to Thailand to begin missionary work.

Oct. 22 — The Church received official recognition in Spain. The first missionaries arrived in June, 1969.

1969
January — Two-month language training missions began. Language training for missionaries prior to their departure to their mission field first began during the early 1960s for Spanish, Portuguese and German language missions.

Jan. 20 — The Tabernacle Choir sang at U.S. President Richard M. Nixon's inauguration in Washington, D.C.

July 20 — *U.S. astronaut Neil Armstrong became the first man to walk on the moon when he descended from the lunar module Eagle; he was followed 18 minutes later by Edwin Aldrin, pilot of the lunar module.*

Nov. 1 — The Southeast Asia Mission formally opened with headquarters in Singapore. In January 1970, the first missionaries were sent to Indonesia, which was part of the mission.

1970
January — A computerized system for recording and reporting Church contributions went into operation.

Jan. 18 — President David O. McKay died in Salt Lake City at age 96.

Jan. 23 — President Joseph Fielding Smith was ordained and set apart as the 10th president of the Church and chose Presidents Harold B. Lee and N. Eldon Tanner as counselors.

March 15 — The first stake in Asia was organized in Tokyo, Japan.

March 22 — The first stake in Africa was organized in Transvaal, South Africa.

October — Monday was designated for family home evening throughout the Church; no other Church activity was to be scheduled during that time.

1971
January — Publication of new Church magazines began: the *Ensign* for adults, the *New Era* for youth and the *Friend* for children.

Aug. 27-29 — The first area conference of the Church was held in Manchester, England. Before the program of holding large area conferences ended in 1980, 63 were held throughout the world.

September — All LDS women were automatically enrolled as members of the Relief Society; dues were eliminated.

1972
Church sports tournaments and dance festivals were directed to be held on a regional basis instead of an all-Church basis.

Jan. 14 — The Church Historical Department was formed in a reorganization of the Church Historian's Office. Church library, archives, and history divisions were created within the new department.

Jan. 18 — The Ogden Temple was dedicated by President Joseph Fielding Smith.

Feb. 9 — The Provo Temple was dedicated by President Smith.

July 2 — President Smith died in Salt Lake City at age 95.

July 7 — President Harold B. Lee was ordained and set apart as the 11th president of the Church, with Presidents N. Eldon Tanner and Marion G. Romney as counselors.

November — The MIA was realigned into the Aaronic Priesthood and Melchizedek Priesthood MIA and was placed directly under priesthood leadership.

1973 A new set of missionary lessons was completed for use in all missions. It was the first change in missionary lessons since 1961.

February — The first Church agricultural missionaries to leave the United States were sent to the Guatemala-El Salvador Mission.

Feb. 4 — The Marriott Activities Center at BYU was dedicated. Seating 22,000, it was the largest such arena on any university campus in the United States.

March 8 — The first stake on mainland Asia was organized in Seoul, Korea.

April 7 — The creation of the Welfare Services Department was announced in general conference. The new organization brought the three welfare units — health services, social services and welfare — into full correlation.

Dec. 26 — President Harold B. Lee died in Salt Lake City at age 74.

Dec. 30 — President Spencer W. Kimball was ordained and set apart as the 12th president of the Church, with Presidents N. Eldon Tanner and Marion G. Romney as counselors.

1974 March 23 — In an exchange of pioneer homes, the Church traded the Brigham Young Forest Farm home in Salt Lake City to the state of Utah for use in the state's Pioneer State Park. The Church acquired the Brigham Young winter home in St. George and the Jacob Hamblin home in nearby Santa Clara, Utah, for use as visitor and information centers.

June 23 — MIA was dropped from the name of Church youth programs.

Sept. 1 — Church College of Hawaii became a branch of Brigham Young University and was renamed Brigham Young University-Hawaii Campus.

Sept. 6 — The First Presidency announced that the Church was divesting itself of its 15 hospitals in three western states and turning them over to a non-Church, non-profit organization, Intermountain Health Care. The Church completed the legal steps for divesting

the hospitals on March 21, 1975.

Oct. 3 — Seventies quorums were authorized in all stakes and all quorums in the Church were renamed after the stake.

Nov. 19 — President Spencer W. Kimball dedicated the Washington Temple at Kensington, Md. Visitors during pre-dedication tours September through November totaled 758,327, topping the previous record of 662,401 at the Los Angeles Temple in 1956.

1975 May 3 — Citing accelerated growth of the Church worldwide, the First Presidency announced the creation of an area supervisory program and the assignment of six Assistants to the Twelve to oversee Church activities while residing outside the United States and Canada. The number of these foreign areas was increased to eight later in the year.

May 17 — A supervisory program for missions in the United States and Canada was announced, along with the assignment of members of the Quorum of the Twelve as advisers and other General Authorities as supervisors of the 12 areas.

June 27 — The end of auxiliary conferences was announced during the opening session of the 1975 June Conference. These conferences would be replaced with annual regional meetings for priesthood and auxiliary leaders.

July 24 — The 28-story Church Office Building in Salt Lake City was dedicated by President Spencer W. Kimball.

Aug. 8-17 — President Kimball spoke to a total of 44,500 members at five area conferences in the Far East, Japan, the Philippines, Hong Kong, Taiwan and Korea

Oct. 3 — President Kimball announced in general conference the organization of the First Quorum of the Seventy, and the first three members of the quorum were sustained.

Oct. 6-11 — Brigham Young University observed its 100th anniversary during homecoming week.

Nov. 7-9 — Incident to the rapid growth of the Church in Mexico, 15 stakes were created in Mexico City in one weekend.

Nov. 18 — The Church Genealogical Department was organized with five divisions, two of which were formerly known as the Genealogical Society.

1976 Feb. 15- March 2 — A total of 53,000 members in the South

Pacific attended nine area conferences in American Samoa, Western Samoa, New Zealand, Fiji, Tonga, Tahiti, and Australia to hear counsel from President Spencer W. Kimball and other General Authorities.

April 3 — Members attending general conference accepted Joseph Smith's Vision of the Celestial Kingdom and Joseph F. Smith's Vision of the Redemption of the Dead for addition to the Pearl of Great Price. These scriptures became part of the Doctrine and Covenants on June 6, 1979.

June 5 — The Teton Dam in southeastern Idaho burst, sending a wall of water, between 12 and 20 feet high, onto the mostly LDS towns below. About 40,000 people, most of them members of the Church, were driven from their homes.

June 18-22 — President Kimball spoke at three area conferences in England and Scotland, which were attended by more than a total of 17,000 members.

June 25 — Missouri Gov. Christopher S. Bond signed an executive order rescinding the extermination order issued in 1838 by Gov. Lilburn W. Boggs.

July 4 — President Kimball spoke at a Church-sponsored U.S. Bicentennial devotional attended by more than 23,000 people at the Capitol Centre in Landover, Md. Numerous additional activities involved Church members in the United States during the year-long Bicentennial observance.

July 31- Aug. 8 — President Kimball addressed a total of 25,000 members from 12 countries in Europe at five area conferences in France, Finland, Denmark, The Netherlands and Germany.

1977
Jan. 1 — The First Presidency announced a new format for general conferences. General sessions would be held on the first Sunday of each April and October and the preceding Saturday. Regional representative seminars would be held on the preceding Friday.

Feb. 5 — The First Presidency announced that the Quorum of the Twelve would oversee ecclesiastical matters and the Presiding Bishopric would have responsibility for temporal programs.

May 14 — A bishops central storehouse, the second in the Church and first outside of Salt Lake City, opened at Colton, Calif. Also, the Young Men program was restructured.

May 22 — Formation of a new Church Activities Committee, with responsibility for coordinating cultural arts and physical activities, was announced.

May 30 — Poland granted legal status to the Church.

July 1 — In response to continued growth in membership worldwide, the geographic subdivisions of the Church, previously known as areas, were renamed zones, and the 11 zones were subdivided into areas. Members of the First Quorum of the Seventy were assigned as zone advisers and area supervisors.

Oct. 1 — The Church published *A Topical Guide to the Scriptures of The Church of Jesus Christ of Latter-day Saints,* the first product of a continuing scriptural-aids project established by the First Presidency.

1978
March 31 — President Spencer W. Kimball announced that semiannual rather than quarterly stake conferences would be held starting in 1979.

April 1 — President Kimball emphasized the four-generation program, which later became the basis for the Church's computerized Ancestral File.

June 9 — In a letter dated June 8 and made public the following day, the First Presidency announced the revelation that worthy men of all races would be eligible to receive the priesthood. On Sept. 30, members accepted the revelation by a sustaining vote at general conference. The First Presidency's announcement is now Official Declaration - 2 in the Doctrine and Covenants.

July 1 — The Relief Society Monument to Women was dedicated in Nauvoo, Ill., by President Kimball.

Aug. 7 — North Dakota became the final state of the United States to have a stake headquartered within its boundaries when the Fargo North Dakota stake was created.

Sept. 9 — A new missionary training program was announced: Missionaries to English-speaking missions would receive four weeks training while those learning other languages would continue to receive eight weeks training at the new Missionary Training Center in Provo, Utah, which replaced the Language Training Mission and the Mission Home in Salt Lake City.

Sept. 16 — Women and girls 12 years of age and over gathered for a first-ever special closed-circuit audio conference, similar to general conference priesthood broadcasts.

Sept. 30 — A new special emeritus status for General Authorities was announced in general conference, and seven members of the First Quorum of the Seventy were so designated.

Oct. 26 — The Missionary Training Center in Provo, Utah, previously the Language Training Mission constructed in 1976, began training all missionaries.

Nov. 9 — Elder and Sister Rendell N. Mabey and Elder and Sister Edwin Q. Cannon arrived in Nigeria as special representatives of the Church to open missionary work in West Africa.

1979

Feb. 3 — The Church Genealogical Department announced a new "family entry system" to allow submissions of names of deceased ancestors for temple work whose birthplaces and birthdates are unknown.

Feb. 18 — The Church's 1,000th stake was created at Nauvoo, Ill., by President Ezra Taft Benson of the Quorum of the Twelve.

June 6 — Joseph Smith's Vision of the Celestial Kingdom and Joseph F. Smith's Vision of the Redemption of the Dead were transferred from the Pearl of Great Price to the Doctrine and Covenants, becoming Sections 137 and 138, respectively.

Sept. 12-14 — The Tabernacle Choir, which celebrated the golden anniversary of its nationally broadcast radio program in July, toured Japan and Korea.

Sept. 29 — A new 2,400-page edition of the King James version of the Bible, with many special features, including a topical guide, a Bible dictionary, and a revolutionary footnote system, was published by the Church.

Oct. 29 — The first two converts of eastern Africa were baptized in Kenya.

Oct. 24 — President Spencer W. Kimball, on a tour of the Middle East, dedicated the Orson Hyde Memorial Gardens on the Mount of Olives in Jerusalem.

1980

Feb. 22 — The Presidency of the First Quorum of the Seventy was reorganized to strengthen the lines of administration at Church headquarters. The executive directors of the Missionary, Curriculum, Priesthood and Genealogy departments became members of the presidency.

March 2 — U.S. and Canadian members began a new consolidated meeting schedule that put priesthood, sacrament, and auxiliary meetings into one three-hour time block on Sundays.

April 6 — Celebrating the Church's 150th anniversary, President Spencer W. Kimball conducted part of general conference from the newly restored Peter Whitmer farmhouse at Fayette, N.Y., the site where the Church was organized. The proceedings in Fayette were linked with the congregation in the Tabernacle in Salt Lake City via satellite, the first time a satellite was used in the Church for transmitting broadcasts of general conference.

May — Missionary work opened in Haiti and Belize.

Oct. 18-Nov. 1 — The last of a series of large area conferences, presided over by the president of the Church, was held in six major cities in the Far East: Manila, Philippines; Hong Kong; Taipei, Taiwan; Seoul, Korea; and Tokyo and Osaka, Japan.

1981

Jan. 20 — The Tabernacle Choir participated in the inaugural festivities for President Ronald Reagan.

April 1 — Plans to build nine smaller temples in the United States, Central America, Asia, Africa and Europe were announced by President Spencer W. Kimball: Chicago, Ill.; Dallas, Texas; Guatemala City, Guatemala; Lima, Peru; Frankfurt, Germany; Stockholm, Sweden; Seoul, Korea; Manila, Philippines; and Johannesburg, South Africa.

April 3 — At the regional representatives meeting, President Spencer W. Kimball outlined three responsibilities to carry out the mission of the Church: Proclaim the gospel, perfect the saints and redeem the dead.

May 5 — The First Presidency publicly voiced its opposition to the proposed basing of the MX missile system in the Utah-Nevada desert.

July 23 — Elder Gordon B. Hinckley was called as a counselor in the First Presidency, the first time since the administration of President David O. McKay that a president had more than two counselors.

Sept. 12 — A smaller, less-expensive ward meetinghouse, called the Sage Plan, was announced by the First Presidency.

Sept. 26 — The first copies of a new version of the Triple Combination (Book of Mormon, Doctrine and Covenants and Pearl of Great Price), with extensive scripture helps, were made available to the public.

Oct. 3 — A network of 500 satellite dishes for stake centers outside Utah was announced.

1982 March 18 — Three Church executive councils were created: the Missionary Executive Council, the Priesthood Executive Council, and the Temple and Genealogy Executive Council.

April 1 — It was announced that Church membership had reached the 5-million member mark.

April 2 — At general conference, major changes in financing Church meetinghouses were announced, shifting construction costs to general Church funds and utility costs to local units. Also, the term of service for single elders serving full-time missions was reduced from two years to 18 months.

Sept. 5 — The Mormon Tabernacle Choir celebrated 50 years of continuous weekly broadcasts over the CBS radio network.

Sept. 10 — U.S. President Ronald Reagan visited Utah to tour a Church cannery and see the Church Welfare Program in action.

Oct. 3 — Elder Boyd K. Packer of the Quorum of the Twelve and a member of the Scriptures Publication Committee announced that a subtitle was being added to the Book of Mormon: "Another Testament of Jesus Christ."

Oct. 30 — A visitors center and historic site opened its doors in the three-story Grandin printing building in Palmyra, N.Y., where the first copies of the Book of Mormon were printed in 1830.

1983 Aug. 5, 9 — For the first time in Church history, two temples were dedicated within a week's time: the Apia Samoa Temple on Aug. 5 and the Nuku'alofa Tonga Temple on Aug. 9; both by President Gordon B. Hinckley.

Oct. 16 — The first of a series of multi-stake (later known as regional) conferences was held in London, England.

1984 Jan. 7 — Premier Zhao Ziyang of the People's Republic of China visited the BYU-Hawaii campus and the adjacent Polynesian Cultural Center during the first visit of a Chinese premier to the United States since the People's Republic of China was formed in 1949.

March 25 — A new program — the Four-Phase Genealogical Facilities Program — was announced, enabling wards and branches to establish genealogical facilities in their meetinghouses.

April 7 — The first members of the First Quorum of the Seventy called for temporary three- to five-year terms were sustained. They were later sustained to the Second Quorum of the Seventy, created in 1989.

June 24 — Members of the First Quorum of the Seventy were appointed to serve as area presidencies in 13 major geographical areas of the Church — seven in the United States and Canada and six in other parts of the world.

Oct. 28 — The Church's 1,500th stake was created 150 years after the first stake was organized in Kirtland, Ohio. The landmark stake was the Ciudad Obregon Mexico Yaqui Stake.

Nov. 26 — The First Presidency announced that, beginning Jan. 1, the term of full-time missionary service for single elders would again be 24 months. It had been shortened from two years to 18 months in April 1982.

1985 Jan. 27 — Latter-day Saints in the United States and Canada participated in a special fast to benefit victims of famine in Africa and other parts of the world. The fast raised more than $6 million.

June 29 — The Freiberg Temple, located in the German Democratic Republic, then communist-controlled, was dedicated by President Gordon B. Hinckley.

Aug. 2 — A new LDS hymnbook, the first revision in 37 years, came off the presses.

Aug. 24 — The Johannesburg South Africa Temple was dedicated by President Hinckley. With the dedication of this building, there was now a temple on every continent except Antarctica.

Oct. 23 — The Church Genealogical Library in Salt Lake City was dedicated by President Hinckley.

Nov. 5 — President Spencer W. Kimball died in Salt Lake City at age 90.

Nov. 10 — President Ezra Taft Benson was ordained and set apart as the 13th president of the Church, with President Hinckley and President Thomas S. Monson as counselors.

1986 April 30 — Church membership was estimated to have reached the 6-million member milestone.

June 22 — The 1,600th stake of the Church was created by President Monson in Kitchener, Ontario.

July 6 — New missionary discussions, which

focus on "teaching from the heart," were approved for use in all English-speaking missions.

Oct. 4 — Seventies quorums in stakes throughout the Church were discontinued.

Oct. 11 — In the first Churchwide Young Women activity, an estimated 300,000 gathered at sites around the world to release helium-filled balloons containing personal messages from the young women.

1987
Feb. 15 — The Tabernacle Choir marked its 3,000th radio broadcast in a series that had become the longest-running network program in the free world.

March 12 — It was announced that the Church-owned Hotel Utah, a landmark in downtown Salt Lake City for 76 years, would close as a hotel Aug. 31 and be renovated as a meetinghouse and office building.

July 15 — The Genealogical Library celebrated the conversion of the last card from its card catalog to computer.

July 24-26 — Church members throughout Britain commemorated the 150th anniversary of the first missionary work in Great Britain. Thirteen General Authorities, including President Ezra Taft Benson and President Gordon B. Hinckley, attended various events, which included dedication of historical sites, firesides and conferences.

Aug. 15 — The Church's Genealogical Department was renamed the Family History Department.

Sept. 4 — A letter from the First Presidency announced the discontinuance of the International Mission. Responsibility for its areas reverted to the respective area presidencies of the Church.

1988
Jan. 30-31 — Seven stakes were created in one weekend in Lima, Peru, by Elder Charles Didier of the Seventy.

May 15 — Elder Neal A. Maxwell of the Quorum of the Twelve organized the Aba Nigeria Stake, the first Church stake in West Africa.

May 28 — The First Presidency issued a statement on the subject of AIDS, stressing chastity before marriage, fidelity in marriage, and abstinence from homosexual behavior, yet extending sympathy to those who have contracted the disease.

June 1 — The Church was granted legal recognition in Hungary, the first of several such steps in Eastern European nations during the next two years.

August — The Church reached the milestone of having completed 100 million endowments for the dead.

The BYU Folk Dancers were the only North American dance company to perform at opening ceremonies of the 1988 Olympic Games in Seoul, Korea, viewed by an estimated 1 billion people worldwide.

Oct. 16 — Elder David B. Haight created the 1,700th stake of the Church. The new stake was in Manaus, Brazil, a city of 1.5 million in the heart of the Amazon jungle.

Oct. 24-28 — President Thomas S. Monson led a delegation of Church leaders that met with the German Democratic Republic's top government officials. It was announced Nov. 12 that the Church had been granted rights to send missionaries to the DDR and for LDS members from the DDR to serve as missionaries in other countries.

1989
El Salvador reached self-sufficiency in local full-time missionaries.

Jan. 28 — Elders Russell M. Nelson and Dallin H. Oaks of the Quorum of the Twelve completed an eight-day visit to China and were assured by high-level Chinese leaders that people are free to practice religious beliefs in that country.

April 1-2 — The Second Quorum of the Seventy was created and all General Authorities serving under a five-year call were sustained as members, along with another eight newly called General Authorities.

May 16 — The BYU Jerusalem Center for Near Eastern Studies was dedicated by President Howard W. Hunter of the Quorum of the Twelve.

June 14 — LDS missionaries and those of the Jehovah's Witnesses were expelled from Ghana, a western Africa nation where 6,000 Church members live. The Church had no advance notice of the ban. The LDS missionaries were able to return to Ghana in 1990.

June 15 — Ground was broken for the first LDS meetinghouse in Poland.

June 25 — The 100th stake in Mexico was created in Tecalco. Mexico became the first country outside the United States with 100 or more stakes.

June 27 — The renovated Carthage Jail

complex in Illinois, where the Prophet Joseph Smith was martyred, was dedicated by President Gordon B. Hinckley, highlighting activities commemorating the 150th anniversary of the Mormon settlement of Nauvoo, Ill.

Oct. 17 — The first LDS meetinghouse in the Republic of Hungary, located in the capital city of Budapest, was dedicated by President Thomas S. Monson.

Nov. 9 — *The Berlin Wall came down, paving the way for eventual unification of East and West Germany.*

Nov. 25 — A major change in policy for financing local Church units in the United States and Canada was announced by the First Presidency. Ward members would no longer have stake and ward budget assessments.

1990 **Feb. 25** — The Church was officially recognized in Kenya. **April 2** — A new Church software package called FamilySearch, designed to simplify the task of family history research, was released by the Church.

May 21 — The U.S. Supreme Court handed down a unanimous decision that money given directly to missionaries was not a deductible donation under federal tax law. The Church encouraged members to follow established procedures of contributing through their wards.

July — New missions in the Eastern European countries of Czechoslovakia, Hungary, and Poland highlighted the record 29 missions created in 1990.

Sept. 13 — Registration of the Leningrad Branch of the Church was approved by the Council on Religious Affairs of the Council of Ministers in the Soviet Union.

November — The First Presidency announced in November a new policy for United States and Canada, effective Jan. 1, 1991, that would equalize contributions required to maintain a full-time missionary.

Nov. 30 — The government of Ghana gave permission for the Church to resume activities in that West African country.

1991 **April 19** — Recognition of the Church in the Ivory Coast, the center of French West Africa, was announced at a special meeting of Church members in Abidjan.

April 27 — Fifty years after the Church began keeping individual membership records, it

completed computerizing membership records worldwide.

May 1 — The 500,000th full-time missionary in this dispensation was called.

May 26 — The 1,800th stake in the Church, the San Francisco de Macoris Dominican Republic Stake, was created.

June 8 — The Tabernacle Choir embarked on a 21-day tour of eight European countries, including five countries in which the choir had not performed before: Hungary, Austria, Czechoslovakia, Poland and the Soviet Union.

June 24 — The Russian Republic, the largest in the Soviet Union, granted formal recognition to the Church following the Tabernacle Choir's concert in Moscow's Bolshoi Theater.

Sept. 1 — Membership in the Church reached 8 million, about two years after membership hit the 7 million mark in December 1989.

1992 **Aug. 15** — Commemorating the "second rescue" of the ill-fated Willie and Martin handcart pioneers, President Hinckley dedicated three monuments in central Wyoming. The Riverton Wyoming Stake researched family histories and performed temple ordinances for those pioneers whose work was not previously done.

Aug. 30 — The Church's 1,900th stake, the Orlando Florida South Stake, was organized by Elder Neal A. Maxwell of the Quorum of the Twelve.

Sept. 26 — The First Presidency authorized the use of humanitarian relief funds to be sent to Somalia and other African nations in the grip of the drought of the century. In an initial response, one million pounds of food was shipped.

Oct. 8 — The Church was legally recognized in Tanzania.

Dec. 6 — The Church reached a milestone of 20,000 wards and branches with the creation of the Harvest Park Ward in the Salt Lake Granger South Stake.

Dec. 15 — A gospel literacy effort sponsored by the Relief Society to help increase literacy throughout the Church was announced in a letter from the First Presidency to priesthood and Relief Society leaders.

Dec. 26 — The Tabernacle Choir left on a tour of the Holy Land. Concerts were later held in Jerusalem, Tel Aviv and Haifa.

1993 The Church received legal recognition in Italy, Madagascar, Cameroon and Ethiopia.

Jan. 6 — Four Church-service missionaries entered Hanoi, Vietnam, to give humanitarian service, teaching English to doctors and staff at a children's hospital and to teachers, staff and children at a school for young children.

April 6 — The centennial of the Salt Lake Temple was observed at a Tabernacle Choir special program, and a special mural was placed in the temple.

June 27 — After being refurbished and remodeled, the former Hotel Utah was rededicated and renamed the Joseph Smith Memorial Building, housing office and meeting facilities for the Church and a theater showing the new film "Legacy."

June 29 — The government of Mexico formally registered the LDS Church, grant-ing it all the rights of a religious organization, including the right to own property.

1994 **Feb. 13** — The First Presidency announced that the 87-year-old Uintah Stake Tabernacle in Vernal, Utah, would be renovated and dedicated as Utah's 10th temple. It was the first existing building to be renovated into a temple.

May 30 — President Ezra Taft Benson, 94, president of the Church for 8 1/2 years, died in Salt Lake City.

June 5 — President Howard W. Hunter was ordained and set apart as the 14th president of the Church. Set apart as his counselors were President Gordon B. Hinckley and President Thomas S. Monson.

Aug. 6 — One-third of the population of the United States has been visited by Church representatives, and 36 percent have friends or relatives who are LDS, the Missionary Department announced.

1995 **Jan. 21** — The Church reached 9 million members.

March 3 — President Hunter died at his Salt Lake City home after serving as Church president for less than nine months, the shortest tenure of any president.

March 12 — President Gordon B. Hinckley was ordained and set apart as the 15th president of the Church. Set apart as his counselors were President Thomas S. Monson, first counselor, and President James E. Faust, second counselor.

April 1 — A new administrative position, Area Authority, was announced by President Hinckley during the priesthood session of general conference. The position of regional representative was discontinued after 28 years.

June 16 — *The International Olympic Committee announced that the site for the 2002 Winter Olympics would be in Salt Lake City.*

Sept. 23 — At the annual General Relief Society Meeting, the First Presidency and Quorum of the Twelve issued a Proclamation to the World on the Family, reaffirming that "the family is central to the Creator's plan for the eternal destiny of His children."

Dec. 18 — President Hinckley was interviewed by CBS television host Mike Wallace on the show *60 Minutes*. The show was broadcast in April 1996.

1996 **Feb. 28** — A milestone was reached as a majority of members, 4,720,000, lived outside the United States, compared to 4,719,000 living within.

April 6 — President Gordon B. Hinckley announced at general conference that a new assembly hall four times the size of the Tabernacle would be built.

May 27-28 — President Hinckley, on a tour of the Orient, became the first Church president ever to visit mainland China. He also visited, from May 17 to June 1, Japan, Korea, Hong Kong, Cambodia, Vietnam, the Philippines and Saipan.

June 17-July 12 — A commemorative wagon train crossed Iowa, retracing the path of the 1846 exodus from Nauvoo, Ill.

Nov. 2 The First Presidency announced the establishment of Latter-day Saint Charities, a charitable, nonprofit corporation designed to help the Church deliver humanitarian aid to the poor and needy of the world.

Nov. 8-16 — President Hinckley spoke to gatherings of Church members and missionaries in Colombia, Peru, Bolivia, Chile, Argentina and Brazil, and broke ground for temples in Bolivia and Brazil.

Nov. 18 — Elder Joseph B. Wirthlin of the Quorum of the Twelve became the first apostle to address Latter-day Saints in Far East Russia when he spoke in Vladivostok, Russia, in the region of Siberia.

1997 **January** — The Church in Africa reached a milestone when the 100,000th member on the continent was baptized. The milestone marked the almost doubling of the membership in Africa in six years.

March 9 — Chile became the fourth nation in the world to have 100 or more stakes, with the creation of the Puerto Varas Chile Stake.

April 5 — During general conference, the organization of the Third, Fourth and Fifth Quorums of the Seventy was announced. Area Authorities were then ordained as Seventies, and their titled changed to Area Authority Seventy.

April 19-21 — The commemorative Mormon Trail Wagon Train, which the worldwide public would view as the centerpiece of the sesquicentennial observance of the Mormon Pioneer trek, left from two locations, Council Bluffs, Iowa, on April 19, and Winter Quarters (Omaha), Neb., on April 21. The two contingents would later merge.

May 8-17 — President Hinckley toured the South Pacific nations of New Zealand and Australia, speaking 15 times in seven cities to a total of more than 55,000 members.

June 1 — A letter from the First Presidency announced significant modifications to the curriculum and gospel study program for the Melchizedek Priesthood and Relief Society, providing a similar meeting and instruction schedule for both organizations.

June 15 — The 100th stake in the Church's Pacific Area, the Suva Fiji North Stake, was created.

July 22 — After 93 days on the trail, the commemorative Mormon Trail Wagon Train from Winter Quarters, Neb., entered Salt Lake City, where they were greeted by about 50,000 cheering people at This Is the Place State Park. There, they heard an address by President Hinckley.

Aug. 7-14 — President Hinckley delivered 12 addresses to about 56,000 people in four nations of South America: Paraguay, Ecuador, Venezuela and Uruguay.

Oct. 4 — It was announced in general conference by President Hinckley that the Church would construct temples in remote areas of the Church that have small LDS populations. The first were to be built in Anchorage, Alaska; in the LDS colonies of northern Mexico; and in Monticello, Utah.

Oct. 10-17 — President. Hinckley addressed a total of 52,500 members in eight islands of the Pacific: Samoa, Hawaii, American Samoa, Tonga, Fiji and Tahiti.

November — Sometime during the first week of November, the Church reached 10 million members, according to Church estimates.

Nov. 8-13 — President Hinckley addressed 42,000 Church members in Mexico City and an additional 12,000 in Puebla, Mexico. On the trip, he met with Mexico's president, Dr. Ernesto Zedillo.

1998

Feb. 14-22 — President Gordon B. Hinckley became the first Church president ever to visit West Africa during a nine-day tour of Nigeria, Ghana, Kenya, Zimbabwe and South Africa. On Feb. 16, he announced plans for the first temple to be built in West Africa, in Ghana.

March 9-15 — President Hinckley addressed more than 53,000 members in 10 cities of northern Mexico: Hermosillo, Ciudad Obregon, Culiacan, Guadalajara, Torreon, Leon, Ciudad Victoria, Monterrey, Chihuahua and Ciudad Juarez.

March 26 — The replica of the Joseph Smith Sr. family log home near Palmyra, N.Y., was dedicated by President Hinckley. The home was the location where the Prophet Joseph Smith was visited in his youth by the Angel Moroni.

March 27 — After 2 1/2 years of reconstruction, the Egbert B. Grandin Building, in Palmyra, N.Y., where the Book of Mormon was published in 1829, was dedicated as a Church historic site by President Hinckley.

April 4 — President Hinckley announced in general conference that the Church would construct an additional 30 smaller temples that would bring the total number of operating temples in the Church to 100 by the year 2000.

July 26 — The Monticello Utah Temple, the prototype for a new generation of small temples in less-populous areas of the Church, was dedicated in southeast Utah by President Hinckley.

Nov. 19-21 — President Hinckley toured areas devastated caused by Hurricane Mitch in Nicaragua and Honduras and spoke to 19,000 members. In all, the Church sent 840,000 pounds of relief supplies to the affected areas.

1999

Feb. 20 — The First Presidency made a landmark announcement that a temple would be built in Palmyra, N.Y.

April 1 — The city of Omaha, Neb., deeded to

the Church the pioneer cemetery at historic Winter Quarters, where some 600 Latter-day Saints are buried.

April 4 — In his closing remarks at general conference, President Hinckley made the surprise announcement that the historic Nauvoo Temple would be rebuilt.

May 24 — The FamilySearch Internet Genealogy Service, which promised to be the greatest boon to family research since the invention of the microfilm, was officially launched by President Hinckley.

June 1 — The Mormon Youth Chorus and Symphony was disbanded, and the chorus, renamed the Temple Square Chorale, became a training choir for the Tabernacle Choir. The symphony orchestra was reorganized under a new name, the Orchestra at Temple Square.

Oct. 2-3 — The last general conference in the Tabernacle on Temple Square — the site of general conferences since 1867 — was held. Future general conferences would be held in the new Conference Center.

Nov. 14 — For the first time in the history of the Church, two temples, both in Canada, were dedicated on the same day. The Halifax Nova Scotia Temple was dedicated by President Hinckley and the Regina Saskatchewan Temple was dedicated by President Boyd K. Packer, acting president of the Quorum of the Twelve.

2000
Jan. 1 — The First Presidency and the Quorum of the Twelve issued their testimonies of the Savior in a document titled "The Living Christ."

Late February or early March — The 100 millionth copy of the Book of Mormon, since it was first published in 1830 was printed. Another milestone was reached in 2000 when the Book of Mormon was printed in its 100th language.

April 1-2 — The first general conference to be held in the new Conference Center convened, with more than 400,000 requests for free tickets, far exceeding the 21,000-seat capacity of the hall.

April 6 — The Palmyra New York Temple, located on what was once the 100-acre Joseph Smith Sr. farm and overlooking the Sacred Grove, was dedicated by President Hinckley. An estimated 1.3 million members participated in the first session, via the Church satellite system.

April 23 — The rebuilt Gadfield Elm Chapel, the oldest LDS chapel in England that was constructed in 1836 by members of the United

Brethren and given to the Church four years later after 600 members of that faith joined the Church en masse, was rededicated by Elder Jeffrey R. Holland of the Quorum of the Twelve.

May 20-21 – Three temples were dedicated in two days, the first time in the history of the Church that had occurred. They were the Tampico Mexico Temple on May 20, and the Villahermosa Mexico and the Nashville Tennessee temples, both on May 21.

September — The Church reached 11 million members and, for the first time in its 170-year history, it had more non-English-speaking members than English-speaking.

Oct. 1 — The 100th operating temple in the Church, the Boston Massachusetts Temple, was dedicated by President Hinckley.

Oct. 7-8 — The new 21,000-seat Conference Center, across the street north of Temple Square, was dedicated during general conference by President Hinckley.

Nov. 5 — Following a procedure established by the Prophet Joseph Smith for the cornerstone laying of the original Nauvoo Temple April 6, 1841, President Hinckley presided over the dedication of the four cornerstones of the Nauvoo Illinois Temple.

Dec. 19 — The government of Kazakhstan, one of the former republics of what was once the Soviet Union, granted the Church official recognition.

2001
Jan. 20 – At the inauguration of U.S. President George W. Bush, the Mormon Tabernacle Choir sang in the inaugural parade in Washington, D.C., the sixth time the choir has participated in presidential inauguration festivities.

Feb. 15 – The First Presidency and Quorum of the Twelve approved a series of guidelines to reaffirm the centrality of the Savior in the name of the Church. Church members, news organizations and others were asked to use the full and correct name of the Church – The Church of Jesus Christ of Latter-day Saints – and to avoid use of the term "Mormon Church."

March 31 – A worldwide Perpetual Education Fund, based on principles similar to those underlying the Perpetual Emigration Fund of the 1800s, was announced by President Gordon B. Hinckley.

Aug. 7 – Sea Trek 2001, an epic voyage of eight tall sailing ships commemorating the 19th century gathering of European converts to Zion, departed from Esbjerg, Denmark, on the first leg of its 59-day journey, which concluded Oct. 4 in New York City.

Aug. 10 — Ricks College in Rexburg, Idaho, was officially renamed Brigham Young University-Idaho and became a four-year university.

Sept. 7-8 – The first two meetinghouses built by the Church in the Ukraine Kiev Mission were dedicated on consecutive dates in the districts of Livoberezhny and Svyatoshinsky.

Sept. 20 — President Hinckley was among 26 religious leaders who met at the White House in Washington, D.C., with U.S. President George W. Bush regarding the terrorist attacks in New York City and Washington D.C., on Sept. 11, 2001.

Nov. 11 — The first meetinghouse built by the Church in the Czech Republic was dedicated in Brno.

Dec. 2 — The first meetinghouse in Sri Lanka was dedicated in the capital city of Colombo.

Dec. 17 — After a 32-month absence of proselytizing missionaries in the Republic of Serbia, six missionaries from the Bulgaria Sofia Mission returned to Serbia. Missionaries were withdrawn from the country in March 1999 because of conflict in the region.

2002
Jan. 19 – The first meetinghouse in Serbia was dedicated in Belgrade.

Feb. 2 – The first meetinghouse in India, the Rajahmundry Branch, was dedicated.

Feb. 8-24 – Salt Lake City hosted the 2002 Winter Olympics, with the Tabernacle Choir performing in the opening ceremonies to an estimated TV viewing audience of 3.5 billion people.

Some 10,000-20,000 Olympic visitors from many nations visited Temple Square each day.

Feb. 8 – During his brief visit to Salt Lake City to formally open the Winter Oympics, U.S. President George W. Bush and his wife, Laura, visited with the First Presidency.

May 22 – The first missionary training center in Africa opened its doors in Tema, Ghana, the 16th missionary training center throughout the world.

June 9 — The first branch of the Church in the Republic of Georgia was formed in Tbilisi.

June 27 – On the 158th anniversary of the martyrdom of the Prophet Joseph Smith and his brother, Hyrum, the rebuilt Nauvoo Illinois Temple was dedicated by President Hinckley.

Sept. 9-10 – President Hinckley became the first Church president to visit Russia and Ukraine.

2003
Jan. 11 — The first-ever global leadership training meeting in the Church by satellite transmission was held for priesthood leaders and transmitted in 56 languages to more than 97 percent of the Church's priesthood leaders.

March 7 — The Church was granted legal recognition by government officials in Benin, a French-speaking West African coastal nation between Togo and Nigeria.

March 15 — The first meetinghouse in Guyana, an English-speaking Caribbean nation, was dedicated in Georgetown, the capital city.

July 9 — The Apia Samoa Temple was destroyed by fire, marking the first time in Church history an operational temple has burned. The First Presidency announced July 16 the Church would rebuild the temple.

Nov. 30 —The first meetinghouse of the Church in Ethiopia was dedicated in the nation's capital of Addis Ababa.

2004
Jan. 25: The first meetinghouse of the Church in Cambodia, a two-story structure in Phnom Penh, was dedicated.

Late January – Membership in the Church passed the 12 million mark.

April 3 – The Sixth Quorum of the Seventy was created in a division of the Fifth Quorum of the Seventy

Aug. 1 – Mexico became the first nation, outside the United States, to reach one million members of the Church.

November – The First Presidency and Quorum of the Twelve introduce "Preach My Gospel," a comprehensive and far-reaching program designed to prepare and strengthen missionaries. The 230-page booklet addresses every aspect of missionary service and is considered the most complete, orchestrated effort in the history of the Church to unify the missionary effort.

2005
During 2005, tens of thousands of Latter-day Saint youth participated in commemorative cultural events across the globe in a worldwide commemoration honoring the 200th anniversary of the birth of the Prophet Joseph Smith and the 175th anniversary of the organization of the Church.

April 19 – Two new quorums of the Seventy were announced. The Seventh Quorum was created in a division of the Fourth Quorum and the Eighth Quorum was organized by dividing the Third Quorum.

July 3 – The first meetinghouse in the southeastern African nation of Malawi, a country of 12 million people, was dedicated in the city of Blantyre.

July 31-Aug. 9 – President Hinckley traveled 24,995 miles on a seven-nation tour of Asia and Africa, holding meetings in Russia, Korea, Taiwan, China, India, Kenya and Nigeria, where he also dedicated the Aba Nigeria Temple. He was the first Church president to visit India.

Oct. 7 – The First Presidency broke ground for a five-story state-of-the-art Church History Library at a site across the street east of the Conference Center in Salt Lake City.

Nov. 12 – The first Church meetinghouse on Kiritimati Atoll, a 248-square-mile coral atoll in the Pacific Ocean, which is part of the Republic of Kiribati and also known as Christmas Island, was dedicated.

Dec. 23 – Culminating a yearlong celebration of the 200th anniversary of the birth of the Prophet Joseph Smith, the Church held a commemorative satellite broadcast that featured segments from the prophet's birthplace in Vermont, as well as from the Conference Center in Salt Lake City. The commemorative program was telecast to 161 countries by satellite and worldwide by Internet, with the proceedings translated into 81 languages.

2006

Jan. 3 – The six-year legal battle over the Church Plaza, located between the Salt Lake Temple and the Church Office Building in Salt Lake City, ended when the deadline passed for the ACLU and its plaintiffs to appeal a decision by the 10th U.S. Circuit Court of Appeals in Denver, Colo. The appeals court on Oct. 3, 2005, upheld the sale of one block of Main Street to the Church.

March 19 – The first meetinghouse constructed by the Church in Malaysia was dedicated in Miri, Sarawak.

April 30 – The Mormon Tabernacle Choir reached a milestone when it aired the 4,000th consecutive network broadcast of its weekly "Music and Spoken Word" program.

Oct. 14 – Ground was broken in Ljubljana, the capital of Slovenia, for the first meetinghouse in the country that will serve the three branches in Slovenia, which was once part of the former country of Yugoslavia.

Oct. 18 – Official recognition of the Church in the central European country of Slovakia was granted by government officials after missionaries gathered the required 20,000 signatures necessary for a new religion to be recognized. Slovakia was once part of Czechoslovakia, but after the Berlin Wall fell in 1989, the country was divided into its two traditional ethnic groups of Czechs and Slovaks. The Czech Republic granted recognition of the Church in 1990.

Nov. 2 – President Hinckley, at 96 years and 133 days, became the longest-lived Church president, a distinction previously held by President David O. McKay.

Nov. 19 – The Mormon Tabernacle Choir was honored as a Laureate of the 2006 Mother Teresa Award for "edifying the world through inspirational choral performances and recordings."

December – The Prophet Joseph Smith and President Brigham Young were included on a list of the top 100 "Most influential figures in American history," printed in the December issue of Atlantic magazine.

2007

March 31 – The 140th-year-old Salt Lake Tabernacle on Temple Square, closed since January 2005 for extensive renovation and remodeling, was rededicated by President Hinckley. During the renovation, the pillars were strengthened and fortified to meet seismic code, and the roof was strengthened with the addition of steel trusses. Seating capacity in the building was reduced about 1,000 to 3,456.

June 21 – The Mormon Tabernacle Choir embarked on a tour of the eastern United States and Canada, performing before a total of 50,000 people in nine concerts in seven cities. The choir returned to Salt Lake City July 3.

June 24 – Church membership has reached 13 million members, President Hinckley announced to 118 mission presidents and their wives during the New Mission Presidents Seminar at the Missionary Training Center in Provo, Utah. He also announced that since the organization of the Church in 1830, an estimated one million missionaries have served throughout the world.

HIGHLIGHTS

INDEX

ADMINISTRATIVE AND POLICY ANNOUNCEMENTS

• **A letter from the First Presidency,** dated March 18, 2008, was sent to priesthood leaders with instruction that members should counsel with their local priesthood leaders, rather than writing or telephoning Church headquarters about doctrinal issues and personal matters.

• The Church released a statement July 14, 2008, that **missionary assignments to Russia** will be limited to those nationalities not needing visas because of legislation by the Russian government requiring all foreigners on humanitarian visas (which includes the Church's missionaries) to leave Russia every three months to renew their visas. Missionaries currently serving in Russia were not withdrawn and the missions are fully staffed, the statement said.

• The Church's administrative areas were consolidated in the eastern United States, Europe, Australia, New Zealand and the Pacific, effective Aug. 1, 2008, the First Presidency announced. The Europe Central and Europe West areas were combined to form the **Europe Area;** the Australia and New Zealand/Pacific Islands areas were combined into the **Pacific Area;** and the North America East Area was divided between the **North America Northeast and North America Southeast areas.**

• Due to unsettled conditions in Bolivia, some 102 **North American missionaries were transferred to Peru.** Evacuation of the missionaries by commercial and charter flights was completed on Sept. 15, 2008. The Church expected missionaries would return to Bolivia when conditions become more settled.

APPOINTMENTS

• **Richard L. Bushman** was appointed the Howard W. Hunter Visiting Professor in Mormon Studies at Claremont Graduate University School of Religion on Oct. 19, 2007, and will play a key role in establishing the first permanent, graduate-level study of Mormonism at a secular university.

• **Richard E. Turley,** managing director of the Family and Church History Department, was named assistant Church historian and recorder on March 12, 2008.

• **Mack Wilberg** was named music director of the Mormon Tabernacle Choir and Orchestra at Temple Square on March 21, 2008. As music director, he oversees all musical and creative aspects of the choir, the orchestra, the Temple Square Chorale and the Bells on Temple Square. He succeeded **Craig Jessop,** who stepped down as music director on March 4, 2008.

• **Elder Paul V. Johnson,** a member of the First Quorum of the Seventy, was named commissioner of the Church Educational System, succeeding **Elder Wm. Rolfe Kerr,** an emeritus General Authority who was called as president of the Logan Utah Temple, it was announced on June 7, 2008.

AWARDS AND HONORS

• **Elder M. Russell Ballard** of the Quorum of the Twelve was given the third annual Junius F. Wells Award by the Mormon Historic Sites Foundation on Oct. 12, 2007, for his many years of support to Church historic preservation projects.

• Honored as being "highly instrumental" in furthering the cause of the American Red Cross, **the Church** was given an Award of Achievement on Oct. 23, 2007, by the American Association of Blood Banks at an event in Anaheim, Calif.

• Utah Supreme Court Chief Justice **Christine M. Durham** was given the 2007 William H. Rehnquist Award for Judicial Excellence by the National Center for State Courts on Nov. 15, 2007. She was presented the award by U.S. Supreme Court Chief Justice John G. Roberts at a ceremony in Washington, D.C.

• Utah State Rep. **Karen Morgan,** D-Utah, a member of the Wasatch 4th Ward, Salt Lake Wasatch Stake, was sworn in as chairwomen of Women in Government's Board of Directors at the 14th annual State Director's Conference in Phoenix, Ariz., on Jan. 3, 2008.

• **Susan Purdon-Sully** of the Chermside Ward, Brisbane Australia Stake, was appointed to the Federal Magistrates Court of Australia, the highest legal position obtained by a member of the Church in Australia, the *Church News* reported on Jan. 5, 2008.

• The Utah House of Representatives passed a resolution on Feb. 26, 2008, honoring the life of **President Gordon B. Hinckley,** who died Jan. 27, 2008.

• A street, located on the north side of the **Campinas Brazil Temple,** was named for the late **President James E. Faust,** the *Church News* reported March 29, 2008. President Faust died Aug. 10, 2007, after serving 12 years in the First Presidency.

• "For building bridges of trust among disparate groups and for playing a key role in the preservation" of Church history, **Elder M. Russell Ballard** of the Quorum of the Twelve received the 2008 Legacy of Life Award on April 17, 2008, from the Deseret Foundation's Heart & Lung Research Foundation at a dinner in Salt Lake City.

• **James Russell III,** professor of atmospheric and planetary science at Virginia's Hampton University and co-director of the Center for Atmospheric Sciences, was one of three scientists in Virginia to receive the state's 2008 Outstanding Scientist Award on April 17, 2008.

• **Elder M. Russell Ballard** was presented the Distinguished Public Service Award from the Washington D.C. Chapter of the BYU Management Society on April 19, 2008, at an event at Georgetown University that was attended by four LDS U.S. senators and diplomats from nine countries.

• Six LDS women represented their states at the annual American Mothers Inc. National Convention April 23-26, 2008, in Lincoln, Neb. They were **Carol Louise Kenley,** Alaska; **Louise Larson,** Arizona; **Kathleen Stevens,** Idaho; **Colleen Haycock,** Nevada; **Cheryl Kay Spencer,** Tennessee; and **Claudia Eliason,** Utah. In addition, six women represented their states as Young Mothers: **Heidi Asay,** Alaska; **Gretchen Zaitzeff,** Illinois; **Heather Lynn Deshler,** Kentucky; **Theresa Huston,** Nevada; **Maria Dowdle,** Oregon; and **Ingrid Sorensen,** Utah.

• During commencement exercises in the Dee Glen Smith Spectrum May 3, 2008, Utah State University awarded an honorary Doctor of Humane Letters degree to **Elder L. Tom Perry** of the Quorum of the Twelve and an honorary Doctor of Laws degree to **Elder W. Eugene Hansen,** an emeritus General Authority.

• **U.S. Navy chaplain Clifford Stuart** was named the Navy's top chaplain of the year, the first time a Church member had received such an honor from any branch of the U.S. military, the *Church News* reported on May 10, 2008.

• **Lindsey Brinton,** 18, a member of the Federal Heights Ward, Salt Lake Emigration Stake, won the America Junior Miss title in Mobile, Ala., on June 28, 2008. In addition, three others who represented their states were LDS: **Hannah Marsh,** Arizona; **Brooke Gibbons,** South Carolina; and **Marianne Miles,** Wyoming.

• **Robert S. Beecroft** of the Kentlands Ward, Washington D.C. Stake, who joined the Foreign Service in 1994, was sworn in by Secretary of State Condoleezza Rice on July 17, 2008, as U.S. Ambassador to Jordan.

• LDS Olympians earned four gold medals and three silvers at the 2008 Summer Olympics in Beijing, China, in August 2008. Winning gold medals were **Ryan Millar** and **Rich Lambourne,** members of the U.S. men's volleyball team, both of whom are former BYU volleyball players; **Natasha Kai** of Laie, Hawaii, a member of the U.S. women's soccer team; and shot putter **Valerie Adams Vili** of New Zealand. The silver medalists were American swimmer **Lacey Nymeyer** of Tucson, Ariz., who with her teammates won the silver medal in the 4x100-meter freestyle relay; and **Tairia Flowers,** a UCLA graduate, and **Laura Berg** of Santa Fe Springs, Calif., members of the U.S. softball team. In addition, 12 other LDS athletes participated in the Olympics.

• **Elder Richard G. Scott** of the Quorum of the Twelve was given an honorary Doctor of Christian Service degree from BYU on Aug. 14, 2008, for his "lifetime of dedicated and selfless service and for his multifaceted excellence and contributions." Elder Scott was the keynote speaker at BYU's commencement exercises.

• **Presiding Bishop H. David Burton** was honored Sept. 9, 2008, by Utah Youth Village, one of the state's oldest welfare agencies, for the Church's work worldwide that benefits children.

• Two LDS athletes won gold medals in the 2008 Paralympic Games in Beijing, China, the *Church News* reported Sept. 27, 2008. **Jason Smyth,** a member of the Londonderry Branch, Belfast Northern Ireland Stake, swept the 100- and 200-meter sprint events, setting world records in both events in his respective competition category. **Jeff Skiba** of Sammamish, Wash., won Paralympic gold in the high jump, setting a world record in the event.

TEMPLE NEWS

• The **Nuku'alofa Tonga Temple,** closed since June 2006 for remodeling, was rededicated Nov. 4, 2007, by Elder Russell M. Nelson of the Quorum of the Twelve in two sessions.

• Ground was broken on Nov. 14, 2007, for the **Cebu Philippines Temple** by Elder Dallin H. Oaks of the Quorum of the Twelve. When completed, the edifice will be the nation's second temple.

• The First Presidency announced on Nov. 18, 2007, plans to build a temple in **San Salvador, El Salvador,** the first temple in that Central America nation.

• The **Rexburg Idaho Temple** – called "the beacon on the hill" – was dedicated Feb.10, 2008, by President Thomas S. Monson. The temple, the third to be dedicated in Idaho, is the Church 125th temple in operation worldwide.

• Two new temples in **Arizona** – one in **Gilbert** and the other in **Gila Valley** – were announced April 26, 2008, by President Monson.

• Nearly a month after announcing two new temples in Arizona, President Monson announced on May 24, 2008, a third new temple in Arizona in **Phoenix,** which, when completed, will bring the total number of temples in operation or in planning or construction stages in the Church to 140.

• In what he called "a long-awaited day," President Monson on June 1, 2008, dedicated the **Curitiba Brazil Temple,** the fifth temple in the country.

Draper Utah Temple

• Ground for the **Manaus Brazil Temple** – the first temple that will be built in the Amazon Basin and the sixth in Brazil – was broken June 20, 2008, by Elder Charles Didier of the Seventy and president of the Brazil Area.

• The traditional gold-leafed statue of the Angel Moroni on July 8, 2008, was lifted into place atop the spire of the **Draper Utah Temple,** which then was nearing completion.

• A 12-foot statue of the Angel Moroni on July 11, 2008, was place atop the **Oquirrh Mountain Utah Temple,** under construction in South Jordan, Utah.

• The **Panama City Panama Temple,** the Church's 127th operating temple and the third in Central America, was dedicated Aug. 10, 2008, by President Monson.

• President Monson on Aug. 24, 2008, dedicated the **Twin Falls Idaho Temple,** located near Snake River Canyon in south-central Idaho's Magic Valley. Two water elements – twin falls – stand at the entrance to the temple grounds, Idaho's fourth temple.

• Signaling the beginning of construction, ground for the **San Salvador El Salvador Temple** was broken Sept. 20, 2008, by Elder Don R. Clarke of the Seventy and president of the Central America Area.

• The First Presidency announced on Sept. 22, 2008, that the **Laie Hawaii Temple** will close Dec. 29, 2008, for approximately 18 months to accommodate a renovation of the temple. Following the renovation, the temple will be rededicated.

• President Monson announced five new temples during the Church's 178th Semiannual General Conference on Oct. 4, 2008. The temples will be in **Kansas City, Mo.; Philadelphia, Pa.; Calgary, Alberta; Cordoba, Argentina; and Rome, Italy.** With 128 temples currently operating and with another 17 in some phase of planning or construction, these five temples bring the worldwide total to 145.

DEATHS OF GENERAL AUTHORITIES

• **President Gordon B. Hinckley,** 97, died Jan. 27, 2008, at his home in Salt Lake City of causes incident to age. He had served as president of the Church since March 12, 1995. Previously, he was a counselor to three Church presidents for 14 years, and served 20 years in the Quorum of the Twelve and three years as an Assistant to the Twelve.

• **Elder J. Thomas Fyans,** 90, who was called to the First Quorum of the Seventy in 1976 and served in the Presidency of the Seventy for nine years, died May 18, 2008, at his home in Sandy, Utah. Before being called as a Seventy, he served two years as an Assistant to the Twelve. He was named emeritus General Authority in 1989.

DEATHS

• **Inis Bernice Egan Hunter,** 93, widow of President Howard W. Hunter, the 14th president of the Church, died Oct.14, 2007, in Laguna Hills, Calif.

• **Georgia Wahlin Bello,** 83, composer of the Primary song, "Popcorn Popping on the Apricot Tree," died Nov. 5, 2007, in Salt Lake City, Utah.

• **Elder Chad Steven Wayman,** 21, of Sandy, Utah, serving in the South Africa Johannesburg Mission, was killed Jan. 11, 2008, in a car accident near Kimberly, South Africa.

• **James LeVoy Sorenson,** 86, LDS inventor, entrepreneur and philanthropist who held more than 40 medical patents and was a co-developer of the first real-time computerized heart monitor, died Jan. 20, 2008, in Salt Lake City, Utah. Among his achievements, he created a worldwide, correlated genetic and genealogical database used in ancestry research.

• **Ruth Wright Faust,** 86, wife of the late President James E. Faust who served 12 years as second counselor in the First Presidency, died Feb. 10, 2008, in Salt Lake City, Utah, exactly six months after he husband died.

• **Elder Eugene Fontanos,** 23, from San Fernando, LaUnion, Philippines, serving in the Philippines Bacolod Mission, was killed Feb. 26, 2008, when struck by a passing motorist while walking in the village of Valladolid.

• **C. Monroe Hart,** 89, the first member of the Church to receive the rank of Rear Admiral in the U.S. Navy and a former member of the Church Military Relations Committee, died April 13, 2008, in Provo, Utah.

• **Elder Matthew Lawrence Knoop,** 20, a missionary serving in the Brazil Salvador Mission from Jeremey Ranch Ward, Park City Utah Stake, died April 21, 2008, from injuries sustained in a hit-and-run accident in Catu, a town in northern Brazil the day before.

• **Sister Lindsey Spjute,** 23, of Farmington, Utah, and a missionary serving in the England Birmingham Mission, died May 10, 2008, while exercising.

• **Sister Karen Deschamps,** 60, of St. George, Utah, a missionary serving with her husband Elder Randall Deschamps as Kirtland Historic Sites missionaries in the Ohio Cleveland Mission, died May 13, 2008, from injuries sustained in an automobile accident in Kirtland, Ohio.

• **Beth (Betty) Burton Stohl,** 91, who served with her husband Clark Stohl as directors of Church Hosting for 14 years, died June 13, 2008, in Salt Lake City. On behalf of the Church, the Stohls hosted heads of state and other government leaders from around the world as they visited Utah.

October 2007-September 2008

Number	Stake	Created	First stake president
2777	**Mesa Arizona Hermosa Vista**	21 Oct 2007	Creg Donald Ostler
2778	**West Jordan Utah Oquirrh Point**	21 Oct 2007	Troy D. Virgin
2779	**Jaen Peru**	4 Nov 2007	S. Guillermo Sanchez Caseaneda
2780	**Tumber Peru**	4 Nov 2007	Victor A. Pereyra Talledo
2781	**Indianapolis Indiana West**	11 Nov 2007	William Garn Cowley
2783	**Guacara Venezuela**	18 Nov 2007	Rigoberto Rodriguez Rojas
2782	**Caucaia Brazil**	18 Nov 2007	Benedito S. de Oliveira
2785	**Palmas Brazil**	2 Dec 2007	Tobias Ferreira Leal
2784	**Pomalca Peru**	2 Dec 2007	Mercedes Edgardo Clavo Chero
2788	**Sullana Peru**	9 Dec 2007	Jose F. Alvardo Arambulo
2786	**Pinhais Brazil**	9 Dec 2007	Imar B. Pires
2789	**Goodyear Arizona**	9 Dec 2007	John Clarence Hayes
2787	**Maceio Brazil Tabuleiro**	9 Dec 2007	Alvis Costa Ponde
2790	**Maricopa Arizona**	9 Dec 2007	Malin Walter Lewis
2791	**San Antonio Texas Hill Country**	27 Jan 2008	Jeffrey Duane Foote
2794	**Lehi Utah Willow Park**	17 Feb 2008	Douglas James Wilcox
2792	**Queen Creek Arizona Chandler Heights**	17 Feb 2008	Russell Lyle Richardson
2793	**Queen Creek Arizona North**	17 Feb 2008	Alyn Michael McClure
2795	**Verona Italy**	2 Mar 2008	Massimo Botta
2796	**Cedar City Utah Cross Hollow**	16 Mar 2008	Gregory James Powell
2797	**Kinshasa DR of Congo**	13 Apr 2008	Sylvain Wily Nyembive-Mutambaie
2798	**Perry Utah**	13 Apr 2008	Bruce O. Tams
2799	**Santo Domingo DR Hainamosa**	13 Apr 2008	Florentino Alcantara
2800	**Santo Domingo DR Las Americas**	13 Apr 2008	Victor de la Cruz
2801	**Henderson Nevada Eldorado**	26 Apr 2008	Russell Timothy Peterson
2802	**Kyle Texas**	4 May 2008	Charles Terry Allen
2803	**Frisco Texas**	4 May 2008	Jonathan Clifford Roberts
2804	**Catarman Philippines**	14 May 2008	Jemmy Dumdum Pedrola
2805	**Payson Utah Mount Nebo**	18 May 2008	Rodney H. Newman
	Mazatenagngo Guatemala East		Miguel Enrique Donis Cornejo
	discontinued 25 May 2008		
	Walnut California		Richard Keith Harder
	discontinued 8 June 2008		
2804	**Harare Zimbabwe Marimba Park**	8 June 2008	Stanley Makaza
2805	**Pachuca Mexico South**	15 June 2008	Jose Raul Serrano Cruz
	Guatemala City Monte Maria		Gerardo Soto Urbina
	discontinued 22 June 2008		
2805	**Washington Utah East**	22 June 2008	Randon Brant Jones
2806	**Nuku'alofa Tonga Harbour**	22 JUne 2008	Hakeai Vehekite Piutau
	Cali Columbia Jardin		Hugo Beltran Solano
	discontinued 29 June 2008		
	Barstow California		William Edward Schmitt
	discontinued 24 August 2008		
2805	**BYU-Idaho 9th** (student married)	24 August 2008	Terry W. Call
2806	**Santo Domingo DR Los Restauradores**	31 August 2008	Paulino Agame Martinez
	Miami Florida (Spanish)		Avimael Arevalo Mendez
	discontinued 7 Sept 2008		
2806	**McAllen Texas West**	7 Sept 2008	Laren Brice Chandler
2807	**Twin Falls Idaho South**	14 Sept 2008	Reed Juan Harris

GROWTH OF CHURCH DURING ADMINISTRATIONS OF THE PRESIDENTS

	At beginning				At end			
	Stakes	Members*	Missions	Temples	Stakes	Members*	Missions	Temples
JOSEPH SMITH, 1830-1844	0	280	0	0	2	26,146	3	1
BRIGHAM YOUNG, 1847-1877	2	34,694	4	2	20	115,065	9	3
JOHN TAYLOR, 1880-1887	23	133,628	10	3	31	173,029	13	4
WILFORD WOODRUFF, 1889-1898	32	180,294	13	5	40	267,251	20	6
LORENZO SNOW, 1898-1901	40	267,251	20	6	50	292,931	21	6
JOSEPH F. SMITH, 1901-1918	50	292,931	21	6	75	495,962	22	6
HEBER J. GRANT, 1918-1945	75	495,962	22	6	149	954,004	38	9
GEORGE ALBERT SMITH, 1945-51	149	954,004	38	9	184	1,111,314	43	10
DAVID O. MC KAY, 1951-70	184	1,111,314	43	10	500	2,807,456	89	15
JOSEPH FIELDING SMITH, 1970-72	500	2,807,456	89	15	581	3,218,908	99	17
HAROLD B. LEE, 1972-73	581	3,218,908	99	17	630	3,306,658	109	17
SPENCER W. KIMBALL, 1973-85	630	3,306,658	109	17	1,570	5,920,000	187	38
EZRA TAFT BENSON, 1985-94	1,570	5,920,000	187	38	1,980	8,689,168	295	47
HOWARD W. HUNTER, 1994-95	1,980	8,689,168	295	47	2,029	9,025,914	303	49
GORDON B. HINCKLEY, 1995 - 2008	2,029	9,025,914	303	49	2,791	13,193,999	348	124
				October 2008				
THOMAS S. MONSON, 2008 -	2,791	13,193,999	348	124	2,807	13,428,061	348	128

* Nearest year-end total

See **LENGTH OF SERVICE** chart on page 128.

LDS Summer Olympians

Year	Name	Event	Medal
1912	Alma Richards, USA	High jump	Gold
1920	Creed Haymond, USA*	Sprints	
1928	Doral W. Pilling, Canada	Javelin	
1932	Jesse Mortensen, USA**	Decathalon	
1936	M. Dale Schofield, USA	400-meter hurdles	
1948	Jay Lambert, USA	Boxing	
	Clarence Robison, USA	5,000 meter run	
1952	Paula Meyers Pope, USA***	Diving	Silver
	Robert Detweiler, USA***	Rowing	Gold
	Jane Sears, USA	Swimming	Bronze
1956	Paula Meyers Pope, USA	Diving	Silver, Bronze
1960	Paula Meyers Pope, USA	Diving	Silver
	Jack Yerman, USA***	400-meter run	
		4x100 relay	Gold
1964	L. Jay Silvester, USA	Discus	
	Dale Elizabeth McClements Kephart, USA***	Gymnastics	
	Walter E. "Ed" Red, USA***	Javelin	
1968	Wade Bell, USA	800-meter run	
	Robert Carmona, Mexico	Decathalon	
	Kresimir Cosic, Yugoslavia	Basketball	Silver
	Jackson S. Horsely, USA	Swimming	Bronze
	Canagasabi Kunulon, Singapore	Sprints	
	Kenneth Lundmark, Sweden	High jump	
	Keith Russell, USA	Diving	
	L. Jay Silvester, USA	Discus	Bronze
	Arnold Vitarbo, USA	Shooting	
1972	Anders Arrhenius, Sweden*	Shot put	
	Kresimir Cosic, Yugoslavia	Basketball	Bronze
	George Greenfield, USA	Gymnastics	
	Debbie Stark Hill, USA	Gymnastics	
	Kenneth James, Australia	Basketball	
	Canagasabi Kunulon, Singapore	Sprints	
	Eddie Palubinskas, Australia	Basketball	
	L. Jay Silvester, USA	Discus	Silver
	Usaia Sotutu, Fiji	Steeplechase	
	Saimoni Tamani, Fiji	400-meter run	
1976	Kresimir Cosic, Yugoslavia	Basketball	Silver
	Lelei Fonoimoana, Fiji	Swimming	
	Richard George, USA	Javelin	
	Henry Marsh, USA	Steeplechase	
	Laman Palma, Mexico	Marathon	
	Eddie Palubinskas, Australia	Basketball	
	L. Jay Silvester, USA	Discus	
	Phil Tollestrup, Canada	Basketball	
	Tauna Kay Vandeweghe, USA	Swimming	
	Allesandra Viero, Italy	Gymnastics	
	Wayne Young, USA	Gymnastics	
1980	Kresimir Cosic, Yugoslavia	Basketball	Gold
	Mark Albert Fuller, USA***	Greco-Roman Wrestling	
	Kenth Gardenkrans, Sweden	Discus	
	Henry Marsh, USA****	Steeplechase	
	Peter Vidmar, USA****	Gymnastics	
	Danny Vranes, USA****	Basketball	
1984	Pedro Caceres, Argentina	Steeplechase	
	Paul Cummings, USA	10,000-meter run	
	Stefan Fernholm, Sweden	Discus	
	Mark Fuller, USA	Greco-Roman wrestling	
	Bo Gustafsson, Sweden	50-kilometer walk	Silver
	Lorna Griffin, USA	Discus, shot put	
	Silo Havili, Tonga	Boxing	
	Henry Marsh, USA	Steeplechase	
	Scott Maxwell, Canada (DS)	Baseball	
	Doug Padilla, USA	5,000-meter Run	
	Otosico Havili, Tonga	Boxing	
	Villiami Pulu, Tonga	Boxing	
	Fine Sanivea, Tonga	Boxing	

Year	Athlete	Sport	Medal
	Timo Saarelainen, Finland***	Basketball	
	Cory Snyder, USA (DS)	Baseball	Silver
	Karl Tilleman, Canada	Basketball	
	Tauna Kay Vandeweghe, USA	Volleyball	Silver
	Peter Vidmar, USA	Gymnastics	2 Gold, 1 Silver
	Walt Zobell, USA	Trapshooting	
1988	Uati Afele, Western Samoa	Wrestling	
	Lucky Agbonsevbafe, Nigeria	Soccer	
	Troy Dalbey, USA	Swimming	2 Golds
	Mike Evans, USA	Water Polo	Silver
	James Bergeson, USA	Water Polo	Silver
	Ed Eyestone, USA	Marathon	
	Tualau Fale, Tonga	Boxing	
	Mark Fuller, USA	Greco-Roman wrestling	
	Bo Gustafsson, Sweden	50-kilometer walk	
	Viliamu Lesiva, Western Samoa	Boxing	
	Henry Marsh, USA	Steeplechase	
	Asomua Naea, Western Samoa	Boxing	
	Doug Padilla, USA	5,000-meter run	
	Fred Solovi, Western Samoa	Wrestling	
	Sione Talia'uli, Tonga	Boxing	
	Troy Tanner, USA	Volleyball	Gold
	Karl Tilleman, Canada	Basketball	
	Palako Vaka, Tonga	Boxing	
1992	Mark Albert Fuller, USA	Greco-Roman wrestling	
	Ed Eyestone, USA	Marathon	
	Julie Jenkins, USA	800-meter run	
	Mike Evans, USA	Water Polo	
1996	Kristine Quance, USA	Swimming	Gold
	Laura Berg, USA	Softball	Gold
2000	Kenneth Andam, Ghana	100-meter run	
	Marsha Baird, Trinidad	Heptathalon	
	Maggie Chan Roper, Hong Kong	Distance runner	
	Jamie Dantzcher, USA	Gymnastics	
	Rulon Gardner, USA	Greco-Roman Wrestling	Gold
	Courtney Johnson, USA	Water polo	Silver
	Ryan Millar, USA	Volleyball	
	Leonard Myles-Mills, Ghana	100-meter run	
	Amy Palmer, USA	Hammer throw	
	Robbie Pratt, Mexico	Pole vault	
	Jason Pyrah, USA	1,500-meter run	
	Arunas Savackas, Lithuania	Swimming	
	Charlene Tagaloa, USA	Volleyball	
	Laura Berg, USA	Softball	Gold
2004	Marsha Baird, Trinidad & Tobago	Track and Field	
	Megan Dirkmaat, USA	Rowing	Silver
	Rulon Gardner, USA	Greco-Roman Wrestling	Bronze
	Rachelle Kunkel, USA	3-meter springboard diving	
	Tiffany Lott-Hogan, USA	Heptathlon	
	Ryan Millar, USA	Volleyball	
	Leonard Myles-Mills, Ghana	100 meters, 4x100 relay	
	John Nunn, USA	Race walking	
	Lucia Fernanda Palerma, Argentina	Rowing	
	James Parker, USA	Hammer throw	
	Mosiah Rodriguez, Brazil	Gymnastics	
	Maggie Chan-Roper, Hong Kong	Marathon	
	Cael Sanderson, USA	Greco-Roman Wrestling	Gold
	Justin Wilcock, USA	3-meter springboard diving	
	Guard Young, USA	Gymnastics	Silver
	Laura Berg, USA	Softball	Gold
	Tairia Mim Flowers, USA	Softball	Gold
2008	Ryan Millar, USA	Volleyball	Gold
	Rich Lambourne, USA	Volleyball	Gold
	Natasha Kai, USA	Women's Soccer	Gold
	Valerie Adams Vili, New Zealand	Shot Put	Gold
	Lacey Nymeyer, USA	Swimming 4x100 freestyle	Silver
	Tairia Flowers, USA	Softball	Silver
	Laura Berg, USA	Softball	Silver

* Injured, unable to compete; ** Declared ineligible; *** Joined Church after competition; **** U.S. boycott, unable to compete; (DS) Demonstration sport